I0322306

Language, Politics and Society in the Middle East

Language, Politics and Society in the Middle East

Essays in Honour of Yasir Suleiman

Edited by Yonatan Mendel
and Abeer AlNajjar

EDINBURGH
University Press

Edinburgh University Press is one of the leading university presses in the UK. We publish academic books and journals in our selected subject areas across the humanities and social sciences, combining cutting-edge scholarship with high editorial and production values to produce academic works of lasting importance. For more information visit our website: edinburghuniversitypress.com

© editorial matter and organisation Yonatan Mendel and Abeer AlNajjar, 2018
© the chapters their several authors, 2018

Edinburgh University Press Ltd
The Tun – Holyrood Road
12 (2f) Jackson's Entry
Edinburgh EH8 8PJ

Typeset in 10.5/13 Gentium Plus by
IDSUK (DataConnection) Ltd

A CIP record for this book is available from the British Library

ISBN 978 1 4744 2153 9 (hardback)
ISBN 978 1 4744 2154 6 (webready PDF)
ISBN 978 1 4744 2155 3 (epub)

The right of the contributors to be identified as authors of this work has been asserted in accordance with the Copyright, Designs and Patents Act 1988 and the Copyright and Related Rights Regulations 2003 (SI No. 2498).

Contents

List of Figures and Tables vii
Acknowledgements viii
Foreword by Carole Hillenbrand ix

Introduction: Words, Language, Message 1
Yonatan Mendel and Abeer AlNajjar

1 The Hauntology of Language and Identity 14
John E. Joseph

2 Transcultural Content and Translingual Reflection: Rethinking the Arabic Language Learning Experience 30
Karin Christina Ryding

3 Metaphorical Recurrence and Language Symbolism in Arabic Metalanguage Discourse 49
Chaoqun Lian

4 Colloquial Moroccan Arabic: Shifts in Usage and Attitudes in the Era of Computer-mediated Communication 69
Eirlys Davies

5 'Arabic is Under Threat': Language Anxiety as a Discourse on Identity and Conflict 90
Ashraf Abdelhay and Sinfree Makoni

6 Code Choice, Place and Identity in Egypt: Evidence from Two Novels 111
Reem Bassiouney

7 Language as Proxy in Egypt's Identity Politics: Examining the New Wave of Egyptian Nationalism 126
Mariam Aboelezz

8 *Rakākah* and the Petit Quarrel of 1871: Christian Authors and the Competition over Arabic 148
Rana Issa

9 Orchestrating Multimodal Protest and Subverting Banal Nationalism in the Linguistic Landscape of the Tunisian Revolution 165
Sonia Shiri

10 The Arab Jews and the Arabic Language in Israel: An Ongoing Ambivalence between Positive Nostalgia and Negative Present 185
Maisalon Dallashi

11 War Names in the Arab–Israeli Conflict: A Comparative Study 207
Muhammad Amara

About the Contributors 228
Index 232

Figures and Tables

Figures

7.1 Suleiman's (2008) conceptualisation of Egyptian supra-nationalisms 128

7.2 Survey participants' agreement/disagreement with the statement 'I think [WM] is a threat to the Arabic language' against the political orientation of the party they voted for in the 2011–12 parliamentary elections 138

Tables

10.1 Knowledge of Arabic among Jews 192

10.2 Attitudes towards Arabic 194

10.3 Attitudes towards Arabic among three generations of Arab Jews 196

11.1 Names of wars between Israel and Arab armies 212

Acknowledgements

This book is a product and culmination of collaboration between many scholars without whom we would not have reached this important milestone. First and foremost, we wish to thank the contributors, thirteen scholars from the Middle East, Europe and the United States, who were unfailingly serious, patient and professional. Their appreciation of and respect for both this project and for Yasir Suleiman made this endeavour truly gratifying. No less importantly, we wish to express our appreciation to additional scholars who made an indelible contribution to this endeavour through the provision of personal consultation, assistance in peer review and through academic support. Specifically, we extend our gratitude to Prof. Yehouda Shenhav, Prof. Bernard Spolsky, Prof. Benjamin Hary, Dr Iman Soliman, Dr Hussien M. ElKhafaifi, Dr Samir Abu-Absi, Abdulkafi AlBirini, Dr Roy Vilozny, Dr Dafna Yitzhaki, Dr Hezi Brosh, Dr Allon Uhlmann and many others who asked to remain anonymous. They were enormously helpful and we are extremely grateful for their thoughtful feedback and assistance.

We are also grateful to Edinburgh University Press and staff who patiently remained true to the project despite some unanticipated delays while ensuring that this project came to fruition. Specifically, we extend our thanks to Nicola Ramsey, who has guided this project from its inception; to Rebecca Mackenzie, who did an incredible job on the book's cover; and to Ersev Ersoy, who gave us a final push to ensure the book's completion.

We also appreciate the assistance of three language editors – Mona Saleh and Asma Alabed at the American University of Sharjah, and to Lisa Richlen in Jerusalem – who assisted us in standardising the language in the chapters and in editing our joint introduction. Many thanks and alf shukr lakun.

Last but not least, we wish to thank our immediate families who have forgiven us for a seemingly endless stream of skype conversations and correspondences. To Ella and new-born David, and to Ahmad, Zeena and Talal for their love and support – we are incredibly fortunate to have you in our lives.

Foreword: About Professor Yasir Suleiman

It is a great honour and pleasure for me to write a foreword in this *Festschrift* in honour of my dear friend and colleague, Professor Yasir Suleiman. This volume, with its contributions from scholars in the UK, USA, Europe, the Arab world and China, is a mark of the deep admiration, respect and affection with which he is viewed by his colleagues around the world.

Let me begin with an outline of some significant biographical landmarks in Yasir's career. He was born in Jerusalem. He studied in the University of Jordan, Amman, where he gained a BA, with First Class honours, in English Language and Literature in 1972. He was awarded a PhD in Linguistics at the University of St Andrews in 1984. He then studied for a second BA in Classical Arabic and Islamic Studies (with Syriac and Classical Hebrew), at the University of Durham, and graduated with first-class honours in 1986. In 1990, Yasir was appointed to the Iraq Chair of Arabic and Islamic Studies at the University of Edinburgh.

I had the great good fortune to work with Yasir at the University of Edinburgh for seventeen years. In that time he worked marvels. He joined a disunited and ineffectual department, and he left it buoyant and highly successful. Indeed, under his leadership, morale was high and colleagues worked happily together. Thanks to Yasir's encouragement and mentoring skills, the Department of Islamic and Middle Eastern Studies in Edinburgh came top in that field countrywide in the Research Assessment Exercise in 2000, the only department to achieve a 5*.

Yasir did not hold himself aloof from senior administrative responsibilities, either within his department or in the wider university context. During his tenure of the Edinburgh Chair (–2007) he served as Head of Department for eight years, as Director of the Edinburgh Institute for the Study of the Arab World and Islam for ten years, was an elected member of the University Court and sat on many important committees.

He was also fully involved in teaching, acting for seven years as the course convener for the MSc in the Practice and Theory of Translation. He supervised postgraduates on different aspects of the Arabic language and he also taught undergraduate classes on modern Arabic literature.

Amongst his many other activities during his time in Edinburgh, Yasir served as a member of the RAE Middle Eastern and African Studies Panel in 1996 and 2000, he organised a series of successful international conferences, and he nominated and welcomed Edward Said to Edinburgh for an honorary degree. Yasir became a Fellow of the Royal Society of Edinburgh (FRSE) in 2000. Just before leaving Edinburgh, he was one of the trio of academics who won the competition to be awarded the honour of establishing the HRH Prince Alwaleed Bin Talal Centre for the Study of Islam and Muslims in the Contemporary World at Edinburgh University in 2007, with a donation of £8 million.

In 2007, Yasir moved to Cambridge to take up the Sultan Qaboos Bin Sa'id Chair of Modern Arabic Studies. At the same time he became a Professorial Fellow of King's College. Soon after his arrival in Cambridge, he led the successful bid, working single-handedly on its academic content, that resulted in 2009 in the establishment of the HRH Prince Alwaleed Bin Talal Centre of Islamic Studies at the University of Cambridge, with a further donation of £8 million.

In Cambridge, Yasir demonstrated once again his outstanding abilities to provide inspirational leadership. He served as Head of the Department of Middle Eastern Studies and he became the Founding Director of the HRH Prince Alwaleed Bin Talal Centre of Islamic Studies at the University of Cambridge. This Centre is one of a number of such centres in the US and the UK funded by Prince Alwaleed with the aim of promoting a better understanding of Islam in the West and of creating more harmony between the faiths. The initiatives undertaken by the Cambridge Centre under Yasir's leadership have made a great impact. For example, the project titled 'Contextualising Islam in Britain' has proved to be an outstanding success. It has helped to inform and enlighten non-Muslims about Islam here in the UK, and has brought together on a regular basis British Muslims, both Sunnis and Shi'ites, as well as Muslims representing a range of different ethnicities now settled in the UK. By dint of Yasir's skilful chairmanship, this highly diverse group has been able to discuss harmoniously a number of really controversial issues affecting Muslim communities in Britain. I have read with great admiration the report that was the result of this venture. It is not surprising that it was singled out for praise in the British Parliament. Yasir has also overseen two path-breaking projects on the subject of conversion to Islam in the UK, seen from both female and male perspectives, examining what has motivated such conversions to take place. There has been enormous public interest in this work, especially in the case of women converts.

Yasir also serves on the panel of judges for the British–Kuwaiti Friendship Society Book Prize. This is the most prestigious prize in Britain in the field of Islamic and Middle Eastern Studies. Yasir chairs this panel extremely well; he has created and maintained a most harmonious atmosphere amongst the judges. Yasir has also chaired the Board of Trustees of the International Prize for Arabic Fiction since 2013. These two public roles have given him considerable gravitas in the world of Arab literary culture, not just in the particular sphere of Britain, but more widely on the global stage.

Yasir's international work to promote inter-cultural understanding has also been remarkable. He has been indefatigable in holding workshops and conferences – for example, in Morocco, Bosnia, China and Tunisia – and in creating partnerships with universities in these countries. It was a great honour for him to be awarded the status of Ambassador of the University of Sarajevo. This kind of work exploits his capacity to offer practical help to higher education institutions in troubled situations abroad, a tradition inaugurated by his successful 'Books for Baghdad' initiative in Edinburgh after the Iraq War.

Yasir has played an important role in educational initiatives in the Arab world; these include his consultancy work on Arabic Language teaching and learning reforms in Qatar, Abu Dhabi, Oman, Bahrain and Egypt during the last seven years. He has spoken regularly on British, American and Arab TV and radio about contemporary issues to do with the Arab world, and he has written articles on Middle Eastern matters in the print media in both English and Arabic.

In 2011, Yasir received the award of Commander of the Order of the British Empire (CBE) for his contribution to scholarship. His numerous publications are indeed an impressive testimony to his dedication and achievement in research in the diverse fields of Arabic language, linguistics, poetry, politics, Arab and Palestinian nationalism, identity and other related subjects. Especially important are his five single-authored monographs: *The Arabic Grammatical Tradition: A Study in Taʿlīl*; *The Arabic Language and National Identity: A Study in Ideology*; *A War of Words: Language and Conflict in the Middle East*; *Arabic, Self and Identity: A Study in Conflict and Displacement*; and *Arabic in the Fray: Language Ideology and Cultural Politics*. He has also edited seven books, and written fifty articles and book chapters. This performance speaks for itself. Moreover, he has also written very lengthy reports for the Supreme Education Council in Qatar on Arabic curriculum matters and Arabic lesson plans.

Without doubt Professor Yasir Suleiman has given exemplary service to higher education and inter-cultural understanding in Britain. He has worked unceasingly and with remarkably inspirational leadership, energy and vision not only in the universities of Edinburgh and Cambridge, but also in the wider field of Islamic and Middle Eastern Studies in the UK, and he has built firm and lasting bonds with universities and public bodies in the Middle East, North Africa and Europe. He is a most prominent and very well-respected public figure on the international stage. His remarkable people skills, his talent for diplomacy and for finding solutions to difficult problems, his capacity to listen and not preach, his wisdom and his finely tuned judgement – all these qualities make him a natural spokesperson on Middle Eastern affairs. He is an exceptionally gifted and public-spirited individual and an ornament to the culture and community that he represents. There is quite simply nobody like him in the field of Islamic and Middle Eastern Studies.

Yasir's most recent successful venture has been the 2016 publication of an edited volume, titled *Being Palestinian: Personal Reflections on Palestinian Identity in the Diaspora.* Yasir's preface to the book is deeply moving. It is both penetrating and informative. Its insights come both from the head and from the heart. This passionate and inspiring book, with its hundred contributions written by exiled Palestinians from many walks of life and countries, has already received high praise both in the UK and the USA. This will be THE book on the Palestinian diaspora for a long time to come.

To end on an all-important personal note, Yasir has been blessed with a very happy and fulfilled, closely-knit family life, with his wife Shahla and their two sons, Tamir and Sinan. They have given him the unfailing love and support which have made it possible for him to do what he has done. May he long continue to shed lustre on the field of Middle Eastern Studies.

Carole Hillenbrand

Introduction: Words, Language, Message

Yonatan Mendel and Abeer AlNajjar

Where is 'Bazra' that is found on the front cover of this book? What lies behind a road sign? And what can we learn from a road sign that indicates three different names, of which none represents the real name of the place? For Yasir Suleiman, language – including ones' verbal and written expression, selected or forgotten terminology, vowels pronounced or not pronounced, and locations written on road signs – provides us with a nuanced, honest and deep analysis of society, of what it tells us and of what it keeps away from us.

For Yasir Suleiman, and as seen in his extensive academic research, language deeply and profoundly exposes social and political realities. We are referring to language in its larger context, including the words which form the building blocks of language, the context in which such words are written and the phraseology selected. Indeed, when we look at Suleiman's contribution to the study of language and society, we find out that in his research language emerges as the 'Black Box' of human social and political journeys. And Yasir Suleiman is one of the world's leading contemporary experts in the study and analysis of these lingual black boxes, particularly in relation to the Arabic language but also regarding other languages and related case studies.

For Yasir Suleiman, therefore, the phrase 'these are just words' is utterly meaningless; rather he would uncover meaning through an examination of the linguistic material – both mundane and profound – in everyday life. Such meanings could be found, for example, in a pamphlet, personal correspondence, a sign in a shop window or, perhaps more 'officially', through a country's linguistic curriculum, language policy or official language status. In other words, Yasir Suleiman's research, publications, lectures, books and teachings reveal the worldviews that make languages and the languages that make worldviews. They expose the worlds that make languages and the languages that make worlds. He focuses on language, yet his work highlights a delicate yet powerful story about who we are, where we are from and about our needs, aspirations, fears and desires.

So what is the story behind the road sign at the entrance to the small Israeli village of 'Bazra', about 20 km northwest of Jaffa? In examining linguistic landscape in *Arabic, Self and Identity* (Suleiman 2011), Yasir Suleiman notes that 'the linguistic landscape and the map as a cartographic text emerge as an arena for ideological contestation through which claims of ownership, identity inscription and identity erasure can be pursued . . .' Indeed, true to Yasir's observation, the case of 'Bazra', and the words written on the road sign to describe this locale in Hebrew, Arabic and English, exemplify this insight.

On the road sign, all three languages refer to the Iraqi city of Al-Baṣrah (البصرة). This, however is not out of celebration to Iraqi Jews who immigrated from the city or to Jewish–Iraqi tradition, nor is it related to Iraqi culture or to the larger Arab region in which Palestine/Israel is situated. Rather, the village name commemorates its twenty-eight founding members, Jewish Zionists who immigrated to Palestine in the 1930s from Germany. During the Second World War, they volunteered for service in the British engineering corps and during active duty, they were stationed next to Iraqi city of Al-Baṣrah. There, not only did they support the British war effort, they also facilitated weapons smuggling into Palestine during the period of the British Mandate in order to strengthen the Zionist military in their impending conflict with the Palestinians. In early August 1946, following their return to Palestine, a Zionist construction and development company (Rassco – Rural and Suburban Settlement Company), founded a decade earlier by the Jewish Agency to facilitate the establishment of new agricultural settlements, created 'Bazra' in their honour. In order to further distance the Iraqi city of Al-Baṣrah (and the Arab world generally) from the Jewish village, a Biblical explanation to the village's name was also given – the name Baṣrah (or Batsra) corresponds with a Biblical verse in Amos 1:12. Anyway, and as published in *Ha-Tsofeh* newspaper, 'Bazra' was truly a Jewish and Zionist project, and the inauguration ceremony of the village was attended by numerous Jewish soldiers who had also served in the British army and who established other colonies (lit. *moshavot*) in the area.

Based on similar such cases during this time period, it is reasonable to assume that the choice of name was driven by the location of 'Bazra' (written in Hebrew as *Batsra* or *Baṣra*) near the Palestinian village of *Tabṣur* located in, what was then, the Ṭūlkarm District. Similar letters of the root of the village – in both Hebrew and Arabic: B.Ṣ.R – are found in the Arabic name of the Arab-Palestinian village of Tabṣur and in the Hebrew name of the Jewish village of 'Bazra' that was established nearby. Almost certainly, the selection of the Hebrew name (*Batsra* or *Baṣra*) served as a politico-linguistic attempt to hide or blur the original Arab-Palestinian ownership of the land; this was a common phenomenon which was described, among others, by Meron Benvenisti's 'The Hebrew Map'. Analysing today's 'Bazra' road sign in this light indicates that the name of the Jewish village both conceals and reveals the long and loud silence of the people of Tabṣur – who, according to PalestineRemembered, today would number over 2,500 people. As such, the ongoing Palestinian Nakba and its denial are also hidden and revealed within the three words written on the road sign.

Furthermore, an analysis of the pronunciation of the Hebrew, Arabic and English names of the village – as written on the road sign – offers a fascinating window into the creation of modern Hebrew, the ideology behind its creation and the status of and power relations between Hebrew, Arabic and English in Israel. In principle, because both Hebrew and Arabic are Semitic languages, the pronunciation of the letter Ṣād should be similar in the two languages – a voiceless post-dental sibilant emphatic sound of 'ṣ'. While pronounced as such by Arabs and Arab Jews throughout the Middle East, in the ideologically charged atmosphere in which the 'revival' or 'revitalisation' of Hebrew took place in mandatory Palestine, the Semitic letter Ṣād, was replaced by the eastern European, Ashkenazi-version of Tsad ('ts' sound). This change in pronunciation is telling in that it reveals power relations and the nature of discussions that took place within the Hebrew Language Academy and other related bodies tasked with the creation of Modern Hebrew (Or 2016). Specific to the road sign, while the written Hebrew name could reflect a pronunciation and orientation of Arab Jews, the Modern Hebrew Israeli pronunciation of the village reflects the influence of Jews of European origin (Ashkenazi Jews). Thus, in present-day Israel, the village's name is pronounced only as Batsra or Batzra, and never as Basra or Baṣra. Therefore, the pronunciation of the name not only demonstrates Ashkenazi hegemony in Israel, it is also far from accurately reflecting the city that inspired its name in the first place.

Another topic related to the road sign is the order of the languages written on it. The Arabic on the sign is clearly inferior to the Hebrew, as in all road signs in Israel. This is consistent with political developments, most notably the creation of Israel following the 1948 War, and the evident decline in the status of the language in historical Palestine. But another striking issue emerges from the road sign. While the Israeli village of 'Bazra' is named after a city with an Arabic name, the Arabic on the road sign is transliterated from the incorrect Hebrew pronunciation. Due to the Israeli non-Semitic (some would say anti-Semitic) usage of the letter Ṣād (or Ṣadi in Hebrew), the pronunciation of the Iraqi Arab city of Baṣrah instead becomes Batsrah in modern Hebrew – a fact which has influenced the way the Arabic letters are written on the road sign. This inverts the political and lingual reciprocal power relations in Israel whereby Arabic is transliterated from Hebrew and not vice versa, even when the original name is in Arabic. Thus, we see the invention of a new and non-existent city named 'Batsrah,' or, as written on the sign, in Arabic: بتسرا

The English version of the village name adds another interesting twist to this narrative. While the city of Al-Baṣrah is known in English as either Basra or Al-Basra, the English on the sign is based on the interests of the Hebrew language planner. Neither the original Arabic name nor its commonly used English name is written; rather the usage of 'Bazra' which emphasises and prioritises a Hebrew–Israeli pronunciation. Perhaps the sign-maker sought to assist English-speakers; instead of forcing them to make the rather odd hissing sound of 'ts', it was assumed that pronouncing 'z' would be easier. Thus, in English as well as in Arabic and Hebrew, a known city in Iraq was transformed into a new and non-existent city named 'Bazra'.

Clearly, this seemingly benign example of a road sign is not only indicative of a specific geographic location. More profoundly, it contains a fundamental message about power relations, historical processes, ideological debates, socio-political developments and economic interests within Israel. While the analysis outlined here may correspond with Yasir Suleiman's work, it almost certainly lacks his incredible depth and his intellectual and academic prowess. Indeed, Suleiman has encouraged us to dig deeper and go further; to fully excavate the load embedded in every word and every location, in acts of code-switching, word choice, accent, transliteration and pronunciation. In his spirit, scholars have attempted to unearth the messages embedded in the Arabic we speak, read and write, in the languages that we do not know, and in those we were forced to forget. In other words, it is the Suleimanian school that further invites us, enables and even dares us to tell a complex and multi-layered story rich with meaning.

Following this, the case of the 'Bazra' road sign emerges as indicative of Jewish–British cooperation, historical Palestine, British Mandatory Palestine, the Jewish–Arab conflict, the 1948 War, the Nakba, the creation of Israel, the Jewish-Israeli modern political 'use' in the Bible, the fight over indigenousness and land ownership in Palestine/Israel, the Israeli disregard of Arab–Jewish culture, Ashkenazi dominance within the Zionist movement and in Israeli-Jewish society in general, Arabic's inferiority, and the special status of English in Israel. Strikingly, this entire story can be observed while driving on road 4 between Haifa and Tel Aviv (previously the Ṭūlkarm District, now part of the Sharon regional council) and passing a seemly innocuous road sign containing just three black words on a white background.

The contents of this book reflect Yasir Suleiman's indelible contribution to the study of language and society. It encompasses diverse academic fields such as linguistics, sociolinguistics and the sociology of language, while also analysing how Arabic finds itself at the crossroads of society, politics, identity, culture and conflict. As Hillenbrand notes in her personal Foreword, it is a challenge to fully encapsulate a scholar's influence, particularly one whose work has had such a tremendous impact on his academic field and larger, related social processes. A Fellow of the Royal Society of Edinburgh and a Fellow of King's College at the University of Cambridge, Yasir Suleiman served as the Head of the Department of Middle Eastern Studies at the University of Cambridge. He is also the Founding Director of the Prince Alwaleed Bin Talal Centre of Islamic Studies at the University of Cambridge, and was the first Chair of HM Sultan Qaboos Bin Sa'id Professor of Modern Arabic Studies at the University of Cambridge. Alongside these achievements, Suleiman serves as Chair of the Panel of Judges of the British–Kuwaiti Friendship Society Book Prize in Middle Eastern

Studies, and is a Trustee on the Boards of the Arab–British Chamber Charitable Foundation, the International Prize for Arab Fiction, the Banipal Trust for Arab Literature and the Gulf Research Centre-Cambridge. He also serves as Chair of the Advisory Board of the Centre for the Advanced Study of the Arab World (CASAW), Chair of the Centre for the Study of the International Relations of the Middle East and North Africa (CIRMENA), is a board member of the Islamic Manuscript Association, a member of the Advisory Board of the Centre for Evaluation and Research in Muslim Education at the Institute of Education, a member of the Advisory Board of the Doha Institute, and many more. Perhaps most significantly, he has been honoured with the status of Commander of the Order of the British Empire (CBE).

Yasir Suleiman's numerous honours attest to the importance of his research and his profound academic excellence. He has shed light on many areas, conflicts and case studies, and many of them are mentioned in this book particularly in relation to Arabic. Perhaps even more important, he has pointed to the ways in which language is situated at the heart of social and political life. Through the work of Yasir Suleiman, the reader is exposed to key insights that can be extracted from the reservoir of language and language use, and from the wells of metaphors, slang, language studies and language acquisition. This has been evident in his five single-authored monographs: *The Arabic Grammatical Tradition: A Study in Taʿlīl*; *The Arabic Language and National Identity: A Study in Ideology* ; *A War of Words: Language and Conflict in the Middle East*; *Arabic, Self and Identity: A Study in Conflict and Displacement*; and *Arabic in the Fray: Language Ideology and Cultural Politics*.

Yasir Suleiman has drawn our attention to the symbolism of language in the context of national conflict, while his work on the role of language in articulating national identity in the Middle East is unmatched. Building on earlier research he conducted on the concept of *Taʿlīl*, and due to his mastery of Arabic grammar, the focus of his work has transitioned from linguistics to 'language', and from sociolinguistics to sociology, society and language. This has laid the groundwork for studying language realities and debates – analysing them through top-down as well as bottom-up developments. His studies have extended to encompass social and political realities, the way language is involved in ideological and cultural debates, and the ideological weight influencing translation. Suleiman's work has further been inclusive of the central role language plays in cognition and how we understand the world. He is interested in the ways in which language facilitates intimidation or protection, the connection between linguistic change and political reality, the ways in which literary productions reflect language ideologies or dismantle them, and how 'minor' linguistic details are actually crucial to gaining a full understanding of a social or political reality.

For example, in his *Arabic in the Fray*, Suleiman examines seemingly random elements of our social life, such as book titles, acknowledgements, epigraphs and jacket copy, and dismantles and deconstructs them. These are then reconstructed and connected to a wider web of conflicts, contemporary political issues, fears, anxieties and desires. His revealing analysis of books in Arabic dedicated to the Arabic language is an eye-opening example of the subtle way in which language serves as a (somewhat 'quiet' and 'sensitive') proxy for (rather 'loud' and 'dramatic') political conflicts, social tensions and identity crises.

Another example is Suleiman's book *Arabic, Self and Identity*, in which he exemplifies these tendencies as it focuses on the linkage between language, ideology and power. Among many other characters, this book introduces us to Elias Koussa, a Palestinian advocate who lived and practised law in Haifa, during the British Mandate in Palestine, but also following the establishment of Israel in 1948. He demonstrates Koussa's capacity for strategically deploying language in order to articulate political arguments and as a marker for political transformation. In 1943, Koussa wrote to the High Commissioner for Palestine to protest the inclusion of Arabic, placed underneath Hebrew text, in a pamphlet announcing the screening of a film. Koussa pointed out that this ordering of the two languages constituted 'a flagrant violation of the provision of Article 22 of the Mandate', which stipulated that in all official documents the order of the languages written should be English, Arabic and Hebrew – in that order. It is clear that Koussa's inquiry was primarily motivated by the larger national and political context in Palestine at the time and that, for him, language served as a proxy of these developments. Accordingly, he wrote: 'The Arabs look upon the matter with serious apprehension lest this instance, and the many other cases in which the same order was adopted, imply a settled policy of subordinating their rights and interests to those of the Jewish community.' Clearly, language and its usage was as an important indicator for a political change in Palestine; it reflected changing power relations – both overt and covert – prevailing during that period. This allegedly 'small' example came to Suleiman's attention and received a thorough and thought-provoking analysis in his book. This is consistent with his tendency to deeply analyse even the seemingly most insignificant examples of language for deeper meaning and as a trigger for discussion, complaint or praise.

When discussing the nature of this book, we made a decision to present Yasir Suleiman's work as broadly as possible. Accordingly, we sought contributions from both senior and junior scholars, and from scholars who are personally very well acquainted with him and his work as well as those whose scholarship has influenced their work. Each chapter underwent peer review by an external professor and, following a series of corrections, was accepted for publication. While the process was lengthy, we were blessed to benefit from the cooperation of many high-ranking scholars, contributors and reviewers. Therefore, we feel confident that the final product is of high quality and we also believe that this book appropriately pays tribute to Yasir Suleiman: a person of many merits who has attracted a generous group of followers, students, supporters and admirers.

Through reading this book, we hope that the reader will embark on a journey into the linguistic situation in the Middle East. More specifically, we attempted to shed light on the unique 'story' that is an outcome of research on language. From Palestine to Israel, from Sudan to Egypt, from Tunisia to Morocco, we believe that language plays a crucial role in the way that humans understand, explain, shape and mediate reality. In other words, and in the spirit of Yasir Suleiman, we hope that the chapters included in this book will expose new aspects of the social and political realities of the Middle East, aspects which, until now, have at times been silenced or hidden. Language, as a most fundamental form of human interaction, is crucial to life in any society. When it is ignored or disregarded, we may miss crucial pieces of the entire picture or understanding the picture incorrectly. Language, perhaps more than other aspect of human interaction, is both the message and the messenger, both the self and the collective, both the dream and the reality, and, uniquely, can tell a story that is greater than the sum of its parts.

This volume aims to shed light on core questions relating to language and society, language and conflict, and language and politics, in relation to a changing Middle East. While the book focuses on Arabic, it goes way beyond a purely linguistic analysis by bringing to the fore a set of pressing questions about the relationship between Arabic and society. For example, it touches on the development of language policy via an examination of administrative mandates (top-down) in contrast to grassroots initiatives (bottom-up); the deeper layers of the linguistic landscape that highlight the connection between politics, conflict, identity, road signs and street names; Arabic studies and Arabic identity and the myriad ways countries deal simultaneously with globalisation while also seeking to strengthen local and national identity, and more. We hope scholars, including linguists and sociolinguists, will find such analyses useful. We would also like to reach a broader audience – individuals seeking to better understand the Middle East through one of its most elusive yet meaningful components: its languages.

The book begins with a Foreword written by Carole Hillenbrand. Focusing on Yasir Suleiman's life, career, achievements, publications and personal qualities, Hillenbrand outlines the tremendous scope of his academic career, which has stretched from Palestine, via Scotland, to Cambridge. Personal and thoughtful in tone, Hillenbrand lists Yasir Suleiman's extraordinary achievements: first and foremost, his central contribution to strengthening and institutionalising Arabic and Islamic Studies in Britain. She also comments on his leadership qualities, his skill as an administrator and his success in forging and nurturing links between institutions in the Arab world, the United States and Europe. Hillenbrand highlights the quality of Yasir Suleiman's scholarship and his research interests, while also pointing to his commitment to his people – the Palestinians (on which he edited his last book titled *Being Palestinian: Personal Reflections on Palestinian Identity in the Diaspora*). Finally, she draws attention to Suleiman's major publications and their impact on the field, while noting that he has served as a guide, philosopher and friend to her and many others.

The book's chapters then divide to two main parts. The first part of the book is dedicated to research that covers a rather general theme about Arabic, while the second part of the book is dedicated to chapters that focus on more specific case studies relating to language and society in the Middle East – in a specific country or at a specific time.

The first research chapter in this book is John E. Joseph's 'The Hauntology of Language and Identity'. Joseph begins his research with a reference to Suleiman by highlighting how language and identity – a connection featured in a considerable part of Suleiman's academic work – are embedded in one another as they occupy what Joseph terms 'the same memory'. Joseph then employs the term *hauntology* (Fr.: *hantologie*), coined by Derrida in his *Specters of Marx*, to explicate linguistic identity. Joseph's argument is further developed in his reference to a paper by Wernberg-Møller (1999) which was published following series of conferences on language and society in the Middle East and North Africa organised by Suleiman at Edinburgh in the late 1990s. Through Wernberg-Møller's paper in which a conversation by a Moroccan family that had been living in Edinburgh for around twenty years is analysed, Joseph demonstrates the value of the hauntological perspective in understanding text and in identifying its hidden meanings. Emphasising the strong emotive component of identity, Joseph urges us to challenge our 'rational comfort zone' through the lens of hauntology's analytical strategies.

Joseph's chapter is followed by Karin C. Ryding's 'Transcultural Content and Translingual Reflection: Rethinking the Arabic Language Learning Experience', comprising Chapter 2. Her chapter argues that while Arabic has garnered increased attention by the American education system over the past decade, the sociolinguistics of Arabic are being neglected in such educational endeavours. This is despite academic research on this topic, including, notably, Yasir Suleiman's *Arabic Sociolinguistics: Issues and Perspectives* (1994). Ryding writes that the complexity of teaching and learning Arabic is related to the transcultural realities of living and working in the Arab world. As she demonstrates, Arabic is particularly challenging as the language must be modified to conform to different types of interaction. Ryding then analyses some of the shortfalls in the field of Arabic language instruction, and argues that because Arabic teaching – due to its distinctive diglossic nature – lacks many traditional models to choose from, it must construct its own, which she refers to as 'the repertoire model'. Ryding summarises by noting that sociolinguistic analyses, like those studied by Suleiman, must be taken into consideration and should force us to come to terms with the linguistic reality of multiple discourse levels and, accordingly, to develop new models for Arabic pedagogy.

Chapter 3 is Chaoqun Lian's 'Metaphorical Recurrence and Language Symbolism in Arabic Metalanguage Discourse'. Lian, a former PhD student of Suleiman, begins by pointing out that in Arabic metalanguage discourse one often encounters metaphors associating the form and situation of Arabic to non-linguistic entities and activities. Many of these metaphors, according to Lian, belong to 'organic metaphors', as they depict Arabic and its varieties as living organisms. In his chapter, Lian investigates the recurrence of 'organic metaphors' in language policy discussions within the Arabic language academies in Damascus and Cairo. By carefully analysing selected cases of metaphor-making, Lian unearths the normally covert link between language perception and socio-political circumstances in the Arabic-speaking world. According to Lian, when these socio-political circumstances are taken into consideration, academic research will be able to produce a more nuanced, dialectic understanding of the 'organic' perception of languages.

Chapter 4 is Eirlys Davies' 'Colloquial Moroccan Arabic: Shifts in Usage and Attitudes in the Era of Computer-mediated Communication'. Davies begins by highlighting a reality whereby, for centuries, the gulf between Colloquial Arabic dialects (CA) and Modern Standard Arabic (MSA) has been a defining characteristic of the Arabic-speech community. Davies then notes that the arrival of mobile phones, the growing use of the Internet and computer-mediated communication, and advertising that corresponds to these trends have revolutionised communication in the Middle East. Consequently, many individuals, particularly among the younger generation, have begun to communicate (in personal SMSs, emails or social media) in CA and they have a strong tendency to use Latin letters instead of Arabic letters. Davies focuses on these trends as they are manifested in Morocco. Highlighting the contribution of Suleiman to the diglossic relationship between CA and MSA, the chapter stresses that this is a bottom-up process. Davies courageously concludes that we must accept change as inevitable, and, instead of resisting such modes of communication, 'it may be better to embrace them, experiment with them and explore their potential as means of solving problems'.

Chapter 5 was jointly written by Ashraf Abdelhay and Sinfree Makoni. Titled '"Arabic is Under Threat": Language Anxiety as a Discourse on Identity and Conflict', the authors lay out a series of critical reflections on the discourses of language anxiety that characterise Arabic as a 'threatened language'. Examining Arabic as a site of social contestation in the Sudan, Abdelhay and Makoni analyse three statements that express a specific set of ideas and social attitudes about language, identity and society. The first statement was made at a rally by President Bashir a few weeks before the southern referendum held in 2011. The second statement comes from an article written by the Sudanese journalist Hussein Khojali. Finally, the third statement is a metalinguistic commentary made by the late South Sudanese leader John Garang de Mabior. Despite the different contexts surrounding their statements and the differences between them, Abdelhay and Makoni demonstrate that all three statements are metalinguistic commentaries which bring language to the fore as a proxy for articulating wider social and political concerns. All statements are ideological; they all link language with the extra-linguistic world of identity politics and power. The authors thus conclude that in contexts of conflict, individuals display awareness of the indexical values of language, 'and they exploit the symbolism of language to articulate social and political issues'.

Chapter 6 begins the more case study-oriented part of the book. Reem Bassiouney's 'Code Choice, Place and Identity in Egypt: Evidence from Two Novels' examines the relationship between place, identity and language in two Egyptian novels: *Qindīl Umm Hāshim* (*The Saint's Lamp*) by Yaḥyā Ḥaqqī (1944) and *Awrāq al-narjis* (*Leaves of Narcissus*) by Sumayyah Ramaḍān (2001). Both novels address questions of identity in Egypt, during and following the British occupation of the country. In the first novel, the protagonist studied in the UK and returned to Egypt during the British occupation, while in the second the protagonist studied in Ireland and returned to Egypt some fifty years after the period of British colonisation ended. Perceptively and convincingly, Bassiouney analyses the role of code choice – between Modern Standard Arabic and Egyptian Colloquial Arabic – in the two novels. Corresponding with Suleiman's extensive work on code-switching in Middle Eastern communities, Bassiouney argues that the authors use code-switching in order to reflect the protagonists' stance towards the self, towards others and towards place. She highlights that in matter of fact, code-switching in the two novels does not reflect real patterns of language use, rather *redefines* and *reconstructs* different stances held by the authors towards their protagonists.

Chapter 7 also focuses on Egypt. Mariam Aboelezz's 'Language as Proxy in Egypt's Identity Politics: Examining the New Wave of Egyptian Nationalism', is a fascinating case study in which the writer focuses on the period following the overthrow of Egypt's Islamist president Mohamad Morsi in 2013. Concurrent with this was a government-supported emphasis on 'Egyptian identity'. Using the concept of *alterity* as highlighted by Suleiman, as well as acknowledging Suleiman's contribution to the study of the role of language as proxy in identity politics, Aboelezz examines how language is used as proxy in this new wave of Egyptian nationalism. She demonstrates how old motifs have been revived by the government – for example, the use of *ʿāmmiyya* and the rejection of *fuṣḥā* as proxies for promoting an Egyptian identity – and establishes a convincing link between language and identity through processes of distanciation, differentiation and identification.

Chapter 8, '*Rakākah* and the Petit Quarrel of 1871: Christian Authors and the Competition over Arabic', by Rana Issa sheds light on a fascinating linguistic battle over the correct modes of Arabic expression between two Arab intellectuals – Ahmad Faris al-Shidyāq (1804–87) and Ibrahim al-Yāzijī (1847–1906) in 1871. At its core, the debate is over the 'correct' writing style, and whether Arab intellectuals suffered from a *rakākah* (solecism) in their use of language. Issa places this debate in the context of other linguistic debates prevailing in the nineteenth century – a period in which languages served as vehicles for constructing national identities. She examines the dynamics of Arabic linguistic ideology through the lenses of Arjun Appadurai's technoscapes and Yasir Suleiman's history of Arabic in his book *The Arabic Language and National Identity*. Following from an analysis of the battle over *rakākah*, Issa highlights that the two sides – al-Shidyāq and al-Yāzijī – represented two competing ideologies regarding Standard Arabic. Whereas for al-Shidyāq, a linguistic error was an aspect of the creative process, for al-Yāzijī, an error cheapened an author's text and was nothing but a *rakākah*. Issa demonstrates that the obsession with *rakākah* reproduced itself in subsequent writings by *nahḍa* authors, and observes that the 'protection of the language against *rakākah*' was also a central part of the Arab language academies.

Chapter 9 is a fascinating case study of linguistic landscape. Sonia Shiri's 'Orchestrating Multimodal Protest and Subverting Banal Nationalism in the Linguistic Landscape of the Tunisian Revolution' is based on a multimodal approach to examining the Tunisian demonstration of 14 January 2011. She explores the way in which protesters exploited a variety of peaceful multimodal strategies in order to subvert the linguistic landscape of the capital city and bring about political change. The study, based on an analysis of slogans and pictures, focuses on a specific and critical demonstration that led to the eventual flight of Tunisian president, Zine al-Abidine Ben Ali. Shiri highlights that demonstrators' usage of multimodal signs eventually helped them to prevail in the transient linguistic landscape.

The last two chapters of the book are taken from a place that is especially important to Yasir Suleiman: Palestine and present-day Israel. Chapter 10, by Maisalon Dallashi, is titled 'The Arab Jews and the Arabic Language in Israel: An Ongoing Ambivalence between Positive Nostalgia and Negative Present'. It is based on a rather tragic survey which demonstrated a significant decline in knowledge of Arabic among Arab Jews following their immigration to Israel. The survey results, presented here in English for the first time, form the backdrop for an analysis of command of Arabic among three generations of Arab Jews in comparison with non-Arab Jews living in Israel. Dallashi's nuanced analysis of the complex relationship between Arab Jews and Arabic demonstrates that language is harnessed to promote two different discourses in Israel: on the one hand, it is a means of connection, while, on the other hand, it is a tool of segregation. By focusing on the Arab-Jewish community in Israel, Dallashi sheds light on processes that have resulted in what she calls 'the dialectical relations in which Arabic concomitantly represents various, contradicting and even dissonant values'.

The final chapter examines a crucial and highly sensitive topic from a unique angle. Muhammad Amara's 'War Names in the Arab–Israeli Conflict: A Comparative Study' analyses the names given to the different wars – from 1948 hitherto – on both the Israeli and Arab sides. Amara surveys and analyses the names given to six wars (in the years 1948, 1956, 1967, 1973, 1982 and 2006), two Palestinian *intifāḍas* (1987 and 2000), and three Israeli attacks on Gaza (2008, 2012 and 2014) in Hebrew and in Arabic. Referencing Suleiman's argument that 'code names offer us snapshots of symbolic meanings along a moving frame . . . However, by tracking the major breaks in this frame, we can identify the major sociopolitical ruptures in society,' Amara highlights how language in the Israeli–Arab conflict not only reflects events in the political arena and on the battlefield, but also shapes the realities of both sides of the conflict.

We wish to conclude on a personal note: editing this book was a tremendously satisfying opportunity, enabling both of us to gain new perspectives on Yasir Suleiman's work and research. Suleiman remains original, thought-provoking and as influential as ever. It was truly our pleasure to revisit some of his work and to be impressed, anew, at his deep reflections – both powerful and crucial – about language.

Furthermore, it was a tremendous honour to edit this book together. Both of us are former PhD students of Yasir. In this unique partnership – one of us is a native Hebrew-speaker, while the other's mother tongue is Arabic, one of us is Jewish and the other Muslim, one was born in Jerusalem and the other comes from a family that was displaced and uprooted from its Palestinian village of ʿImwās[1] – we did our best to give a broad perspective on Yasir Suleiman's contribution to the field of language and society, but also to his unique interests and personal life story. In relation to Yasir Suleiman's Palestinian origin and his connection to Palestine, we can only hope that one day his research – followed by ours – will include an analysis of the language of justice and equality, of return and of reconciliation, in the Middle East generally, and in Palestine/Israel specifically.

With much appreciation and great admiration, we dedicate this book to Professor Yasir Suleiman. We truly hope that he will continue to explore and discover new worlds using his unique and original language compass.

Note

1. A small village on the road between Jerusalem and Ramallah that was completely evacuated and destroyed by the Israeli military in June 1967. Currently, the village is the host of Canada Park, which was created and named to change and erase the Palestinian identity of the village and the whole area.

References

Or, Iair G., *Creating a Style for a Generation: The Beliefs and Ideologies of Hebrew Language Planners* (Tel Aviv: Ov– Z.A.P, 2016, in Hebrew).

Suleiman, Y., *Arabic Sociolinguistics: Issues and Perspectives* (Richmond: Curzon, 1994).

Suleiman, Y., *The Arabic Grammatical Tradition: A Study in Taʿlīl* (Edinburgh: Edinburgh University Press, 1999).

Suleiman, Y., *The Arabic Language and National Identity: A Study in Ideology* (Edinburgh: Edinburgh University Press, 2003).

Suleiman, Y., *A War of Words: Language and Conflict in the Middle East* (Cambridge: Cambridge University Press, 2004).

Suleiman, Y., *Arabic, Self and Identity: A Study in Conflict and Displacement* (Oxford: Oxford University Press, 2011).

Suleiman, Y., *Arabic in the Fray: Language Ideology and Cultural Politics* (Edinburgh: Edinburgh University Press, 2013).

Suleiman, Y. (ed.), *Being Palestinian: Personal Reflections on Palestinian Identity in the Diaspora* (Edinburgh: Edinburgh University Press, 2016).

Wernberg-Møller, A., 'Sociolinguistic meaning in code-switching: The case of Moroccans in Edinburgh', in Y Suleiman (ed.), *Language and Society in the Middle East and North Africa: Studies in Variation and Identity* (Richmond: Curzon, 1999), pp. 234–58.

CHAPTER 1

The Hauntology of Language and Identity[1]

John E. Joseph

Introduction

A few months ago, in a tea shop in the historic district of Taipei, something a tour guide said started a train of thought that led me to Yasir Suleiman. The guide was explaining how in the traditional three-room Taiwanese house we were in, the front room was the shop, where business transactions were carried out, including the serving of tea. The middle room was the family's dwelling, where their meals were prepared and consumed, children conceived, and other recreation and rest enjoyed. The back room was the storehouse for the shop and for the family's own provisions. It struck me how close this is to the layout of the mind as conceived from ancient times until the sixteenth century, not entirely giving way until the end of the eighteenth century, and first set out analytically by the three great medical writers of the tenth and early eleventh centuries, Rhazes, Haly Abbas and Avicenna, all Persians who wrote in the Arabic language (Joseph 2017).

They explained how the brain is composed of grey and white matter that surrounds fluid-filled cells, or ventricles, one in the back, one in the centre and two side-by-side in the front. Because the grey and white matter are cold, being run through by a limited blood supply, it was assumed that the activity of the brain could not be conducted there, but rather in the ventricles, and that the fluid they contained must be various types of spirit (natural, vital and animal) whereby information is transmitted from the sensory organs to the mind, and from the mind to the muscles of the body. As Haly Abbas lays out the cell theory of the brain, the two front ventricles are the location of *phantasia*, imagination; the middle ventricle of *cogitatio*, the reasoning faculty; and the rear ventricle of *memoria*, memory. It is through *phantasia* that the mind represents the outer world to the inner, as the shop is the part of the house where the family transacts with the public. *Cogitatio* is the private inner sanctum of thought, and *memoria* the storehouse serving *phantasia* and *cogitatio*. The picture becomes slightly more complicated with Avicenna, but the three cells remain attached to these three mental functions.

The revival of anatomical observation in the sixteenth century brought about the decline of cerebral ventricular theory and a shift to locating mental functions in the brain matter, rather than the fluid-filled cavities within it, though it still took centuries to develop clear evidence of this. How the functions were conceived meanwhile remained intact. *Cogitatio*, in fact, would in the seventeenth century become the basis for the modern conception of self, who a person is – his identity – through the general understanding of what Descartes meant by his *Cogito ergo sum* (although, as shown by Baker and Morris (1996), this general understanding was some distance from what Descartes actually maintained).

The constellation of the Arabic-language treatises with the question of identity brought Yasir Suleiman out of the storehouse of my *memoria* and into the front room of *phantasia*, that imaginative part of the mind that perceives not just whatever is before one's eyes, or ears or touch, but also what is not. The room in which I can conduct a conversation with a friend halfway across the world, despite having left all electronic devices behind. Perception is not a passive process; the brain is not a screen onto which reality is projected like a film. Perception takes much active mental work on the perceiver's part; the project of phenomenology includes trying to separate out such work from things-in-themselves, and to investigate the possibility of knowing them. Knowledge is social in the sense that something is real if available to anyone's *phantasia*, or at least to that of more than a single person; it is political in the sense that it can be imposed on others by persuasion, by appeal to the *cogitatio* in the case of rational persuasion, by appeal to *memoria* in historical argumentation, by appeal directly to *phantasia* in propaganda and pornography, but also in more respectable aesthetic forms, including art, music, dance and poetry.

The 'storehouse' also figures prominently as a metaphor in writings about language in the nineteenth and twentieth centuries. The *Cours de linguistique générale* (Saussure 1916) contains a number of words translatable as storehouse: *trésor*, *casier*, *magasin*, *dépôt*. It is used as a way of conceiving that part of the brain in which is stored an individual's knowledge of a language. At the same time, Saussure insists that a language is a historical product, and a social fact. The storehouse is haunted, as it were, by voices from the past, and the imagined totality of voices from the present. In fact, the concept of the language as social fact is itself haunted by that imagined totality: Bourdieu (1982: 23) makes a link between the use of *trésor* by Saussure and by Auguste Comte, who Bourdieu says 'offers an exemplary expression of the illusion of linguistic communism that haunts the whole of linguistic theory'.[2]

Language and identity – a conjunction about which Suleiman (2003, 2011) has written so insightfully – are rooted in one another because they occupy the same memory. Chomsky, starting in his 1962 address to the International Congress of Linguists (Joseph 2002), tried to move knowledge of language out of the storehouse of memory and relocate it to the front room, as a mental grammar that is a module of the reasoning faculty, but already by the late 1960s he was returning more and more of it to the 'lexicon', our knowledge of words rather than of rules for combining them and interpreting the syntactic combinations. It is the storeroom of memory that lexicon inhabits. More recent work in philosophy, psychology and linguistics has been focused on extending the mind from the brain outward through the whole of the nervous system (as David Hartley had already done in the eighteenth century, with Alexander Bain professing a modernised version in the nineteenth century) and potentially beyond, to the devices we use as extensions of our minds, starting with the blind person's cane (an example that goes back to Descartes) and continuing perhaps – this part remains controversial – to the mechanical devices on which I Google things I cannot recall. But the brain remains the nerve centre, literally. Not all of language can be accounted for by cerebral activity alone, but while not sufficient, it is necessary. And memory haunts it.

Language and identity

Language and identity is a topic in which contemporary perspectives cannot be neatly separated from historical ones. Identity, even in the here and now, is grounded in beliefs about the past: about heritage and ancestry, and about belonging to a people, a place, a set of beliefs and a way of life. Of the many ways in which such belonging is signified, what language a person speaks, and how he or she speaks it, rank among the most powerful, because it is through language that people and places are named, heritage and ancestry recorded and passed on, beliefs developed and ritualised.

No language exists in a homogeneous or unchanging form. So-called dead languages come closest, being no longer in daily use across a large population, yet even Latin or Old English are known to us through texts showing massive linguistic variation from writer to writer. It is through variation that the identity of individuals is indexed and interpreted – regardless of whether it is deliberately signalled, which is ultimately unknowable (hence, of less interest than its interpretation). Of course, even these languages are not really dead: Latin lives on in the Romance languages, and Old English in Modern English. They evolved steadily over centuries, and the events that punctuated this evolution by re-identifying the Latin of the Iberian peninsula as the Spanish, Portuguese and Catalan languages, for example, were the political and cultural ones that were bound up with the identity of new 'nations' in the early modern period.

The evolution of sounds, words and grammatical forms has been a history of changes that started small, in some particular town or village or hamlet, and spread out through contact with people from other towns and villages. Until the nineteenth century, literacy was very limited, as was education, so writing was a less important factor than we might now imagine. Even the development of mass communication has not put an end to local differences in language use, so that, now as in the past, how people speak indexes where they are from. Even in a given locale, the reality of constant linguistic innovation has meant that different generations speak somewhat differently; and other cultural differences, including religious or sectarian ones, and those associated with gender, and with occupation or education, are indexed as well. Because change does not occur in wholesale fashion, it results in something like layers of time in a language. Any members of the younger generation who resist some new word or pronunciation or intonation used by their age mates, sticking instead to the way their grandparents speak, are likely to have this difference interpreted by others as signifying something deeper about their identity – who they are, what they care about and like, what they aspire to. That is what is meant by 'indexing', and it can have both positive and negative consequences.

Identities are manifested in language as, first, the categories and labels that people attach to themselves and others to signal their belonging; second, as the indexed ways of speaking and behaving through which they perform their belonging; and, third, as the interpretations that others make of those indices. The ability to perceive and interpret the indices is itself part of shared culture. Every individual has a repertoire of identities of various kinds – some combination of national, ethnic, religious, generational and gender identities, together with those relating to social class, sexual orientation, profession and various levels of sub- and supranational belonging. Culture and identity are never entirely separable: it is a defining feature of the concept of a 'culture' that whatever beliefs, values, inclinations, tastes, practices and texts constitute it also serve an identity function for those who participate in the culture. On the other hand, no group can be expected to be culturally homogeneous. The urge to tribalise is too deeply rooted in human nature, indeed in animal behaviour generally, which testifies to how deep it runs in our evolutionary heritage.

So, for instance, within Christian or Muslim religious identity there are various ways of 'being Christian' and 'being Muslim', in other words a variety of Christian and Islamic cultural identities. They are subsumed under the umbrella of a religious identity that itself admits of variants, Orthodox, Catholic and Protestant, Sunni and Shia, and within the latter, Sufis, each with their distinctive practices and texts, even if most of their central beliefs are shared.

'Heritage languages' is a relatively recent term that gets applied to two kinds of minority languages: on the one hand, the language of an immigrant minority in a diaspora setting (for example, Cantonese in the south Chinese community of Cardiff), and, on the other hand, the traditional language of a place that has become a minority language there, its place taken over by some more widely spoken language (for example, Welsh in Cardiff). Heritage languages possess for their speakers and partisans the ability to form a connection to the past, to origins, to ancestors both real and imagined. The philologist and novelist J. R. R. Tolkien considered Welsh to be his 'native language' even though he could not speak it and had no Welsh family background – just a spiritual connection that he felt to the language. 'It is the native language to which in unexplored desire we would still go home' (Tolkien 1963: 41).

There is also an ethical dimension to heritage: as Appiah (2005) has shown, it has the potential to be oppressive. Immigrant parents sometimes try to force a heritage identity on children who identify more with the new country in which they were brought up. He objects to Kymlicka's (1995) stress on recognising and preserving identity groups and cultures, which contributes more to reifying them, constraining the individual's rights, than to liberation.

> When multiculturalists like Kymlicka say that there are so many 'cultures' in this or that country, what drops out of the picture is that every 'culture' represents not only difference but the elimination of difference: the group represents a clump of relative homogeneity, and that homogeneity is perpetuated and enforced by regulative mechanisms designed to marginalise and silence dissent from its basic norms and mores. (Appiah 2005: 152)

We should not, Appiah says, 'ask other people to maintain the diversity of the species at the price of their individual autonomy. We can't require others to provide us with a cultural museum to tour through' (ibid., p. 268).

Marks and spectres

The word *hauntology* (Fr. *hantologie*) was coined by Jacques Derrida in his *Specters of Marx* of 1993. This many-faceted book was his response to the fall of the Berlin Wall in 1989, the collapse of the Soviet Union two years later, and the best-selling *The End of History and the Last Man* (1992), written in reaction to those events by Derrida's one-time student of comparative literature, Francis Fukuyama. Originally a seminar, *Specters of Marx* is framed within reflections on a play by Karl Marx's favourite author. That play opens with its title character confronting the ghost of his father. Both of them are called Hamlet.

Derrida relates how he announced the title of his seminar before opening Marx' and Engels' *Communist Manifesto* for the first time in twenty years, and was startled to read its first sentences: 'A spectre is haunting Europe – the spectre of communism. All the powers of old Europe have entered into a holy alliance to exorcise this spectre.' Derrida realised that this text had been haunting his memory. He was already well aware of being haunted by decades of his own principled resistance to Marxism, which had made life difficult for him in the academic world of 1960s Paris (Peeters 2012).

To the countless occurrences of spectres, spirits, ghosts and phantoms in the *Communist Manifesto* Derrida adds the ongoing spectral existence of Marx's own texts, and the spectres of Marxism that have haunted Europe since the 'death' of Marxism. They may yet rematerialise, as the 'end of history' proves to be less final than Hegel, or indeed Marx, would lead us to think. At the moment that remains hard to imagine. On the other hand, thirty years ago it was hard to imagine that such European 'ghost' nation-states as Serbia, Bosnia-Herzegovina, Montenegro, Macedonia, Ukraine, Belarus, the Baltic and Caucasian republics, and indeed a united Germany, might again become living political realities. My *Oxford World Atlas* from 1988 is now a historical relic, whereas the atlas volume of my 1929 *Encyclopaedia Britannica* is hauntingly up-to-date, apart from the Soviet Union and the Levant.

The term 'historical memory' figures prominently in studies of national and ethnic identity, but it is an odd concept. Memory can only be historical, unless it is false memory, in which case historians would resist calling it 'memory' at all, preferring 'delusion' or 'propaganda'. Yet historians know full well that the historical memories that underpin identity are always partial, in both senses of the word: incomplete and biased. The term 'historical memory' suggests that they are shared across a population in the same form, which is sure to be an illusion except, to a degree, in the case of images that have been captured and widely reproduced. But this means that cinematic representations of events are more likely to form historical memory than the events themselves.

It would be more accurate to call such memories 'spectres'. They are the ghosts that haunt us and the places we inhabit, ghosts that go on defining the places they once peopled, even after globalisation, and go on defining who we are, even in diaspora. The 'we' I am using is spectral: a spirit giving the illusion of material existence. These ghosts manifest themselves in the choice of languages we speak and write, the way we speak and write them and the judgements we make about others based on their speech and writing. We are all expert linguistic hauntologists.

To reassure any rationalists who may be reading this, hauntology is not about believing that your house is haunted by spooks who appear in the night and hide your keys and phone. In the words of Jameson (1999: 39):

> Spectrality does not involve the conviction that ghosts exist or that the past (and maybe even the future they offer to prophesy) is still very much alive and at work, within the living present: all it says, if it can be thought to speak, is that the living present is scarcely as self-sufficient as it claims to be; that we would do well not to count on its density and solidity, which might under exceptional circumstances betray us.

This is a minimalist stance, designed so as not to frighten the children, horses or social scientists. I am not sure how 'exceptional' the circumstances are in which 'the living present' exposes its metaphorical nature. And 'hard' scientists would have little trouble recognising 'density' or 'solidity' as illusory when it comes to time, and our perceptions of it as linear.

Pace Jameson, we are all haunted. That is another way of conceiving of the multiple identities we . . . what? Perform? Inhabit? I grope for the ghost of a verb that has never existed, like Dickens' Ghost of Christmas Yet to Come. Not *have* – more like *do*. More still like *are*, except that if you say 'Your identity is who you are', you risk being misunderstood as claiming that your identity limits what you can be.[3] The haunting fact is that every sentence you utter is haunted by its possible interpretations, some of which may run exactly counter to what you, its author, think. You can try to act like an exorcist, slaying the demonic misinterpretations by which your innocent sentences are possessed. At best, though, you can only hope to slay those you become aware of. They multiply as you push your thinking forward. As Davis (2005: 378–9) writes, 'For Derrida, the ghost's secret . . . is not unspeakable because it is taboo, but because it cannot not (yet) be articulated in the languages available to us. The ghost pushes at the boundaries of language and thought.'

And after you are gone, the things you have written carry on, the spectres of your once-living thought. So do the things you have spoken: the founding text of modern linguistics was assembled from notes taken by the students of Ferdinand de Saussure, and published in his name three years after he died. How spectral is that?

Not just our sentences but our *voices* are haunted, by the ghosts of those we grew up among. The people may still be living, but it is their younger selves whose spectral presence abides in our accents. The sociolinguistic indices of where we are from, geographically and socially, are the spectres of, not Marx, but marks – those others made on us, on our *habitus*, to use the medieval term conjured up again by Bourdieu. And what is your *habitus*, if not the ghost of you, insofar as you are the social product of your upbringing? An upbringing that developed very rapidly when you were a child, but not definitively. Your upbringing continues still today, as does mine.

Unheimlichkeit and otherness

In a long footnote to *Specters of Marx* (pp. 274–5n.), Derrida discusses Freud's 1919 essay 'Das Unheimliche', a difficult title to translate. *Unheimlich* is the opposite of *heimlich*, 'homely' in the sense of familiar, of the family. It is sometimes translated as 'uncanny', but 'an *unheimlich* house' appears in the standard translations as 'a haunted house'. Returning to the mind–house analogy I drew at the start of this chapter, the house that is the Freudian mind has a secret subterranean chamber, accessible through the back room of memory. There ghosts from our early childhood abide alongside ghosts from human prehistory, directing the movements on the floor above as in a magnetic puppet theatre.

Approaching *unheimlich* from two directions – a cross-linguistic etymological study of the word, and examples of what arouses the feeling – Freud finds that 'both courses lead to the same result: the uncanny is that class of the frightening which leads back to what is known of old and long familiar' ([1919] 1955: 220), in other words, to what is *heimlich*. 'Thus *heimlich* is a word the meaning of which develops in the direction of ambivalence, until it finally coincides with its opposite, *unheimlich* . . . [T]he *unheimlich* is what was once *heimlich*, familiar; the prefix "*un*" is the token of repression' (ibid., pp. 226, 245). He notes also that 'In Arabic and Hebrew "uncanny" means the same as "daemonic", "gruesome"' (ibid., p. 221).

Derrida ([1993] 1994: 196n.) remarks on how, for Freud, the ghosts in *Hamlet*, *Macbeth* and *Julius Caesar* are 'wholly devoid of any power of *Unheimlichkeit*'. They are not 'spooky', not horror film ghosts, but familiar, people the characters have known, part of the family, the home. They are also real actors, agents, *the* real actors pushing the living characters into action, most obviously in the case of Hamlet. Derrida (ibid.) comments: 'Explanation: literature, theatrical fiction. According to Freud, we adapt our judgment to the conditions of fictive reality, such as they are established by the poet, and treat "souls, spirits and specters" like grounded, normal, legitimate existences.' Derrida is puzzled by this explanation, given that all the examples Freud gives of *Unheimlichkeit* in the essay are also drawn from literature.

It is evident why Freud would take a particular interest in these Shakespearean ghosts: as the spectral manifestations of the unconscious minds of Brutus, Macbeth and Hamlet Jr. The service they did Freud has been repaid. Despite all the revolutions in religion and psychology of the last 400 years, and particularly of the twentieth century, these continue to rank as three of the great pieces of literature of any time or culture, owing more than a little to how the rise of psychological enquiry helped to raise and underpin their reputation, even as European society as a whole was becoming steadily more materialistic.

It is psychology too – social psychology – that has turned identity, including its linguistic dimension, from something of interest to social anthropologists studying national cultures, to an enquiry into the beliefs, behaviours and practices of individuals, and of their more local group belongings. The work of the late Eric Hobsbawm helped to smooth the passage, against the current of a lingering association of national, ethnic and religious identities with racism, oppression and bigotry (see, e.g., Hobsbawm 1990). Fifteen years ago it was still thought dangerous to investigate such things, as if grappling with them would lend them academic respectability, rather than lessen their power. I have been told by some younger American academics that to study any manifestation of race or ethnicity was to acknowledge the social force of these categories, and so to underwrite their reality. I believe the opposite: to bury one's head in the sand and pretend the categories do not have social force is to give them support, by letting them operate unquestioned and unopposed. In the zombie movie, I am not the guy who thinks we're safe locking the doors and windows; I am the one going for the baseball bat and shotgun. Even we who take 'race' to be a ghastly social construction with no active essentialist force would be fools to ignore its spectres.

Derrida was by profession a philosopher, yet it was in literary studies that his insights first gained an international audience. There, writes Davis (2005: 373):

> Derrida's rehabilitation of ghosts as a respectable subject of enquiry has proved to be extraordinarily fertile. Hauntology supplants its near-homonym ontology, replacing the priority of being and presence with the figure of the ghost as that which is neither present nor absent, neither dead nor alive. Attending to the ghost is an ethical injunction insofar as it occupies the place of the Levinasian Other: a wholly irrecuperable intrusion in our world, which is not comprehensible within our available intellectual frameworks, but whose otherness we are responsible for preserving.

The Levinasian Other is very familiar to those of us who come to the study of language and identity from a social psychological-*cum*-anthropological direction. It is Emmanuel Levinas' version of what Henri Tajfel called the in-group/out-group dichotomy (Levinas 1980; Tajfel 1978). For Tajfel, identity is grounded as much in difference from an out-group as in solidarity with our in-group. This is a Saussurean dichotomy, based on value generated by difference, within which there is an inherent tension. If those we say we keep out are still shaping us, then they remain somehow *within*, as a force shaping the essentialist identity that we erect in order to ensure that they stay out. Well, are they in or out? It is a classic deconstruction scenario: they are both and neither. As with the *(un)heimlich*, the dichotomy cannot exorcise the spectral presence of the Other.

When we say with Anderson (1991), following Renan (1882), that a nation is an imagined community – not the physical land or even the people, but their shared practice of remembering and forgetting – we are identifying the nation as a spiritual entity, with an economy of ghosts that are conjured up and exorcised as needed.

When with Billig (1995) we speak of the particular force of 'banal nationalism' – the everyday symbols that are only half-perceived, and are all the more psychologically powerful on that account – now we are in the company of Freud's ghosts who lack *Unheimlichkeit*, spectres we accept as having 'normal, legitimate existences' because 'we ply our judgements according to *fictive* reality', the reality of a national identity that is a tissue woven of fictive threads, texts, selective memories, stories of ghosts conjured and exorcised.

Haunted by otherness

Reading Bassiouney (2009: 61) I was struck by an example she took from a 1999 paper by Alison Wernberg-Møller. It involves a Moroccan family who had been living in Edinburgh for around twenty years. The daughter Samia (S.A.) is describing to Wernberg-Møller a book she has been reading, when her mother Z.A. walks in.

S.A.: it's based on a girl it's like it goes through different ... it's like ... y'know it goes through in stages like y'know you've got a seed time, harvest time ... em ...
Z.A.: *qulha b-l'Arabiyya*! [TELL HER IN ARABIC!]
S.A.: *man 'arafshi kayfsh ngulha b-l'Arabiyya* [I DON'T KNOW HOW TO TELL HER IN ARABIC] ... and those times y'know are sort of like ... it's like a circle y'know how things change.

It seemed familiar to me, as if I had lived it myself. I finally realised that I had heard this paper when it was first presented at a conference back in 1997. It had not lodged itself firmly in my memory, perhaps because of how Weinberg-Møller's considerable analytical nous was limited by the vocabulary available to us for treating issues of language and identity. Weinberg-Møller frames the text in terms of 'code-switching', specifically as 'an example of a situational switch', in which 'Z.A. may be thought of as attempting to redefine the situation in terms of the primary purpose of the session, which is to record S.A. speaking in Arabic. In this case Z.A. only manages a partial redefinition before S.A. switches back to English again.'

Research into code-switching is frequently bound up with Conversation Analysis, a very strict methodology that forbids the analyst from bringing any psychological explanations into the analysis; everything must be grounded very directly in the linguistic interchanges between speakers. To Wernberg-Møller's credit, she pushes such restrictions to their limit, and does not deprive readers of her very astute insights into the conversations that she personally witnessed and recorded. At times, she gives what appear to be her empathetic readings of what the speakers were experiencing, as when she talks about *obligations*: 'when S.A. switches her attention to Z.A. she is aware of an obligation to reply in Arabic since this would usually be her normal linguistic behaviour with her mother'. She says too that Samia's 'use of English is *dictated* by the difficulty S.A. encounters in speaking of certain topics in Arabic' (my italics). In between these statements about dictates and obligations Wernberg-Møller says that 'The fact that S.A. is responding to a command already in Arabic does not necessarily mean her response will also be in Arabic, but ... there is an increased likelihood that it will be', because of the 'obligation' imposed by what 'would usually be her normal linguistic behaviour with her mother'. This is confusing: is the 'obligation' about obeying her mother, speaking Arabic to her mother or behaving consistently? What kind of 'obligation' manifests itself as 'an increased likelihood'? And is the choice of English *certainly dictated* by what she is saying?

Certainly, the switch to Arabic is *not* dictated by what her mother tells her, for although Samia replies to her in Arabic, it is to say that she *is not* about to speak in Arabic as ordered. She invokes the content of what she is telling, but it is unconvincing: she is not talking about things that it would be hard to express in Arabic if she were telling them to her mother. So, yes, addressee is primary in the switch, which is probably what is meant by labelling it 'situational'.

One might also approach the passage from a language and identity perspective: Samia evidently wants to project her identity as a British or Scottish girl – there is at least an index of Scottishness indicated by her pausing with *em* instead of *um*; other such indices occur elsewhere in her speech. Z.A. wants her daughter to project her identity as someone of Moroccan heritage, with all that this is bound up with in terms of culture, religion, values and behaviour in addition to language. Today, at least, Samia is rejecting this unequivocally.

What more might a hauntological perspective help us to say about the passage? One can sense ghosts present here: a mother haunted by what her own grandmother and mother might have thought of this Europeanised Samia, and by the ghosts of English-monolingual Grandchildren Yet to Come. Of her own culture, and maybe religion, fading into a spectral presence in her own family, within her lifetime, through a decision to emigrate in which she was complicit. In the Arabic-speaking countries of the Middle East and North Africa, globalisation has been connected with significant social changes, none of which lacks precedents in earlier history. For centuries, people from these lands have emigrated northward and westward – as well as to south of the Sahara, and eastward deep into Asia – usually without returning, which was a possibility only for a small, privileged pre-revolutionary élite. Their princely life in their homeland could never be matched by a middle-class existence in Europe or the New World.

For the emigrating masses the reverse was the case. Despite their abiding love for the homeland of their memoryscape, it was a place of relative constraint, limitations on education, on opportunity, on whom one might associate with and marry. It may not have been a life of poverty or squalor, but one easily squeezed at the whim of a ruler or even of a corrupt local official. The comforts and chains of tradition stood in stark contrast to the *modernity* represented by the West. What has changed with the globalisation trend of the last two decades is that, first, more of the children of the middle class went to Europe or the Americas for their university education and professional training, and, second, more of them have returned home. Adding to this trend, the expansion of overseas universities into the region has meant that a Western education, in a Western language, has been available without leaving the homeland.

Increasingly, the language has been English, whereas in previous periods it was at least as likely to be French. The rise of English has been marked even in the former French colonies of North Africa, where the French linguistic heritage remains strong. Suleiman has written of how, in North African Francophone writing of the colonial period,

> French carries in its social and cultural DNA, so to speak, a set of ideological meanings and historical experiences of domination and hegemony that clash with the ideological meanings of Arabic as a covert and absent language. And by virtue of being endowed with symbolic meaning, language choice acts as proxy for accessing the hidden myths of the two languages . . . (Suleiman 2013: 208)

Another way of saying this is that North African Francophone writing is doubly haunted: by the guilty ghost of the French language's experience of domination and hegemony, and by the ghost of the repressed Arabic, each voicing its myths in a clashing cacophony. A third ghost might be included, that of Berber, dominated and repressed by both French and Arabic (Saadi-Mokrane 2002).

English has ghosts of its own in the Middle East, and even in North Africa, but their lamentations are not so loud as to cancel out how the language is indexed for 'modernity', 'technology' and 'education', with all the associations – negative as well as positive – that those terms carry. Amongst the positive associations are those of democracy, even though there is no logical reason why that concept is not perfectly compatible with Arabic or any other language. We are dealing here with an indexation that is essentially historical, and based on a semiotics of difference: if the region's traditional cultures are associated with autocracy, paternalism and the like, and if Arabic is their traditional language of expression, then English will be perceived and felt as embodying the opposite features.

Across the Middle East and North Africa, the Internet has become a social force every bit as powerful as in Europe and the Americas. Indeed, it allows for the constant, real-time existence of a pan-Arabic-language culture that extends across the globe, interweaved with a pan-English-language culture that runs still further and deeper. It is important to remember, though, that the 'polyphony' that this suggests is not an unprecedented development, let alone a 'post-modern' one (whatever that may mean). In fact, the term polyphony was first used in this context in the 1930s by Bakhtin, to designate a condition of language generally: that dialects and voices are always intermingled, and always have been (Bakhtin 1981). No language can ever be 'pure' of the ongoing influence of the other languages with which it co-exists in the repertoires of bilingual speakers.

What about Samia: trying to drive a stake through the heart of this vampire-mother who would force her into what, for her, is a spectral world of old people's memories, foreign enough to be *Unheimlichkeit*, and yet not so foreign as to be completely not a part of her? She must spend part of her life exorcising her Moroccan spirits so as to project an identity to her peers that she is one of them, and part of her life feeling guilt for that, and a deep sense of loss, not just of a heritage that at some level she must value, but of the closeness to her mother that must inevitably wane in adolescence, as our child-self becomes a ghost we both flee and regret.

And yet – what is Samia reading? A book about a girl going through the stages of life, compared with seed time and harvest time – not something modern Edinburgh children know much about, unless they come from an Indian or African background, where rural life is only one or two generations distant, rather than three or four. *It's like a circle y'know how things change*. They do indeed, but their ghosts remain, often in one's mother's voice.

Rereading Bassiouney hauntologically sent me back to Wernberg-Møller's article, where I found another example that must have made little impression on me in 1997.

Z.A. had been talking about a cousin of hers in Morocco who had been possessed by a *jinn*; she and her daughter gave me a lengthy and rather excited account of how the *jinn* affected her cousin and what was done in the end to get rid of the *jinn*. Z.A. describes the girl under the influence of the *jinn*:

> *khasha* [SHE NEEDED (NEEDS)] seven people! . . . they canna' . . . they canna' hold her . . . *taqtilhum! Sita, saba', taqtilhum! . . . kay anna l'afrit li f-ha huwa li kiykhadimha!* [SHE WOULD KILL (KILLS) THEM! SIX, SEVEN, SHE WOULD KILL (KILLS) THEM! . . . AS IF THE DEMON INSIDE HER (HE) IS THE ONE WORKING (CONTROLLING) HER]. (Wernberg-Møller 1999: 248)

I know now how Derrida felt when, after choosing the title *Specters of Marx*, he opened *The Communist Manifesto* to find the word *spectre* three times in the opening lines. This time it is Z.A. switching into English – Scottish English (*canna'*) – in her excitement and eagerness to relay this story of demonic possession. Her own Scottish ghost has made itself heard. Note that Samia too was joining in excitedly: for this Moroccan *jinn* has brought old-fashioned mother and modern daughter together, narratively and linguistically, and brings them closer thematically to the Algerian Derrida.

We naturally assume that belief in ghosts belongs to a pre-modern age. At the end of the First World War Max Weber (1919) lamented how modernism was bringing about an *Entzauberung*, an un-magicking or disenchanting of the world. It was only partially successful: we *profess* to be materialistic empiricists, but our rhetoric gives us away (see further Joseph 2014).

Conclusion

The power of Yasir Suleiman's work comes from the vast knowledge he brings to bear in his linguistic analysis from so many domains of the social sciences and humanities. Such breadth has become ever rarer as linguistics has strived for a scientific narrowness that gives the appearance of precision, but surrenders any hope of capturing the full complexity of language. Suleiman has resisted and continues to resist such narrowness.

I have done my best in this chapter to emulate Suleiman's intellectual breadth by proposing that hauntology, a set of ideas originating in the writing of Derrida, has much to offer us by way of insights into linguistic identity. In Joseph (2004) I argued against what had become a strong tendency to eliminate any considerations of essentialism from the analysis of identity, on the grounds that national or ethnic essences are fictive constructs, and have yielded disastrous consequences in the form of racism and genocide. My argument was that, however fictive they may be, those consequences prove their real power; and that we cannot understand their essentialist nature without getting our hands dirty with some analysis of how essences get constructed. In a similar vein, since identities are not purely rational (or purely irrational), but have a strong emotional component – not that a stark dichotomy between the rational and the emotional will stand up to much prodding – a fuller understanding of them can be gained if we expand and enrich our rational comfort zone with the not-irrational set of analytic concepts that hauntology bids us to consider.

Notes

1. I am grateful to Reem Bassiouney and the participants in her seminar at Georgetown University for listening to the first version of this chapter and engaging in helpful discussion of it. I reminded them that, much as Edinburgh is the home of the creators of both the ultra-empiricist Sherlock Holmes and the mystical Harry Potter, and where British sociolinguistics had its start in the 1970s, Georgetown, that epicentre of American empiricist sociolinguistic work, has made no greater contribution to world culture than *The Exorcist*.
2. My translation. Original: 'offre une expression exemplaire de l'illusion du communisme linguistique qui hante toute la théorie linguistique'. Bourdieu bases this judgement on a citation from Comte (1852: 254).
3. This is how one sociolinguist friend of mine initially reacted to my book *Language and Identity* (Joseph 2004), which begins, 'Put as simply as possible, your identity is who you are.' When I told him that I was simply trying to define what we mean when we talk about 'identity', he accepted that this was a more obvious reading, and went on to write one of my more positive reviews.

References

Anderson, B., *Imagined Communities: Reflections on the Origin and Spread of Nationalism*, 2nd edn (London and New York: Verso, [1983], 1993).

Appiah, K. A., *The Ethics of Identity* (Princeton, NJ: Princeton University Press, 2005).

Baker, G. and Morris, K. J., *Descartes' Dualism* (London and New York: Routledge, 1996).

Bakhtin, M. M., *The Dialogic Imagination: Four Essays*, ed. M. Holquist, trans. C. Emerson and M. Holquist (Austin, TX: University of Texas Press, 1981).

Bassiouney, R., *Arabic Sociolinguistics* (Edinburgh: Edinburgh University Press, 2009).

Billig, M., *Banal Nationalism* (London: Sage, 1995).

Bourdieu, P., *Ce que parler veut dire: L'économie des échanges linguistiques* (Paris: Fayard, 1982).

Comte, A., *Système de politique positive, ou Traité de sociologie, instituant la religion de l'humanité*, vol. 2 (Paris: chez l'auteur; chez Carilian-Gœury & Dalmont, 1852).

Davis, C., '*État présent*: Hauntology, spectres and phantoms', *French Studies* 59(3) (2005): 373–9.

Derrida, J., *Spectres de Marx: L'État de la dette, le travail du deuil et la nouvelle Internationale* (Paris: Galilée, 1993; English version, *Specters of Marx: The State of the Debt, the Work of Mourning, and the New International*, trans. Peggy Kamuf, London and New York: Routledge, 1994).

Freud, S., 'Das Unheimliche', *Imago: Zeitschrift für Anwendung der Psychoanalyse auf die Geisteswissenschaften* 5 (1919): 297–324; English version, 'The uncanny', trans. J. Strachey, in collaboration with A. Freud, assisted by A. Strachey and A. Tyson, in J. Strachey (ed.), *The Standard Edition of the Complete Psychological Works of Sigmund Freud, vol. XVII: 1917–1919* (London: Hogarth Press and the Institute of Psycho-Analysis, 1955), pp. 217–52.

Fukuyama, F., *The End of History and the Last Man* (New York: The Free Press, 1992).

Hobsbawm, E. J., *Nations and Nationalism since 1780: Programmes, Myth, Reality* (Cambridge: Cambridge University Press, 1990).

Jameson, F., 'Marx's purloined letter', in M. Sprinkler (ed.), *Ghostly Demarcations: A Symposium on Jacques Derrida's* Specters of Marx (London and New York: Verso, 1999), pp. 26–67.

Joseph, J. E., *From Whitney to Chomsky: Essays in the History of American Linguistics* (Amsterdam and Philadelphia: John Benjamins, 2002).

Joseph, J. E., *Language and Identity: National, Ethnic, Religious* (Basingstoke and New York: Palgrave Macmillan, 2004).

Joseph, J. E., '"The wolf in itself": The uses of enchantment in the development of modern linguistics', in R. Bod, J. Maat and T. Weststeijn (eds), *The Making of the Humanities, vol. III: The Modern Humanities* (Amsterdam: Amsterdam University Press, 2014), pp. 81–95.

Joseph, J. E., *Language, Mind and Body: A Conceptual History* (Cambridge: Cambridge University Press, 2017).

Kymlicka, W., *Multicultural Citizenship: A Liberal Theory of Minority Rights* (Oxford: Oxford University Press, 1995).

Levinas, E., *Le temps et l'autre* (Montpellier: Fata Morgana, 1980; English version, *Time and the Other*, trans. R. A. Cohen, Pittsburgh: Duquesne University Press, 1987).

Peeters, B., *Derrida* (Paris: Flammarion, 2012; English version, *Derrida: A Biography*, trans. A. Brown, Cambridge: Polity, 2013).

Renan, E., *Qu'est-ce qu'une nation? Conférence faite en Sorbonne, le 11 mars 1882* (Paris: Calmann Lévy, 1882).

Saadi-Mokrane, D., 'The Algerian linguicide', in A.-E. Berger (ed.), *Algeria in Others' Languages* (Ithaca, NY: Cornell University Press, 2002), pp. 44–78.

Saussure, F. de, *Cours de linguistique générale*, ed. C. Bally and A. Sechehaye, with the assistance of A. Riedlinger (Paris and Lausanne: Payot, 1916; English version, *Course in General Linguistics*, trans. W. Baskin, New York: Philosophical Library, 1959).

Suleiman, Y., *The Arabic Language and National Identity: A Study in Ideology* (Edinburgh: Edinburgh University Press, 2003).

Suleiman, Y., *Arabic, Self and Identity: A Study in Conflict and Displacement* (Oxford: Oxford University Press, 2011).

Suleiman, Y., *Arabic in the Fray: Language Ideology and Cultural Politics* (Edinburgh: Edinburgh University Press, 2013).

Tajfel, H., 'Social categorization, social identity and social comparison', in H. Tajfel (ed.), *Differentiation between Social Groups: Studies in the Social Psychology of Intergroup Relations* (London: Academic Press, 1978), pp. 61–76.

Tolkien, J. R. R., 'English and Welsh', in H. Lewis (ed.), *Angles and Britons: O'Donnell Lectures* (Cardiff: University of Wales Press, 1963), pp. 1–44.

Weber, M., *Wissenschaft als Beruf* (Munich: Duncker & Humblot, 1919).

Wernberg-Møller, A., 'Sociolinguistic meaning in code-switching: The case of Moroccans in Edinburgh', in Y. Suleiman (ed.), *Language and Society in the Middle East and North Africa: Studies in Variation and Identity* (Richmond: Curzon, 1999), pp. 234–58.

CHAPTER 2

Transcultural Content and Translingual Reflection: Rethinking the Arabic Language Learning Experience

Karin Christina Ryding

> Civilizations have never occurred or survived for long simply by fighting off all the others: beneath a superficial level of defensive propaganda, every great civilization is made up of endless traffic with others.
>
> Edward Said, 2000

In terms of civilisations both fending off and trafficking with others, Said's words above have never been truer. An intricate and difficult inter-cultural dialogue is taking place between the Muslim world and the West. This dialogue has long been fraught, but it increases in both complexity and depth with the addition of neo-Islamic terrorist threats to safety and security. It has never been more important to understand the Arab world and its cultures, and certainly the path to understanding culture lies through language. Not short-term programmes and measures to meet 'tactical needs', but long-term strategies to increase the quality and quantity of intellectual engagement with other cultures through extended study of language and culture.[1] American institutions of learning have paid increasing attention to the teaching of Arabic in the past fifteen years, but little consultation or agreement has ensued among those who see the learning of Arabic as the intersection of national needs with practical skills, those who know and understand the sociolinguistics or the linguistic ethnography of Arabic, those who prepare and publish learning materials, and those who see language education essentially as a path to literary appreciation and expertise. In particular, the sociolinguistics of Arabic remains a neglected aspect of language education, despite the key contributions of Yasir Suleiman and others to understanding the inner and outer dimensions of Arabic language, culture, society and identity.[2] Arabic and other discourse communities are built both on continuities that are strongly sensed among members, and also on comfort levels in differentiating private and public discourse events. This ease of shift from one realm to another seems natural to native speakers of a language, but is among the hardest things to learn for newcomers to the language, even after several years of formal instruction. In Arabic, the complexities of discourse calibration and the distance between acrolect and basilect have both deterred and discouraged empirical analysis of vernacular discourse and have ultimately impoverished the resources for curriculum planning and teaching Arabic as a foreign language.[3] But it may be time for a shift of perspective, because as Homi Bhabha has observed, 'Learning to work with the contradictory strains of languages *lived*, and languages *learned*, has the potential for a remarkable critical and creative impulse' (emphasis in original) (Bhabha [1994] 2012: x). The lived Arabic language is the mother tongue, the vernacular; the learned Arabic language is *fuṣḥā*, the language of writing.

The Arabic vernacular system, which covers all forms of spoken Arabic, maintains itself through a kind of fluid stability. The allotropic complexity of Arabic discourses requires that Arabic learners be aware of this system in order to deal with the transcultural realities of living and working in the Arab world using appropriately variant forms of Arabic for all types of interaction. Writing and reading in Standard Arabic are appropriate activities; informal discourse conducted in Standard Arabic is not. Teaching minimal oral skills in one dialect (often, Egyptian) is a step forward, but teaching the essentials of the vernacular system, and the pragmatics and procedures of negotiated discourse in vernacular Arabic is important knowledge for those who aim for advanced and enlightened expertise in Arabic studies. There is reason to be pragmatic in our approach to a skill area that is an ever-moving target: the daily 'drift' of contemporary spoken Arabics reflects the fact that they are unanchored by any central authority or authoritative vernacular text, and the spoken Arabics of today are shifting and drifting dramatically as speakers deal with emergent vernacular literacy in social media and take their place in the fast-moving culture of technology and social order, the new 'vernacular cosmopolitanism' (Bhabha [1994] 2012: ix).[4] Grasping the central nodes of oral expression that allow adequate communication to take place between native speakers and non-native speakers is more and more the key for Arabic second-language acquisition (ASLA). Researching and teaching discourse negotiation skills, including the ability to use an appropriate mid-level or mesolect form of spoken Arabic that travels efficiently throughout the Arab world, remains a salient issue in ASLA programme and curriculum development today (as it has been for well over a decade), along with inter-cultural pragmatics. Linguistic flexibility, interactive discourse pragmatics and 'symbolic competence' need to be considered as part of standard academic practice.[5]

The false Arabic parallel and reverse privileging

Many academic programmes in the US, and even many government training programmes, claim to focus on communicative competence through the outmoded construct of teaching standard-Arabic-only for all forms of interaction, including conversation, listening, negotiating and other spoken discourse functions, as well as for reading and writing. A false parallel with more commonly taught languages (French or German, for instance) has been established under the misleading assumption that the standard written language is also the standard spoken language (or at least close). But there is no standard spoken Arabic; there are regional spoken Arabics, and although there are definite similarities among them, there is no normed, overall standard vernacular Arabic, nor are any of the regiolects normed or anchored in codified grammatical rules.[6] Moreover, as we know through the pioneering work of Elsaid Badawi, performance hierarchies and mixed levels of discourse are found in every regional dialect area.[7] Negotiating discourse appropriateness in Arabic is a skill that is rarely formally taught, but it is an essential component of proficiency, performance and translingual reflection.

Along with the false parallels to more commonly taught languages, Arabic pedagogical tradition has reversed both the importance and sequence of spoken and written language knowledge. Rather than approach language acquisition gradually through basic interactive communicative skills, Arabic learners are normally introduced to the language through the written form only. Although this strategy is often justified as teaching 'the hard parts' (see Perkins 2009: 79), as a prelude to teaching the (reputedly easier) spoken forms, it is not necessarily so. As I have noted elsewhere (Ryding 2006b, 2013a, 2015), the privileging of the written form results in building false confidence in the learner and may also lead to communicative dysfunction if and when learners try to use literary Arabic for ordinary discourse. I have labelled this kind of pedagogical practice 'reverse privileging' (see Ryding 2006b, 2017b). Dismissive attitudes towards Arabic vernacular speech have long prevailed in Arabic studies. But these attitudes are both out of line and outmoded because they are based on the fallacy of easy access; that is, the mistaken idea that colloquial Arabic is infinitely simpler to acquire and use than the written variety, and that the best way to learn it is by in-country exposure subsequent to instruction in *fuṣḥā*, without 'wasting' time on teaching colloquial Arabic in the formal classroom. However, new approaches to discourse-in-context take into account the multiple factors involved in interaction, and open the teaching of spoken language to multiple layers of analysis. There are, for example, a range of paralinguistic behaviours that occur in interactive discourse, but which are absent from any study of the literary form. As Asif Agha states:

> Events in which we look at discourse-in-context are invariably events in which perceivable linguistic signs (or tokens of 'discourse') are accompanied by a range of nonlinguistic signs. Attempts to study discourse are, in effect, attempts to study

> the co-deployment of linguistic and nonlinguistic signs in social interaction. (Agha 2005: 1)

In addition to paralinguistc behaviours, discourse contexts of use can be determining factors in the choice of discourse level and style. Construction grammar theorists include these elements as part of the 'grammar' of any language:

> In a discourse approach to constructions, context features [such as age, gender, education, lifestyle, genre, text-type and speech community values] are not outside of constructions, but part of the constructions. Together with the internal features, they specify resources for language users in an ordinary constructional fashion. When looked at in this manner, 'contextual features' that affect variability are not seen as being outside grammar, but as being part of grammar. (Östman and Truesdale, 2013: 488)

Using Arabic discourse: the Arabic repertoire

Yasir Suleiman's extensive work in Arabic sociolinguistics has opened a gateway to Arabic discourse analysis, identity issues, indexicality and interdiscursive relations.[8] An important further step for the Arabic linguistics community is to incorporate such insights into academic work for those who learn Arabic as a foreign language. Of course, not everything can be taught about a culture's interactive discourse practices, but sociolinguistics and linguistic anthropology have much to offer Arabic pedagogy, especially in terms of analysis of social processes that involve language. Because social processes have been largely divorced from Arabic instruction, there is a significant skills gap between what students learn in the classroom and what they need to do in order to be able to comprehend the world outside the classroom. Not only is there a gap between written and spoken Arabic, but there is much to be done in terms of studying connections and relationships between spoken language and spoken language actions; in other words, semiosis writ large. This chapter is therefore a call for more extensive interdisciplinary research that connects Arabic language instruction with culturally embedded interdiscursive relations. It is also a call for more considered examination of the ecology of linguistic difference in the Arab world.

For example, the idea of 'native speaker' in Arabic as a construct towards which to direct language learning goals is, as Blommaert and Rampton express it, almost 'impossible to reconcile with the facts of linguistic diversity, mixed languages and multilingualism . . . Instead [sociolinguists] work with the notion of linguistic repertoire' (2011: 4).[9] As Michael Geisler has put it:

> Let's re-evaluate the primacy of the native-speaker ideal and its pedagogical implications: to clone, in the language classroom, fully inculturated speakers of French or Italian or Japanese.[10] Without an Archimedean point, anchored in the learner's

> identity, coupled with the awareness of the liminality involved in every cultural crossover phenomenon, all we get are very articulate parrots. (We have all encountered the occasional very gifted near-native speaker of a foreign language who has nothing to say but says it beautifully.) That is why the MLA ad hoc committee's report[11] calls for 'translingual and transcultural competence' (237); translingual and transcultural competence implies liminality (see also Bhabha), not a complete exchange of identities. (Geisler 2008: 235)

The idea of teaching an Arabic language repertoire rather than *fuṣḥā* only, is one that deserves serious attention from Arabic linguistics researchers. It requires a repositioning of perspective, a rethinking of curricula, materials and methods; but it may be the only valid way to access the variation that is not only inherent in, but also continually emergent in, Arabic communities of practice, placing situated discourse at the core of the curriculum. Such systematic repositioning would reflect the idea that 'an ecological analysis of multilingual interactions enables us to see interactions in multilingual environments as complex dynamic systems' (Kramsch and Whiteside 2008: 667). Arabic linguistic interaction in particular, is characterised by constant calibration and recalibration, or 'soft assembly' of discourse resources, and adaptation to 'all aspects of context' (Larsen-Freeman and Cameron 2008: 169). As Blommaert and Rampton (2011: 5) suggest:

> Linguistics has traditionally privileged the structure of language and treated language use as little more than a product/output generated by semantic, grammatical and phonological systems ... This commitment to system-in-language has been challenged by a linguistics of communicative practice ... This approach puts situated action first, it sees the linguistic conventions/structures as just one (albeit important) semiotic resource among a number available to participants in the process of local language production and interpretation.

What is Arabic? The tensions of variance

The unique history and spread of Arabic has resulted in its being a composite, multi-functional mosaic of spoken and written variants that have been blended under one term. Jonathan Owens has said that the general use of the term 'Arabic' actually refers to what he calls 'holistic Arabic'; stating that 'Arabic has in a sense two histories, one the literary language, one the "holistic" language' (Owens 2006: 37–8), which covers the written language as well as all forms of vernacular. This important differentiation is key for re-examining the learning goals and outcomes for students of the language, and especially for curriculum redesign and progress in developing effective language programmes, both academic and governmental. In academic curriculum design, the term 'Arabic' is often put on a (false) par with other languages that have a centralised, normed standard as well as a range of 'dialects'. But is the Arabic language similar to other languages in terms of its sociolinguistic structures? How can the consistently wide range of variation in spoken Arabic be explained and comprehended in historical terms? More to the point for this study, how can 'Arabic' skills be approached pedagogically so that learners achieve 'not mastery but attainable, reasonable degrees of control' (Swaffar and Arens 2005: 38)? One approach to understanding the Arabic language complex is to examine theories of the evolution of the term 'Arabiyya'.[12] In his definitive 2013 article, 'What is Arabic?' Jan Retsö discusses the term 'Arabiyya' and its implications because, as he notes, 'the Arabic language appears as an extremely variegated phenomenon', but 'the Arabiyya [i.e., *al-fuṣḥā*] has a special position, not only being a second language for everyone but also because of its typological features, many of which set it apart not only from all the modern spoken varieties but also from the epigraphic languages' (2013: 434). It is Retsö's thesis that 'there were many dialects and languages in Arabia at the time of the Prophet that we today would probably call Arabic but that are referred to in the contemporary sources as *ʾaʿjamī*, that is, 'non-*ʿarabī*" (2013: 434). In other words, the pre-Islamic languages of the Arabian peninsula were certainly Semitic, but not all were of the 'Arabiyya' type.[13] These languages were ultimately absorbed into the Arabiyya spectrum because of the influence of Islam, its political dominance and the prestige of the Qurʾānic language. Retsö proposes that 'languages and dialects from the peninsula were spread outside the area by successive waves of conquest and migration that established them as mother tongues of people who otherwise had no connection with Arabia' (Retsö 2013: 436). What does this have to do with contemporary Arabic? It provides conceptual underpinning for the valorisation of spoken forms as well as the written, for the vernaculars as well as the standard. Without detracting from the extraordinary importance of the Arabiyya for the culture, history, religion and society of the Arabic-speaking world, Retsö's theory sets the vernaculars in their historical context, as forms of spoken communication that came to be part of the extensive Arabiyya complex (in Owens' terms, 'holistic Arabic'), and which subsequently developed lives of their own in very different geographical contexts. The main point is this: rather than deteriorated forms devolved from the literary language, the vernaculars can be seen essentially as remnants of Arabian civilisation which have legacies of their own, constituting key components of the Arabiyya.

In important respects, Retsö's approach relates to Charles Ferguson's idea of the Arabic koinè, wherein Ferguson (1959) posited that linguistic levelling of dialect differences occurred during the expansion of the Islamic empire, when soldiers whose peninsular mother tongues were dissimilar needed to communicate with each other as well as with local populations, adjusting their spoken language(s) in systematic ways, and thereby developing an 'Arabic' lingua franca comprehensible to all. Ferguson's koinè theory is one way of accounting for the many similarities among contemporary urban Arabic vernaculars in phonology, morphology and lexicon, similarities among the vernaculars that are not reflected in the literary language. As the vernacular levelling effect gradually took place, the powerful Arabiyya used for formal, literary, liturgical and official purposes anchored Arabic literacy and prepared the way for the written and spoken languages to become a linguistic whole, albeit in a multi-functional way, with each variant serving specific purposes and developing along its particular path for the future. The Arabiyya became codified and standardised; the vernaculars did not. They became more localised and conventionalised; they developed into rich repositories of indigenous culture; they experienced contact with other languages and emerged as distinctive communities of Arabic practice.

Horizontal and vertical variation

One of these communities of practice was Egypt. The sociolinguistic situation in Egypt today, as in many other Arab countries, not only reflects its complex history, it also reflects what Elsaid Badawi has referred to as the horizontal and vertical aspects of language use. In his classic work on levels of Egyptian Arabic (*Mustawayāt al-ʿarabiyya al-muʿāṣira fī miṣr*), Badawi described the tension between the vertical and horizontal axes of Arabic language variation:

> the horizontal expanse of the language . . . linguistic activity [which] extends horizontally within society and diversifies into what are called geographical dialects . . . and the vertical: a linguistic activity at any delimited geographical point extends vertically and differentiates into what are called [social] class dialects (such as the dialect of the common people and the dialect of the educated), superimposed upon each other, varying . . . each from the other, from the lowest class level represented by the poor[est] of the common people, up to the highest class level represented by the educated elite, passing by in our ascent, [multiple] levels of the middle, and the middle of middles, and the middle of the middle of middles. (Badawi 1973: 8)

If one considers the horizontal/vertical structure of linguistic variation, one looks not only at the extremes of variation but also at the great middle ground, as Badawi says, 'the middle of the middle of middles', which is where ordinary discourse intersects with everyday life for the great majority of educated Arabic-speakers. Badawi named this middle ground *ʿāmmiyyat al-muthaqqafīn*, 'the vernacular of the educated', more widely known as 'educated spoken Arabic', or ESA.[14] Since the time that this label was coined for this concept by Badawi (1973), it has been an area of controversy and unease, because although it occupies a certain area on the language spectrum, nonetheless it consists not of a particular variety but rather of controlled, intuitive acts of constant improvisation on the part of educated native Arabic-speakers.

Because of its adaptability, in many ways it is this area of the spectrum, ESA, that represents the most logical form of interactive vernacular speech to teach to learners of Arabic. It is flexible, it travels well, it is not marked as overly literary, and yet is equally unmarked as overly familiar. T. F. Mitchell has stated that: 'The question may reasonably be posed as to which form of Arabic the foreign learner should first be taught and the right answer in the current situation is undoubtedly pan-Arabic' (1962: 12).[15] But discovery and exploration of the principles and processes of ESA in order to develop textbooks and training procedures has been a conflicted area of research, and is difficult to conceptualise for language instruction.[16] This is undoubtedly because of its status as an improvised option for native speakers, rather than being anchored in any way to text or consistent practice. Educated native Arabic-speakers learn how to communicate in ESA, but not in any formal way; the process and skills involved are acquired through exposure and practise, as a variant of their mother tongues, to the Arabic regional vernaculars.

Elite closure in Arabic

ESA is a particularly useful option for Arabic learners when learning to interact with native Arabic-speakers because it is not a familiar or intimate register, and allows users to talk to each other in a polite, formal manner that is not stilted. This is ideologically important because, when it comes to the post-colonial experience, and to interaction between Arabic-speakers and non-Arabic-speakers, the powerful solidarity and intimacy of common vernacular Arabic speech can be used to 'wall out' those who are not insiders. Outsiders include the ranks of Arabic language learners, those who study Arabic in the classroom and then try to make the transition to interactive discourse with native speakers. More often than not, the initial attempts to do this are discouraging; sometimes they are embarrassing. This process of exclusion has been noted and labelled 'elite closure', according to sociolinguist Carol Myers-Scotton. It occurs when people 'establish or maintain their powers and privileges via linguistic choices' (1993: 149). And it can have the effect of not only protecting a particular in-group, but also excluding those who would wish to join. Elite closure can happen under many different kinds of circumstance and in many different cultures, but, for learners of Arabic, it happens most often and most directly when they endeavour to make contact with native Arabic-speakers in informal situations. It is as if spoken Arabic were an intimate and exclusive island where native speakers can be themselves, and where the foreigner is intrusive. Is there a key to this situation for learners of Arabic? Would teaching colloquial Arabic help? Yes and no.

I turn to a passage from a Moroccan author, Abdel Fattah Kilito, which I have cited in a previous article, and which illustrates the sense of transgression experienced by a native Arabic-speaker confronted with an American woman who speaks fluent colloquial Moroccan (Ryding 2015: 70–1):

Kilito states 'Thou shalt not speak my language' (*lan tatakallama lughatii*), and makes it the title of one of his most popular books (Kilito 2002, 2008), expressing frankly this feeling: 'One day I realized that I dislike having foreigners speak my language' (Kilito 2002: 100).[17] Hearing an American woman speak fluent colloquial Moroccan Arabic, he confesses to feeling that 'the American woman robbed me of it', and that because of her skill, 'my language is slipping away from me' (Kilito 2008: 91). This feeling is intensified because of her ease and control not only of the language, but of the pragmatics of Moroccan discourse, as she utters the deeply Moroccan phrase '*wallahila*' at one point, astounding her listeners with her fluency, but not winning any friends by doing so. Kilito admits that he feels transgressed: 'it was as though using it ("*wallahila*") were an exclusive right to Moroccans and forbidden to others' (Kilito 2008: 92).

What are Arabic educators supposed to make of this? Is this sense of unease and estrangement upon hearing a non-Arab use the vernacular fluently experienced by most native Arabic-speakers? By some? By many? Does it depend on the discourse context? Discourse alienation is an under-researched area of Arabic psycho-linguistics and language attitudes. But perhaps it provides a conceptual wedge to linguists who would study the acquisition of Arabic as a second language: under what circumstances can a non-native speaker use the vernacular in order to join a conversation, and how can she or he do this effectively, with appropriate cultural sensitivity?[18] As Americans, we normally expect that visitors to our country will have adequate, if minimal, English skills and we are comfortable with that. This comfort level, however, may be the exact opposite for speakers of other languages, who are not only surprised but perhaps discomfited by hearing their native language spoken by foreigners.

We are confronted with three challenging aspects of Arabic discourse for learners, all of which revolve around the ability to calibrate between linguistic codes: Standard Arabic, Vernacular Arabic, and the hybrid ESA.

1. How does one develop adequate vernacular skills to participate politely and effectively in daily interaction?
2. How does one calibrate one's interactions with native Arabic-speakers so as to be neither closed out, nor judged to be intrusive?
3. How can a learner grasp the nature of hybridity and its appropriate use?

Educated spoken Arabic fills many discourse functions, but not all. Teaching learners the options involved in developing their own Arabic language repertoires, and in recognising how and when to use them seems to be the key that provides the synergy required for full linguistic performance, including cultural and social appropriateness.

The synergy of discrepant perspectives

As concern about ultimate achievement and communicative skills in Arabic increases, it is responding to real pressures from the speech community, from learners and from the language situation. It is responding to the accumulation of outcome anomalies in traditional Arabic language programmes, and responding to the problem of years of formal instruction that yield only partial results. These anomalies include, for example, significant disparities in skills acquisition; the inappropriate use of formal Arabic for ordinary discourse; learners' lack of comprehension in most interpersonal discourse contexts; and their inability to communicate basic needs despite years of formal language study. Such anomalies reflect inconsistencies within a system that, when accumulated over time, can exert pressure for change in the disciplinary matrix.[19]

A carefully conceived, situated discourse-in-use paradigm for Arabic language study could resolve the tensions between learner communicative needs and traditional pedagogical practice, resulting instead in a synergy of perspectives and practices based in linguistic reality. To this end, it may be useful to consider the most effective forms of language that could fit into an academic curriculum as well as the possibility of teaching declarative knowledge about the complexities of Arabic language-in-use.[20] It is very possible that the traditional taboo against teaching 'about' the language, rather than 'in' the language has held back Arabic pedagogical practice and has held back the ability of learners to grasp the cultural roots, the indexical implications and the cultural meanings of Arabic discourse. For example, an Arabic dialect survey course, or a course in sociolinguistic distinctions in Arabic language use (heavily illustrated with Arabic examples and role-plays), might give learners a sense of ballast and direction in their approach to Arabic studies. For specific ideas and examples of teaching Arabic culture in context and Arabic cultural area studies, see Ryding (2013b: 219–29, 2015).

Suggestions for incorporating the Arabic vernacular system into academic work

A reviewer of an earlier draft of this chapter suggested that more explicit and pragmatic ideas be offered here for teaching spoken Arabic proficiency. Although I do not pretend to offer a definitive solution to the problems of incorporating the Arabic vernacular system into academic work, I provide the following suggestions based on my own experience, with the caveat that they are just that: suggestions that may encourage further discussion and experimentation. First, Arabic teaching programmes need to start out with a heavy emphasis on spoken Arabic in addition to the written language (approximately a 2:1 ratio of spoken to written). In my experience, the most effective way to introduce spoken and written variants is to teach them on parallel tracks, not mixed into one class, especially in the early stages of language learning. An example of this would be an intensive two-track course consisting of six credit hours of spoken Arabic and three credit hours of written Arabic, per semester. This equals a nine-credit course, which would be given for two semesters as the intensive introductory course in Arabic. The second year course could then consist either of the same ratio of spoken-to-written, or of an equal number of credit hours, say three credit hours of spoken Arabic and three of written, yielding a six-credit course. After the second year, learners could focus on the areas where they want to specialise, and they would also be better prepared to hit the ground running if they choose to spend a semester or year in study abroad.

The separate tracks allow the learner to concentrate on developing speaking and listening skills, as well as reading and writing abilities that will strengthen rapidly and will ultimately converge as equals, instead of the usual practice of simply adding a vernacular course here and there to round out more extensive core *fuṣḥā* courses. This initial privileging of spoken Arabic also responds to learner motivations and desires to be able to speak and practise Arabic outside the classroom, which is difficult when *fuṣḥā* is one's only option. I believe that the key to valorising the vernacular system as a legitimate academic pursuit lies in the content of such courses, which should be directed not only towards proficiency as it is generally understood, but also towards a critical understanding of the key elements of educated Arabic discourse, the meanings and definitions of 'Arabiyya', and of popular Arab culture. Such courses would focus on translingual and transcultural competence through the study of cultural values and aesthetics, including analysis of social media technologies that incorporate and expand the new vernacular literacies, such as Facebook.

Second, curriculum developers and teacher trainers need to work in tandem to create faculty resources that contribute to the skills of linguistic navigation in Arabic and to interpersonal communication at all levels. Outside-the-box thinking might include cultural and linguistic content courses in combined written and spoken Arabic; two-track training in both spoken and written Arabic; spoken-language-heavy summer courses; or a fifth year of full-time Arabic (both spoken and written) to accelerate acquisition – to name just a few options.

Third, serious and long-term study of Arabic proficiency guidelines needs to be undertaken on a profession-wide basis in order to clearly establish the key role of vernacular competence within the oral proficiency testing system, and to constantly calibrate tester training and inter-rater reliability. In order to explore any of these ideas, I encourage Arabic language professionals to think in terms of grant funding for experimental curriculum design that focuses on vernacular proficiency and content-based instruction. This research and experimentation is critically needed, but for most programmes and researchers, the resources needed to develop new ideas is not usually available without external funding.

Boundary conditions and the Arabic linguistic ecotone

Boundary conditions in mathematics 'are the parameters that define the space within which one seeks solutions' (Appiah 2016: 2). As Appiah notes, this theme offers 'an invitation to reflect together on the parameters within which our profession takes place' (ibid.). I think that Arabic can be viewed as having parameters distinct from other, more commonly taught languages, and even from most world languages. This is because of the extraordinary indexical load of spoken language variants in the Arab world: one's dialect or regional vernacular is part of one's identity to an unusually strong degree, as is the equally powerful sense of belonging to the greater Arab community through knowledge of *fuṣḥā*. To what extent can this complex, multimodal practice be opened up for sharing with non-native speakers? Is there a boundary area that can be readily shared with speakers of Arabic as a foreign language? In other words, is there a linguistic 'ecotone', or common ground of merged discourses with its own characteristics?[21] Studies of linguistic 'bivalency' and 'hybridity' suggest that rather than seeing the traditional dichotomy between spoken and written language variants as the norm, that 'syncretic and bivalent language practices' are actually at the heart of language (Woolard 1999: 8). The idea is that educated Arabic-speakers simultaneously 'inhabit' multiple roles as they engage in discourse, and that these roles often merge into the great middle space identified by Badawi (above). As Woolard notes: 'A frame that places hybridity and simultaneity at the center may help us theorise the ambiguities of interference rather than avoid it. Code-switching, bivalency, and interference are subtly different ways of choosing both languages [variants] at once' (1999: 15). Rubdy and Alsagoff refer to this as follows: 'notwithstanding its quotidian nature, hybridity is a helpful concept because it provides a profoundly reflexive perspective in transcending binary categories' (2013b: 9).

It would seem that a hybrid, polyfunctional language strategy, involving the understanding and use of formal Arabic, colloquial Arabic and ESA, would be useful in helping learners make their way into the hybridity at the centre of the Arabic language spectrum.[22] ESA's effectiveness, in particular, depends on the awareness of both teachers and learners alike that this mesolect register of language occupies a continuum, not a discrete space, and will shift with the sociolinguistic situation.[23] This may not be as daunting as it seems, if users are aware of the core features of both spoken and written Arabic and are able to adjust to sociolinguistic context variation. Mejdell expresses the following opinion:

> I do not believe that the intermediate forms of the language, CS [code-switching] and mixed styles of Arabic, will ever turn into an autonomous variety in the normal sense, implying a certain structural cohesion. The native notion of *lughat al-muthaqqafīn* or *lugha wusṭā*, is similarly if impressionistically defined as mixing and interaction between the high norm and the vernacular, a mode of speaking, at best a heterogeneous variety. (Mejdell 2011/12: 37)

It is probable that an approach to teaching variation in context will be the most effective way to ease Arabic learners into interactive dialogue, and help them to establish strong and productive interdiscursive identities.[24] Strategies for conceiving and implementing new models for ASLA along these lines would require significant departures from standard contemporary language teaching methodologies and would acknowledge that Arabic is indeed distinctive in its levels and the multiple possibilities of variation. In order to be truly 'communicative' in its aims and its approaches, Arabic language pedagogy would need to voice a higher order conceptualisation of language performance, to rely on sophisticated knowledge of interactional pragmatics, and on knowing and navigating the parameters of the Arabic language continuum. In other words, spoken Arabic is an activity, not a state of affairs. It reflects communicative strategies selected from a repertoire of options that apply in a range of situated discourse contexts. Although classical Arabic and modern Standard Arabic are close enough together to be considered one solid element, *fuṣḥā*; as soon as spontaneous speech begins, fluidity becomes the norm rather than solidity, and spoken Arabic flows among its speakers like a river, a river of language. And just as one cannot – according to Heraclitus – step into the same river twice, spoken Arabic cannot be pinned down to one singular set of rules; it must be navigated. It is this navigation skill that has been missing from Arabic pedagogical practice, and that needs to become a conscious component of Arabic instruction.

The repertoire model

Arabic teaching does not have many traditional models to choose from because of its distinctive diglossic nature, so it must construct its own: the repertoire model. In order to do this, one needs to take into account the myriad facets of Arabic language performance, the sociolinguistic insights of researchers such as Yasir Suleiman and Gunvor Mejdell, and the practicalities of goal-oriented second-language ultimate attainment. Redefining, redesigning and creating Arabic-specific models of instruction will be major contributions not only to the teaching of Arabic as a foreign language, but to the field of second-language acquisition studies as a whole, constituting a new and unprecedented branch of curriculum modelling and development where hybridity occupies its rightful place. This does not at all imply abandoning the legacy and vitality of *fuṣḥā*; it means coming to terms with the linguistic reality of multiple discourse levels and doing the intellectual work of designing new models for Arabic pedagogy. As Edward Said has stated: 'May our . . . models for the years ahead combine the richness of the past with the . . . excitement of the new. One must not only hope, but also do.' (Said 2000: 91)

Notes

1. See Saussy (2007: 60): 'Language policy should aim at preparing a large class of people to work closely, bidirectionally, with the languages and cultures of the world.'
2. See especially Suleiman (2012, 2014) for analysis of Arabic language ideologies and anxieties.
3. I use the term 'vernacular' here because I believe it is the most applicable to the Arabic-language situation. I therefore take a tack different from Suleiman, who argues that the term 'vernacular' does not accurately apply to the Arabic situation, because it 'evokes an emerging language on a par with the rise of the European languages as competitors of Latin in the print, ethnic or national identity domain in past medieval times,' (2013a: 269). But I believe that this specific use of 'vernacular' to refer to the emergent Romance languages does not invalidate its broader meaning, as thus defined by LePage: 'the everyday spoken language or languages of a community, as contrasted with a standard or official language' (LePage, 1997: 6).
4. On 'drift' see Sapir (1949): 'Language moves down time in a current of its own making. It has a drift.' On the characteristics of contemporary Arabic as used in social media, see Sinatora (2016).
5. On 'symbolic competence', see Kramsch (2011) and Kramsch and Whiteside (2008).
6. On 'Arabics', see Eid (2008).
7. See Badawi's pivotal work on defining Arabic language levels and the Arabic language continuum (1973, 1985).
8. See, for example, Suleiman (2011, 2013a, 2013b). These works provide a foundational shift of framework and scholarship for the study of Arabic discourse.
9. Language is 'a repertoire: a culturally sensitive ordered complex of genres, styles, registers, with lots of hybrid forms, and occurring in a wide variety of ways big and small'. Such 'forms of variation matter in social life – they function as powerful sources of indexical meanings' (Blommaert 2007: 115).
10. Geisler's endnote here reads: 'This re-evaluation is all the more appropriate since there is an ongoing discussion among applied linguists about the native-speaker ideal as a pedagogical concept. See, for instance, Cook [1999].'
11. The MLA ad hoc committee report was the result of three years of deliberation and was published in 2007 (see references).
12. See also Owens on 'Arabic and the dialects', where he reviews the theories of Brockelmann, Fück and Blau, in particular (2006: 43–7).
13. For more on the historical interpretation and etymology of '*ʿarab*', see Retsö (1989/90).
14. For more on ESA, see Ryding (2006a).

15. 'pan-Arabic' is Mitchell's term for ESA.
16. I have published textbooks and several articles on ESA (which I referred to as FSA, 'formal spoken Arabic'). See Ryding (1991, 1995); Ryding and Zaiback ([1993] 2004); and Ryding and Mehall (2005), for example.
17. '*fī yawm-in min al-ayyām-i tabayyana lī anna-nī lā uḥibb-u an yatakallam-a l-ajānib-u lughat-ī.*'
18. In a recent article I comment this topic as follows: 'I appreciate Kilito's honest confession of discomfort, but I also take it as a challenge. Would most native Arabic-speakers prefer to hear foreigners speak in a less directly intimate style? In a more "educated", formal, or psychologically distant style? I imagine that protected intimacy or elite closure varies with the speech community and the speech situation; that in certain situations the [+intimacy] register is acceptable on the part of non-native speakers, but in others, it needs to be more [+formal]. I believe that his attitude of protected intimacy is an as-yet unarticulated issue in generalised resistance to teaching ordinary spoken Arabic, and empirical studies are sorely needed in order to delineate its character, to explore its relationship to teaching Arabic, and to enhance our understanding of the role of pedagogy in transferring socially appropriate Arabic discourse skills to learners of Arabic as a foreign language' (Ryding 2017a).
19. On the accumulation of anomalies and the 'disciplinary matrix', see Kuhn (1970).
20. For more on educated spoken Arabic, see Ryding (1991, 1995, 2006a, 2012, 2013a), as well as Mejdell (2006, 2008, 2011/12, 2012), on variation, *lugha wusṭā*, polyfunctionality and mixed Arabic.
21. The term 'ecotone' is borrowed from the discipline of landscape ecology. It refers to the transition area between two biological communities where they meet and integrate (such as forest area merging into open land). This area may be of varying size, and it may be local (the zone between a field and forest) or regional (the transition between forest and grassland ecosystems). An ecotone may be seen as a gradual blending of the two communities across a broad area, or it may manifest itself as a sharp boundary line. See at: www.eoearth.org/view/article/152345 for more detail and for references. I propose that linguistic 'ecotones' exist between distinct language areas where characteristics of one level of discourse are shared or mixed with those of another. Such discourse ecotones can be relatively stable or they can shift over time.
22. ESA or formal spoken Arabic (FSA), as I have referred to it elsewhere (see Ryding (1991); Ryding and Mehall (2005): Ryding and Zaiback ([1993] 2004)).
23. See Mejdell (2008) about dialect continua and polyfunctionality.
24. On interdiscursive identities, see Bauman (2005).

References

Agha, A., 'Introduction: Semiosis across encounters', *Journal of Linguistic Anthropology* 15(1) (2005): 1–5.

Appiah, K. A., 'Boundary conditions', *MLA Newsletter* 48(1) (2016): 2.

Badawi, Elsaid M., *Mustawayāt al-ʿ arabiyya l-muʿāṣira fii miṣr* (Cairo: Dār al-maʿārif, 1973).

Badawi, Elsaid M., 'Educated spoken Arabic: A problem in teaching Arabic as a foreign language', in Kurt R. Jankowsky (ed.), *Scientific and Humanistic Dimensions of Language* (Washington, DC: Georgetown University Press, 1985), pp. 15–22.

Bauman, R., 'Commentary: Indirect indexicality, identity, performance: Dialogic observations', *Journal of Linguistic Anthropology* 15(1) (2005): 145–50.

Bhabha, Homi K., 'How newness enters the world', in *The Location of Culture* (London: Routledge, 1994, first Indian reprint, 2012), pp. 303–37.

Blommaert, J., 'Sociolinguistics and discourse analysis: Orders of indexicality and polycentricity', *Journal of Multicultural Discourses* 2(2) (2007): 115–30.

Blommaert, J. and Rampton, B., 'Language and superdiversity', *Diversities* 13(2) (2011): 1–20.

Cook, V., 'Going beyond the native speaker in language teaching', *TESOL Quarterly* 33(2) (1999): 185–209.

Eid, M., 'Arabic or Arabics: The core and the variable', Presentation at the Arabic Linguistics Society Symposium, XXII, March 2008.

Geisler, Michael E., 'The MLA report on foreign languages: One year into the future', *Profession* 2008: 229–39.

Kilito, Abdelfattah, *Thou Shalt Not Speak My Language*, trans. Waïl S. Hassan (Syracuse, NY: Syracuse University Press, 2008).

Kilito, Abdelfattah. 2002. *Lan tatakallam-a lughat-ī* (Beirut: Dār al-ṭalīʻa li-l-ṭabāʻa wa-l-nashr).

Kramsch, C., 'The symbolic dimensions of the intercultural', *Language Teaching* 44(3) (2011): 354–67.

Kramsch, C. and Whiteside, A., 'Language ecology in multilingual settings: Towards a theory of symbolic competence', *Applied Linguistics* 29(4) (2008): 645–71.

Kuhn, Thomas S., *The Structure of Scientific Revolutions* (Chicago, IL: University of Chicago Press, 1979).

Larsen-Freeman, D. and Cameron, L., *Complex Systems and Applied Linguistics* (Oxford: Oxford University Press, 2008).

LePage, R., 'Introduction', in Andrée Tabouret-Keller, Robert LePage, Penelope Gardner-Chloros and Gabrielle Varro (eds), *Vernacular Literacy: A Re-evaluation* (Oxford: Oxford University Press, 1997), pp. 1–19.

Mejdell, G., *Mixed Styles in Spoken Arabic in Egypt: Somewhere between Order and Chaos* (Leiden: Brill, 2006).

Mejdell, G., 'Is modern *fusha* a "standard" language?' in Zeinab Ibrahim and Sanaa Makhlouf (eds), *Linguistics in an Age of Globalization: Perspectives on Arabic Language and Teaching* (Cairo: American University in Cairo Press, 2008), pp. 41–52.

Mejdell, G., 'Diglossia, code-switching, style variation and congruence', *Al-Arabiyya* 44/45 (2011/12): 29–39.

Mejdell, G., 'The elusiveness of *lugha wusṭā* – or, attempting to catch its true nature', in Reem Bassiouney and Grahahm Katz (eds), *Arabic Language and Linguistics* (Washington, DC: Georgetown University Press, 2012), pp. 157–67.

Mitchell, Terrence F., *Colloquial Arabic: The Living Language of Egypt* (London: English Universities Press, 1962).

Modern Language Association (MLA), Ad Hoc Committee on Foreign Languages, 'Foreign languages and higher education: New structures for a changed world', *Profession* 2007: 234–45.

Myers-Scotton, Carol, 'Elite closure as a powerful language strategy: The African case', *International Journal of the Sociology of Language* 103 (1993): 149–63.

Östman, J. and Trousdale, G., 'Dialects, discourse, and construction grammar', in Thomas Hoffman and Graeme Trousdale (eds) *The Oxford Handbook of Construction Grammar* (Oxford: Oxford University Press, 2013), pp. 476–90.

Owens, J., *A Linguistic History of Arabic* (Oxford: Oxford University Press, 2006).

Owens, J. (ed.), *The Oxford Handbook of Arabic Linguistics* (Oxford: Oxford University Press, 2013).

Perkins, David N., *Making Learning Whole: How Seven Principles of Teaching can Transform Education* (San Francisco, CA: Jossey-Bass, 2009).

Retsö, J., 'The earliest Arabs', *Orientalia Suecana* 38/9 (1989/90: 131–9).

Retsö, J., 'What is Arabic?' in Jonathan Owens (ed.), *The Oxford Handbook of Arabic Linguistics* (Oxford: Oxford University Press, 2013), pp. 433–50.

Rubdy, R. and Alsagoff, Lubna (eds), *The Global-Local Interface and Hybridity: Exploring Language and Identity* (Clevedon: Multilingual Matters, 2013a).

Rubdy, R. and Alsagoff, Lubna, 'The cultural dynamics of globalization: Problematizing hybridity', in Rani Rubdy and Lubna Alsagoff (eds), *The Global-Local Interface and Hybridity: Exploring Language and Identity* (Clevedon: Multilingual Matters, 2013b), pp. 1–14.

Rubdy, R. and Ben Said, S. (eds), *Conflict, Exclusion and Dissent in the Linguistic Landscape* (Basingstoke: Palgrave Macmillan, 2015).

Ryding, Karin C., 'Proficiency despite diglossia: A new approach for Arabic', *Modern Language Journal* 75(2) (1991): 212–18.

Ryding, Karin C., 'Discourse competence in TAFL: Skill levels and choice of language variety in the Arabic classroom', in Mahmoud Al-Batal (ed.), *Teaching of Arabic as a Foreign Language: Issues and Directions* (Provo, UT: American Association of Teachers of Arabic, 1995), pp. 223–32.

Ryding, Karin C., 'Educated Arabic', in Kees Versteegh (ed.), *Encyclopedia of Arabic Language and Linguistics* (Leiden: Brill, 2006a), vol. 1, pp. 666–71.

Ryding, Karin C., 'Teaching Arabic in the United States', in Kassem Wahba, Zeinab Taha and Liz England (eds), *A Handbook for Arabic Language Teaching Professionals in the 21st Century* (Mahwah, NJ: Lawrence Erlbaum, 2006b), pp. 13–20.

Ryding, Karin C., 'Educated spoken Arabic: Defining a functional standard in middle/mixed Arabic', in Lidia Bettini and Paolo La Spisa (eds), *Au-dela de l'arabe standard: Moyen arabe et arabe mixte dans les sources médiévales, modernes, et contemporaines, Quaderni di Semitistica 28* (Florence: Dipartemento di scienze dell'antichità, medioevo e rinascimento e linguistica, Università di Firenze, 2012), pp. 307–21.

Ryding, Karin C., *Teaching and Learning Arabic as a Foreign Language: A Guide for Teachers* (Washington, DC: Georgetown University Press, 2013a).

Ryding, Karin C., 'Second language acquisition', in Jonathan Owens (ed.), *The Oxford Handbook of Arabic Linguistics* (Oxford: Oxford University Press, 2013b), pp. 392–411.

Ryding, Karin C., 'Arabic language learning: If diglossia is the question, then what is the answer?' *Annals of Japan Association for Middle East Studies (AJAMES)* 31(2) (2015): 63–82.

Ryding, Karin C., 'Future research directions in Arabic as a foreign language', in Kassem Wahba, Zeinab Taha and Liz England (eds), *A Handbook for Arabic Language Teaching Professionals in the 21st Century*, 2nd edn (Mahwah, NJ: Lawrence Erlbaum, 2017a forthcoming), pp. 11–19.

Ryding, Karin C., 'Teaching Arabic in the United States, II', in Kassem Wahba, Zeinab Taha and Liz England (eds), *A Handbook for Arabic Language Teaching Professionals in the 21st Century*, 2nd edn (Mahwah, NJ: Lawrence Erlbaum, 2017b forthcoming), pp. 399–405.

Ryding, Karin C. and Mehall, David J., *Formal Spoken Arabic*, 2nd edn (Washington, DC: Georgetown University Press, 2005).

Ryding, Karin C. and Zaiback, A., *Formal Spoken Arabic: FAST Course* (Washington, DC: Georgetown University Press, [1993] 2004).

Said, Edward W., 'Presidential address 1999: Humanism and heroism', *PMLA* 115(3) (2000): 285–91.

Sapir, E., *Language: An Introduction to the Study of Speech* (New York: Harcourt Brace Jovanovich, 1949).

Saussy, H., Contribution to 'Forum on language policy and the politics of language', *ADFL Bulletin* 1/2 (2007): 56–65.

Sinatora, Francesco L., 'Language Change and Identity in Syria: Evidence from Social Media', dissertation, Georgetown University, Washington, DC, 2016.

Suleiman, Y., *Arabic, Self and Identity* (Oxford: Oxford University Press, 2011).

Suleiman, Y., 'Ideology and the standardization of Arabic', in Reem Bassiouney and E. Graham Katz (eds), *Arabic Language and Linguistics* (Washington, DC: Georgetown University Press, 2012), pp. 201–13.

Suleiman, Y., 'Arabic folk linguistics: Between mother tongue and native language', in Jonathan Owens (ed.), *The Oxford Handbook of Arabic Linguistics* (Oxford: Oxford University Press, 2013a), pp. 264–80.
Suleiman, Y., *Arabic in the Fray* (Edinburgh: Edinburgh University Press, 2013b).
Suleiman, Y. , 'Arab(ic) language anxiety', *Al-Arabiyya* 47 (2014): 57–81.
Swaffar, Janet and Arens, Katherine, *Remapping the Foreign Language Curriculum: An Approach through Multiple Literacies* (New York: Modern Language Association, 2005).
Woolard, Kathryn A., 'Simultaneity and bivalency as strategies in bilingualism', *Journal of Linguistic Anthropology* 8(1) (1999): 3–29.

Online source

www.eoearth.org/view/article/152345.

CHAPTER 3

Metaphorical Recurrence and Language Symbolism in Arabic Metalanguage Discourse

Chaoqun Lian

In Arabic metalanguage discourse, we often come across metaphors associating the form, variation, use and situation of Arabic to non-linguistic entities and activities. Many of these metaphors belong to what may be termed as 'organic metaphors', as they depict Arabic and its varieties as living organisms, subject to the same force of nature and the same pattern of interrelations as those manifested in the worlds of plants, animals and human beings. Two sets of these organic metaphors – one conveys the idea of inalienability between *fuṣḥā/faṣīḥa* (Standard Arabic) and *ʿāmmiyya* (Colloquial Arabic), while the other highlights antagonism – seem to be recurrent in the discourse on Arabic diglossia, that is, the co-existence of *fuṣḥā* and *ʿāmmiyya* with structural and functional disparities between each other. This phenomenon – what may be termed 'metaphorical recurrence' – is worthy of investigation, not because of the co-recurrence of two seemingly contradictory perspectives, but the metaphor-making process that endows Arabic diglossia with enduring socio-political significance in Arab society.

This chapter investigates the recurrence of the above sets of 'organic metaphors' in language policy discussions within the Arabic language academies in Damascus and Cairo, arguably the most representative strands of intellectual discourse on language in the Arabic-speaking world. I begin with two extracts of discourse in the 1920s by Syrian academicians to illustrate that, when employing 'organic metaphors', they consciously and unconsciously framed the relationship between *fuṣḥā* and *ʿāmmiyya* with perspectives according with the socio-political contexts of the time. In doing so, they endowed the seemingly linguistic phenomenon of Arabic diglossia with extra-linguistic significance, making it a resource and proxy for nation-building and anti-colonialism in symbolic terms. I then move on to examine the reproduction and reiteration of this 'language symbolism' through 'organic metaphors' recurrent in the discourse of the Cairo Academy in later periods and in other contexts – the rise of pan-Arabism in the 1950s, widespread social trauma following the 1967 defeat, and the dominance of state interests over pan-Arab solidarity in the 1990s. While the changing socio-political contexts pulled this symbolism in various directions, the content of the 'organic metaphors' and the perspectives they generated tended to be stable. In the last section, I reason out this stability by distinguishing between the epochal and the *longue durée* contexts, and attribute the recurrence of 'organic metaphors' to the latter.

A caveat should be added here concerning methodology. The chapter does not aim to cover the phenomenon of metaphorical recurrence in a thorough manner. It is not based on any corpus or list of 'organic metaphors', but on careful analysis of selected cases of metaphor-making. My purpose here is to reveal the often covert link between language perception and socio-political circumstances in the Arabic-speaking world, rather than offering a systematic description exhausting all variants of 'organic metaphors' in Arabic metalanguage discourse. Accordingly, I do not select the cases according to any 'objective', statistical criterion, but to their discursive significance as representing the foregrounded language ideologies in the various socio-political contexts.

Metaphor and framing

Approaches to metaphor vary. While Kövecses (2002: vii) points out that metaphor is most commonly understood as 'a figure of speech in which one thing is compared to another by saying that one is the other', Schön (1993: 137) holds that metaphor 'refers both to a certain kind of product – a perspective or frame, a way of looking at things – and to a certain kind of process – a process by which new perspectives on the world come into existence'. The difference between Kövecses and Schön as I understand it is that the former talks about what metaphor is while the latter focuses on what metaphor does. To illustrate, let us consider the following extract of discourse.

In 1923, ʿAbd al-Qādir al-Maghribī, a member of the Syrian Science Academy (now the Arabic Language Academy in Damascus), wrote a formal reply on behalf of the Academy to the enquiry of the Syrian Ministry of Education on how to promote *fuṣḥā* in Syrian society. When arguing that it is not feasible and unnecessary to reshape the grammar of *ʿāmmiyya* in line with *fuṣḥā* as a means of promoting the latter, he states (1923: 236):

Extract 1

> It is clear that every eloquent (*faṣīḥa*) human language has on its part a language born (*muwallada*) of it, which is the colloquial (*ʿāmmiyya*) language or the popular (*dārija*) language. This colloquial language is, in fact, the daughter (*ibna*) of the

> eloquent. Moreover, some people claim that the former is an abridged (*ikhtizāl*), shortened and deviated form of the latter and is more suitable to the contexts [of communication]. It is, therefore, improper to cast pessimism over the colloquial language to the extent of fighting (*muḥāraba*), destroying (*mulāshā*) and killing (*imāta*) it.

This extract contains two organic metaphors. The first seems to fit Kövecses' description, as it compares the relationship between *faṣīḥa* and *ʿāmmiyya* to that between the parent and the daughter by saying that '*ʿāmmiyya* is the daughter of *faṣīḥa*'. But 'one is the other' is not the only surface realisation of this comparison, the passive participle '*muwallada*' is another. As for the second metaphor, it does not contain any 'one is the other' structure, but uses the verbal nouns '*muḥāraba*', '*mulāshā*' and '*imāta*' to suggest a comparison: *ʿāmmiyya* is our enemy. These two metaphors show that a metaphor may have diverse and flexible surface realisations. To go beneath this surface diversity, Lakoff and Johnson (1980) propose the Conceptual Metaphor Theory (CMT), which understands any metaphor as inherently a cognitive association of different concepts or conceptual domains. According to CMT, the two metaphors in extract 1 associate 'language variation' with 'kingship' and 'language standardisation (in the form of decreasing the use and status of *ʿāmmiyya*)' with 'fight', respectively. However, although CMT deepens our understanding of metaphor from mere comparison to conceptual association, it is still an answer to 'what metaphor is' without explaining the purpose, function and effect of metaphor.

This latter issue, or 'what metaphor does', is the concern of the pragmatics of metaphor. Traditionally, metaphor is understood to serve aesthetic or rhetorical purposes to move the heart or persuade the mind. Modern pragmatics of metaphor goes a step further to explore the mechanism behind such moving or persuasive effect of metaphor. Schön's explanation of metaphor above belongs to this branch of enquiry. He understands metaphor as both a perspective-generating process and its end product. This process, which he terms 'framing', is to transfer, often selectively, certain experience associated with a domain as a frame of evaluation and judgement into another in order to express a perspective or position on the latter.

Now let us re-examine extract 1 in line with the theory of 'framing'. The first metaphor frames the relationship between *faṣīḥa* and *ʿāmmiyya* as that between the parent and the daughter. This brings in two perspectives. One is that, like the kinship between the parent and the daughter, *ʿāmmiyya* is inalienable from *faṣīḥa*. This perspective is in tune with what al-Maghribī explicitly argues: the existence of *ʿāmmiyya* is a natural phenomenon whose elimination is impossible. However, there is another, less explicit perspective also generated by the parent–daughter metaphor. A daughter is no doubt a descendant of her parent, inheriting the latter's physical, behavioural and intellectual qualities. More often than not, she is dearly loved, protected and cultivated by her parent. However, in the Middle Eastern context, where patriarchy is not yet challenged but permeates deeply into familial and social relations, female descendants in a family are generally considered to be less perfect than, if not inferior to, their brothers to become legitimate heirs of the family and are generally excluded from its orthodox pedigree. Imperfectness of female lineage is a key perspective carried over from the domain of family to that of language. Beneath the justification of the inalienability of *ʿāmmiyya* from *faṣīḥa* is the acknowledgement of the flawed, unorthodox nature of *ʿāmmiyya*. This latter view is clearly revealed by the use of 'abridged, shortened and deviated' to describe *ʿāmmiyya* in extract 1.

The second metaphor frames *ʿāmmiyya* in a conflict situation, as if *ʿāmmiyya* was among the enemies 'we', the language users, are fighting against in the battlefield until we end its 'life'. Similar to the first metaphor, this one also brings in two perspectives. One is explicitly in line with al-Maghribī's main argument to reveal the absurdity of *ʿāmmiyya*-phobia, while the other is to recognise, if not himself believe in, a popular view that *faṣīḥa* and *ʿāmmiyya* are in conflict. Obviously this latter perspective is implicit.

Whether a perspective is more explicit or more implicit is decided by the degree of frame awareness – an issue Schön does not clarify too much. Inspired by Cameron's (2008: 202) differentiation between 'deliberate' and 'automatic' metaphors, I understand the framing process as on a continuum between deliberate framing and automatic framing. If one uses a metaphor to generate the perspectives that frame the discursive act he or she participates in with full awareness of this generation process, then this is deliberate framing. If one uses a metaphor automatically without any awareness of the perspectives it brings in to frame his discursive act, then this is automatic framing. Most metaphorical processes, like the two cases in extract 1, are mixtures of both types of framing. So when al-Maghribī deliberately uses the parent–daughter metaphor to argue for the inalienability between *faṣīḥa* and *ʿāmmiyya*, he also automatically activates the perspective of imperfectness and inferiority associated with the image of female descent. Similarly, when he uses the battle metaphor to oppose excessive antagonism towards *ʿāmmiyya*, he could not avoid reproducing this antagonism as a result of automatic framing.

Context and symbolism

The perspectives that develop out of the above framing processes are also attested elsewhere in the Arabic metalanguage discourse with the use of metaphors differing from the above. The following extract of discourse, also produced in the 1920s, is an example.

In 1923, the Syrian Science Academy asked its member Ilyās Qudsī to write a reply to a call published in a French newspaper for writing Arabic and other oriental languages in Latin script. In this reply, when showing the advantages of Arabic script, Qudsī argues that using diacritics rather than letters to represent short vowels has succeeded in separating *fuṣḥā* from the influence of *ʿāmmiyya*. To demonstrate that this separation is necessary to maintain the integrity of *fuṣḥā*, he gives the following metaphor (1923: 180–1):

Extract 2

> Due to the separation of *fuṣḥā* from *ʿāmmiyya*, the integrity of its [*fuṣḥā*] grammar, vocabulary, and derivational principles has been maintained for fifteen centuries and will continue to be preserved as God wishes. *Fuṣḥā* looks like a gorgeous garden (*ḥadīqa ghannāʾ*) where both fruitful and fruitless trees exhibit their dazzling beauty; the chief guardians of the garden are the Noble Qurʾān and the literary legacy we have inherited, including the *Jāhiliyya* poetry, scholastic books, and other materials adopted by Arabic dictionaries. *ʿĀmmiyya* is a big area of thickets (*ghiyāḍ*) that surrounds the garden, mixed with thorns (*shawk*) and brambles (*ʿawsaj*), growing and multiplying in a disorderly way, and obtaining water and nutrition from the garden. This area of thickets prevents the thorns from penetrating into the garden and damaging the beautiful trees, and the guardians also forbid any plant that does not attain the resemblance of the garden trees enter from outside into the garden.

Qudsī's metaphor frames the relationship between *fuṣḥā* and *ʿāmmiyya* in the symbiosis of different species in the world of plants. This metaphor explicitly advocates the thesis of separation between *fuṣḥā* and *ʿāmmiyya* by showing that *fuṣḥā* is the most refined variety of Arabic, while *ʿāmmiyya* is unrefined, immature and mixed with non-Arabic elements. This is most evident in the contrast between 'trees', on the one hand, and 'thickets' (*ghiyāḍ*), 'thorns' and 'brambles', on the other. The verbal form of *ghiyāḍ* is *ghāḍa*, meaning 'to decrease and diminish'. Its verbal noun *ghayḍ* means 'prematurely born foetus' and 'small amount'. It is clear that *ghiyāḍ* refers to those small plants that are not developed enough to be counted as 'trees'. As for thorns and brambles, they are intruders not belonging to the original ecosystem of *fuṣḥā* and *ʿāmmiyya*, that is, linguistic elements of non-Arabic origins. Not coincidently, the term *ikhtizāl* used by al-Maghribī in extract 1 also carries similar perceptions of *ʿāmmiyya*. In modern usage, *ikhtizāl* means 'abridgement', so *ʿāmmiyya* is an abridged form of *fuṣḥā*. In old usage, *khazal*, the lexical root of *ikhtizāl*, means sluggishness and disruption in walking, as if there are 'thorns pricking the feet [of the pedestrian]' (Ibn Manẓūr 1885: 216). Due to this 'sluggishness' and 'disruption', the pedestrian should frequently 'halt' his feet, 'terminate', or even 'cut short' his journey, and thence comes the meaning of 'abridgement'. Here, *ʿāmmiyya* contains 'thorns' and 'brambles' that prevent using Arabic in its complete (*salīm*) and eloquent (*faṣīḥ*) manner.

This sharp contrast between *fuṣḥā* and *ʿāmmiyya* aside, which Qudsī purposefully constructs to support his separation thesis, it is noteworthy that, in this metaphor, he also, in a relatively implicit manner, depicts the mutual reliance between the two language varieties: the *fuṣḥā* 'trees' supply the *ʿāmmiyya* 'thickets' with water and nutrition, while the 'thickets' protect the 'trees' from external intrusions.[1] This image of mutual reliance reminds us of the inalienability thesis in the parent–daughter metaphor in extract 1.

The metaphorical framing processes in extracts 1 and 2 bring in perspectives similar in their contents but different in their explicitness. The explicit perspectives of inalienability and anti-antagonism/separation in extract 1 are implicit in extract 2, while the implicit perspectives of *ʿāmmiyya* inferiority and pro-antagonism/separation in extract 1 are explicit in extract 2.

Does this different explicitness indicate two different positions on the issue of *fuṣḥā* and *ʿāmmiyya*? It is hardly so, because these two extracts are both taken from formal replies of the Syrian Science Academy published in the same year to language policy enquiries. Although the authors of the two replies might hold different views on *fuṣḥā* and *ʿāmmiyya*, when writing on behalf of the Academy, they more or less had to accommodate their views to the official position and agenda of the Academy on this issue.

The difference lies in the fact that the two replies address the relationship between *fuṣḥā* and *ʿāmmiyya* in two different contexts. Al-Maghribī (1923) discusses this relationship as part of the issue of 'promoting *fuṣḥā*', which belongs to the making and promotion of a standard national language as necessary to the construction of a coherent national community in the nascent Syrian state. The Syrian government intended to adopt a *fuṣḥā*-only policy, whose legitimacy lay in (1) the principle of 'one nation, one language' as part of the nation-state model imported from Europe;[2] (2) the unchallenged literary, elitist status of *fuṣḥā* as the language of the long-ingrained learned tradition in Syria and the Arabic-speaking world, which can be easily adapted to promote mass literacy as a prerequisite for the integration of different segments in a national community; and (3) the fact that *fuṣḥā* has been taught and acquired throughout the entire Arabic-speaking world, making it a symbol of pan-Arabism – the founding ideology of Fayṣal's (d. 1933) short-lived Arab Kingdom of Syria (March–July 1920) continuously endorsed, at least partially, by the following Syrian regimes.

As a leading intellectual of the time, al-Maghribī could not be unware of the above political significances of the promotion of *fuṣḥā* to national integration at both state-territorial and pan-Arab levels. As a member of the Syrian Science Academy, he was aware that the Academy, as a state-sponsored institution, should naturally support and justify language policies of the government. However, as a linguist, he was also aware that it was technically impossible to enforce linguistic unification in the direction of *fuṣḥā* over a short time span. To appease potential conflicts of views triggered by his multiple social roles, al-Maghribī tactically juxtaposed the parent–daughter and the battle metaphors to justify the idea '*ʿāmmiyya* is inalienable to *fuṣḥā*' without articulating it directly, on the one hand, and to support the government agenda of linguistic-*cum*-national integration, on the other.

This latter purpose was achieved through the association that the two metaphors mediated between linguistic integration–separation and national integration–fragmentation. On the state-territorial level of national integration, seeing *fuṣḥā* as the parent of *ʿāmmiyya* refracts the elitist, top-down pattern of state-formation in Syria and other Arab states, where the ruling elites often perceive the rule as 'fathering' their subjects (e.g., see ʿAbd al-Laṭīf (2012) on the father metaphor in Anwar Sadat's political speeches). On the pan-Arab level of national integration, a pattern of perception similar to the parent–descent frame was adopted to describe the relationship between the Arab nation and the territorial Arab states as that between the body and its organs. Darwīsh al-Miqdādī, in his textbook[3] *Tāʾrīkh al-ʾumma al-ʿarabiyya* (*History of the Arab Nation*), first published in 1931, considers the 'Arab Island' to be 'a living body' of which the 'head' is the Fertile Crescent, the 'heart' is central Arabia, and the 'extremities' are the Arabian coastlands from the Gulf of Aqaba to the Gulf of Basra (Dawn 1988: 69; see also Choueiri 2000: 34). As for the battle metaphor in extract 1, this is easily reminiscent, in the 1920s, of the internal, sectarian feuds across the Middle East and the First World War as the great war of nations. Framing the antagonism between *fuṣḥā* and *ʿāmmiyya* in these disturbing, pessimistic experiences, this antagonism is seen as a refraction of the conflicts and political fragmentation in or involving the Arabic-speaking world. Alleviating this antagonism, therefore, is in accordance with the agenda of national integration which aspires at integrity, solidary, stability and prosperity of both individual Arab states and the Arab nation as a whole.

By contrast, Qudsī (1923) was set in a different context. It was a refutation of the suggestion of Latinising the Arabic script published in a French newspaper. For many Arab intellectuals, the calls to use Latin script and for elevating *ʿāmmiyyas* to the status of national languages of individual Arab states were both colonial conspiracies aimed at weakening Arab solidary by politically fragmenting the Arabic-speaking world.[4] Therefore, in dealing with these conspiracies, *ʿāmmiyya* was not seen as an index and component of Arab identity, but as an entity that is originally Arab but penetrated and exploited by external powers to become a proxy for their evil agendas for controlling and subjecting the Arabic-speaking world. Qudsī's description of *ʿāmmiyya* as thickets mixed with thorns and brambles fits the above association between *ʿāmmiyya* and foreign conspiracies. This also explains why Qudsī makes the 'separation of *fuṣḥā* from *ʿāmmiyya*' thesis more explicit.

The above analysis shows that both al-Maghribī and Qudsī in their deliberate metaphorical framing processes consciously associate the issue of *fuṣḥā* and *ʿāmmiyya* with the contexts of national integration and the perceived colonial conspiracy, respectively. This association between language and socio-political concerns is also evident in automatic framing. For example, in extract 1, the battle metaphor seems to have encoded the context of internal feuds and external invasion already, and the use of the word '*muwallada*' in the parent–daughter metaphor may also activate a hidden judgement of *ʿāmmiyya*s, embedded in this word, as 'contaminated' by foreign languages, which is in accord with the conspiracy theory about *ʿāmmiyya*.

'*Muwallada*' has a negative connotation in traditional Islamic literature. As a term of Islamic history, it refers to 'a cross-breed, half-caste or even . . . one who, without being of Arab origin, has been born among the Arabs and received an Arabic education' (Chalmeta and Heinrichs 1993: 807). As a term of linguistics, it refers to the words and expressions that are used by those 'cross-breed' Arabic-speakers and are not found in the orthodox corpus of the Arabic language (the Qurʾān and pre-Islamic poetry). This ethnic-*cum*-linguistic hybridity appeared following the Arab conquest of Mesopotamia, Great Syria and Egypt in the seventh and eighth centuries, due to intensive contact between Arab emigrants and the local people in the conquered lands. From then on, until roughly the tenth century, only some Bedouin tribes remaining in Arabia who had minimal contact with non-Arabs were regarded as ethnically pure; their use of Arabic set the highest standard of *fuṣḥā*. The Arabic languages spoken in the conquered lands, by contrast, were perceived to be corrupted, thus not trustworthy for grammar-making. These metaphorical and allusive meanings of *muwallad* reveal al-Maghribī's attitude towards *ʿāmmiyya*, which is hidden behind his words: *ʿāmmiyya* is a set of hybrid language varieties of *fuṣḥā* and foreign languages.

So far it has been clear that the metalanguage discourse on *fuṣḥā* and *ʿāmmiyya* has been deeply affected by the socio-political contexts of the Arabic-speaking world. Accordingly, the seemingly 'linguistic' issue of Arabic diglossia has been endowed with extra-linguistic significance, linking it to the national cause of self-integration and anti-colonialism. Such extra-linguistic significance and the process of its endowment belong to what Suleiman (2011, 2013) proposes as 'language symbolism': the use of Arabic as a symbolic resource and a proxy for identity negotiations and power struggles in conflictual and turbulent situations. In certain situations, this symbolic use of Arabic is conscious and deliberate, whereas in others, it is automatic, appearing to be 'a result of complex historical and structural forces that shape the social system within which individuals must act' (Tollefson 2011: 367). Metaphor, due to its deliberate and automatic framing effects that link the experiences of the linguistic and the socio-political together, severs as a mediator, generator and container of language symbolism.

Metaphorical recurrence

Realising this role of metaphor in Arabic metalanguage discourse, we can now move on to examine and explain the phenomenon of metaphorical recurrence in this discourse. In what follows, I will conduct a limited review of the recurrence of the above-mentioned organic metaphors in the discussion of the Cairo Language Academy on *fuṣḥā* and *ʿāmmiyya*. I have chosen this Academy because, since its inauguration in 1932, it has overshadowed its Syrian precedent and the latecomers in other Arab states as the leading forum for language policy debates in the entire Arabic-speaking world. My review is diachronic but not historical, as my purpose is to illustrate this recurrence phenomenon via case studies, but not to provide a chronicle of all the organic metaphors and the pragmatics of their making. Due to the connection between metaphor and language symbolism, I will consider each recurrence within its most relevant socio-political context. This will help to explain the socio-political significance of this recurrence in the end of the chapter.

In 1957, Muḥmaad Riḍā al-Shabībī, a member of the Cairo Academy made a speech at the annual conference of the Academy arguing for unifying all the *ʿāmmiyya*s of Arabic in order to promote linguistic unification around *fuṣḥā* in the Arabic-speaking world as a prerequisite for the ultimate Arab unity. In his speech, he denied the claims of *ʿāmmiyya* supporters about elevating *ʿāmmiyya*s to the status of national languages of Arab states. He associated these claims, first, to the colonial conspiracies aimed at fragmenting the Arabs and, then, to the rise of state-territorial nationalism that stressed the value of *ʿāmmiyya* to the formation of state identities. He then argued that state-territorial nationalism is an ephemeral political trend, while pan-Arab unity is the ultimate destiny for the Arabs. Now that the age of pan-Arab unity has come, he argued, it is necessary to promote linguistic unity of the Arabs based on *fuṣḥā*. In this context he made the 'unifying *ʿāmmiyya*s' proposal.

This proposal was radical and was not feasible in linguistic terms. However, it suited the political atmosphere of the 1950s, when pan-Arabism in its Nasserist and Baʿathist variations swept over the Arabic-speaking world. Al-Shabībī establishes a cause–effect correlation between linguistic and political unity–fragmentation on both instrumental and symbolic grounds. The instrumental dimension lies in that, for him, unifying *ʿāmmiyya*s is a first step towards the reunion of spoken and written Arabic around *fuṣḥā*. However, since it is nearly impossible to enforce the unification of *ʿāmmiyya*s in real language use, and al-Shabībī would be aware of this, his proposal was largely symbolic, using linguistic unification as a 'proxy' (Suleiman 2013: 16) to serve the political agenda of pan-Arabism.

Against this background, we can better understand the framing effects of the following organic metaphors extracted from his speech. When demonstrating how *ʿāmmiyya*s proliferated in the age of the decline of the Arabs (referring to their loss of grip on the Islamic empire following the collapse of the Abbasid dynasty) as a result of the rise of non-Arab peoples such the Persians and the Turks, al-Shabībī laments that ([1957] 1962: 85):

Extract 3

> In this period, many [Arabic] dialects began to split from *fuṣḥā*. Even if they did not triumph over (*taghallab ʿalā*) their mother (*umm*) in writing and composition, they prevailed/tyrannised over (*ṭāghā ʿalā*) her in general conversation and daily communication.

In extract 3, we come across the two familiar metaphors of the descent and the battle. Yet here al-Shabībī employs the two metaphors in a single narrative to create a composite metaphor. Although his comparison of *fuṣḥā* to the mother of *ʿāmmiyyas* still frames the relationship between the two sets of language varieties as inalienable kinship, the main framing effect that he deliberately uses this composite metaphor to activate is the image of a mother betrayed, attacked and abused by her children. This frame continues when al-Shabībī describes how, in the early twentieth century, *fuṣḥā* emerged out of the attack by *ʿāmmiyya* supporters 'triumphantly' (*ẓāfira*) with 'full dignity' (*mawfūrat al-karāma*), and how the call to replace *fuṣḥā* with *ʿāmmiyya* 'failed in awful disgrace' (*bāʾat bi-khizy faẓīʿ*) (al-Shabībī [1957] 1962: 86), as if the 'mother' finally defended herself against the matricide-like attacks by her 'children' and their accomplices. At this point, the audience may ask: 'What is the mother going to do after her triumph? Will she abandon her own children?' Following this line of thinking, the frame further develops when al-Shabībī informs us that, in recent years, the *ʿāmmiyyas* in various Arab regions became closer to *fuṣḥā* than before, and people started to call for the reconciliation (*al-tawfīq wa-l-iṣlāḥ*) between *fuṣḥā* and *ʿāmmiyya* (ibid.: 87). Now the framing effect is strong enough to guide the mind of the audience without further 'framing'. They may possibly answer to themselves: 'No, she will not. She will let them repent and seek reunion with her.' In this way, the audience will naturally sympathise with al-Shabībī's proposal of unifying *ʿāmmiyyas* and bringing them back to *fuṣḥā*. That was why, in the discussion following his speech, although many members of the Academy did not agree with his proposal, they challenged only its instrumental infeasibility but not its underlying idea – the inalienable link between varieties of Arabic and their ultimate reunion with *fuṣḥā*. For example, although Tammam Ḥassān commented on the proposal by saying that 'two members of a family (*ʿāʾila*) do not speak in the same way' in order to demonstrate that dialectal diversity is a natural phenomenon (ibid.: 91), the adoption of the 'family' metaphor only revealed the framing effect of al-Shabībī's metaphors on his mind.

Reading the above metaphorical frame in the context of the prevailing pan-Arabism in the 1950s, the symbolic association between the frame and the context is obvious. The feuds and reconciliation between the mother and her children that the frame activates to depict the situation of *fuṣḥā* and *ʿāmmiyya* can be easily applied to the situation of the Arab nation and the individual Arab states. This shows that al-Shabībī's choice of metaphor is not random. His choice should be able to associate linguistic and political unity–fragmentation together. This choice is partly due to the resonance of his own political inclination with pan-Arabism, but is also partly due to the structuralising force of pan-Arabism that makes this resonance inevitable and automatic.

In 1978, the Cairo Academy set the theme of its annual conference as 'the relationship between *fuṣḥā* and *ʿāmmiyya*', and invited a number of its members coming from different Arab countries to present the situation of Arabic diglossia in their home countries. Ibrāhīm Sāmrāʾī, an Iraqi member of the Academy, set out to present the case of Iraq. At the beginning of his speech, he clarified his purpose of studying *ʿāmmiyya* as to serve the cause of recovering the past, centuries-long 'status, power and ability' of *fuṣḥā* (1978: 35). He stated that 'we need to pay attention to *ʿāmmiyya*, because it harms (*taḥmīl al-ḍaym ʿalā*) our *fuṣḥā*', which was now on the path of recovery and revival (ibid.). This set the tone of his speech. Although he mentioned that *ʿāmmiyya* lives 'side by side' (*jiwār*) with *fuṣḥā* in Iraq (ibid.: 37) and that '*ʿāmmiyya* has taken and is still taking a great many from *fuṣḥā*' (ibid.: 39), which is reminiscent of the thesis of mutual reliance or even inalienability discussed before, his overall attitude towards *ʿāmmiyya* was negative.

This negativity first lies in his observation that the Iraqi *ʿāmmiyya* had been and continued to be significantly influenced by foreign languages, especially Persian. Such influence had left a mark of alienness (*wasm aʿjamī*) on this *ʿāmmiyya*. Yet a more evident negativity is reflected in his use of a series of 'battle' or 'confrontation' metaphors to describe the relationship between *fuṣḥā* and *ʿāmmiyya*. For example, he depicted *fuṣḥā* as 'not content with defence (*muqāwama*) and resistance (*wuqūf*), so it does retreat (*tanḥasir*) in front of *ʿāmmiyya*' (ibid.). He cited certain new usages in *fuṣḥā*, such as treating *raʾs* 'head' as grammatically feminine, and explained these as *ʿāmmiyya* 'marching against' (*zaḥf ʿalā*) (ibid.: 40) or 'attacking' (*ghazā*) (ibid.: 41) *fuṣḥā*. He described the improper use of language in a draft law in Iraq as the 'assault' (*sṭwa*) of *ʿāmmiyya* on *fuṣḥā* and the 'tyranny' (*jawr*) of the former over the latter (ibid.). Finally, he concluded his speech by stating that 'the *Law of the integrity of Arabic* has been issued in Iraq to defend this language from the havoc (*ghāyla*) of *ʿāmmiyya*' and that 'we can can only guard (*ʿāṣim*) this noble language by paying serious, organised efforts' (ibid.: 42).

Why did Sāmrāʾī choose to employ the battle metaphor to this extent of density? It seems that, in his speech, the balanced co-existence of the perceived inalienability and antagonism between *fuṣḥā* and *ʿāmmiyya* that we witnessed in the earlier extracts is broken, and the emphasis is now exclusively on defending *fuṣḥā* against the tyranny of *ʿāmmiyya*. How do we explain this pronounced antagonism? Did it have any relation to the socio-political circumstances of the time?

The reason lies in the deep trauma and malaise the Arabs began to suffer following the defeat of the Arab coalition in the 1967 War with Israel. Ṭarābīshī (2005) explains why this defeat was traumatic as follows (cf. Suleiman 2011: 131). First, this defeat was unexpected given the Arabs' feeling of self-confidence and invincibility before the war. Second, the humiliation created by the fact that a massive coalition of Arab armies lost the war at the hands of the Israeli army, which was numerically small and belittled by the Arabs before the war, made many Arabs believe that Arab society was backward at all levels. Third, the wounds of the 1967 defeat were not healed by any meaningful Arab victory over the Israelis in the following confrontations between the two (e.g., the 1973 Arab–Israeli War, the 1982 Lebanon War, the two Palestinian uprisings (*intifāḍa*), etc.), leaving an impression that defeats were repetitive and the Arab backwardness was endemic. Fourth, these repetitive defeats implanted a sense of victimhood into the Arab psyche, revealed as both envying and resisting the powerful, dominant Other in international and inter-cultural relations.

This trauma had already affected the tone of the metalanguage discourse in the Arabic-speaking world, especially in the language policy circles. For example, the resolution issued by the Second Arabisation (*taʿrīb*) Conference (1973) states that (Aḥmad 1999: 208):

Extract 4

> The deficits that have afflicted the Arabic language in recent times do not come from the language itself but from the linguistic invasion (*al-ghazw al-lughawī*) launched against it in various forms, from distancing it from its users, to arousing suspicion about its capability, to isolating it from life and society.

In the post-1967 context, the concept of 'linguistic invasion' in the above extract of discourse carries a straightforward reminiscence of the continual military defeats the Arabs suffered as a whole.[5] Framing the situation of Arabic in such traumatic experience of the Arabs establishes a clear, symbolic correlation between this language and the Arab nation.

Since this correlation did exist in the post-1967 discourse, we may consider the signification of Sāmrāʾī's excessive use of the battle metaphor along similar lines. In order to do so, we need to figure out what *fuṣḥā* and *ʿāmmiyya* symbolised respectively in the post-1967 context. This drives us to answer the following question first: who should take the blame for the 1967 defeat? There were two parties to blame: one included Zionists and their sponsors in the 'West', and the other included individual Arab states who in their state-building and modernisation endeavours failed to either empower the Arab people or recover their past might and glories. Not coincidently, *ʿāmmiyya*, as I have discussed before, had been symbolically tarnished by colonial conspiracy and state-territorial nationalism, both of which were blamed for the political fragmentation of the Arabic-speaking world. By contrast, *fuṣḥā* was no doubt the most legitimate symbol of the Arab nation, its glorious past and the might of its solidarity. So, when *ʿāmmiyya* was described as attacking and tyrannising *fuṣḥā*, this was reminiscent of how foreign troops invaded Arab lands and how the territorial Arab states hijacked the cause of Arab renaissance to serve their own political interests and agenda, which led to the total failure in the 1967 War.

Certainly, this is only reminiscence. This might not be what Sāmrāʾī deliberately aims to convey through the battle metaphors he uses. However, considering these metaphors together with his statement of reviving the glory of *fuṣḥā* at the beginning of his speech, it is against intuition if we consider his speech innocent of the post-1967 trauma discussed above. As least we could say that this trauma plays a structuralising function that makes his use of the battle metaphors an automatic choice.

The antagonism towards *ʿāmmiyya* represented by Sāmrāʾī (1978) dwindled in the metalanguage discourse of the Cairo Academy with the waning of pan-Arabism as a political agenda, the consolidation of the multi-state system in the Arabic-speaking world, and the wave of economic opening-up and liberalisation in favour of the West-led capitalist world system from the late 1970s onwards. Entering the last decade of the twentieth century, the end of the Cold War and Iraq's invasion of Kuwait only reinforced the above tendencies of socio-political change. The former rendered the 'West' as being perceived as the only dominant core of the world system, while the latter announced the triumph of territorial-state interests and identities over pan-Arab causes in the Arabic-speaking world. In this context, the descent and battle metaphors gained new significance in the discourse on *fuṣḥā* and *ʿāmmiyya* in the Academy.

In 1990, the Academy once again themed its annual conference as '*fuṣḥā* and *ʿāmmiyya*'. In the opening ceremony, Aḥmad Fatḥī Surūr, then Egyptian Minister of Education (1986–1990), explained this renewed interest by arguing that it is 'a desired national goal' to 'bring *fuṣḥā* and *ʿāmmiyya* close to each other in individual Arab countries', and then to 'bring all the *ʿāmmiyya*s close together within the compass of *fuṣḥā*', as this would buttress 'the convergence of Arab societies' (1990: 10). This statement indicates the association between linguistic and national integration.

Along this line of argument, Ibrāhīm Tarzī, the chief editor of the official journal of the Academy, wrote a preface for Issue 65 of the journal, which contains a selection of the papers presented at the 1990 annual conference. He depicts the situation of *fuṣḥā* and *ʿāmmiyya* as follows (1990: 7–8):

Extract 5

> Many elements prevailing in our *ʿāmmiyyas* stem from the womb (*raḥim*) of our *fuṣḥā*. However, only a few of these elements retain their belonging and loyalty to their mother language (*lughatuh al-umm*), whereas the rest have been attacked (*iʿtarā*) by deviation, distortion, deletion or addition . . . as well as baseness (*hujna*) and foreignness (*ʿujma*), since the spoken variety of Arabic was mixed (*ikhtalaṭat*) with the languages of those who were subjected during the Islamic Conquests; crowds (*afwāj*) of people converted to the religion of Allah and dedicated themselves to the learning of Arabic – the language of the Holy Qurʾān and the Noble Hadith.
>
> Whereas the status of *fuṣḥā* as a language of science and literature remained safe and well-protected, oral communication became the domain of intimate contact (*liqāʾ ḥamīm*) between Arabic and the languages of the Muslim peoples, which led to cross-pollination (*talāquḥ*) that gave birth to (*wallad*) a lot of words and phrases prevalent in our *ʿāmmiyyas*.
>
> Then, in the recent ages, our Arab world suffered various raids (*ghazawāt*) on its heartland, followed by raids (*ghazawāt*) on our *ʿāmmiyyas*, bringing to them more baseness and foreignness and driving them away from their uncontaminated, eloquent (*faṣīḥa*) pedigree (*nasab*). As a result, there appeared hybrids (*khalīṭ*) of Arabic and Turkish or of Arabic and some European languages such as English, French and Italian!

The metaphors of descent and battle in extract 5 differ from what I analysed before in that they are used to arouse sympathy for *ʿāmmiyyas*. The use of 'womb' together with 'mother' brings in a very intimate relationship between *fuṣḥā* and *ʿāmmiyya*. The 'womb' suggests the pure pedigree of *ʿāmmiyya*; and its deviation and distortion had nothing to do with this pedigree, but was caused by contact with non-Arabic languages. Moreover, attaching the pronoun 'our' to both *fuṣḥā* and *ʿāmmiyya* only confirms and reinforces this sense of intimacy and pure pedigree. This attitude towards *ʿāmmiyya* is repeated in the battle metaphor. Now the battle is not between *fuṣḥā* and *ʿāmmiyya*, nor does the latter tyrannise against the former. Instead, *ʿāmmiyya* becomes the victim of raids and attacks. All the above metaphorical meanings convey one central message: *ʿāmmiyya* is part of 'us'.

This message is the product of metaphorical framing that is both deliberate and automatic. It is deliberate as Tarzī wants to use the above metaphors to demonstrate the inalienability between *fuṣḥā* and *ʿāmmiyya* and the victimhood of the latter, so he can go on to justify the necessity of bringing *ʿāmmiyya* back to *fuṣḥā* in the form of linguistic integration as Minister Surūr calls for. Since this integration is seen as a national cause, it can be argued that 'bringing *ʿāmmiyya* back' conveys a symbolic correlation with bringing the detached, deviated individual Arab states back to their mother – the Arab nation. Evidently, here linguistic integration serves as a proxy to alleviate the anxiety over the increasingly inward-looking tendencies of the Arab states and their indifference to Arab solidarity. As this anxiety works on collective psychology in Arab society in the same manner of the post-1967 trauma, the above framing is somehow inevitable as an automatic response to the anxiety.

The epochal and the *longue durée*

From al-Maghribī (1923) and Qudsī (1923), to al-Shabībī ([1957] 1962), to Sāmrāʾī (1978), then to Tarzī (1990), we witness a number of metaphors that depict *fuṣḥā* and *ʿāmmiyya* as living organisms. These metaphors seem to be recurrent over time in two regards. One is the recurrence of the domains of experience that these metaphors transfer to the perception of the relationship between *fuṣḥā* and *ʿāmmiyya*. These domains include descent, neighbour, symbiosis of plants and battle. The other regard is the recurrence of the 'frames' that these metaphors generate, including the purity and refinement of *fuṣḥā* and the defectiveness and hybridity of *ʿāmmiyya*, on the one hand, and the inalienability–mutual reliance and the antagonism–separation of *fuṣḥā* and *ʿāmmiyya*, on the other.

The reason for employing these metaphors together with exploiting their framing effects is because the frames they generate fit the language symbolism that establishes symbolic correspondences between the situation of *fuṣḥā* and *ʿāmmiyya*, on the one hand, and the seemingly epochal socio-political contexts of the Arabic-speaking world in different periods, on the other. As the above metaphorical analyses illustrate, al-Maghribī (1923) constructs the image of the authentic parent (*fuṣḥā*) and the deviating children (*ʿāmmiyya*) in order to echo with the national language-making agenda of the Syrian government based on *fuṣḥā* as a step towards building a coherent national community of Syria in an elitist, top-down manner as part of an expected, unified pan-Arab polity. Qudsī (1923) depicts a symbiosis of *fuṣḥā* and *ʿāmmiyya*, but highlights the latter's inferiority and mixture with alien elements to hint at the colonial penetration into the interior of the Arab lands, thus colouring his refutation of the Latinising Arabic script proposal with anti-colonialism – a stance he could not openly articulate when Syria was under the French mandate (1923–46). Al-Shabībī ([1957] 1962) presents a scene of reconciliation between a mother (*fuṣḥā*) and her rebellious children (*ʿāmmiyyas*) to highlight the symbolic correspondence between linguistic reunion of Arabic and political reunion of the Arab nation in line with the ideology of pan-Arabism prevailing in the 1950s and 1960s. Sāmrāʾī (1978), affected by the collective trauma of the 1967 defeat, stresses the importance of defending *fuṣḥā* against the tyranny and enmity of *ʿāmmiyya* to allude to his concern over the failing territorial Arab states and the continuing colonial presence in the Arabic-speaking world. Tarzī (1990) reproduces the family and battle metaphors, but foregrounds the intimacy and inalienability between *fuṣḥā* and *ʿāmmiyya* and the victimhood of the latter to alleviate the growing anxiety over the waning pan-Arabism and the consolidated fragmentation of the Arabic-speaking world in the last decade of the twentieth century.

Under the influence of these epochal contexts, every recurrence of the organic metaphors is a reiteration, that is, reprocessing the contents and frames of these metaphors to construct or adjust the symbolism of *fuṣḥā* and *ʿāmmiyya* in accord with the dominant socio-political concerns in Arab society in a certain period. However, the general lines of the metaphorical contents and frames remains stable for a long time, at least from the 1920s to the 1990s as shown by the cases studied in this chapter. This *longue durée* stability may be explained by the unchanged aspects of all the above-mentioned epochal socio-political contexts: the persisting rapture between state and society or the elites and the commoners as a result of the unfinished mission of state–social integration in individual Arab states, the duality of pan-Arab and territorial-state national identities as a result of the increasing political fragmentation in the Arabic-speaking world, and the enduring sense of coloniality and external threats in Arab society as a result of the long-term subjection of the region to the hierarchical power relations in the modern, capitalist world system. These *longue durée* circumstances cultivate the symbolic associations between *fuṣḥā* and elitism, state authority and pan-Arab solidarity, between *ʿāmmiyya* and the lower social strata, ethnic impurity and foreign conspiracy, between the inalienability of *fuṣḥā* and *ʿāmmiyya* and national integration at both state-territorial and pan-Arab levels, and between the antagonism of *fuṣḥā* and *ʿāmmiyya* and defending Arabness (*ʿurūba*) against fragmentation from within and enmity from without. These symbolic meanings of *fuṣḥā* and *ʿāmmiyya* will keep resurfacing as long as these *longue durée* circumstances remain unchallenged, and the recurrence of the organic metaphors discussed in this chapter will not stop, as the following example shows.

On 7 December 2014, El Sawy Culturewheel (*Sāqiyat al-Ṣāwī*), an influential private cultural centre in Cairo opened its sixth Festival of Colloquial Poetry under the banner '*ʿāmmiyya* is the daughter of *fuṣḥā*' to observe the United Nations Arabic Language Day (18 December). In his opening address of the festival, Muhammad al-Ṣāwī, founder and director of the centre, explained the choice of this banner by saying:

> Many people imagine (*taṣawwar*) that a battle (*maʿraka*) is going on between *fuṣḥā* and *ʿāmmiyya* as if these two were in conflict (*ṣirāʿ*). Quite the contrary, *ʿāmmiyya* . . . is the daughter (*bint*) of *fuṣḥā*; it is an indivisible part of *fuṣḥā*, enriching and empowering the latter by reaching those domains of expression that *fuṣḥā* does not in the age and circumstances we are living in. ('Mahrajān al-Sāqiya' 2014)

Here the recurrence of the parent–daughter and conflict metaphors seems to be a conscious response to the state media's depiction of Egyptian *ʿāmmiyya* as a sign of the political illegitimacy of the protesters and the perceived foreign plots against Egypt during the Egyptian Revolution in 2011 (Bassiouney 2014: 294–340). Once again, the situation of *fuṣḥā* and *ʿāmmiyya* is related to intra-state feuds and foreign enmity.

Together, the epochal and the *longue durée* socio-political contexts in the Arabic-speaking world confine the perception of the relationship between *fuṣḥā* and *ʿāmmiyya* to a stable dialectic of inalienability and antagonism. The above discussion shows how this dialectic is vividly articulated by the two recurrent sets of 'organic metaphors' in Arabic metalanguage discourse. Like the natural world witnessing both symbiosis and 'survival of the fittest' as the logic underlying the relationships between plants, animals and human beings, so do languages and language varieties in metalanguage reflections. Yet contemporary eco-linguistics, sustained by a morality of multi-culturalism, tend to over-emphasise the 'symbiosis' dimension of intra- and inter-language relations in diglossic and multilingual language communities.[6] This tendency is in its nature no less idealistic than the 'one nation, one language' ideology prevailing in the age of nationalism. Both could be blamed for their detachment from a contextual examination of language situations and ideologies in line with the socio-political circumstances of the language communities in question. When we consider these circumstances, we may arrive at a more nuanced, dialectic understanding of the 'organic' perception of languages, such as that I have shown in this chapter concerning Arabic diglossia.

Notes

1. Again, not coincidentally, Muḥammad Ḥasan ʿAbd al-Laṭīf, a current member of the Cairo Language Academy, told me in a personal interview (19 June 2012) that the Arabic language is always developing, but the developments are mostly revealed in *ʿāmmiyya*.
2. The principle of 'one nation, one language' is central to both of the two main variants of the European nation-state model – what Fishman (1968) terms as 'nationalism' and 'nationism', respectively, and Wright (2012) terms as 'ethno-linguistic nationalism' and 'civic-contractual nationalism', respectively. The two variants interacted with pan-Arabism and territorial-state nationalisms in the Arabic-speaking world in complicated ways, with the above principle remaining an underlying logic in many situations. See Lian (2015: 88–101) for a detailed discussion.
3. Al-Miqdādī's book was 'selected as the text for the teaching of Arab history in the secondary schools of Palestine, Syria and Iraq, where it continued to be the standard text of Arab youth for several student generations' (Faris 1954: 156–7; cf. Choueiri 2000: 222).

4. The notorious proponents of *ʿāmmiyya* include: (1) Wilhelm Spitta (1853–83), a German Orientalist, who published *Grammatik des arabischen vulgärdialectes von Aegypten* (*The Grammar of Arabic Colloquial in Egypt*) in 1880; (2) William Willcocks (1852–1932), a British engineer, who published *Syria, Egypt, North Africa, and Malta speak Punic, not Arabic* in 1883 and *Why is There No Power of Invention among the Egyptians Now?* in 1893 to call for abandoning *fuṣḥā* and adopting *ʿāmmiyya*; (3) John Selden Willmore (1856–1931), a British judge, who published *The Spoken Arabic of Egypt* in 1901; (4) Salāma Mūsā (1887–1958), an Egyptian Copt, who advocated Egyptian Colloquial as the official language of Egypt in order to seek an Egyptian political identity independent of the Arab one; and (5) Anīs Furayḥa (1903–1992), a Lebanese linguist, who proposed using Latin script to write *ʿāmmiyya* as well as making *ʿāmmiyya* the official language(s) of Arab states. For detailed critiques of these pro-*ʿāmmiyya* views and corresponding polemics, please refer to Suleiman (2003, 2004, 2013).
5. I am aware that this argument, suggesting an analogy between the Arab defeat by the Israelis and the perceived foreign invasion of the Arabic language, does not sound strong enough to be considered convincing. With respect to the resolution quoted here, there is an additional piece of evidence supporting the possible existence of this hidden analogy therein. The resolution of the First Arabisation Conference (1961) did not mention anything in relation to a 'linguistic invasion' (Aḥmad 1999: 207), thus making the adoption of this concept in the Second Conference too striking for us to downplay the influence of the 1967 trauma on the perception of language. Yet direct, even 'physical', evidence is always in short supply. This is natural as connections between conceptions of language and the sociopolitical contexts of their formation are often covert and occluded by the banalisation of language ideologies, and a widespread apolitical reading of language as mainly an instrument and medium of thought and communication. Therefore, readers should bear in mind that my analysis is only one interpretation of such connections in the Arabic-speaking world, but by no means the only one. This applies to all the case studies in this chapter, including the following explanation of Sāmrāʾī's excessive use of the battle metaphor.
6. See Edwards (2009: 230–45) for a critique of the new ecology of language.

References

Works in Arabic

ʿAbd al-Laṭīf, Muḥammad Ḥamāsa, Interview by Chaoqun Lian, digital recording, Cairo University, 19 June 2012.

ʿAbd al-Laṭīf, ʿImād, *Istīrātījiyyāt al-iqnāʿ wa-l-taʾthīr fī al-khiṭāb al-siyāsī: khuṭab al-raʾīs al-Sadāt namūdhajan* (Cairo: al-Hayʾat al-Miṣriyya al-ʿĀmma li-l-Kitāb, 2012).
Aḥmad, Aslamū Walad Sayyidī, 'al-Taʿrīb . . . min khilāl tajribat Maktab Tansīq al-Taʿrīb', *Majallat Majmaʿ al-Lugha al-ʿArabiyya* 84 (1999): 198–219.
Ibn Manẓūr, Muḥammad ibn Mukarram, *Lisān al-ʿarab*, vol. 13 (Cairo: al-Maṭbaʿa al-Mīriyya, 1885).
al-Maghribī, ʿAbd al-Qādir, 'Aqrab al-ṭuruq ilā nashr al-lugha al-fuṣḥā', *Majallat al-Majmaʿ al-ʿIlmī al-ʿArabī* 3(8) (1923): 231–8.
'Mahrajān al-Sāqiya li-shiʿr al-ʿāmmiyya 2014 (umsiyyat al-iftitāḥ),' YouTube video, 56:49, posted by 'El Sakia TV Festivals,' 19 January 2015, available at: https://www.youtube.com/watch?v=FH3Sofq4osQ.
Qudsī, Ilyās, 'Tabdīl al-ḥurūf al-ʿarabiyya', *Majallat al-Majmaʿ al-ʿIlmī al-ʿArabī* 3(6) (1923): 177–84.
al-Sāmrāʾī, Ibrāḥīm, 'Qiṣṣat al-ʿāmmiyya fī al-Irāq: Tārīkhuhā wa-wāqʾiʿuhā', *Majallat Majmaʿ al-Lugha al-ʿArabiyya* 41 (1978): 35–42.
al-Shabībī, Muḥammad Riḍan, 'al-Lahjāt al-qawmiyya wa-tawḥīduhā fī al-bilād al-ʿarabiyya', *Majallat Majmaʿ al-Lugha al-ʿArabiyya* 14 ([1957] 1962): 85–99.
Surūr, Aḥmad Fatḥī, 'Kalimat al-ustādh al-duktūr Aḥmad Fatḥī Surūr wazīr al-taʿlīm', *Majallat Majmaʿ al-Lugha al-ʿArabiyya* 66 (1990): 9–10.
Ṭarābīshī, George (Jūrj), *al-Maraḍ bi-l-gharb: al-Taḥlīl al-nafsī li-ʿuṣāb jamāʿī ʿarabī* (Damascus: Dār Petra li-l-Nashr wa-l-Tawzīʿ, 2005).
al-Tarzī, Ibrāhīm, 'Taṣdīr.' *Majallat Majmaʿ al-Lugha al-ʿArabiyya* 66 (1990): 7–8.

Works in English

Bassiouney, R., *Language and Identity in Modern Egypt* (Edinburgh: Edinburgh University Press, 2014).
Cameron, L., 'Metaphor and talk', in Raymond W. Gibbs (ed.), *The Cambridge Handbook of Metaphor and Thought* (Cambridge: Cambridge University Press, 2008), pp. 197–211.
Chalmeta, P. and Heinrichs W. F., 'Muwallad', in C. E. Bosworth, E. van Donzel, W. P. Heinrichs and Ch. Pellat (eds), *Encyclopaedia of Islam*, 2nd edn) (Leiden: Brill, 1993), vol. 7, pp. 807–8.
Choueiri, Youssef M., *Arab Nationalism, a History: Nation and State in the Arab World* (Oxford: Blackwell, 2000).
Dawn, C. E., 'An Arab nationalist view of world politics and history in the interwar period', in Uriel Dann (ed.), *The Great Powers in the Middle East, 1919–1939* (New York: Holmes & Meier, 1988), pp. 355–69.
Edwards, J., *Language and Identity: An Introduction* (Cambridge: Cambridge University Press, 2009).
Faris, Nabih A., 'The Arabs and their history', *Middle East Journal* 8 (1954): 155–62.

Ferguson, C., 'Diglossia', *Word*, 15 (1959): 325–40.

Fishman, Joshua A., 'Nationality-nationalism and nation-nationism', in Joshua A. Fishman, Charles A. Ferguson and Jyotirindra Das Gupta (eds), *Language Problems of Developing Nations* (New York: Wiley, 1968), pp. 39–51.

Kövecses, Zoltán, *Metaphor: A Practical Introduction* (Oxford: Oxford University Press, 2002).

Lakoff, G. and Johnson, M., *Metaphors We Live By* (Chicago, IL: University of Chicago Press, 1980).

Lian, C., 'Language planning and language policy of Arabic language academies in the twentieth century: A study of discourse', PhD dissertation, University of Cambridge, 2015.

Schön, Donald A., 'Generative metaphor: A perspective on problem-setting in social policy', in Andrew Ortony (ed.), *Metaphor and Thought*, 2nd edn (Cambridge: Cambridge University Press, 1993), pp. 137–63.

Suleiman, Y., *The Arabic Language and National Identity: A Study in Ideology* (Edinburgh: Edinburgh University Press, 2003).

Suleiman, Y., *A War of Words: Language and Conflict in the Middle East* (Cambridge: Cambridge University Press, 2004).

Suleiman, Y., *Arabic, Self and Identity: A Study in Conflict and Displacement* (Oxford: Oxford University Press, 2011).

Suleiman, Y., *Arabic in the Fray: Language Ideology and Cultural Politics* (Edinburgh: Edinburgh University Press, 2013).

Tollefson, James W., 'Language planning and language policy', in Rajend Mesthrie (ed.), *The Cambridge Handbook of Sociolinguistics* (Cambridge: Cambridge University Press, 2011), pp. 357–76.

Wright, S., 'Language policy, the nation and nationalism', in Bernard Spolsky (ed.), *The Cambridge Handbook of Language Policy* (Cambridge: Cambridge University Press, 2012), pp. 59–78.

CHAPTER 4

Colloquial Moroccan Arabic: Shifts in Usage and Attitudes in the Era of Computer-mediated Communication[1]

Eirlys Davies

Introduction

Ever since Ferguson's (1959) seminal paper, the language situation of the Arabic-speaking countries has been cited as a textbook example of diglossia. The sharp functional division between a high variety (H), referred to as *fusḥa*, Classical Arabic or Standard Arabic (henceforth SA), and a low variety (L), the local unwritten dialect acquired as a mother tongue, has remained in place for centuries. However, this is not to say that there has been no argument about the situation. Nationalists, modernisers, educators and psychologists have long debated the relations between colloquial Arabic and SA.

Attempts to manipulate this language situation have been legion, as can be seen from the surveys provided by Suleiman (2003, 2004). For instance, in the twentieth-century Middle East, Sati Al-Husri insisted that SA must serve as the cement of Arab unity, while Salama Musa considered SA a handicap and argued that Egypt should adopt as its language the colloquial dialect, and Lutfi Al-Sayyid called for the development of a middle Arabic bridging the gulf between H and L. Calls for the adoption of the Roman alphabet for Arabic were made by Abdelaziz Fahmi, Salama Musa and Said Aql, among others; in fact, according to Mahmoud (1980), over 300 proposals for reform of the Arabic writing system were submitted to the Arabic Language Academy in Cairo between 1938 and 1964.

Further west, in the North African countries colonised by France, the Arabisation policies implemented after independence sought to eradicate French from schools and administrations, and tried to make people use new terms derived from Arabic roots, rather than borrowings from French (Bentahila 1983). More recently, psycholinguists have stressed the need for early education to be in the mother tongue. Thus, there have been impassioned pleas for the use of colloquial Moroccan Arabic (henceforth MA) as a medium of instruction, at least in primary schools; however, in May 2015, the latest commission on reform of the Moroccan education system rejected this possibility. At the other end of the educational spectrum, attempts have been made to present highbrow literature through MA via translation; recently we have seen Rilke's *Duino Elegies* translated into MA by Mourad Alami, while Abderrahim Youssi has translated Coleridge's *The Rime of the Ancient Mariner*, and Hakima Berrada has translated La Boétie's sixteenth-century philosophical work, *Discours de la Servitude Volontaire* (Elinson 2013; Miller 2013).

The common feature of all these attempts to bring about changes in the use of and attitudes towards Arabic is that they are very much top-down initiatives. Scholars, politicians and ideologists have considered it their right and/or duty to try to influence how the masses should speak and write. Most of these attempts have also been relatively, if not entirely, ineffectual. Children still begin school speaking only the dialect and are immediately expected to learn to read and write in SA; MA remains full of borrowed words from European languages; French is still very much used in Morocco's corridors of power; and no Arab state has approved a reformed writing system for Arabic. As for the translation projects, Moroccans who are educated enough to be able to appreciate these works are unlikely to feel the need for MA versions, since they can already read the works in other languages.

However, over the last couple of decades, a new scenario has emerged simultaneously across many countries of the Arabic-speaking world. The tendency for the distinction between SA and the colloquials to correspond almost exactly to that between writing and speech seems to be weakening. We are now seeing more and more use of the dialects in writing. In some cases this writing is in Arabic script, but the most dramatic development has been the writing of colloquial Arabic using the Roman alphabet – a phenomenon variously referred to across the region as Arabizi, Arancia, Franco-Arabic or just Franco, but which we will here label Romanised Arabic (RA). Linked to this development is a further trend: the type of code- switching between colloquial Arabic and French or English, which has long been a common feature of everyday speech across the Arab world (Bentahila and Davies 1983), is now also seen in RA discourse.

These trends will be explored in this chapter. The focus will be on the current situation in Morocco, but there are certainly parallels with what is happening in other parts of the Arab world. Previous studies have examined the use of RA in Egypt (Warschauer, El Said and Zohry 2002; Aboelezz 2009, 2012), the UAE (Palfreyman and Al Khalil 2003), Saudi Arabia (Alabdulqader et al. 2014), Jordan (Al-Tamimi and Gorgis 2007; Bianchi 2012) and Morocco (Hall 2015). The sources used in these studies included instant messaging, emails, Facebook posts and Internet forum posts. Looking beyond CMC, some studies have reported on its use in other media, including classroom notes (Palfreyman and Al-Khalil 2003), billboard advertising (Hall 2015) and magazines (Aboelezz 2012).

In fact, writing dialectal Arabic is in itself nothing new. For example, in the days before telephones became widespread, Moroccans studying abroad kept in touch with their families back home via handwritten letters, often written in MA so that their illiterate parents would understand when the letters were read out to them. Belnap and Bishop (2003) similarly report the use of colloquial Arabic in personal correspondence by Arabic-speaking students resident in the USA. More generally, Dürscheid and Frehner (2013) argue that the oral features associated with emailing are not new, but have been seen for centuries in the written correspondence of the semi-literate. But instances of such private uses of language are not readily available to researchers, and so it is impossible to estimate the extent to which colloquial Arabic has been used for such purposes.

Nor indeed is the writing of Arabic in Roman script a revolutionary step. The French protectorate in Morocco left the country with the legacy of a bilingual administration system, and today all place names and personal names still have standard versions in Roman script as well as Arabic script. Morocco's linguistic landscape reflects this, with road signs, business and shop signs drawing on both alphabets. The official transliteration system used for proper names in Morocco is, naturally enough, influenced by French orthography; so, for instance, /u/ is represented by 'ou', /ʃ/ by 'ch', and /ʒ/ by 'j'.

The new trend for using RA can be contrasted with what went before in a number of ways. First, RA is now being used, not just because a sender or receiver is unable to communicate effectively in SA, but also between highly educated people who could if they wished opt to write in SA or a European language. Second, rather than being confined to private correspondence, texts written in MA are now highly visible in the public domain. And, third, the orthography used by today's RA writers differs from the officially approved transliteration inherited from colonial times; rather than being imposed from above, it seems to have been devised at ground-level by the users themselves. Most importantly, the changes we are now witnessing are not a response to official recommendations, or the endeavours of academics or activists. Rather, they constitute a bottom-up trend, apparently arising from ordinary people's responses to changing communication needs – and above all to the rise of computer-mediated communication (CMC).

The development of CMC has encouraged the use of the written medium in contexts where previously people might have relied on oral communication. For instance, instead of making a phone call, many people now prefer to send a text message. However, when SMS services first became widely available on mobile phones, the ASCII code they relied upon was not adapted to represent alphabets other than the Roman one. Those whose languages used other scripts, including Arabic-speakers, therefore solved the problem by representing these languages in Roman script. The same solution was adopted for writing Arabic on computers.

Naturally enough, given its origins in popular reaction to a problem that needed a rapid solution, the RA currently used across the Arab world has not been subject to any standardisation. Variations are therefore seen; some of these have historical roots, depending on whether English or French orthography is taken as a starting point (u versus ou, i versus ee, sh versus ch), but there may also be variation between users in the same region, and indeed within a single user's repertoire. The most obvious contrast between RA and the classic transliteration used for proper names is that the former uses numerals to represent certain phonemes for which the Roman alphabet offers no obvious symbols. Thus, in Morocco, 7 is commonly used for ح , 3 for ع, 9 for ق , etc., these choices being inspired by formal similarities between the numerals and the Arabic letters they now represent. A detailed discussion of RA orthography and its variations can be found in Palfreyman and Al Khalil (2003).

Thanks to Unicode, it is now easy to type in Arabic script on computers and phones, so we might well expect to see a return to greater use of Arabic script in CMC; M. O. Al-Khalil (personal communication) reports that this is indeed happening among Egyptians and Syrians. However, in Morocco RA seems to have become an entrenched habit, which has not so far been abandoned in favour of the Arabic alphabet.

In fact, it could be argued that RA is not the ideal script for use on today's smartphones, where shifting between numerals and letters involves extra manipulations. On earlier cell phones, of course, it was faster to type numerals than letters, since the latter required repeated key taps, and this may have encouraged the initial incorporation of numerals into RA. Interestingly, then, a writing system originally adopted to meet temporary needs has been maintained even now that the original motivation for it has gone. The fact that it facilitates written code-switching between MA and French, English or Spanish, which is a discourse pattern much favoured by Moroccans, may be one factor behind its maintenance in Morocco. Indeed, there are signs that its use is now spreading beyond the domain of CMC which spawned it.

Uses of RA in Morocco today

The range of domains in which RA is currently being used in Morocco can perhaps best be suggested by a quick snapshot survey of some current examples.

For instance, millions of young people send RA text messages every day, often including switching into French and/or English. The following example, which features the use of French and English as well as RA, was sent by a female student to a classmate:

1. salut habibti bghit ngulek makaynch l cours demain fsba7 walakin kayn exam dyal translation friday f 15h

   Hi dear, I want to tell you there is no class tomorrow morning but there's the translation exam on Friday at 3pm

The author of this message could equally well have expressed the same information in SA, French or English alone, but for less educated users, RA may be the only feasible option. Such users may be encouraged to try writing in RA because the absence of any clear rules means they do not need to worry about making errors. The following message was sent by a plumber to a client:

2. ana machi nduz 3andek fl3chiya wajdni dak lflus 3afak wa salam
   I'll come to see you this afternoon, get that money ready for me please, bye

Curiously, resources are available to help people who may struggle to express themselves effectively in RA. For example, the website www.sms-d-amour-poeme.com_claims to offer 1,000 love texts in RA, thus proposing a public resource to help people send eminently private sentimental messages. The following are representative examples:

3. chhal men 9amar f lkawn 2 wahad f smaa owahad tay9ra f had sms
   How many moons are in the universe? Two: one in the sky, and one who is reading this SMS

4. ach iswa lil bdoun qamar ach iswa l3oud bdoun watar ach tswa l3ayoun bdoun basar ach tswa hyati bdounek ya aghla lbachar
   What is the night worth without a moon? What is a lute worth without strings? What are eyes worth without sight? What is my life worth without you, o dearest person?

RA also features widely in social media communications directed to a wider audience, not merely friends. A recently trending Twitter feed, where people post photos of cars badly parked by inconsiderate drivers, is titled #Alerte7mar ('Warning: donkey'). Internet forums often feature long posts composed in RA, such as (5), where a female participant asks for advice on a weight-loss diet.

5. salam alebnat ana rani brit nkteb likoum nhar tlat walakine kan 3andi mouchkil fi la connextion w nhar larb3a mabrach yethal liya le site galouliya almaw9e3 fi halat seyana wlyouma halitlu wethal ana hayedt lhlawi mab9itch kanechri men zan9a bezaaaaaaaaaaaaf bhal lawel w rah hayedt 400g bezez b9iiit mdarba m3aha hta hayedt bechwiya bechwiya wman3awedhoumch bedoubel dyalhoum kayna ola la haga ana brit ndir regime dyal 3jour nhar 8danoun mesous w nhar 1kg d pomme2terre w 1kg de pommme chno ra2y dyalkoum fihe wach 3ando ijabiyat wla silbiyat iwa lahi 3awen ljami3
   Hi girls, I wanted to write to you on Tuesday but I had a problem with the connection, and on Wednesday the website wouldn't open, they told me the site was protected. Today I opened it and it opened. I gave up sweet things, I don't buy them from shops as much as I used to, and I lost 400g. I was forced

> to keep on struggling with this until I lost the weight little by little, so as not to regain double what I lost. There's one important thing: I want to do a 3-day diet, one day you eat 8 sugar-free yoghurts, one day you eat 1 kg of potatoes, and 1 kg of apples. What's your opinion on this? Does it have positive or negative effects? Well, may God help us all. (posted on www.beautymaroc.com, 21 February 2008)

And while Arabic language websites have always had to devise web addresses using the Roman alphabet, we now see more use of RA in webpage content too.

6. beddal sawtek w'd7ak m3a s7abek
   Change your voice and laugh with your friends
   (from Moroccan telecom company Inwi's website, www.inwi.ma, November 2015)

7. Marhba bikoum au McDo Ain Sebaâ
   Welcome to McDonald's of Ain Sebaâ
   (from the website www.mcdonalds.ma, November 2015)

8. SME3 LE MORNING DE MOMO W RBE7 W L3EB F PENALTY AVEC LE MDJS
   Listen to the Morning of Momo, win and play Penalty with the MDJS (le Morning de Momo being the name of a radio show, Penalty a game, and MDJS a sports organisation)
   (from the website of Moroccan radio station Hit Radio, www.hitradio.ma, 20 March 2016)

Nowadays RA also crops up quite frequently outside the domain of CMC. Graffiti in RA can be seen scrawled on the walls in Moroccan cities, while posters stuck on lamp posts advertise events such as a play titled 'F7ali f7alek' ('Like me, like you'), or a performance by a duo called 'Betweenatna' (a blend of English 'between' and MA *binatna* ('between us'). Even before the spread of CMC, the names of Moroccan popular songs could be found written in the Roman alphabet on cassette and CD sleeves, and now RA is extensively used in this domain. Moroccan state television recently broadcast a daily 3-minute programme called 'NT7ARKO' ('Let's move'), aimed at encouraging viewers to do more sport. And one can even purchase a T-shirt with the slogan 'Keep calm and 3awen lfari9' ('help the team').

Print advertisements using RA have now become commonplace on billboards, in flyers and brochures, and in magazines. Some promote ordinary everyday products: a Moroccan brand of biscuits, Bimo, is advertised with the slogan 'Li3andou 3andou' ('If you've got it, you've got it'), while a supermarket leaflet announces 'les promos dial l7ma9' ('crazy bargains').

Telecom companies were among the first to adopt RA in their advertisements, perhaps in response to their clients' predilection for sending SMSs in RA, but many other companies now use it to promote both local and global products. Banks have opted to use RA in the names of some of their services, such as Wafasalaf's 'Dima maak' ('Always with you'), and Crédit du Maroc's 'Koun-hani' ('Don't worry') and 'Imposta7il' (a blend of two synonyms: French 'impossible' and MA 'mousta7il' 'impossible'). And while initially RA seemed associated with everyday products accessible to all, it is now used to promote luxury goods too.

9. WACH NDADRAK KAYJIW M3A STYLAT DYALEK?
   NDARTAK TANIYA NA9SSA B-50%
   MEN 16 NOVEMBRE 2015 TAL 31 JANVIER 2016
   Do your glasses suit your style?
   Your second pair of glasses with a 50% reduction
   From 16 November 2015 to 31 January 2016
   (advertisement for Ray-Ban and Vogue sunglasses, observed in an optician's window, November 2015)

It is noticeable that in many of these examples RA is combined with French and/or English, either elsewhere on the page, or within structures exhibiting the kind of code-switching typical of everyday conversation, as in examples (7), (8) and (9).

The views of some current users of RA

To investigate the habits and attitudes of one section of Moroccan society, a survey was administered via a printed questionnaire. Approximately 350 questionnaires were distributed, and 248 were collected, though in some of the collected forms one or more questions were left unanswered. The informants were all Moroccan university students; there were thirty postgraduates and 218 undergraduates, all attending prestigious selective schools in which the main medium of education is French or English. There were 130 females and 118 males, with ages ranging from 18 to 28. Obviously, the findings reported here cannot be taken as valid for this age group as a whole, since the respondents belong to an elite, well-educated minority. However, these students do represent an interesting case, for theoretically at least they are not forced to resort to RA, but are quite capable of expressing themselves in SA, French and in many cases also English. The fact that all of them do choose to write in this variety is therefore worthy of attention.

The survey included questions about where and why they used RA, the way they had learned it, their use of code-switching within RA, and their attitudes to these habits. Responses were elicited via multiple choice questions, which allowed the selection of more than one response where appropriate, and space was also provided for comments explaining their choices. The final question provided a list of statements expressing beliefs and attitudes, which the informants were asked to rank on a five-point scale, where 5 represented total agreement and 1 total disagreement.

Unsurprisingly, 99 per cent said they used RA (either often or sometimes) to write text messages on their phones, 99 per cent used it for instant messaging on computers, 71 per cent for Internet forum contributions, and 62 per cent for Facebook posts. Interestingly, only 22 per cent said they used RA in emails (21 per cent sometimes and only 1 per cent often). This is in contrast to the findings of some earlier studies, such as Warschauer et al. (2002), Palfreyman and Al Khalil (2003), and Al Tamim and Gorgis (2007), which found RA to be frequently used in emails. This difference seems likely to be due to developments in technology and to a shift in CMC habits since these earlier studies; our respondents tend to rely more on smartphones than on desktop or laptop computers for their everyday CMC, and they apparently communicate with their peers largely via Facebook and instant messaging, while reserving emails for more formal correspondence, such as with teachers or potential employers. This is a further illustration of how the available technology continues to influence our modes of communication.

More striking is the fact that 31.5 per cent of the informants claimed to use RA for handwritten notes in class, either to record information from the teacher or to communicate with classmates; 15 per cent said they did this often, 16.5 per cent sometimes. Moreover, 15 per cent also claimed to use handwritten RA in other circumstances, citing examples such as notes left for their parents, lists of things to do and diary entries. While still confined to a minority of the group, this trend would seem to constitute a significant development, representing as it does an expansion of the use of RA from typing to handwriting.

Every one of the informants said they used RA to communicate with friends and classmates, while 69 per cent said they also used it to people of their age whom they did not know personally, such as online acquaintances or Internet forum participants. Those who claimed not to use RA with people they did not know often explained that to do so would seem impolite or disrespectful. Naturally enough, 92.5 per cent said they used RA only with Moroccans, most of them giving as a reason the fact that other people would not understand it; the few who did claim to use it with non-Moroccans cited Algerians and Tunisians, whose dialects are more or less mutually intelligible with MA. A majority (63.6 per cent) also said they did not use it with people of their parents' generation, suggesting in their comments that this would not be polite or that such people might not readily understand it. Nevertheless, a sizeable minority, 36.4 per cent, of this admittedly elitist group did claim to use it with older people, mostly parents, aunts and uncles, but in some cases even grandparents. It may be that these older people were among the original users of RA, who have evidently not discarded it as they have grown older, and therefore presumably do not perceive RA as merely 'a funky language for teenz to use' (Palfreyman and Al Khalil 2003), and as appealing only to the 'We are young. We are trendy' generation (Aboelezz 2012). The overall view among our respondents seems to be that RA is best used with peers and intimates, rather than with people to whom respect is due, and this is corroborated by their strong agreement (mean score 4.79, mode 5) with the statement that 'RA should be used just among friends, not for professional correspondence or with strangers'.

Asked how they had learned to write RA, 77.6 per cent of the informants said they had copied the way they had seen others write, in text messages or on Internet forums, and 42.9 per cent said that other people, often older siblings, had given them advice on how to write it. Interestingly, a small number (8.7 per cent) claimed that they had invented their own way of writing RA, and many pointed out that, since RA did not have any rigid rules, they felt free to write it however they wanted, provided it was comprehensible. As one respondent commented, 'the beauty of this way of writing is that there are no rules to worry about'. Finally, 1 per cent said they did not remember how they had learned it. These results suggest that learning to write RA is more akin to the acquisition of a mother tongue than to formal language learning: a gradual process based on observation and imitation, with some advice from more experienced writers if available.

Responses to a list of suggested reasons for using RA revealed a generally down-to-earth, pragmatic perspective. Thus, 85 per cent agreed that RA could be written faster, and 84 per cent that it was easier to write: 'I don't have to waste time looking for the right word', and 'it just comes naturally' were typical of the added comments. In addition, 79 per cent agreed that it was easier to read MA in the Roman alphabet than in Arabic script. Some of these pointed out that, for the words to be easily recognisable, MA in Arabic script needs vocalisation and, of course, this is not easy to provide on a phone or computer. Among those who did not think RA was easier to read, some cited the problems faced by older people who are simply not used to RA and therefore find it hard to decipher. Others noted the somewhat paradoxical fact that writing RA requires people to master a foreign alphabet in order to write in their mother tongue – something which represents a real obstacle for those Moroccans who received a very minimal formal education, learning a modicum of Arabic but no French. In fact, then, while writing and reading RA may be easy tasks for the respondents themselves, many of them are aware that the medium is not equally accessible to less educated Moroccans.

Only half of the informants (50.6 per cent) claimed that they used RA because it was specific to young people, and rather less than half (41.7 per cent) felt that it could be used as a means of preventing other people, such as the older generation, from understanding what they wrote – a motive identified by the respondents of Palfreyman and Al Khalil (2003). But, of course, the original users of RA, from the time of Palfreyman's and Al Khalil's study, are now older, and if they are still using this way of writing, then its image as a resource exclusively exploited by young people will naturally be weakening. It remains to be seen whether the use of RA will gradually extend further up the age range or be abandoned by some age groups.

A majority of the informants rejected the idea that RA could serve to project a positive image. Only 36.5 per cent felt that it was cool and fashionable, and only 32.5 per cent that it could be a marker of identity. Again, our findings differ from those of Palfreyman and Al Khalil (2003) and of Aboelezz (2012), who found, in a study of Egyptian teen magazines published in 2008, that RA 'has become a commodity with symbolic and commercial power' (2012: 69). Many of our respondents commented that the language that symbolised their identity was SA, not RA, and that if they wanted to sound cool or sophisticated, they would use French. However, it should be borne in mind that these views may be specific to the well-educated group surveyed here. Not all Moroccan users of RA can be assumed to share the perspective of this elite group; for those barely able to write in SA or French, it is quite possible that RA may suggest trendiness and sophistication.

Quite a number of our respondents added comments indicating a further reason for using RA which did not feature among the multiple choices offered. Some made remarks like 'it's our language, after all' and 'it's the best way to express your feelings'. Others stressed that in choosing RA they were considering the needs of their addressees, rather than their own preferences. According to them, using RA was simply the surest and most reliable way of getting a message across: there were several comments to the effect that 'it's the only way to be sure people will really understand what you write' – a rather damning indictment of the Moroccan education system! These remarks fit in with the respondents' overall agreement with the statement 'For me the choice of alphabet is not important, what matters is simply to communicate' (mean score 3.70, mode 5). These findings suggest that now the newness of RA has worn off, these Moroccan informants' decision to use it is a matter, not of image, but of practicality for both sender and receiver.

Finally, responses to the statement rating test suggested that these students did not accept the negative views of RA sometimes expressed in the media. There was clear disagreement with the claim that 'The use of RA suggests a lack of education' (mean score 2.0, mode 1), but strong agreement with the claim that 'The use of RA is perfectly normal and acceptable among young people' (mean score 4.51, mode 5). An appreciation of the liberating effect of RA is suggested by their endorsement of the statements 'My way of writing is a personal choice, not the business of others' (mean score 3.97, mode 5), and 'I feel freer when I write in RA than when I write using the Arabic alphabet' (mean score 3.85, mode 5). Given the pressures on Moroccan students to achieve proficiency in SA, French and in many cases also English, and the special emphasis placed on correctness and eloquence when writing SA, the chance to express themselves in RA must surely constitute something of a relief. It offers them a medium where they do not have to worry about rules of grammar or orthography, but are free to convey their message in the simplest, most natural way, confident that their readers will readily understand it.

Questioned about the tendency to switch between MA and other languages when writing in RA, 97.1 per cent admitted mixing French and MA, 77.7 per cent said they mixed English and MA, and 67.4 per cent said they sometimes incorporated all three of these languages within one message (as in example 1, above). Moreover, 90.7 per cent agreed that code-switching when writing facilitated communication, and 83.2 per cent said it was normal behaviour. On the other hand, a sizeable minority of 42.7 per cent agreed that written code-switching was 'regrettable and to be avoided', and the statement 'We are free to mix RA with other languages' left a majority undecided (mean score 3.46, mode 3). Given that 97.1 per cent admitted using this 'regrettable' strategy, it would seem that there is some conflict between ideals and reality here. In fact, negative views of code-switching, and claims that it is a marker of carelessness or ignorance, have been reported from many speech communities where the phenomenon is nevertheless widely used, including Morocco (Bentahila 1983; Davies and Bentahila 2013).

Significantly, in contrast to the general readiness to mix MA with European languages just noted, only 26.9 per cent admitted mixing MA and SA when writing in RA, even though combining elements from SA and MA is quite a common strategy in oral communication (Davies, Bentahila and Owens 2013). This apparent reluctance to mix the high and low varieties of Arabic when writing in the Roman alphabet may be related to a general reticence towards adopting the Roman alphabet for SA, reflected in their disagreement with the statements 'The Roman alphabet could also be used to write SA' (mean score 2.64, mode 1) and 'Romanized Arabic could one day replace the use of the Arabic alphabet' (mean score 1.90, mode 1).

Moreover, these informants also seem reluctant to write MA using the Arabic alphabet: 61.3 per cent said they never did this, with comments to the effect that this was simply impossible as the result was incomprehensible. Among the 38.8 per cent who admitted sometimes writing MA in Arabic script, two explanations emerged. Some commented that they wrote MA in Arabic script when it was the only solution, because they knew their addressees would not be able to read the Roman alphabet. The others observed that writing MA in Arabic script usually created a humorous or ironical effect. It would appear that, for this group at any rate, the informality of MA is felt to be somehow incompatible with the high prestige associated with writing in Arabic script, so that combining the two produces a kind of incongruity which provokes amusement.

In fact, then, the fact of writing RA does not appear to blur the distinction between MA and SA. On the contrary, the use of the Roman alphabet for MA and the Arabic alphabet for SA allows a clear visual differentiation between the two.

It appears that, for these respondents, RA is not seen as encroaching upon the domain of SA, for which they still express respect, as shown by their endorsements of the statements 'We have a duty to protect Standard Arabic, its alphabet and orthography' (mean score 4.08, mode 5), and 'Using RA does not imply that we are neglecting SA' (mean score 4.18, mode 5). To use a distinction drawn by Suleiman (2011: 31), we can say that these young people identify themselves as part of the SA linguistic community as well as members of the RA speech community. Both are important to them, and attachment to one does not entail abandoning the other.

A wider view of the phenomenon

In contrast to the objective, scientific studies on the use of RA referred to above, remarks about RA made by the general public and in the media are often dramatic and highly emotive. RA has been described as 'a malignant language', whose use is 'a crime against our mother language' (Ghazal 2014); it is said to be 'a threat to the Arabic cultural identity' (Al-Fawaz 2014), and even as 'a war against the Arabic language to make it disappear in the long run' (Ghanem 2011). In a TED talk titled 'Don't kill your language', Lebanese language activist Suzanne Talhouk (2012) fervently exhorts her audience not to 'write Arabic with Latin letters mixed with numerals'. Even those who use RA sometimes admit to having negative views of it: Muhammed et al. (2011) found that, although 80 per cent of their respondents claimed to use RA, 40 per cent felt its use had a negative impact on their identity as Arabs.

Those who evoke such metaphors of cancer, crime and war seem to be in a state of panic, viewing RA, with its Western writing system, lack of standardisation and extensive code-switching, as an act of rebellion against tradition and established cultural values. It is not unusual for heavy symbolic significance to be attached to script choice, as is pointed out by Suleiman (2013: 36), who cites the example of Turkey's shift from Arabic to Roman script in 1928, which was perceived by the Arabs as a move to distance the Turks from Islam and the Arab world. It could be that some of those vehemently protesting against RA are recalling Turkey's dramatic choice.

A glance at the wider literature on CMC, however, quickly reveals that the trends observed in the Arab world are by no means unique; very similar developments have taken place in many other speech communities. In particular, the strategy of using the Roman alphabet for languages not standardly associated with it seems to be a very general trend, attested in languages from Russian (Mironovschi 2007) to Farsi (Androutsopoulos 2007). The case of Greeklish, the Romanised version of Greek (Koutsogiannis and Mitsikapoulou 2007; Tseliga 2007) shows many parallels with RA; here, too, the adoption of numerals to represent certain Greek letters is based on visual similarities, as when 8 is used in place of θ. The Romanised Cantonese used in Hong Kong also incorporates numerals, but in this case the parallel is not visual but aural, since the numerals are used to represent words whose pronunciation resembles that of the numeral (Lee 2007).

A number of situations can be distinguished here. On the one hand, we find instances where languages with a well-established writing system and a prestigious written heritage, such as Greek and Chinese, are now being written in a Romanised form for CMC by people who are perfectly able to use the conventional writing system. The case of Greek has aroused feelings very similar to those noted here concerning RA. The Academy of Athens spoke out against the spread of Romanised Greek, and Koutsogiannis' and Mitsilipoulou's (2007) survey of media reaction reveals many panic-stricken comments of the type illustrated above for RA; but they also report more measured reactions from commentators who view Greeklish as a technical question, and are open to exploring its possibilities. Tseliga's (2007) respondents said they continued to use Greeklish out of habit, because it was convenient, and a number of them insisted that it should not be standardised.

A second case concerns languages where the adoption of a Romanised writing system actually offers access to writing for people who have not mastered the language's recognised writing system. For instance, British Muslims who cannot write Arabic make use of RA, and American-born Russians for similar reasons write a Romanised form of Russian (Angermeyer 2012). Sindhi is currently written in Arabic script in Pakistan and Devanagari script in India, but the recent introduction of Romanised Sindhi in CMC opens up the possibility of using the language online for Sindhi diaspora members who do not know either of these traditional scripts. Sarwar (2012) argues that the adoption of this Romanised script, far from killing the language, as some have suggested, is a way of keeping it alive among expatriate communities.

Finally, there are cases where a language hitherto little used in writing is becoming a favoured medium for CMC. In Senegal, for instance, French has long been the medium of education and the normal vehicle for writing, with Wolof serving as an oral lingua franca. Lexander (2012) describes how people are now using Wolof extensively in text messaging; but instead of using the official orthography, they have adopted a system more influenced by French orthography, which they claim is easier to use and read.

This range of examples suggests that the development of a Romanised writing system need not automatically represent a threat or display of disrespect to a language. In many circumstances, it can be seen as a positive step that promotes the use of the language in question, empowers its users and strengthens group bonds, particularly across a diaspora. As for the comparison of RA with Turkey's change of script, clearly the two are not the same thing at all. Choosing to write colloquial Arabic in the Roman alphabet is not an act of removal and replacement, since it did not have an established writing system before; it is rather an act of addition, the creation of a new option that can be exploited where convenient, but is not imposed.

Comments in the media often complain that the users of RA tend to write in the way they would speak, the implication being that such careless discourse is not fit to be written down. This kind of objection is no doubt rooted in the diglossic tradition that is so strong in the Arabic-speaking world. However, similar comments have been made about CMC in many other languages; it has been described as 'written speech', 'speech in writing' and 'talking in written form'. Such descriptions often seem to imply that CMC varieties are relatively simple, unsophisticated, stripped-down forms of expression. Thurlow (2006) shows that media commentaries often present caricatured versions of CMC in an attempt to prove its negative effects on young people's powers of expression, and notes that even apparently scholarly discussions are sometimes quick to make such assumptions. In fact, Thurlow and Poff (2009: 171) report on a number of studies that suggest that the innovations of CMC do not necessarily have detrimental effects on their users' performance in other types of writing, and some that even suggest 'a positive relation between texting and literacy'.

On the other hand, Crystal (2006: 272), after attempting a systematic examination of the extent to which what he terms 'Netspeak' – the English used in CMC – resembles speech and writing, concludes that, although the variety shows similarities with both, ultimately it is 'something fundamentally different from both writing and speech', which cannot be assimilated to either, any more than sign language can. He goes so far as to claim that it needs to be recognised as 'a new medium of linguistic communication' (ibid.). If this dramatic view is adopted of CMC in Arabic, so that RA is seen as something new rather than a degradation of a previously existing variety, then criticising RA for not meeting the norms expected of writing may seem less justifiable.

It is also clear that RA is not alone in being perceived as an act of rebellion against norms. Lists of the features commonly observed in CMC are offered by Crystal (2004, 2006) and Herring (2012), among others. They include abbreviations and acronyms, symbols representing words, simplifications of grammar, exaggerated spelling and punctuation patterns, unconventional uses of capitals, and avoidance of punctuation and capitalisation. Contrastive studies in this area would be welcome; for instance, Bieswanger (2006) draws some comparisons between English and German CMC, but it would be interesting to have larger-scale contrastive projects to see how universal these features are, and whether they share common motivations. For the moment all we can say is that similar patterns are attested in a number of varieties of CMC. Anis (2007) reports on the extensive use of orthographical neologisms in French CMC, and links this trend to a desire to contest standards, mark group identity and convey a counter-culture stance; he notes that the use of such neologisms on web forums has even provoked the creation in France of a 'committee fighting SMS language and deliberate errors' (Anis 2007: 88). Sebba sees orthography as 'an ideal site for ideological struggle and rebellion of various kinds' (2003: 152), and describes the Internet as 'orthographic frontier country' (ibid.: 168).

On the other hand, the tendency to favour innovation and norm violation may also be partly motivated simply by the amusement they offer. There is a playful aspect of CMC, nicely surveyed by Danet (2001), which has been noted in communities all over the world, from Japan (Nishimura 2007) to Israel (Vaisman 2014). Mixing languages and scripts is one such source of enjoyment; thus Su (2007) shows how Taiwan users of CMC amuse themselves by using Chinese characters to represent stylised English words; Lee (2007) illustrates playful aspects of the Romanised Cantonese used by people in Hong Kong; and Androutsopoulos (2013) describes how Germans of Turkish origin opt to spell German words in accordance with Turkish orthography, so that 'Deutsch' is written as 'doyc'. If young people in the Arab world are enjoying experimenting in this way, they are no different from their peers in other parts of the world.

In fact, the phenomenon we have here examined in the context of Moroccan Arabic seems to be just one manifestation of a worldwide trend, and commentators from the Arab world are not alone in expressing their puzzlement, alarm or dismay at these linguistic innovations. As Suleiman (2011: 24) observes, 'language-linked anxieties, as reflexes of the English-language-dominated globalisation of recent times, are not an Arab-specific phenomenon'. In fact, these reactions may illustrate a case of what Suleiman (2004) has called language as proxy, when talk about language really represents talk about other preoccupations: in this case, perhaps, a fear that cultural values are under threat from global forces. When RA is set within a wider perspective, it looks much less like a specific revolution against the norms of Arabic-speaking communities. Instead, it can be seen as but one instance of how the users of a language respond to changing needs and circumstances.

Certainly, for the type of Moroccan users we addressed in our survey, RA does not appear to represent any kind of threat to existing varieties of Arabic, written or spoken. For these young people, RA is a supplementary tool, welcomed for the freedom from constraint it offers, and for the ease with which it can be produced and processed. In the appropriate circumstances, they can make the effort to produce elaborate, careful discourse in SA; but for spontaneous, everyday written communication, RA offers an alternative that may save them from producing the sort of careless SA discourse that would attract criticism. Far from posing a threat, then, it might almost be seen as offering a kind of shield for SA.

Conclusion

Discussions of the impact of the Internet on the world have often compared its effects to those of the advent of printing. Both of these fundamentally changed people's perspectives on the world; both vastly facilitated people's access to knowledge and information. In one respect, however, they contrast sharply. The revolution brought about by the spread of printing in the sixteenth century paved the way for the standardisation of orthography and grammar in many languages, whereas the arrival of CMC seems to have set people free from the norms imposed in other contexts. CMC has blurred the distinction between speech and writing, and that between public and private discourse, and in so doing it seems to be providing a communication platform that is free from long-established conventions. Ordinary people, with no particular talent for writing and no connections to the powers-that-be, would previously have had very little chance of finding a large audience for their words, but the Internet now offers them a global platform. A catchy remark by an obscure individual can end up trending on Twitter; amateur writers can easily self-publish, and some of them achieve fame. The gatekeepers have been removed, the gates have fallen. It is hardly surprising, then, if these new communicators adopt new ways of expressing themselves, far removed from the regulations of received systems.

We have looked here at the views and habits of just one category of user, in one corner of the Arab world, but we cannot fail to be impressed by the parallels to be seen not just in other Arab countries, but in many other parts of the world. The same patterns of rebellion against established writing systems, the same adoption of innovative and playful styles of writing, with extensive code-switching and other features hitherto associated only with speech, are now cropping up in diverse contexts, from the vast Anglophone speech community to small groups using minority languages. This suggests that a much wider revolution is under way.

The most striking feature of these new trends is the fact that they are very much the result of a bottom-up process. Scholars, social reformers and members of powerful elites have long sought to manipulate the language situation in the Arabic-speaking world. Their top-down attempts to promote or modify either SA or the colloquials have often had very little long-term impact. In contrast, a couple of decades seems to have been enough to to allow RA and written code-switching to become firmly established in the repertoires of a whole generation of Arabic-speakers. Such naturally evolving changes seem unlikely to be easily controlled by laws or educational policies.

And the process of change may still be ongoing. Early experiments in the use of RA in CMC were associated with young trendsetters who were eager to use their mother tongue in electronic communications, while older, less computer-literate people looked on, mystified. The findings of this study suggest that the use of RA is now spreading across wider segments of Moroccan society and becoming less exceptional and more of a normal, convenient resource. Along with increased CMC and the expansion of RA use to other domains too, attitudes to this phenomenon may also be changing.

As for the issue of diglossia with which we opened this chapter, the responses of our informants suggest that the distinction between H and L varieties of Arabic is still alive and well. MA is certainly making incursions into the written medium, but at the same time the users of RA seem to be conscious of a clear division between this and SA, and the adoption of the Roman rather than the Arabic alphabet for writing colloquial Arabic can be seen as an affirmation of this distinction. The respondents generally reject the idea of writing SA in the Roman alphabet, and recognise the need to preserve the high variety. Far from destroying the tradition, then, recent trends could even be seen as reaffirming the diglossic distinction: if RA is the domain of colloquial MA, code-switching, unregulated and relaxed communication, then SA, along with the concern for correctness and eloquence that goes with it, can be preserved alongside it.

Ultimately, we must surely admit that change is inevitable, in communication patterns as in other human behaviour. Instead of protesting against new ways of communicating, it may be better to embrace them, experiment with them and explore their potential as a means of solving problems. The uses of RA surveyed here arose largely as a response to changing communication technologies, but these technologies are continuing to change, and will no doubt impact upon future discourse styles. It remains to be seen whether RA will survive the expansion of voice- and video-over-IP, or whether it will be abandoned as no longer convenient by a future generation.

Note

1. I would like to thank Muhamed Osman Al Khalil for his helpful and insightful comments on an earlier version of this chapter.

References

Aboelezz, M., 'Latinised Arabic and connections to bilingual ability', in S. Disney, B. Forchtner, W. Ibrahim and N. Miller (eds), *Papers from the Lancaster University Postgraduate Conference in Linguistics & Language Teaching*, 2009, 3, pp. 1–23.

Aboelezz, M., '"We are young. We are trendy. Buy our product!" The use of Latinized Arabic in printed edited magazines in Egypt', *United Academics Journal of Social Sciences* 2012: 47–72

Alabdulqader, E., Alshehri, M., Almurshad, R., Alothman, A. and Alhakbani, N., 'Computer mediated communication: Patterns and language transformations of youth in Arabic speaking populations', *International Journal of Information Technology & Computer Science* 17(1) (2014): 52–66.

Al-Fawaz, N., 'Purists alarmed at increasing use of Franco-Arabic', *Arab News*, 26 December 2014, available at: http://www.arabnews.com/news/679926, last accessed 25 March 2016.

Al-Tamimi, Y. and Gorgis, D. T., 'Romanised Jordanian Arabic e-messages', *International Journal of Language, Society and Culture* 21 (2007): 1–12.

Androutsopoulos, J., 'Language choice and code switching in German-based diasporic web forums', in B. Danet and S. C. Herring (eds), *The Multilingual Internet: Language, Culture, and Communication Online* (Oxford: Oxford University Press, 2007), pp. 340–61.

Androutsopoulos, J., 'Code-switching in computer-mediated communication', in S. C. Herring, D. Stein and T. Virtanen (eds), *Pragmatics of Computer-mediated Communication* (Berlin: Mouton de Gruyter, 2013), pp. 667–95.

Angermeyer, P. S., 'Bilingualism meets digraphia: Script alternation and hybridity in Russian-American writing and beyond', in M. Sebba, S. Mahootian and C. Jonsson (eds), *Language Mixing and Code-switching in Writing: Approaches to Mixed-language Written Discourse* (New York: Routledge, 2012), pp. 255–71.

Anis, J., 'Neography: Unconventional spelling in French SMS text messages', in B. Danet and S. C. Herring (eds), *The Multilingual Internet: Language, Culture, and Communication Online* (Oxford: Oxford University Press, 2007), pp. 87–115.

Belnap, R. K. and Bishop, B., 'Arabic personal correspondence: A window on change in progress?', *International Journal of the Sociology of Language* 163 (2003): 9–25.

Bentahila, A., *Language Attitudes among Arabic–French Bilinguals in Morocco* (Clevedon: Multilingual Matters, 1983).

Bentahila, A. and Davies E. E., 'The syntax of Arabic–French code-switching', *Lingua* 59 (1983): 301–30.

Bianchi, R. M., '3arabizi: When local Arabic meets global English on the internet', *Acta Linguistica Asiatica* 2(1) (2012): 89–100.

Bieswanger, M., '2 abbrevi8 or not 2 abbrevi8: A contrastive analysis of different shortening strategies in English and German text messages', in T. Hallett, S. Floyd, S. Oshima and A. Shields (eds), *Proceedings of the Symposium about Language and Society*, Austin, TX (SALSA XIV), 2006, available at: http://studentorgs.utexas.edu/salsa/proceedings/2006/Bieswanger.pdf, last accessed 15 March 2016.

Crystal, D., *The Stories of English* (London: Allen Lane, 2004).

Crystal, D., *Language and the Internet* (Cambridge: Cambridge University Press, 2006).

Danet, B., *Cyberpl@y: Communicating Online*, New York: Berg, 2001).

Davies, E. E. and Bentahila, A., 'Language attitudes in the Maghreb countries of North West Africa', in H. Giles and B. Watson (eds), *The Social Meanings of Language, Dialect and Accent* (New York: Peter Lang, 2013), pp. 84–104.

Davies, E. E., Bentahila, A. and Owens, J., 'Codeswitching and related issues involving Arabic', in J. Owens (ed.), *The Oxford Handbook of Arabic Linguistics* (Oxford: Oxford University Press, 2013), pp. 326–48.

Dürscheid, C. and Frehner, C. (2013), 'Email communication', in S. C. Herring, D. Stein and T. Virtanen (eds), *Pragmatics of Computer-Mediated Communication* (Berlin: Mouton de Gruyter, 2013), pp. 35–54.

Elinson, A. E., 'Darija and changing writing practices in Morocco', *International Journal of Middle East Studies*, 45 (2013): 715–30.

Ferguson, C., 'Diglossia', *Word*, 15 (1959): 325–40.

Ghanem, R., 'Arabizi is destroying the Arabic language', *Arab News*, 20 April 2011, available at: http://www.arabnews.com/node/374897, last accessed 26 Mach 2016.

Ghazal, M., 'Arabizi popularity threatening Arabic proficiency among native speakers, experts warn', *Jordan Times*, 28 December 2014, available at: http://www.jordantimes.com/news/local/arabizi-popularity-threatening-arabic-proficiency-among-native-speakers-experts-warn, last accessed 26 March 2016.

Hall, J. L., 'Debating Darija: Language ideology and the written representation of Moroccan Arabic in Morocco', PhD thesis, University of Michigan, 2015.

Herring, S. C., 'Grammar and electronic communication', in C. Chapelle (ed.), *Encyclopedia of Applied Linguistics* (Malden, MA: Wiley Blackwell, 2012).

Koutsogiannis , D and Mitsikipoulou, B., 'Greeklish and Greekness: Trends and discourses of glocalness', *Journal of Computer-Mediated Communication* 9 (2007): 116–60.

Lee, C. K. M., 'Linguistic features of email and ICQ instant messaging in Hong Kong', in B. Danet and S. C. Herring (eds), *The Multilingual Internet: Language, Culture and Communication Online* (Oxford: Oxford University Press, 2007), pp. 184–208.

Lexander, K. V., 'Analyzing multilingual texting in Senegal: An approach for the study of mixed-language SMS', in M. Sebba, S. Mahootian and C. Jonsson (eds), *Language Mixing and Code-Switching in Writing: Approaches to Mixed-Language Written Discourse* (New York: Routledge, 2012), pp. 146–69.

Mahmoud, Y. 'On the reform of the Arabic writing system', *Journal of Reading* 23(8) (1980): 727–9.

Miller, C., '"Du passeur individuel au 'mouvement linguistique": Figures de traducteurs vers l'arabe marocain', *2eme Rencontre d'Anthropologie Linguistique: Des passeurs au quotidien, January 2012, Tunis*, 2013, available at: https://halshs.archives-ouvertes.fr/halshs-00822723, last accessed 30 March 2016.

Mironovschi, L., 'Russian SMS compliments', *Written Language and Literacy* 10:1 (2007): 53–63.

Muhammed, R., Farrag, M., Elshamly, N. and Abdel-Ghaffar, N., 'Summary of Arabizi or romanization: The dilemma of writing Arabic texts', Jīl Jadīd Conference, University of Texas at Austin, February 2011.

Nishimura, Y., 'Linguistic innovations and interactional features in Japanese BBS communication', in B. Danet and S. C. Herring (eds), *The Multilingual Internet: Language, Culture and Communication Online* (Oxford: Oxford University Press, 2007), pp. 163–82

Palfreyman, D. and Al Khalil, M., 'A funky language for teenzz to use: Representing Gulf Arabic in instant messaging', *Journal of Computer-Mediated Communication* 9 (2003): 1; reprinted in B. Danet and S. C. Herring (eds), *The Multilingual Internet: Language, Culture and Communication Online* (Oxford: Oxford University Press, 2007), pp. 43–63.

Sebba, M., 'Spelling rebellion', in J. K. Androutsopoulos and A. Georgakopoulou (eds), *Discourse Constructions of Youth Identities* (Amsterdam: John Benjamins, 2003), pp. 151–73.

Su, H-Y., 'The multilingual and multiorthographic Taiwan-based internet: Creative uses of writing systems on college-affiliated BBSs', in B. Danet and S. C. Herring (eds), *The Multilingual Internet: Language, Culture and Communication Online* (Oxford: Oxford University Press, 2007), pp. 64–86.

Suleiman, Y., *The Arabic Language and National Identity* (Washington, DC: Georgetown University Press, 2003).

Suleiman, Y., *A War of Words: Language and Conflict in the Middle East* (Cambridge: Cambridge University Press, 2004).

Suleiman, Y., *Arabic, Self and Identity: A Study in Conflict and Displacement* (Oxford: Oxford University Press, 2011).

Suleiman, Y., *Arabic in the Fray: Language Ideology and Cultural Politics* (Edinburgh: Edinburgh University Press, 2013).

Sarwar, S. R., 'Does changing the script kill the language?' *The Alternative*, 2012, available at: http://www.thealternative.in/society/romanized-sindhi-does-changing-the-script-kill-the-language, last accessed 22 July 2017.

Talhouk, S., 'Don't kill your language!', TED talk, 2012, available at: https://www.ted.com/talks/suzanne_talhouk_don_t_kill_your_language?language=en, last accessed 27 March 2016.

Thurlow, C., 'From statistical panic to moral panic: The metadiscursive construction and popular exaggeration of new media language in the print media', Journal of Computer-Mediated Communication 11 (2006): 667–701.

Thurlow, C. and Poff, M., 'Text messaging', in S. C. Herring, D. Stein and T. Virtanen (eds), *Pragmatics of Computer-Mediated Communication* (Berlin: Mouton de Gruyter, 2009), pp. 163–90.

Tseliga, T., '"It's all Greeklish to me!" Linguistic and sociocultural perspectives on Roman-alphabeted Greek in asynchronous computer-mediated communication', in B. Danet and S. C. Herring (eds), *The Multilingual Internet: Language,*

Culture and Communication Online (Oxford: Oxford University Press, 2007), pp. 116–41.

Vaisman, C., 'Beautiful script, cute spelling and glamorous words: Doing girlhood through language playfulness on Israeli blogs', *Language and Communication* 34(1) (2014): 69–80

Warschauer, M., El Said, G. R. and Zohry, A. (2002), 'Language choice online: Globalization and identity in Egypt', *Journal of Computer-Mediated Communication* 7 (2002): 4; reprinted in B. Danet and S. C. Herring (eds), *The Multilingual Internet: Language, Culture and Communication Online* (Oxford: Oxford University Press, 2007), pp. 303–18.

CHAPTER 5

'Arabic is Under Threat': Language Anxiety as a Discourse on Identity and Conflict

Ashraf Abdelhay and Sinfree Makoni

Introduction

This chapter provides a set of critical reflections on the discourses of language anxiety that articulate Arabic as a 'threatened language'. Arabic, notwithstanding its largely dominant position in the Arab world, is systematically imagined by some social institutions as an endangered language. Discourses of language anxiety emerge in conditions of social stratification and conflicts. The chapter is designed to achieve two goals: the first is to situate the discourses of language anxiety within the cultural political frame of ideological analysis. In doing so, we sketch the social conditions and ideological elements of these discourses. As a second objective, we intend to explore the social indexical functions of discourses of language anxiety by engaging with metalinguistic commentaries on the social values of Arabic in Sudan. In doing so, we argue that one of the functions of instrumental ideologies of language is to fix the image of Arabic as a proxy for doing politics in the dynamic context of the struggle for power and material resources. We demonstrate that the effectivity of explicitly formulated discourses on Arabic hinges on their capacity to operate through other cultural discourses on religion and/or self. We argue that discourses of language anxiety that urge for linguistic uniformity contribute dialectically to the maintenance of the late-modern conditions of inequality (social diversity); hence, Arabicisation is always an unfinished business. Arabicisation as a linguistic ideology can be enacted only in a symbolic reality that enables peripheralised ethnicities to survive the 'loss' of their linguistic instruments of communication.

The remaining content of the chapter is organised as follows: in the next section, we situate the discourses of language anxiety within the cultural political frame of ideological analysis. In the third section, we engage in an analysis of some data to test the conceptual model outlined. We use metalinguistic commentaries as our data. The final section concludes the chapter.[1]

Doing cultural politics through discourses of language anxiety

Processes of economic and cultural globalisation have resulted in the emergence of new forms of social relations and hybrid linguistic structures (Blommaert 2010; Vertovec 2011).

Unsurprisingly, these late-modern conditions have generated discourses of language anxiety on the part of (pan-)nationalist groups and local speech communities that viewed the emergent structures as a threat to their historically established identities, heritage and power (Suleiman 2013, 2014). Language anxiety is not a new phenomenon, and it can be observed particularly in contexts of cultural and linguistic diversity. For example, the Biblical account of the Tower of Babel is designed to account for linguistic diversity, which is viewed as a divine punishment of humans for their arrogance (Machan 2009). At the synchronic level, discourses of language anxiety are strongly present in narratives that condemn internally structured linguistic variability within the 'same' language.

In the Arab world, we encounter a corpus of metalinguistic commentaries produced by different institutions and figures lamenting the diglossic stratification of Arabic into a set of ethnically ordered styles; views that portray Arabic in its various '-lects' as an effect of a process of linguistic corruption. For example, one of the leading figures in the Khartoum Arabic language academy stated that 'Arabic is subject to a daily aggression' because school teachers instruct in Arabic dialects rather than the standard.[2] It may be said that these examples illustrate a discourse of language anxiety that appears to be 'about Arabic' on the surface, although it need not be constructed 'in Arabic'. Other accounts represent Arabic as a threatened language. For instance, we quite often encounter statements such as 'Arabic is in danger' or 'Arabic is being slaughtered by the tools of its sons'.[3] These value-assigning statements are made under the assumption that Arabic is subject to Western conspiracy or linguistic incursion into its intellectual and semiotic landscapes, and against which they urge institutional language-planning intervention to protect it. The overarching objective of Arabic-language academies, for example, is motivated by a will to construct an ideal monolingual translocal order using Standard Arabic.

In contexts of colonialism, counter-hegemonic discourses of language anxiety have used Arabic as an 'instrument of discursive resistance' (Suleiman 2013: 2). In these cases, the discourse of language anxiety, which intends to resist and transform the status quo, is articulated 'through Arabic'. Not all of these discourses are motivated or generated to achieve exclusively linguistic pragmatic goals such as promoting communicative efficiency. For example, a senior figure in the National Coalition for the Arabic Language in Morocco argued that the subordination of Arabic by French in Morocco is a 'coup' not 'against a means of communication, but as a coup against all the justifications for national existence'.[4]

Situating discourses of language anxiety within the cultural political frame of ideological analysis allows us to address a constellation of conceptual issues, including linguistic diversity as a field shaped by symbolic power and conflict, linguistic symbolism, multi-functionality and complexity, discursive strategies and processes, and effects of strategically-oriented social actions. In the remaining part of this section, we engage with some of these conceptual issues, since they constitute the conditions and features of discourses of language anxiety. Before doing so, a working definition of language ideologies is in order. The concept of linguistic ideologies refers to cultural conceptions about language forms, linguistic practice and speakers (Irvine 1989; Woolard and Schieffelin 1994; Silverstein 1996; Mertz and Yovel 2009; Suleiman 2013). Cultural notions of language constitute the socially shared schemes of interpretation of the nature, value, structure and use of a language (Schieffelin, Woolard and Kroskrity 1998; Blommaert 1999; Irvine and Gal 2000; Joseph 2006). As interpretive frames, ideologies of language are the interfacing complex of beliefs about who typically uses what in what distinctive ways, and as such they produce stereotyped styles of language (Irvine 1989; Morford 1997; Silverstein 2003).

One of the significant sites in which cultural conceptions of language operate explicitly is folk-linguistic views that embody 'myths' about the logicality, purity, beauty, superiority or corruption of a language (Milroy and Milroy 1985; Niedzielski and Preston 2000). These ideological views quite often appear in metalinguistic reflections by educated laypeople. Therefore, metalinguistic (or meta-pragmatic) commentaries are one of the favourite domains of language ideologies (for a detailed review of sites of Arabic language ideology, see Suleiman 2013). Discourses of language anxiety as metalinguistic statements anchor language with particular contexts, histories and subjectivities. Hence, they are fundamentally discourses about cultural and political concerns that are articulated on the terrain of language (we use 'politics' here in the broader sense of the term). The anxiety concerns the dynamic nature of the nexus of language and the extra-linguistic worlds of politics and social interaction (Duchene and Heller 2007; Suleiman 2013, 2014). Generally, discourses of language anxiety manifest themselves in forms of relatively socially shared feelings of linguistic insecurity, worries, complaints or concerns about the potential 'loss' or 'corruption' of a so-called 'pure' language associated with a majority or a minority population. Thus, discourses of language anxiety embody linguistic ideologies and, as such, they provide valuable data regarding how language and identity are socially constituted in a context structured by relations of power and conflict.

In the context of the Arab world and beyond, the ideological inspection of discourses of language anxiety compels us to place 'Arabic in the social world' (Suleiman 2013: 1). It also allows us to bring a (dynamic) conflict perspective to the (synchronic) structural functionalist evaluations of the sociolinguistic situation in the Arabic world. Hence, linguistic diversity as a stratified sociolinguistic order is a condition and a constituent feature of discourses of language anxiety, since they emerge in contexts invested with patterns of domination and subordination. Any discourse of language anxiety is informed by a degree of 'cultural essentialism', which refers to 'a system of belief grounded in a conception of human beings as "cultural" (and under certain conditions territorial and national) subjects, i.e. bearers of *a* culture, located within a boundaried world, which defines them and differentiates them from others' (Grillo 2003: 158, emphasis in the original).

Linguistic symbolism is the most important resource for discourses of language anxiety. These discourses illustrate how 'language symbolism is linked with the deployment of language as proxy in society' (Suleiman 2013: 4). The inspection of metalinguistic commentaries that project a given language as corrupted or threatened requires a particular understanding of language as a symbolic resource articulated with ideologically charged meanings in a context of power conflict. The concept of 'power' refers not just to the material aspects of social relations, but also to the discursive, since it involves the power to represent someone or something in a particular way from within a particular position (Foucault 1972; Hall 1997; Joseph 2006). This cultural definition of power can help us to understand how power operates at the micro-physical level of interaction. The active concept of language as a symbolic resource constitutes the core of the cultural political perspective on language, which directly politicises linguistic practice by situating it in its historical conditions of constitution and interpretation. It focuses on how language as a symbolic practice is deployed to 'do politics' in society in times of political and social conflicts (Suleiman 2013: 2). It explores how language is mobilised by 'ideological brokers' (in Blommaert's 1999 sense of circulators of ideas) as a proxy for undertaking identity work. It is precisely this social constructionist principle of language as a proxy that makes semiotic sociolinguistics possible. The study of discourses of language anxiety, even when they focus on corpus-planning (technical) issues, should be addressed by culturally or symbolically oriented studies of language in society (Suleiman 2006). Language rights activists seem to miss this point when they equate a language with its dictionary (instrumental function) (Edwards 2009).

Most importantly, language in the traditional sense of an autonomous linguistic structure for the expression of propositional meaning is simply invisible on the street. The focus on the symbolic dimensions of language should guide us to see how social individuals use language not just to reflect established social relations, but also to appropriate the hegemonic discourse to construct alternative forms of social reality. Hegemony involves the intra-/inter-cultural struggles to govern by the proxy of discourse; it is about 'doing politics' by culture (Gramsci 1972; Suleiman 2013). In conditions of hegemony, discourses of language anxiety render language 'visible' (thus socially 'marked'). Schieffelin stated:

> For many, language is often invisible, out of awareness in everyday activities and lives. We engage in our mundane interactions with an expected seamlessness of talk. Language often only becomes noticeable when something sounds different, like an accent we are not used to or phrase that is not quite right. (Schieffelin 2002: 152).

As Gramsci put it bluntly, any visibility of language is an index of wider patterns of social relations:

> Every time the question of language surfaces, in one way or another, it means that a series of other problems are coming to the fore: the formation and enlargement of the governing class, the need to establish more intimate and secure relationships between the governing groups and the national-popular mass, in other words, to reorganise the cultural hegemony. (Gramsci 1985: 183–4)

Language as a symbolic practice is not a given, but is itself a dialogical site of conflict over meaning (Voloshinov 1973; Bakhtin 1984). As a construction, language is 'imagined' and deployed as a resource in the creation of 'imagined communities' (Anderson 1991). Blot (2003: 8) captured succinctly this dialectic when he noted, 'language practice and identity categories are being constructed simultaneously'. Hegemonic and counter-hegemonic movements bank on the dynamic nature of language when they engage in language ideological debates (Blommaert 1999). This renders socially contested linguistic items (such as language, nation and identity) semantically layered (Bakhtin 1984).

In contexts of the struggle for resources, discourses of language anxiety that draw on language both as a means and as an object (a language and a metalanguage) contribute to the production of multi-layered values of linguistic forms and, by extension, to polycentric identities (Blommaert 2010). Since we can occupy multiple normatively distributed positions, our identities are by no means a monolithic whole, but are rather contingent, hybrid and fragmented (Bhabha 1994). The point here is that we need to take the macro-level questions of ideologies, power conflict and subjectivity very seriously; however, we are simultaneously required to consider them, as Erickson (2001: 135) cautions, 'as they are at work within the conduct of local discourse practices'. Discourses of language anxiety as signifying practices are the domains in which language ideologies can be observed in action. A significant qualification should be entered here. For any ideological construction of identity to be effective, it has to be recognised; or, to phrase it in Althusser's (1971) words, individuals have to respond to 'interpellation'. However, the dimensions of our identities that would be hidden or made relevant in a local interaction order, and how they are 'cued' (Gumperz 1982) and interpreted, cannot be determined *a priori* with any absolute certainty. In other words, although our subjectivities are essentially polycentric as an effect of the multiple locations that we occupy simultaneously in social life, they can never be present in a single interaction event as a complete package (Erickson 2001). For example, we cannot say that the term 'Arabic' readily symbolises or indexes a Muslim identity unless the indexical correlation enters into a particular ideological frame of reference at a particular point in time and place.

Furthermore, viewing the symbolic aspect of language as inherently dialogical and multi-accentual should allow us to understand not just how macro-level structuring ideologies operate in action, but how to 're-language' the same representation from within a counter-discursive position. This perspective does not deny the existence of social inequality, power differentials, stratified repertoires, and patterns of expectations and constraints that normatively define how we should use language. Nor does it claim that the effect of 'translanguaging' (Garcia 2009) the pre-existing structures from within an oppositional discourse can change the entire social system once and for all (see Gramsci's 1971 'war of manoeuvre'). What it consistently rejects, however, is that cultural patterns of regimentation can completely determine the emergent nature and the unfolding dynamics of a social interaction (Rampton 2005). Interactional sociolinguistics argues emphatically that the local production, negotiation and appropriation of dominant ideologies through discursive practice is a source of innovation (Erickson 2001; see also Gramsci's 1971 'war of positions'). In other words, it fully exploits the Hymesian contextual principle of form-value co-variation to understand how participants interpret meaning 'in context' using various appropriation strategies (Hymes 1996; Canagarajah 1999).

Moreover, discourses of language anxiety manipulate the capacity of language as a proxy for articulating what is publicly forbidden or taboo. For example, discursive processes of proxification can render historically constructed ethnic and racial distinctions on the basis of language recognisable and acceptable (Suleiman 2003). As Woolard and Schieffelin (1994: 62) noted, 'symbolic revalorisation often makes discrimination on linguistic grounds publicly acceptable, whereas the corresponding ethnic or racial discrimination is not'. One key function of these discourses is to rationalise (justify) the linguistic choices people should or should not make. In the case of Arabic, the metalinguistic commentaries that defend the use of Standard Arabic in all domains of social life are rationalised on an ideological basis, which necessarily correlates language with theology and/or (pan-)nationalism (Suleiman 2013). Another function of discourses of language anxiety is that they naturalise the historical nature of both the linguistic and social orders with the potential result that they are self-evidently taken for granted. The fact that most laypeople are unaware of the historical constructedness of Standard Arabic (*fuṣḥā*), or the fact that discourses of language anxiety are always taken as unproblematically clear illustrate the naturalising effect of linguistic ideologies embedded in these discourses. It is in this sense that discourses of language anxiety are politically interested because they intend to have specific (perlocutionary) effects on their addressees.

To summarise the discussion so far, linguistic symbolism and its 'language-as-a proxy' companion are one of the key ideological elements of discourses of language anxiety. Relatively shared feelings about the nature or status of a language are illocutionarily made with a particular 'task-orientation' (Suleiman 2013). Discourses of language anxiety as communicative acts are manipulated 'to do things' (in Austin's 1962 terms) in the social world; for instance, to get their intended audience to believe that a given identity or religion is under attack, and to effectively galvanise them into action (for example, to support a particular political vision). Therefore, discourses of language anxiety are strategic in the sense that they are consciously deployed to achieve certain ends. To validate their constructions, ideological brokers draw on a number of semiotic strategies, including 'erasure' (Irvine and Gal 2000) through which dispreferred differences are eliminated from a cultural representation, 'distanciation' (Suleiman 2013) whereby social distinctions are linguistically created, and 're-articulation' (Hall 1997) through which existing linguistic forms are invested with new values. All of these semiotic strategies operate on the symbolic aspect of language, which gradually shapes the instrumental aspect. The motivation for strategic action, however, depends on some kind of language awareness (whether accurate or not) of linguistic markets (Bourdieu 1991), which define the values of languages in a given society (Errington 1985). Since the main ideological function of discourses of language anxiety is rhetorical (or 'task-oriented' in Suleiman's 2003 words), they shape and effect or resist social change in the long run.

To understand how this process of proxification operates, we need to appreciate the complexity and multi-functionality of language: the fact that language has multiple co-existing functions (Irvine 1989; Suleiman 2003; Edwards 2009). Here, two basic functional aspects of language can be differentiated: the instrumental and the symbolic. The instrumental (or referential) function views language as a linguistic means of communication to get things done (hence, the canonical definition 'language as a means of communication'). The symbolic (or social indexical) dimension of language, on the other hand, links linguistic structure to political and cultural considerations such as identity formation and mechanisms of social control (Suleiman 2013). All empirically informed theories of linguistics, whether or not they were originally conceived within a semiotic ideological frame of analysis, address the symbolic dimension of language (Woolard and Schieffelin 1994). The main issue here is not only that the instrumental function of language is given pride of place in popular and professional strands of linguistics, the problem is that it is considered the only legitimate function of language. Consequently, linguistic homogeneity is assumed by this ideology of language as a basis for efficient communication (Irvine 1989). This is one of the paradoxes of the referential ideology of language: although a society changes, language is assumed to be uniform and static (Williams 1992). As metalinguistic forms of speech, even when discourses of language anxiety claim to function 'realistically' (referentially), they simultaneously operate at a symbolic level of construction to motivate people to resist the current sociolinguistic arrangements, for example. Thus, a socially derived motivation is another key element of discourses of language anxiety.

Most importantly, in language ideological contestations, discourses of language anxiety manipulate tropes of crisis and wars to enforce and circulate a particular version of social reality (Suleiman 2013). Although they deploy imported metaphors from other discursive domains to achieve specific effects, discourses of language anxiety do not flag themselves up as ideological. One way to account for this is that linguistic ideologies are inscribed in the structure of language. In other words, language as both a means and an object of metalinguistic reflection is materialised in the same morphosyntactic patterns. To illustrate this observation with a concrete example, laypeople tend to mistake overt grammar (as a set of formalised rules constructed by language specialists) for covert grammar (the intuitive system of language use) (Suleiman 2013). Since both are indistinguishable at the micro-level of social interaction, the identification of discourses of language anxiety as a second-order ideological structuring becomes a tall order for laypeople. This is why most educated laypeople are unaware of the creative indexicality (the capacity of language to transform elements of social reality), and this limited awareness affects their view of the power of language in the construction of their identities and their situations (Mertz and Yovel 2009). Suleiman (2013: 145) cogently formulated this principle when he noted, 'for most people, language ideology remains invisible, as if it were a category of nature'. Language ideologies are invisible not because they are 'absent' from interaction; on the contrary, they are invisible precisely because they are self-evidently present in the quotidian structure of language usage, but are unnoticed as an effect of the processes of naturalisation and normalisation. This is why, as Suleiman (2013: 145) reminds us, 'the quotidian is full of meaning and that it is only by looking at it afresh, as if to make the familiar unfamiliar, that we can extract the meanings it carries'. Even when ideologies of language are largely implicit, they are intertextually recalled as the contextualising frame of interpretation. One of the advantages of studying discourses of language anxiety is that they alert us to the nature of the authoritative order of normativity or to the ideological frame of reference prevalent in a given speech community, and of the various social indexicalities the breaking of a communicative regime may generate.

In short, the above discussion has sketched the key conditions and features of ideological discourses of language anxiety. The list of ideological elements includes, but is not restricted to:

1. Social diversity: discourses of language anxiety emerge in conditions of inequality and conflict; hence, they are indexical of social distinctions, and because they are politically interested and positioned, they are partial and multiple, which is why they co-vary with concrete practice.
2. Metalinguistic awareness: in contexts of struggle and conflict, people who construct discourses of language anxiety and those who oppose them become aware of the symbolic role of language in the articulation of specific forms of self-definition.
3. Multi-functionality: because of the awareness of the stratified sociolinguistic reality, languages, besides their basic instrumental function, are imbued with additional symbolic dimensions related to identity and power relations.
4. Strategic social action: consciousness of patterns of socio-political asymmetry, particularly in the conditions of conflict and struggle characteristic of globalised modernity and nation-state-based politics, motivates individuals and groups to take task-oriented actions, as such ideological discourses of language anxiety are inscribed/enacted in intersubjective interaction.
5. Effect: discourses of language anxiety are materialised in purposive action, and they intend to achieve specific effects. To achieve a higher degree of effectivity, ideological brokers deploy tropes and figurative language.

Taken together, these elements constitute our guiding interpretive frame for the analysis of some metalinguistic commentaries (as our data) in the context of Sudan. Because discourses of language anxiety are always situated, the interpretive exercise we perform does not purport to provide a sufficient explanation of why discourses of language anxiety continue to emerge. By the same token, our analytic reflections on the data obviously cannot explicate the entire range of the social indexical values of Arabic at intra- and inter-group levels. Consequently, although we may detect certain parallels and contrasts, we have tried to avoid, as far as possible, making unwarranted, sweeping generalisations.

Arabic as a site of social struggle in the Sudan

> If south Sudan secedes, we will change the constitution and at that time there will be no time to speak of diversity of culture and ethnicity ... Sharia (Islamic law) and Islam will be the main source for the constitution, Islam the official religion and Arabic the official language.[5]

> I wish to witness the day when the roṭanat of the Halfawyeen, Danagla, Masaleet, Zaghawa, and Hadandawa become extinct, and that the *Ḍād language* [Arabic language]

> will prevail instead. 'The Tongue of him who they wickedly point to is notably foreign, while this is Arabic tongue, pure and clear.' This is a serious intellectual battle that should be openly fought in favour of a centralised culture. I say battle because we are fed up with trifling articles that are far from convincing anybody. Yes I wish the domination of Arabic. God damn peoples who envy us for our noble pursuit.[6]

> We are a product of historical development. Arabic (though I am poor in it – I should learn it fast) *must be the national language in a new Sudan* and therefore we must learn it. We are as frank and as sharp in everything. Arabic cannot be said to be the language of the Arabs. No, it is the language of the Sudan. English is the language of Americans, but that country is America, not England. Spanish is the language of Argentina, Bolivia, Cuba and they are those countries, not Spain. Therefore I take Arabic on scientific grounds as the language of the Sudan and I must learn it. So, next time, I will address you in Arabic if Daniel Kodi, my Arabic teacher, does his job well and if I am a good student. (Garang 1992: 133, emphasis original)

To make sense of the above statements, we need to situate them in their conditions of constitution. The simple contextualising procedure here is to pose the following general set of questions: (1) what is the nature of the statement (for example, is it a metalinguistic commentary)?; (2) in what linguistic variety is it made?; (3) by and for whom?; (4) how are the (dis)preferred choices rationalised and legitimised?; (5) how is language mobilised to achieve specific effects?; (6) what are these intended effects?; (7) how does this style of language contribute to the reproduction or reconstitution of cultural identities, including national identity?; (8) what is the nature of the language ideology embodied in the statement?; and (9) is the flagged linguistic ideology related to or amalgamated with other forms of ideologies in the same statement?

To begin with, the three statements express a specific set of ideas and social attitudes about language, identity and society. Technically, they are metalinguistic commentaries. They were all made by Sudanese figures whose biographies were shaped by more or less stratified symbolic resources, historical trajectories and differentiating political power. The first statement was made at a rally by President Beshir a few weeks before the southern referendum that was held in 2011. In this statement, he openly expressed his negative attitude towards cultural diversity, which was viewed as a threat to Arabic and Islam. He promised to redress this situation if the south seceded by reconstituting a socially contested monolingual and monocultural policy based on Islam and Arabic as the twin pillars of self-identification at the national level. Beshir's ruling regime, which is supported by the Islamist Movement, overturned a democratic government in June 1989. It has since started to implement an ideological project called *al-mashrūʿ al-ḥaḍārī* (literally 'the Civilisation Project'). *Al-mashrūʿ al-ḥaḍārī* is a state-supported modernisation scheme proposed by the late Islamist leader

Hasan al-Turabi to restructure the existing cultural and national identities using the moulding policies of Islamisation and Arabicisation (for a detailed review of these policies, see Abdelhay et al. 2011).

For al-Turabi, Western modernity is not to be sought wholesale, but in articulation with the principles of Islam, in the hope that both would be transformed in this dialogical process (Ibrahim 1999). Thus, a key objective of this ideological project is the reconstitution of national identity. The medium of teaching in the majority of universities was mainly English. This is viewed by the ideological project as a colonial legacy; hence, a policy of Arabicisation was implemented aggressively in the early 1990s. Arabic is seen here as a significant marker of national identity, and the language ideology embodied in the linguistic policy of Arabicisation is amalgamated with the ideologies of the free market and a particular scheme of political governance. Situating President Beshir's metalinguistic statement within this wider historical context, we can see that Beshir projects Arabic as a defining ingredient of national identity (the other ingredient is Islam). However, his expressed feelings of language anxiety are not strictly about the status of Arabic or even Islam, as they relate more to the effects of the complex political issues at the time, including the potential separation of the southern region. President Beshir was aware that the peace accord with the south provided his regime with some legitimacy, which would be in doubt were the south to secede. Thus, President Beshir's metalinguistic statement was oriented to mitigate the effects of this massive political and economic development (most of the oil wells are in the south). The national identity, according to this position, would be 'purified' of any non-Arabic–Islamic connotations if/when the southerners were to vote for independence. In this case, we see the semiotic strategy of erasure in operation: the northern part is presented as a socio-politically and linguistically homogeneous entity.

The second commentary was made by the Sudanese journalist Hussein Khojali in an Arabic article dated 11 August 2011. It is a metalinguistic formulation in the sense that it comments on the cultural and political value of Arabic in relation to local languages within a stratified sociolinguistic order. It instantiates a discourse of anxiety about linguistic diversity in Sudan in which not just Arabic but the centralised culture (including Islam) is perceived as being threatened by this diversity. The language ideological battle that he initiates is not strictly about language, it is about complex social, cultural and political concerns instead. In more detail, three short remarks about Khojali's position can be made. First, Khojali's statement involves a particular economy of interpretation: he positions the potential reader to see Arabic in contrast to other linguistic varieties. His position itself is deeply enunciated: he is one of the intellectual members of the Islamic ruling regime, an owner of a satellite TV channel (Omdurman Channel), an editor and an owner of a daily newspaper. What he articulates are precisely the principles of *al-mashrūʿ al-ḥaḍārī* we indicated above. Thus, the voice in his text stems from a position of institutional authority. In other words, his intention to see 'the end of diversity' is ideologically constructed. Khojali sees the communicative resources of four territorially anchored ethnicities as the core obstacle to national integration: these ethnicities are Halfawyeen and Danagla (in the very north), Masaleet, Zaghawa (in the west) and Hadandawa (in the east). Some of these groups (such as Halfawyeen and Danagla) are currently involved in the serious business of standardising their linguistic varieties under the motivated pretext that they are targeted by the hegemonic cultural project of Arabicisation and Islamisation (*al-mashrūᶜ al-ḥaḍārī*).

The second remark is that the centre is interpreted by Khojali as essentially a single linguistic unit. As a backdrop that is strategically erased by Khojali, the centre has become sociolinguistically extremely diverse as a result of, among other conditions and factors, conflict-induced internal displacement from peripheralised and war-ridden zones. Khojali's phrase 'centralised culture' is significant not only because it carries an assimilationist ideology of language, but also because it is intended to subvert the legitimacy of the current federalist arrangement at the political level, which, he believes, generates tribal conflicts. Hence, the discourse of language anxiety in this case is also a discourse on identity and conflict. Khojali has manipulated the discursive strategy of erasure to assert the existence of a cultural core based on Islam and Arabic that is monolithic, fixed and static, and which 'ought to' be shared uniformly by all sectors of the populations in the Sudan. He also exploited the strategy of distanciation to dissociate a particular social group from the rest; although Arabic features in the repertoires of groups he excluded.

Third, and most significantly, Khojali expressed his position using three key discursive legacies: Islam, nationalism and the ideology of monolingualism. Mobilising the Qurʾānic verse that the Qurʾān is revealed in Arabic (Classical/Standard Arabic), he set up an indexical relation between language (Arabic), religion (Islam) and self (Muslims). Thus, Arabic is reframed as a 'sacred language' by this ideological position. It is in this sense that 'ethnicity' (Arabism) and 'theology' (Islam) join hands to theorise monoglossia in society. It should be remarked that 'Qurʾānic Arabic' is considered in both the commonsensical consciousness and academic discourse as the mother of all standard languages ('the most eloquent form of Arabic'). However, this formulation of 'standardness' is rationalised precisely in non-linguistic terms. Neither religion nor monolingual nationalism is, strictly speaking, an internal-structural feature of a standard language. They are ideological properties. Khojali draws on a widely reiterated Qurʾānic verse with the intention that readers activate religion as a pre-textual (ideological) frame within which the argument can be perceived as self-evidently true. In a sense, Khojali reiterates an existing ideology of language in the Arab world to achieve a specific effect: the correlation he strategically (or knowingly) draws between language and theology is intended to convey the message that the conspiracy against Arabic is a conspiracy against Islam by proxy. The same conspiracy theory is activated (indexed by 'people who envy us' and 'our noble pursuit') as the rationalising pattern within which his statement is intended to be interpreted (for a review of conspiracy theory, see Billig 1988).

Most importantly, Khojali's metalinguistic commentary encodes the ideological trope of war (*maʿraka*) in order to inspire readers to take action. It is this amalgamation of ideologies derived from different emotional sources that makes linguistic ideologies invisible (common sense or taken for granted). Khojali also tried to press the linguistic dimension of instrumentality into ideological service (*lisān ʿarabī mubīn*). Khojali's goal-oriented argument that Arabic is an object of conspiracy is again an ideological statement about a bundle of political and social concerns. His position provides support for the argument that Arabicisation is not just a matter of official education policy, but is a cultural discourse for imposing uniformity on disparate cultures and histories. The ideology of monolingualism is not only active in state apparatuses, it is also embedded, in the case of Khojali, in the individual utterance. The representation of Arabicisation in purely instrumental terms 'using Arabic a medium of instruction' implies that the process is non-ideological and is an entirely civic territorial requirement for building a modern nation-state. This conception is misleading because it indicates that a monoglot standard (Silverstein 1996) can consensually build a neatly homogenised social reality with egalitarian relations of communication. This centripetally ideological view was forcefully pursued with regard to the former Southern Sudan, and it is still in action in other parts of the Sudan. Most significantly, linguistic uniformity can paradoxically only be imagined through diversity, and this is why Arabicisation is always an unfinished business. Arabicisation, as a linguistic ideology, can be enacted only in a symbolic reality that enables peripheralised ethnicities to survive the loss of their linguistic instruments of communication. Appropriating Suleiman's (2013) words, the ideological project of Arabicisation cannot do its job without enemies.

A final point to mention about the nature of Khojali's linguistic anxiety is that it is inter-textually hybrid (it draws on texts from various sources), and it articulates Arabic with semiotically multi-layered values: Arabic as an instrument of communication, as a marker of religious identity and as symbol of a unitary culture. Khojali exploits the multi-functionality of language to raise a number of issues in the same structure. Thus, the language anxiety expressed by Khojali is in fact anxiety about deep-seated socio-political problems formulated on the terrain of language. Khojali's metalinguistic ideology of language generated much controversy, particularly on social media; a condition which indicates that Khojali was conscious of the potential effects his statement could produce.

The third metalinguistic commentary was made by the late South Sudanese leader John Garang de Mabior. To understand Garang's position towards Arabic, a brief historical note about the south–north relations before the separation of

Southern Sudan in 2011 is in order. Sudan was a British colony (1898–1956). For around four decades, the British colonial regime implemented a divisive policy that intended to govern the south and the north of Sudan as two separate spatialised cultural identities using the conceptual system of binary oppositions: a Christian South with local vernacular and English against a Muslim North with Arabic (for a review, see Abdelhay, Makoni and Makoni 2016). Within the southern region, colonial rule outlawed nearly everything that was particularly devalued by Christian missionaries as being 'Arabic'. Arabic was systematically projected as a dangerous language and was consistently coupled with Islam and the northern part. Even names and dress viewed as Arabic (thus indexically Islamic) were strictly forbidden and eliminated from Southern Sudan. In other words, during the British colonial period, Arabic was seen as indexical of a northern ethnicity and its desire to dominate its southern counterpart. These ethnicities, which were in essence historical constructions, were later seriously considered to be part of the natural order of things. The sociolinguistic outcome of this semiotic exercise was a deceptive image of multiculturalism.

Following independence in 1956, post-colonial (Northern) governments tried to create a unifying national culture using the centralising model of Westminster as a grid. The designed policies intended to dismantle the colonially constructed ethnic particularisms through both hegemony and coercion. A number of assimilative nationalist projects were designed to Arabicise and Islamise the South as a way of erasing the colonially created differences. Consequently, South–North relations went through a protracted civil conflict punctuated by a short-lived peace accord called the Addis Ababa Peace Agreement (1972–83). John Garang (1945–2008) was a veteran of Anya-Anya guerrillas in the civil war in the 1960s. He held a BA and a doctorate in economics from an American university. In 1983, he was sent to Bor in the Upper Nile to end a mutiny, but he joined the mutineers in the bush instead and created a guerrilla army under the name of the 'Sudan People's Liberation Movement/Army' (SPLM/A). Unlike its predecessors, the SPLM was an armed movement with a coherent ideological project called 'the New Sudan', which fought for a united Sudan but under a radically different set of terms. The SPLM signed a peace accord with President Beshir's Islamist ruling party (the National Congress Party, NCP). The peace agreement is called the Comprehensive Peace Agreement (CPA) or the Naivasha Peace Agreement. The accord contained a significant policy statement stipulating: '(1) All the indigenous languages are national languages which shall be respected, developed and promoted; (2) The Arabic language is the widely spoken national language in the Sudan; (3) Arabic, as a major language at the national level, and English shall be the official working languages of National Government business and languages of instruction for higher education; (4) In addition to Arabic and English, the legislature of any sub-national level of government may adopt any other national language(s) as additional official working language(s) at its level; and (5) The use of either language at any level of government or education shall not be discriminated against' (CPA 2005: 26–7).

A final contextualising point here is that before the emergence of Garang's movement, the majority of Southerners regarded Arabic as a symbol of northern Islamic domination. What is interesting about Garang's metalinguistic statement is that he problematised the universalising representation of Arabic not by dispossessing it as an ex-colonial language, but by radically inflecting it as a Sudanese national language. Thus, Arabic has been transformed by this cultural re-translation into an ethnic language: an emblem of a geographically bounded collectivity. However, to (re-)ethnicise Arabic, Garang conceptualised language and identity in radical terms as historical constructions. By situating Arabic within the ideological project of the 'New Sudan', Garang tried to articulate not just Arabic, but also indexically the category of national identity. This is how the polysemous nature of the concept of Arabic is strategically exploited, and this polysemy indicates that we are dealing with a socially stratified form of variation.

Garang's ideological view of language was a nuanced roadmap for transforming the established sociolinguistic regime in which Arabic is too readily indexically associated with Islam and Arab identity. It involved connoting the label 'Arabic' with a more locally inclusive value: Arabic as 'the' marker of a civic-territorially bounded national identity. Thus, Arabic is distanciated from race and the cultural project of pan-Arabism. In other words, Garang had no problem with Arabic in its instrumental capacity, because he spoke a localised variety of Arabic; furthermore, he was deeply motivated to develop a repertoire in Standard Arabic. His metalinguistic commentary was strategically oriented to achieve two perlocutionary effects simultaneously: using the strategies of re-articulation and distanciation, Garang tried to assure both the southerners and the northerners that Arabic would be the marker of national self-identification as a territorially defined form of citizenship dissociated from Arabism and race. We have described his action as strategic because it was socially derived in the sense that Garang was aware of the symbolic value of Arabic within the authoritative order of normativity in the northern part of the Sudan. Garang's position has parallels in other contexts in the Arabic world, such as in Egypt (for a detailed review of the local ideologies of language in Egypt and the Levant, see Suleiman 2003).

To summarise, despite the different conditions in which they were made, the three statements share a number of features. They are all metalinguistic commentaries that bring language to the fore as a proxy for articulating wider social and political concerns. Their authors are ideological brokers: both President Beshir and Khojali reiterated the linguistic and theological dimensions of *al-mashrūʿ al-ḥaḍārī*, while Garang was disseminating the project of the New Sudan through the proxy of outlining part of its national language policy. The statements were all made in a context shaped by power and a struggle concerning the relationship between the self and the state. As such, each links language with the extra-linguistic world of identity politics and power in its own way (centralised culture, Islam, New Sudan and so forth). Thus, they illustrate the observation that, in semiotic ideological reflections, language is invoked to stake serious non-linguistic claims. Another significant commonality is that the commentaries deploy existing, collectively shared symbolic resources to construct their stances regarding the nature of the cultural and linguistic diversity in the Sudan. They are all politically, economically and socially motivated positions to achieve objectives that are ostensibly contradictory (the centralised political system versus a federalist system), and they all draw on language to wage their ideological battle. Crudely, at the statutory level, the voices belong to named individuals (Beshir, Khojali and Garang); however, at the societal level, they are all deeply ideological.

The metalinguistic statements, however, differ in a number of respects. One significant difference concerns the nature of the (dis)preferred social and political system. Both Khojali and President Beshir are hostile to linguistic diversity as a basis for self-identification. Instead, they advocate the linguistic uniformity of Arabic as a symbol of religious and national identity. Although both subscribe to the same political ideology, they differ with regard to the preferred structure of the political system: President Beshir is a supporter of a federalist structure even though the system remains centralist in ideological content; Khojali advocates a centralist system, since he believes that the current federalist system is constructed along tribal lines and consequently encourages separatist tendencies. The point here is that although President Beshir and Khojali broadly share the same ideological orientation, this shared political ideology is by no means unitary. It is true that Khojali partly rationalised his defence of Arabic in instrumental terms (for clear and effective communication); however, the overall matrix of rationality is ideological to the core because it essentially couples Arabic with the Qurʾān. Furthermore, his discourse of anxiety makes full use of the trope of war and a version of conspiracy theory to realise his intended effects. Both Beshir and Khojali believed that the 'eradication' of political and cultural resistance could be accomplished once and for all (cf. Gramsci's war of manoeuvre), while Garang's view was that the entrenched political Islamic system could be subverted by redefining the ideological architecture of the system.

For Garang, social diversity is a product of history and, as such, it is a symbolic resource that should be managed within a collectively shared political project. Unlike President Beshir and Khojali, Garang problematised this essentialised one-language one-religion connection, and re-appropriated Arabic as a marker of a territorially defined national identity. With regard to the nature of the linguistic medium and its social function, Khojali's statement is written in a version of Modern Standard Arabic (MSA), while Beshir's statement is addressed to a rally in a variety of Sudanese Arabic (Khartoum Arabic). Thus, their linguistic anxieties are expressed through Arabic. Garang expressed his unease about the hegemonic Arabic language ideology in the Sudan in speech scripted 'in English' (we are collapsing here). Although the linguistic form is a variant in each case, they each reflected on the status of Arabic to orient the intended audience towards their ideological visions of Sudan. A final significant point of contrast concerns the way they conceptualised the ontology of language. Both Khojali's and President Beshir's commentaries are structured by a particular cultural conceptualisation of language that views (only) Arabic as part of the 'natural order of things', while Garang understood both Arabic and identity as historical constructions. All of these discourses of language anxiety draw on a varying degree of essentialism as a basis for the process of linguistic proxification. Even Garang's view of a territorially bounded Arabic presupposed a version of cultural essentialism. As an effect of discursive contestation over the definition of national identity, what we have here is at least two ideologically contradictory values of the same external reality. Ideological brokers have manipulated various semiotic mechanisms (such as erasure, distanciation and re-articulation) to construct a particular representation of social life in Sudan.

Conclusion

This chapter has focused on the conditions and elements of discourses of language anxiety. We have situated these discourses within the cultural political frame of language ideologies. We have used metalinguistic commentaries that embody cultural conceptions of language as our data to test the sketched conceptual frame of analysis. The cases we have examined are strategically designed to defend or resist social change according to different ideological agendas. We have shown that all of them were deployed to perform identity work within a particular political vision of reality. Since educated laypeople are relatively unaware of the fact that the images of social reality portrayed by these discourses do not pre-exist these discourses, the metaphorical ideology of language becomes relatively successful in shaping their orientation towards a particular action plan. However, as we have illustrated, in contexts of conflict, individuals display language awareness of the indexical values of language and their speakers, and they exploit the symbolism of language to articulate social and political issues. Thus, they are not 'dupes' (victims of deception). Since for any discourse of language anxiety to be recognised or heard it has to be made by authorised figures (a politician, a journalist, a resistance movement leader and so on), it is involved in questions of power relations and oriented social action.

We have also demonstrated that social reality is polysemous as a result of ideological struggle in/through discourse using micro-ethnographic mechanisms of construction such as erasure, distanciation and re-articulation. As an effect of discursive contestation over the definition of national identity, what we have here is at least two ideologically contradictory values of the same external social reality.

Ideological brokers have manipulated various semiotic mechanisms to construct a particular representation of social life in Sudan. One of the advantages of studying discourses of language anxiety is that they allow us to understand the semiotic (structuring) nature of language: how the complex material social reality is discursively constructed by differentially located social agents.

The study of discourses of language anxiety has significant implications for scholars and practitioners in the applied sociolinguistic fields of (educational) language policy and language maintenance. For example, with regard to minority-language rights, activists should be alert to the fact that the 'school' is not the only site for the reiteration of hegemonic ideologies of language. Changing the medium of instruction through a top-down policy intervention is not a guarantee to transforming the established political and economic relations of asymmetry because ideologies operate at the micro-sociological level of interaction, manipulating linguistic symbolism to 'do politics' through culture. A minority-language-oriented identity can indeed survive through the majority discourse; however, there is a need for historical and local-level studies of the trajectories, conditions and discursive strategies involved in these processes of self-definition.

Notes

1. The selection, explication and inspection of this topic in the context of Sudan is deeply inspired by Yasir Suleiman's *Arabic in the Fray: Language Ideology and Cultural Politics*, which is the most authoritative account on the symbolic role of Arabic in the structuring of different forms of subjectivity in contexts of struggle and conflict. We would like to thank the editors of this volume (Yonatan Mendel and Abeer AlNajjar) for the kind invitation to contribute to this significant project. We are also grateful to the reviewers for their useful comments.
2. See at: http://www.aljazeera.net/home/print/f6451603-4dff-4ca1-9c10-122741d17432/c3330aa0-ced6-405f-825d-aa6f118d4fe8, last accessed 25 March 2017.
3. See at: http://www.aljazeera.net/home/print/f6451603-4dff-4ca1-9c10-122741d17432/c3330aa0-ced6-405f-825d-aa6f118d4fe8, last accessed 25 March 2017.
4. See at: http://www.aljazeera.net/home/print/f6451603-4dff-4ca1-9c10-122741d17432/77813246-b87b-4bbd-89be-17aa6bd727a3, last accessed 25 March 2017.
5. See at: http://uk.reuters.com/article/uk-sudan-bashir-islam-idUKTRE6BI0SX20101219, last accessed 3 May 2016. The Arabic version of the statement that is widely circulated and debated in the media is as follows:
   'في حالة انفصال الجنوب سنقوم بتعديل الدستور لذلك لا مجال لحديث عن التعدد الثقافي والإثني. ستكون الشريعة والإسلام هي المصدر الرئيسي للدستور.. وسيكون الإسلام هو الدين الرسمي للدولة وستكون اللغة العربية هي اللغة الرسمية للدولة'
   (http://www.alarabiya.net/views/2010/12/22/130475.html)

6. This provocative statement is widely publicised and available on many social network websites, see at: http://arabic-media.com/newspapers/sudan/alwan.htm, last accessed 26 February 2014. The Arabic version of the statement in Arabic script is:

'أتمنى أن يأتي اليوم الذى تنقرض فيه رطانات الحلفاويين والدناقلة والمساليت والزغاوة والهدندوة وتسود لغة الضاد الموحدة فلسان الذي يلحدون إليه أعجمي وهذا لسان عربي مبين .هذه معركة ذات نطع وغبار أطلقها في الهواء الطلق لصالح الثقافة المركزية ، نعم معركة فلقد سئمنا المقالات المسطحة التي لا تكسب الفكر عدواً ولا صديق'.

References

Abdelhay, A., Makoni, B. and Makoni, S., 'The colonial linguistics of governance in Sudan: The Rejaf Language Conference, 1928', *Journal of African Cultural Studies* 28(3) (2016): 343–58.

Abdelhay, A., Makoni, B., Makoni, S. and Mugaddam, A., 'The sociolinguistics of nationalism in the Sudan: The Arabicisation of politics and the politicisation of Arabic', *Current Issues in Language Planning* 12(4) (2011): 457–501.

Althusser, L., *Lenin and Philosophy and Other Essays*, trans. B. Brewster (New York: Monthly Review Press, 1971).

Anderson, B., *Imagined Communities*, 2nd edn (London: Verso, 1991).

Austin, J., *How to Do Things with Words* (Oxford: Clarendon Press, 1962).

Blot, R., 'Introduction', in R. Blot (ed.), *Language and Social Identity* (Westport, CT: Praeger, 2003), pp. 1–10.

Bakhtin, M., *Problems of Dostoevsky's Poetics*, ed. and trans. C. Emerson (Minneapolis, MN: University of Minnesota Press, 1984).

Bhabha, H., *The Location of Culture* (New York: Routledge, 1994).

Billig, M., 'Methodology and scholarship in understanding ideological explanation', in C. Antaki (ed.), *Analysing Everyday Explanation* (London: Sage, 1988), pp.199–215.

Blommaert, J. (ed.), *Language Ideological Debates* (Berlin: Mouton de Gruyter, 1999).

Blommaert, J., *The Sociolinguistics of Globalisation* (Cambridge: Cambridge University Press, 2010).

Bourdieu, P., *Language and Symbolic Power* (Cambridge, MA: Harvard University Press, 1991).

Canagarajah, S., *Resisting Linguistic Imperialism in English Teaching* (Oxford: Oxford University Press, 1999).

Duchene, A. and Heller, M. (eds), *Discourses of Endangerment: Ideology and Interest in the Defence of Languages* (New York: Continuum, 2007).

Edwards, J., *Language and Identity: An Introduction* (Cambridge: Cambridge University Press, 2009).

Erickson, F., 'Co-membership and wiggle room: Some implications of the study of talk for the development of social theory', in N. Coupland, S. Sarangi and C. Candlin (eds), *Sociolinguistics and Social Theory* (New York: Routledge, 2001), pp.152–81.

Errington, J., 'On the nature of the sociolinguistic sign: Describing the Javanese speech levels', in E. Mertz and R. Parmentier (eds), *Semiotic Mediation: Sociocultural and Psychological Perspectives* (Orlando, FL: Academic Press, 1985), pp. 287–310.

Foucault, M., *The Archaeology of Knowledge and the Discourse on Language*, trans. S. Smith (New York: Pantheon, 1972).

Garang J., *The Call for Democracy in Sudan*. ed. M. Khalid, rev. edn (New York: Kegan Paul, 1992).

Garcia, O., 'Education, multilingualism and translanguaging in the 21st century', in A. Mohanty, M. Panda, R. Phillipson and T. Skutnabb-Kangas (eds), *Multilingual Education for Social Justice: Globalising the Local* (New Delhi: Orient Blackswan, 2009), pp. 128–45.

Gramsci, A., *Selections from the Prison Notebooks of Antonio Gramsci*, ed. and trans. Q. Hoare and G. N. Smith (London: Elecbook, 1971).

Gramsci, A., *Selections from Cultural Writings*, trans. W. Boelhower (London: Lawrence & Wishart, 1985).

Grillo, R., 'Cultural essentialism and cultural anxiety', *Anthropological Theory* 3(2) (2003): 157–73.

Gumperz, J., *Discourse Strategies* (Cambridge: Cambridge University Press, 1982).

Hall, S. (ed.), *Representation: Cultural Representations and Signifying Practices* (London: Sage and Open University, 1997).

Hymes, D., *Ethnography, Linguistics, Narrative Inequality: Toward an Understanding of Voice* (London: Taylor & Francis, 1996).

Ibrahim, A., 'A theology of modernity: Hasan al-Turabi and Islamic renewal in Sudan', *Africa Today*, 46(3/4) (1999): 195–222.

Irvine, J., 'When talk isn't cheap: Language and political economy', *American Ethnologist* 16(2) (1989): 248–67.

Irvine, J. and Gal, S., 'Language ideology and linguistic differentiation, in P. Kroskrity (ed.), *Regimes of Language: Ideologies, Polities and Identities* (Santa Fe, NM: Advanced School Press, 2000).

Joseph, J., *Language and Politics* (Edinburgh: Edinburgh University Press, 2006).

Machan, T., *Language Anxiety: Conflict and Change in the History of English* (Oxford: Oxford University Press, 2009).

Mertz, E. and Yovel, J., 'Metalinguistic awareness', in D. Sandra, J.-O. Östman and J. Verschueren (eds), *Cognition and Pragmatics* (Amsterdam: John Benjamins, 2009), pp. 250–71.

Milroy, J. and Milroy, L., *Authority in Language: Investigating Language Prescription and Standardisation* (London: Routledge & Kegan Paul, 1985).

Morford, J., 'Social indexicality in French pronominal address', *Journal of Linguistic Anthropology* 7(1) (1997): 3–37.

Niedzielski, N. and Preston, D., *Folk Linguistics* (Berlin: Mouton de Gruyter, 2000).

Rampton, B., *Crossing: Language and Ethnicity among Adolescents*, 2nd edn (Manchester: St Jerome Publishing, 2005).

Schieffelin, B., 'Language and place in children's worlds', *Texas Linguistic Forum* 45 (2002): 152–66.

Schieffelin, B., Woolard, K. and Kroskrity, P. (eds), *Language Ideologies: Practice and Theory* (Oxford: Oxford University Press, 1998).

Silverstein, M., "Monoglot standard' in America: Standardization and metaphors of linguistic hegemony', in D. Brenneis and R. Macauley (eds), *The Matrix of Language: Contemporary Linguistic Anthropology* (Boulder, CO: Westview Press, 1996), pp. 284–306.

Silverstein, M., 'Indexical order and the dialectics of sociolinguistic life', *Language and Communication* 23 (2003): 193–229.

Suleiman, Y., *The Arabic Language and National Identity: A Study in Ideology* (Edinburgh: Edinburgh University Press, 2003).

Suleiman, Y., 'Arabic language reforms, language ideology and the criminalization of Sibawayhi', in L. Edzard and J. Watson (eds), *Grammar as a Window onto Arabic Humanism: A Collection of Articles in Honor of Michael G. Carter* (Wiesbaden: Harrassowitz, 2006), pp. 66–83.

Suleiman, Y., *Arabic in the Fray: Language Ideology and Cultural Politics* (Edinburgh: Edinburgh University Press, 2013).

Suleiman, Y., 'Arab(ic) language anxiety: tracing a "condition"', *Al-Arabiyya: Journal of the American Association of Teachers of Arabic* 47 (2014): 57–81.

Vertovec, S., 'The cultural politics of nation and migration', *Annual Review of Anthropology* 40 (2011): 241–56.

Voloshinov, V., *Marxism and the Philosophy of Language*, trans. L. Matejka and I. R. Titunik (New York: Academic Press, 1973).

Williams, G., *Sociolinguistics: A Sociological Critique* (London: Routledge, 1992).

Woolard, K. and Schieffelin, B., 'Language ideology', *Annual Review of Anthropology* 23 (1994): 55–82.

Online source

The Comprehensive Peace Agreement between the Government of the Sudan and the Sudan People's Liberation Movement/Sudan People's Liberation Army (English version, 2005), available at: http://nec.org.sd/en/wp-content/uploads/sites/2/2013/09/Comprehensive-Peace-Agreementxxx.pdf, last accessed 23 February 2015.

CHAPTER 6

Code Choice, Place and Identity in Egypt: Evidence from Two Novels

Reem Bassiouney

This chapter examines the relation between place, identity and language in two Egyptian novels, published during and after the British occupation of Egypt. The two novels are *Qindīl Umm Hāshim* (*The Saint's Lamp*) by Yaḥyá Ḥaqqī (1944) and *Awrāq al-narjis* (*Leaves of Narcissus*) by Sumayyah Ramaḍān (2001). *The Saint's Lamp* was written at a time when Egypt was still under British domination; its protagonist studies in the United Kingdom and then returns to Egypt. Ramaḍān's novel, *Leaves of Narcissus*, was published some fifty years after the end of British colonisation; in it, too, the protagonist studies abroad (in Ireland) and then subsequently returns to Egypt.

In both novels, the protagonists embark on a journey and are then forced to tackle issues of identity imposed upon them: they are forced to explain their own identity in relation to others and in relation to places and their access to them. Places are intertwined with linguistic codes, and therefore access to places is related, first and foremost, to one's access to languages and varieties.[1]

As Blommaert (2005: 203) contends: 'When abroad, we discover ourselves talking a lot about that country, living up to its stereotypes, defending its values and virtues, and in return receiving flak because of the mistakes it made or makes.' Being an uprooted Egyptian in a foreign land also means that the Egyptian identity, with all of its accompanying stereotypes and ideologies, is highlighted and brought to the forefront.

It is worth noting that both during and after the British colonisation of Egypt, places, as well as access to those places, became symbols of affiliations, identities and ideologies. Judgements about the language of these places were also part of this conflict. The public space 'serves as a tool in the hands of different groups for the transmission of the messages as to the place of different languages in . . . geographical and political entities and for influencing and creating de facto language realities' (Shohamy 2006: 11). Laying claim to different locations was also essential to the conflict.

In both novels, social variables that demarcate Egyptian identity are present, including, significantly, the variable of location, while code-switching is employed as a linguistic resource that reflects a stance related to identity and to the 'Other' or the 'non-Egyptian outsider'.

Language in the Arab world more generally is loaded with symbols and ideologies that do not reflect reality in most cases. Suleiman calls it the 'the Arab "obsession" with language as a cultural product and as a symbol of belonging and alienation, of closed and open meanings, of despotism and freedom and of dictatorship and democracy' (2011: 141). Since Egypt is a diglossic community – a community in which two codes exist: Standard Arabic (SA) and Egyptian Colloquial Arabic (ECA) – the role played by code choice in novels is of utmost importance. This chapter will demonstrate how authors use code choice and code-switching in dialogue in two Egyptian novels in which identity issues are prevalent. Note that access to place, together with access to linguistic codes, is essential in the Arab world in general and in Arabic literature in particular.

This chapter attempts to answer the question of why writers in Egypt use SA in dialogue and why they alternate their usage of SA and ECA, depending on stance and place. I will argue that writers use code choice and code-switching between SA, ECA and English in dialogue as a device that does not *reflect* real patterns of language use, but rather *redefines* and *reconstructs* different stances for the protagonists, according to the different people and locations in which they find themselves. This reconstructed stance can be understood by reference to the indexes (see Silverstein 2003) of different codes. According to Johnstone (2010: 31), indexical forms can imply and construct identity. The concept of indexicality refers to the creation of semiotic links between linguistic forms and social meanings (Ochs 1992; Silverstein 1996, 2003). This chapter aims to shed light on the associations of SA and ECA in dialogues throughout these two novels. Fowler (1977: 197–8) argues that, in literary work, authors tend to 'project a diversity of individual world views' by conjuring up associations connected to the belief systems and values shared by the protagonists and their respective communities in literary works. Coupland (2001: 198) adds that: 'Sociolinguistics can borrow back this awareness of how multiply textured styles (or "mind-styles") can be creatively constituted in social texts for its interpretations of dialect style variation.' That is, the role played by literary texts is essential to understanding the function of a dialect or code in a community more generally. Before delving into analysis of the two novels, I would like to elaborate on the indexes of SA and ECA.

Jannis Androutsopoulos (2012: 303), in his article 'Repertoires, characters and scenes: sociolinguistic differences in Turkish–German comedy', delineates the role of language ideology and the perception of language usage by an audience who are part of a community. He argues that: 'Cinematic language indexes language ideological assumptions about how certain groups or types represented in the film use language.' In other words, producers and scriptwriters need to consider the shared assumptions and ideologies of their audience before employing code-switching in their work. The same is true for novels as well. However, as will be made clear, the two Egyptian novels that are analysed in this chapter contribute a new dimension to work on code-switching and performance more generally, as it demonstrates the intricate relation between social context, stance-taking process and code choices.

Indexes can be established and negotiated through talk about language, as well as through the use of language. The importance of metalinguistic discourse has been highlighted by linguists in the field of sociolinguistics generally, especially in the work of Agha (2005), Johnstone (2010) and Jaffe (2009), to name but a few. However, talk about language and reflecting on one's language use in the Arab world is a relatively new phenomenon. Although, as was mentioned earlier, Arabic codes are loaded with political, social and economic indexes, talk about language has been, at least for some, less reflective and more didactic in nature. It is, in fact, due to Suleiman (2003, 2004, 2011) that talk about Arabic codes has taken a more scientific and less prescriptive path. Suleiman's work delineates the relation between different Arabic codes and political events and contexts in Arab countries and related discourse about Arabic identity, whether national or individual. Ferguson's work (1959) already associated SA with the notions of authority, formality, legitimacy and power, while connecting ECA with informality, intimacy and the emotions. However, Ferguson did not account for the overlap of function, nor did he take into consideration the code-switching that occurs between both. However, other linguists researching Arabic did so (see Bassiouney 2009). In order to better understand the associations of codes, one also needs to reflect on language use. Agha (2007) and Rampton (2015) argue that reflexivity is inherent in the definition of style, register, variety or dialect. As a process, reflexivity is reflected in the studies of linguists themselves and not just in the interaction between speakers (see Johnstone 2006; Cameron 2012). Suleiman, in his book *Arabic, Self and Identity* (2011), reflects on his own use of code and the associations of this code and its significance for him, both as a researcher and as an Arab. Suleiman discusses his interaction with a group of Arabic teachers in Qatar (whom he is training). Suleiman chooses to communicate with the teachers in SA and not in his own colloquial. However, he also chooses to drop case and mood marking. When reflecting on his choices, Suleiman argues that he made the intentional decision to use SA, rather than his Palestinian dialect, because he is aware of the negative associations his dialect may conjure up. By using SA, he appeals to the shared cultural heritage of all Arabs, rather than a particular local identity (2011: 50). He argues that his choice of SA 'was also a way of dealing with my personal marginality . . . It was a mode of cultural and psychological resistance against marginality in my personal life and hegemony in the public sphere' (Suleiman, 2011: 56).

Drawing on metalinguistic discourse and examples of public discourse in Egypt, diglossic switching has been explained in terms of indexes; it was established that SA holds both positive and negative associations, and ECA also holds both positive and negative associations (Bassiouney 2014). The indexes of both will be discussed below in relation to identity construction and places.

Analysis

The first novel analysed, *Qindīl Umm Hāshim* (*The Saint's Lamp*) by Yaḥyá Ḥaqqī (1944), deals with issues of identity in Egypt during the first half of the twentieth century. The protagonist is Ismāʿīl, who originally comes from Sayyidah Zaynab – an old and crowded lower-class area in Cairo. The area was named after the mosque, which presumably holds the tomb of Zaynab – the Prophet's granddaughter. Ismāʿīl is originally from this area and is then sent to the United Kingdom to study medicine by his parents, who have spent all their money on his education. However, when he returns to Egypt, Ismāʿīl is a different man. He is more aware of the abject state of both medicine and society in Egypt, and is highly critical of his family, community and country more generally. As an eye specialist, he is shocked to discover that his cousin, Fāṭimah, uses oil to treat her eye disease in the belief that this oil, which comes from the lamp of the mosque of Zaynab, will cure her. Ismāʿīl is disgusted by this custom and tries to cure her with modern medicine, but Fāṭimah, surprisingly, does not respond to his medication and goes blind. Following this incident, Ismāʿīl re-evaluates his life and chooses to embrace his local community and, indeed, all of Egypt, despite its shortcomings. He manages to cure Fāṭimah only when he comes to understand and respect her beliefs. Indeed, he fails when trying to impose his new beliefs on his community. Instead, he is forced to embrace their beliefs and to identify with his local community and with Egyptians more generally. He comes to realise that, in embracing an identity, one should not compare states, cultures, East or West. He begins to understand that an identity is not a rational calculation, but an emotional state of belonging. Ismāʿīl constructs his identity through an evaluation and interpretation of his surroundings and context, as well as through his close association with his local area. Bauman (2000: 1) defines identity as:

> An emergent construction, the situated outcome of a rhetorical and interpretive process in which interactants make situationally motivated selections from socially constituted repertoires of identificational and affiliational resources and craft these semiotic resources into identity claims for presentation to others.

That is, the agency of an individual in the process of identity construction is pertinent.

Ḥaqqī, the author himself, posits that he was a product of the first generation of the twentieth century – the generation that was searching for a distinctive identity different from that of the colonising powers. At the end of the novel, Ismāʿīl realises the strength, stamina and special characteristics of Egyptians. His perception of the Egyptian collective identity changes to become more like of the intellectuals at the time that took pride in Egypt's resilience, even through difficult and challenging circumstances. It is difficult to separate locality from identity throughout the novel. Ismāʿīl's local area has emotional and historical significance, which he and his community share. After his final moment of enlightenment, Ismāʿīl is ready to accept all the negative traits of the members of his community, because he belongs to the same quarter as them. Note the following example (1944: 118):

تعالوا جميعا الى! فيكم من آذاني، و من كذب علي، و من غشني، و لكني رغم هذا لا يزال في قلبي مكان
لقذارتكم و جهلكم و انحطاطكم، فأنتم مني و أنا منكم، و أنا ابن هذا الحي و أنا ابن هذا الميدان. لقد جار عليكم الزمان، و
كلما جار و استبد، كان إعزازي لكم أقوى و اشد

> Come to me, all of you. Some of you have done me harm, and some of you have lied to me and cheated me, yet even so there is still a place in my heart for your filth, your ignorance, and your backwardness, for you are of me and I am of you. I am the son of this quarter, the son of this square. Time has been cruel to you, and the more cruel it is the stronger my affection is for you. (Ḥaqqī 1973: 85)

The imperative here is used to show his informal relation with members of this quarter. However, it also shows Ismāʿīl's patronising and powerful tone towards them. They are not perfect; in fact, they are far from it. But Ismāʿīl understands that he is part of their quarter, which acknowledgement overrides all their differences. Their state is abject, but this does not lessen his closeness to them. Significantly, the internal dialogue between Ismāʿīl and his community is in SA, with all its powerful and authoritative indexes. Earlier in the novel, when Ismāʿīl destroys the lamp of Umm Hāshim, members of the community attack him and are poised and ready to kill him. Sheikh Dardīrī, a respected man in the community, commands them to stop their violence, because Ismāʿīl is the son of a good man, Sheikh Rajab, and because he belongs to their quarter (1944: 105).

اتركوه! انني اعرفه. هذا سي اسماعيل ابن الشيخ رجب من حتتنا. اتركوه. ألا ترون انه مريوح

> 'Leave him!' He said. 'I know the man – it's Ismāʿīl, the son of Sheikh Ragab. He's one of us (From our quarter). Let him be. Don't you see he's possessed?' (Ḥaqqī 1973: 78)

The appeal to relational identification (Van Leeuwen 1996) and to a shared local area renders Ismāʿīl a member of their community and thus saves his life (see Milroy 1987). Using the term of address 'Sheikh' to refer to the father of Ismāʿīl implies that he is a respected man in the community.

In Ḥaqqī's novel, *Qindīl Umm Hāshim*, Ismāʿīl engages in a number of conversations with his family and neighbours. He also overhears several monologues and dialogues. These conversations are not all in the same code. What is interesting is that in the film adaptation of *Qindīl Umm Hāshim*, all of the dialogues are spoken in ECA. As a consequence, the linguistic diversity of the novel is lost. This is because the film, unlike the novel, attempts to reflect realistic linguistic habits, and an individual in this situation would be unlikely to converse in SA. Indeed, it is not the spoken code of any country in the Arab world. Thus, it is more likely for them to converse in a local dialect or in ECA (a Cairene standard dialect).

Ismāʿīl's linguistic repertoire includes two codes, SA and ECA, in the novel. As mentioned above, in the film adaptation, it is reduced to ECA only. In the novel, when Ismāʿīl speaks to his foreign ex-girlfriend, their conversations are in SA. One would expect Mary, his ex-girlfriend, to address Ismāʿīl in English, but the author 'translates' the statement into SA. Unlike Mary, Fāṭimah, his Egyptian cousin, speaks only in ECA and never takes a position or even gives her opinion about any issue. Fāṭimah is, as is established from the beginning of the novel, going blind. Indeed, it is no coincidence that Ismāʿīl's professor in the UK calls Egypt 'the country of the blind'. Before he leaves Egypt, Ismāʿīl does not know that Fātimah has a serious eye condition and returns to find her almost completely blind. Thus, Fāṭimah clearly represents 'Egypt' throughout the novel.

When Ismāʿīl, towards the end of the novel, comes to realise the importance of the Egyptians' belief system, he addresses Fāṭimah for the first (and last) time in SA (1944: 118–19):

تعالي يا فاطمة! لا تيأسي من الشفاء. لقد جئتك ببركة أم هاشم! ستجلي عنك الداء، و تزيح الأذى، و ترد إليك بصرك فإذا هو حديد...

و فوق ذلك، سأعلمك كيف تأكلين و تشربين، و كيف تجلسين و تلبسين، سأجعلك من بني آدم.

> 'Come here, Fāṭimah. Do not despair of being cured. I have brought you the blessings of Umm Hāshim. She will drive away your illness and restore your sight as good as new.'
>
> 'And on top of that, I will teach you how to eat and drink, how you should sit, and how you should dress – I'll make a lady of you.' (= Ḥaqqī 1973: 86)

Once again, Ismāʿīl uses the imperative with SA to render his authority and power over Fāṭimah. The content of this excerpt is also significant, as it clearly demonstrates Ismāʿīl's patronising character and attitude.

When Ismāʿīl sees his mother putting oil in Fāṭimah's eyes, he is outraged and code-switches between ECA and SA, which reflects the conflicted relationship between Ismāʿīl and his mother (1944: 99–100) (SA is set in italics):

ما هذا يا مي؟
هذا زيت قنديل أم هاشم. تعودت أن اقطر لها منه كل مساء
لقد جاءنا به صديقك الشيخ درديري. انه يذكرك و يتشوق اليك. هل تذكره؟ أم تراك نسيته؟
حرام عليك الأذية. حرام عليك. انت مؤمنة تصلين فكيف تقبلين أمثال هذه الخرافات و الأوهام؟
صمتت امه...
اسم الله عليك يا اسماعيل يا بني. ربنا يكملك بعقلك هذا غير الدوا و الأجزا. هذا ليس إلا من بركة أم هاشم.
أهي دي أم هاشم بتاعتكم هي اللي ح تجيب للبنت العمى سترون كيف أداويها فتنال على يدي أنا الشفاء الذي لم تجده عند الست أم هاشم.
يا أبني ده ناس كثير بيتباركوا بزيت قنديل أم العواجز جربوه و ربنا شفاهم عليه. إحنا طول عمرنا جاعلين تكالنا على الله و على أم هاشم.ده سرها باتع
انا لا اعرف أم هاشم و لا أم عفريت.
والده: ماذا تقول؟ هل هذا كل ما تعلمته في بلاد برة؟ كل ما كسبناه منك أن تعود إلينا كافرا؟

'What's that, mother?'

'It's oil from the lamp of Umm Hāshim. Every evening I pour some of it into her eyes. Your friend Sheikh Dardiri brought it to us. He remembers you and longs to see you again. Do you remember him, or have you forgotten him?'

'You should be ashamed of yourself at the harm you're doing.' He shouted at his mother at the top of his voice 'Shame on you! *And you a believer who says her prayers, how can you accept such superstitions and humbug?'*

'I take my refuge in God,' and then said to him, 'God protect you, my son Ismael. May the lord keep you in your right mind. *This is nothing to do* with medicine, though. *This is just the blessing of Umm Hāshim.'*

'So this is Umm Hāshim, the one that will make the girl blind! *You'll see how I'll treat her and how I'll cure her when Umm Hāshim failed.'*

'My son, many people seek blessings through the oil of Umm Hāshim, the mother of the destitute. They tried it, and the lord cured them through it. All our life, it is God and Umm Hāshim that we put our trust in. her secret powers are invincible.'

'I know neither Umm Hāshim nor Umm of the fairies!'

Father: '*What are you saying? Is this what you learned* abroad? *Is all we have gained to have you return to us an infidel?'*

Ismāʿīl's question is spoken in SA and is followed by his mother's answer, which is also in SA. The mother accommodates to the son in an attempt to win his approval. She then refers to a common friend to stir up old memories and emotions in her son. Ismāʿīl responds by switching to ECA to show his clear disapproval. By using both ECA and negation to deny any knowledge of this common friend and any respect for the oil that she uses, he shows his distinct stance towards his mother and her traditions. Although distance is associated with SA, in this context in which the mother uses SA, the son is expected to accommodate to her, which he does not.

The switching between both codes reflects the mounting tension between son and mother, Ismāʿīl and his community, and Ismāʿīl and his country. This mounting tension is understood more thoroughly by recognising that, in reality, the dialogue would occur completely in ECA. This dialogue, unrealistic as it is, is innovative and is an integral part of the creative process of the author.

Androutsopoulos provides a similar example (2012: 307) from a Turkish–German comedy, *Kebab Connection* (2004), in which a Turkish father and his son engage in a dispute about identity and inter-ethnic marriage between Germans and Turks, prompted by the son's relationship with a German woman. The father uses both German and Turkish throughout the dispute, while the son simply uses German. When the father code-switches between German and Turkish, the son does not accommodate and simply uses German. In response, the father switches to only utilising Turkish, in order to index his disagreement and uneasiness with his son's stance towards inter-ethnic marriage and towards his identity within the code used. This uneasiness and conflict is also apparent in the dialogue between Ismāʿīl and his mother.

As Androutsopoulos (2012: 305) argues, speakers/audience identify a code and decipher its indexes. This is why, according to Androutsopoulos, dubbed language in films loses a lot of its indexes, because the dubbing process cannot render the variation found within the linguistic codes of the original movie with the indexes of these codes. The same is true for literature in the Arab world, especially because of the diglossic linguistic situation. It becomes challenging to translate a novel such as the one analysed above and render the associations of SA and ECA in a different language that has its own indexes and communities.

To recap, while he is living and studying in the UK we assume that Ismāʿīl uses English. He renders all dialogues between himself and the people he interacts with in the UK in SA, as this is code associated with translation from English to Arabic. In Egypt, his only important communication is related only to people in his quarter, and his conflicted attitude towards them is apparent in his code choice and in switching between SA and ECA. However, when he leaves the quarter in dismay after his quarrel with his mother, there are no dialogues that take place between himself and others; he becomes an outsider. Only inside the quarter can he find his true identity, and only by going back to his local space can he find peace of mind.

In Ramaḍān's novel, *Leaves of Narcissus* (2001), Kīmī, the female protagonist, is unsure of her identity. She expresses a conflicted stance throughout most of the novel. As a female Egyptian student abroad, she is confronted with prejudices, stereotypes and negative perceptions. An Egyptian upper-class girl, Kīmī travels to Ireland to study for a doctorate in English literature at the end of the 1970s/beginning of the 1980s. Kīmī's sense of belonging is, to a great extent, influenced by her experience; when abroad, Kīmī is forced to take a stance, from which she evaluates herself in relation to her original local area (Egypt at large) and her new location (Ireland) (for stance-taking, see Jaffe 2009; Bassiouney 2014). Because of her identity in relation to her abstract local area, Egypt, those around her stereotype her as, alternatively, an Egyptian, an Arab and a Muslim. Whether she likes it or not, Kīmī is also forced to defend the identity of Egyptians more generally. In her painful search for one coherent identity for all Egyptians, she loses her mind and ends up in an asylum. In despair, she claims that it is impossible to summarise the 'people of Egypt' in a few words or even within the space of a book. Kīmī's only hope of recovery comes when she returns 'home' towards the end of the novel. It is only when Kīmī identifies a 'home' and, thus, her identity in relation to a large local area – Egypt – that she is at last able to recover.

Kīmī, unlike Ismāʿīl, does not have an attachment to her local area and people, and thus we, as readers, are unsure that she will be as confident of her identity. What she considers 'home' is not a local area, but one specific person – her servant in Egypt – who serves as her alter ego. Abstract and geographically vast areas are imposed on her as making up part of her identity by outsiders; places that she cannot relate to in the same way that Ismāʿīl relates to his square in Sayyidah Zaynab. She calls these places 'fantastic' and 'illusionary'; they include an entire continent – Africa – a region – the Middle East – and a vast and geographically diverse area – the Muslim world. While her local area is less well defined than Ismāʿīl's, her linguistic repertoire in the novel is wider, including English, ECA and SA, although she claims that she does not master SA, as will be made clear below.

In *Leaves of Narcissus*, Kīmī's sense of identity at the beginning of the novel, when she is in Ireland working on her doctorate, is extremely conflicted. The conflict within Kīmī is caused partly by her identification with more than one language, English and Arabic – especially, but not only, ECA. Kīmī declares that all languages are her language, and that is why she has no language; likewise, all countries are her country, which is also why she has no home. Kīmī does not regard linguistic diversity in a positive light. In fact, it is this diversity that confuses her.

In the case of Kīmī, she does not have a choice. Even though she masters English, she is still regarded as an 'Egyptian' by non-Egyptians. Thus, as a social variable, language comes *after* locality. Interestingly, Kīmī is not just regarded as an Egyptian; instead, her putative identity straddles all Muslim countries, including Iran. While she does not share a language (Kīmī speaks Arabic, while Iranians primarily speak Persian or Turkish dialects) or location with Iran, she is perceived as sharing a religion with Iranians and therefore as belonging to their 'community'. It would seem that for the 'outsiders' in Ireland, religion, rather than locality, is the salient social variable that marks identity. For Egyptians, in public discourse, the issue of religion is a complex one.[2] This difference in perception between Kīmī and the non-Egyptians that she encounters make her linguistic choices and talk about language more complex.

Kīmī's attitude towards other Arabs, Africans and the Irish is also complicated. When her Irish friends make fun of Libya and its political system, she feels the urge to make clear that Egypt is not Libya, that it is different. However, she also feels offended by their remarks and, to a great extent, she feels an affinity with the Libyans, given that they share a language and a continent. While Kīmī considers herself as simply Egyptian, those whom she encounters in Ireland do not distinguish Egyptians from either Libyans or Iranians.

Kīmī states, in despair, that it is impossible to summarise the 'people of Egypt' in a few words, sentences or even whole books. Note the following example – entirely in SA – in which her Irish colleagues verbally attack her:

> 'What a life you Muslim women have! What a religion! fascists. Nazi. You remind us of how some people once behaved here – but we've rid ourselves of all that! Look at yourselves. You remind us of our own past.'
>
> 'This passport that you folks carry – Why it's soaked in blood!'
>
> So I (Kīmī) defend it. 'My passport is Arab, not Iranian.'
>
> 'All of you over there hate Jews. Racists!'
>
> My passport is Egyptian. I defend it. What is it that I am trying to defend? Whatever loyalties I have are judged suspicious in advance. What am I defending? My passport? My language? My faith? This is a religion, I say, that took from and build upon your religion. That's all there is to the matter. (Ramaḍān 2002: 76)

Kīmī is not entirely sure what she is trying to defend; that is, which aspect of her identity is under attack and which aspect is being perceived in a negative way. She lists different aspects of the identity that she tries to defend. This list includes: a passport (a national identity), a language (a marker of this identity) and a faith (another marker of this identity). In this novel, places are imposed upon Kīmī by outsiders who do not necessarily share her assumptions or ideologies; places with which she may not have an affiliation and others to which she may not be completely sure of her affiliation. Once in the asylum, Kīmī declares in SA that she has been reduced to a 'thing' with no characteristics:

> A thing, nothing more. Without voice, without story, indeed without language. A body that hears and sees only . . . how do you resist your fate through writing if writing is your fate? I clutch my pen. Before me, the white page takes on the blurred outlines of a phantom. I see small black letters in a highly ornate font: hospital for Mental and Nervous Disorders. Even if I knew how to write, my language would be unreadable: all languages are foreign and the tongue of my people is suitable only for telling stories. (Ramaḍān 2002: 62)

Kīmī tries to write her own story, but is unable to. She says simply that the tongue of her people – meaning ECA – is only fit for *telling* stories, not for writing them. Her language, ECA, is not to be read by anyone. In her impaired state of mind, it is difficult for her to write in any other language except her mother tongue – what she refers to as 'the tongue of my people'. The possessive pronoun 'my' makes her the owner of the people and also of the tongue. But she claims to be the owner of a deficient language in which she cannot express herself; a language that, to a great extent, she looks down upon. Her conflict with herself is amplified by the diglossic situation in Egypt. Indeed, her split identity may even be the result of this diglossic situation.

While Kīmī may feel this way, it is not clear whether the author of this novel, Sumayyah Ramaḍān, shares these views. Kīmī uses SA in her dialogues. However, what Kīmī claims to do, or not do, and her linguistic repertoire are, in fact, different. Her use of codes are related directly to her state of mind. Kīmī's inability to write her story in her mother tongue and declare what 'all Egyptians are' is significant on multiple levels. Kīmī's ideology is shared by many – the belief that ECA is a code that is not fit for writing (see Suleiman 2003). The author, though, unlike Kīmī, challenges these ideologies and uses both SA and ECA creatively in her work. The schizophrenia that Kīmī suffers from is also reflected in the split of codes that is difficult for her to overcome – a spoken code that is not taken seriously and a formal code that she cannot master or utilise.

When asked to define her homeland, Kīmī is unsure how to do so. This highlights the difference between her and Ismāʿīl, who shares a local area with his family and community. Kīmī, on the other hand, finds it difficult to summarise 'a homeland' in a few words. She is forced, as a single individual, to represent an entire homeland. Kīmī refers to places and codes as two markers of this homeland. Locality also interacts with perceptions of identity. Kīmī posits, again in SA:

> I am African, too. Why do I remain something illusionary, fantastic, that is constantly under threat of being transformed into a continent in its own entirety, or an ignorant nation, or a submissive people, or even a more ancient civilization? ... 'We Egyptians', 'people in my country' ... who is that 'we'? Precisely which 'people' in that country? I am them, and I am not them, I am that 'we' and I'm also 'I' – just 'I'. (Ramaḍān 2002: 45)

Kīmī's juxtaposition of herself in relation to 'we', Egyptians, is important in her search for a collective identity. She is forced, by outsiders, to identify with all Egyptians. Whether she likes it or not, she represents her country and all of its peoples once she goes abroad. When asked to define her homeland, Kīmī is not sure it is even possible. She finds it challenging to summarise a homeland in a few words. She is then forced to be one individual representing an entire continent.

Most of Kīmī's conversations are either in SA or a mixture of ECA and SA. There is only one character in the novel that addresses, and is addressed by, Kīmī in ECA – namely, Āminah. Āminah, a servant from the countryside, accompanies Kīmī throughout her life, even in the asylum, and is portrayed as Kīmī's alter ego.

Kīmī has a distorted relationship with everyone around her, except for Āminah, who provides her with a 'home': Āminah smells like Kīmī's mother, tells Kīmī stories, believes in Kīmī, and also shares Kīmī's secrets and frustrations. Āminah is almost not human, but rather acts as a symbol of a home that Kīmī is not sure she can reach. It is possible that Āminah also stands for, like Fāṭimah in *Qindīl Umm Hāshim*, the 'authentic Egypt'. Āminah, like Fāṭimah, consistently uses ECA in her interactions with Kīmī, conjuring up the informal, intimate and authentic indexes of ECA. By way of contrast, Kīmī addresses her mother in SA, and her mother also always replies likewise in SA (Ramaḍān 2001: 89).

ECA indexes intimacy, while SA indexes detachment and formality in this novel. Again, as with *The Saint's Lamp*, if *Leaves of Narcissus* were to be translated, the novel would have only one code and the richness of linguistic diversity within the text would be lost. What is, indeed, interesting about this novel is the metalinguistic discourse of the protagonist, who finds it difficult (if not impossible) to write in ECA – her mother tongue – and reflects the negative indexes associated with ECA as a written code in her discourse.

Discussion and conclusions

In his book *Arabic in the Fray*, Suleiman argues that 'the cognitive role of Arabic has been used to express a variety of perspectives on the mediating role that the language plays in influencing thought and interpreting reality' (Suleiman 2013: 270). In this chapter, this mediating role is discussed in relation to code choice in novels. Access and lack of access to language as a social resource has been also discussed. Heller, in her book *Paths to Post-Nationalism* (2011: 192–3), addresses the problem of diversity and inequality. She argues that 'to understand nation we need to understand the structural relations of difference and inequality that sediment over time'. She also adds that access to linguistic resources is related to access to discursive space. Linguistic resources carry their own indexes and so do places. In the case of Kīmī in *Leaves of Narcissus*, her access to language and place overwhelms her. She masters English and ECA but not SA and therefore cannot write her story. Her relation to place is both illusionary and abstract. However, Ismāʿīl does not have the same problem; rather, his access to language and place is made much clearer throughout *The Saint's Lamp*. Although he has a conflicted relation to place at the beginning of his journey of self-discovery, Ismāʿīl's quarter remains something tangible and concrete. Language is never an impediment in his attempts at communication. While at the beginning he considers his quarter of Cairo inferior to the UK – which, at the time, was still dominating Egypt – he manages to overcome this judgement through the help of his local community. Kīmī, on the other hand, never overcomes her feeling of inferiority, and this is reflected in her lack of access to SA. In terms of access and resources, identity construction remains, for both protagonists, an ongoing struggle; a struggle of both inclusiveness and exclusiveness.

In order to be able to interpret the protagonists' stances in these two novels, as well as their identification processes in relation to local areas, one needs empirical evidence of conventional associations of codes and meanings gained from both ethnographic and sociolinguistic data. One also needs knowledge of a speaker's repertoire and the range of their linguistic performance (see Schilling-Estes 1998). That is to say, to understand the stance being adopted in a specific moment by a specific speaker, interpreters need to assess the particular moment of 'linguistic performance against that speaker's choices and performances in other contexts and at other moments' (Jaffe 2009: 56). I argue that understanding stance means that one should understand identity formation at multiple indexical levels. The indexes of SA and ECA specifically have been discussed in relation to code choice, code-switching and the metalinguistic discourse of protagonists.

Hodson (2014: 190) argues that writers usually manipulate 'style-shifting' to convey protagonists' state of mind, feelings and relation to others, as well as protagonists' identity more generally. Hudson also contends that the use of dialect in literature is usually the result of the author's aim to reflect 'everyday living' in a 'realistic way'. While this may be true for literature written in English, it is not the case in Arabic literature. This is because SA is not the spoken code of any community. Therefore, by using SA in literature, authors are not reflecting reality, which is why when these novels are translated into a different language or adapted into movie versions, the linguistic repertoire of the protagonists decreases to only one code.

Code-switching is used as a device by authors to reflect protagonists' stances towards the self, others and place. In the two novels discussed in this chapter – *The Saint's Lamp* and *Leaves of Narcissus* – the codes ECA and SA are used in dialogue as a linguistic resource that reflects identity. That is, these two authors, when constructing their dialogues, did not reflect realistic linguistic habits. Instead, they constructed a different linguistic context in which ideologies, attitudes and perceptions are more prominent. Language is abstracted from its function of communication to a social variable that carries valuable indexes.

Notes

1. Both of these novels were discussed in Bassiouney 2014.
2. Perhaps the fact that Kīmī studies in Ireland is also significant. It could be that in Ireland, where religious tensions between Catholics and Protestants persist, perceptions of the self are directly related to religion. This proposition is not mentioned directly in the novel, but may be worth investigating in future research, especially because outsiders' beliefs can influence an insider's perceptions of identity markers.

References

Primary texts

Ḥaqqī, Y., *Qindil Umm Hashim* (Cairo: al-Hayah al-Misriyah al-Ammah lil-Kitab, [1944] 1997).

Ḥaqqī, Y., *The Saint's Lamp and Other Stories* (Leiden: Brill, 1973).
Ramaḍān, S., *Awraq al-narjis* (Cairo: Dar Sharqiyat, 2001).
Ramaḍān, S., *The Leaves of Narcissus*, trans. Marilyn Booth (Cairo: American University in Cairo Press, 2002).

Secondary references

Agha, A., 'Voice, footing, enregisterment', *Journal of Linguistic Anthropology* 15(1) (2005): 38–59.
Agha, A., *Language and Social Relations* (Cambridge: Cambridge University Press, 2007).
Androutsopoulos, J., 'Repertoires, characters and scenes: Sociolinguistic difference in Turkish-German comedy', *Multilingua* 31(2) (2012): 301–26.
Bassiouney, R., *Arabic Sociolinguistics: Topics in Diglossia, Gender, Identity, and Politics* (Washington, DC: Georgetown University Press, 2009).
Bassiouney, R., *Language and Identity in Modern Egypt* (Edinburgh: Edinburgh University Press, 2014).
Bauman, R., 'Language, identity, performance', *Pragmatics* 10(1) (2000): 1–6.
Blommaert, J., *Discourse: A Critical Introduction* (Cambridge: Cambridge University Press, 2005).
Cameron, D., *Working with Spoken Discourse* (Los Angeles, CA: Sage, 2012).
Coupland, N., 'Language, situation, and the relational self: Theorizing dialect-style in sociolinguistics', in Penelope Eckert and John R. Rickford (eds), *Style and Sociolinguistic Variation* (Cambridge: Cambridge University Press, 2001), pp. 185–210.
Ferguson, C., 'Diglossia', *Word* 15 (1959): 325–40; reprinted in Pier Paolo Gligioli (ed.), *Language and Social Contexts: Selected Readings* (Harmondsworth: Penguin, 1972), pp. 232–51.
Fowler, R., *Linguistics and the Novel* (London: Methuen, 1977).
Heller, M., *Paths to Post-Nationalism: A Critical Ethnography of Language and Identity* (Oxford: Oxford University Press, 2011).
Hodson, J., *Dialect in Film and Literature* (Basingstoke: Palgrave Macmillan, 2014).
Jaffe, A., 'The sociolinguistics of stance', in Alexandra Jaffe (ed.), *Stance: Sociolinguistic Perspectives* (Oxford: Oxford University Press, 2009), pp. 3–28.
Johnstone, B., 'Reflexivity in sociolinguistics.' in Anne H. Anderson, Keith Brown et al. (eds), *Encyclopedia of Language and Linguistics*, 2nd edn (Oxford: Elsevier, 2006), vol. 10, pp. 463–4.
Johnstone, B., 'Locating language in identity', in Carmen Llamas and Dominic Watt (eds), *Language and Identity* (Edinburgh: Edinburgh University Press, 2010), pp. 29–36.
Milroy, L., *Language and Social Networks*, 2nd edn (Oxford: Blackwell, 1987).
Mitchell, T., *Colonising Egypt* (Berkeley, CA: University of California Press, 1988).

Ochs, E., 'Indexing gender', in Alessandro Duranti and Charles Goodwin (eds), *Rethinking Context: Language as an Interactive Phenomenon* (Cambridge: Cambridge University Press, 1992), pp. 335–58.

Rampton, B., 'Contemporary urban vernaculars', in Jacomine Nortier and Bente A. Svendsen (eds), *Language, Youth and Identity in the 21st Century: Linguistic Practices across Urban Spaces* (Cambridge: Cambridge University Press, 2015), pp. 24–44.

Schilling-Estes, N., 'Investigating "self-conscious" speech: The performance register in Ocracoke English', *Language in Society* 27(1) (1998): 53–83.

Shohamy, Elana G., *Language Policy: Hidden Agendas and New Approaches* (London: Routledge, 2006).

Silverstein, M., 'Indexical order and the dialectics of sociolinguistic life', in C. B. Paulson and R. G. Tucker (eds), *Salsa III: Proceedings of the Third Annual Symposium about Language and Society* (Austin, TX: University of Texas, Department of Linguistics, 1996), pp. 266–95.

Silverstein, M., 'Indexical order and the dialectics of sociolinguistic life', *Language & Communication* 23(3/4) (2003): 193–229.

Suleiman, Y., *The Arabic Language and National Identity: A Study in Ideology* (Edinburgh: Edinburgh University Press, 2003).

Suleiman, Y., *A War of Words: Language and Conflict in the Middle East* (Cambridge: Cambridge University Press, 2004).

Suleiman, Y., *Arabic, Self and Identity: A Study in Conflict and Displacement* (Oxford: Oxford University Press, 2011).

Suleiman, Y., *Arabic in the Fray: Language Ideology and Cultural Politics* (Edinburgh: Edinburgh University Press, 2013).

Van Leeuwen, T., 'The representation of social actors', in Carmen Caldas-Coulthard and Malcom Coulthard (eds), *Texts and Practices: Readings in Critical Discourse Analysis* (London: Routledge, 1996), pp. 32–70.

CHAPTER 7

Language as Proxy in Egypt's Identity Politics: Examining the New Wave of Egyptian Nationalism

Mariam Aboelezz

Gramsci famously once said that 'every time the question of language surfaces, in one way or another, it means that a series of other problems are coming to the fore' (Gramsci 1985). Nowhere is this statement more true than in the sphere of identity politics. The role of language in 'classical' Egyptian nationalism dating to the early twentieth century has been well documented by Yasir Suleiman (see Suleiman 1996, 2003, 2008), where advocating *ʿāmmiyya* and rejecting *fuṣḥā* acted as proxy for promoting an Egyptian identity and rejecting an Arab identity. This Egyptian nationalist current espousing Pharaonism is generally considered a thing of the past; superseded by pan-Arab nationalism in the mid-twentieth century. However, waning pan-Arab feelings have now given way to a new wave of Egyptian nationalism in Egypt that has received little scholarly attention to date. This new wave has had linguistic manifestations, such as the establishment of *Wikipedia Masry* in 2008 (Panović 2010), the only official version of the online encyclopaedia in a regional variety of Arabic. This is the same year that saw the formation of the Liberal Egyptian Party, an Egyptian nationalist political party that aimed to standardise Egyptian Arabic. More recent political changes in Egypt appear to have spurred on this new nationalist wave, with a government-backed emphasis on 'Egyptian identity' in the wake of the military deposal of Egypt's Islamist president, Mohamad Morsi, in 2013. Recalling the concept of *alterity* (Suleiman 2008, 2013), this emphasis appears to be an attempt by the new government to distance itself from Islamist ideology (which very easily bleeds into pan-Arab ideology) as well as from its symbols (including *fuṣḥā*). In this chapter, I examine how language is used as proxy in this new wave of Egyptian nationalism. I begin by surveying the history of Egyptian nationalism in Egypt before I describe the new wave of nationalism and explain how recent political changes have played in its favour. I then demonstrate how old motifs are revived and show how the language-identity link is established through processes of distanciation, differentiation and identification (Suleiman 2013).

Introduction

Language disputes have overshadowed many a political crisis over history. When political issues grow too sensitive or controversial to openly discuss, language is often deployed by stakeholders as a proxy to express political views. This has long been the case in identity politics. In this chapter, I address the role of language as proxy in the identity of politics of Egypt with particular focus on Egyptian nationalism. I begin by reviewing the history of what I term 'classical' Egyptian nationalism, which is generally seen to have been overtaken by pan-Arab nationalism. However, I argue that Egyptian nationalism has been revived and provide a detailed survey of evidence to support this. I then attempt to qualify the new wave of Egyptian nationalism using some of the concepts introduced by Yasir Suleiman in the study of language and national identity. In doing so, I highlight the similarities and differences between the two waves of Egyptian nationalism and take account of the factors that have contributed to the revival of Egyptian nationalism in Egypt.

The roots of Egyptian nationalism

In 1798, Napoleon Bonaparte led a French expedition against Egypt. In a way, the roots of Egyptian nationalism may be traced back to this expedition. While the expedition itself was very short-lived and proved to be too adventurous to sustain – the French were driven out of Egypt in 1801 – it marked the beginning of an important period of cultural influence from Europe. Europe had already gone through the Renaissance, the Reformation and the Industrial Revolution, which had given birth to many technologies and intellectual ideals. These were eagerly taken up by Muhammad Ali, a Turkic-Albanian Ottoman whose lineage ruled Egypt from 1805 to 1952, and who had a great zeal for European learning and culture (Brugman 1984). Muhammad Ali sponsored educational missions to Europe to gain specialised knowledge in various educational fields. His reign saw the beginning of the Arabic *nahḍa* or Renaissance (Chejne 1969).

One clear influence of Western ideas during the Arabic *nahḍa* was in the rise of intellectual nationalism. This took different forms: while many thinkers wrote of an Islamic community (*umma*) with Islam as the unifying factor, others wrote of pan-Arab nationalism. There were also those intellectuals who placed 'an emphasis on the special character of Egyptian society, history and culture', sometimes writing of an Egyptian nation (*waṭan*) which transcends the Muslim *umma* (Versteegh 2001: 176). These nationalist currents may be mapped onto the 'concentric nationalist circles' that Suleiman (2008: 39) uses to describe nationalism in Egypt (Figure 7.1). Significantly, he uses the epithet 'Egyptian' at the beginning of each label because of the central role that Egypt is perceived to play in each of these nationalisms. It is worth noting that he distinguishes between two types of Egyptian nationalism.

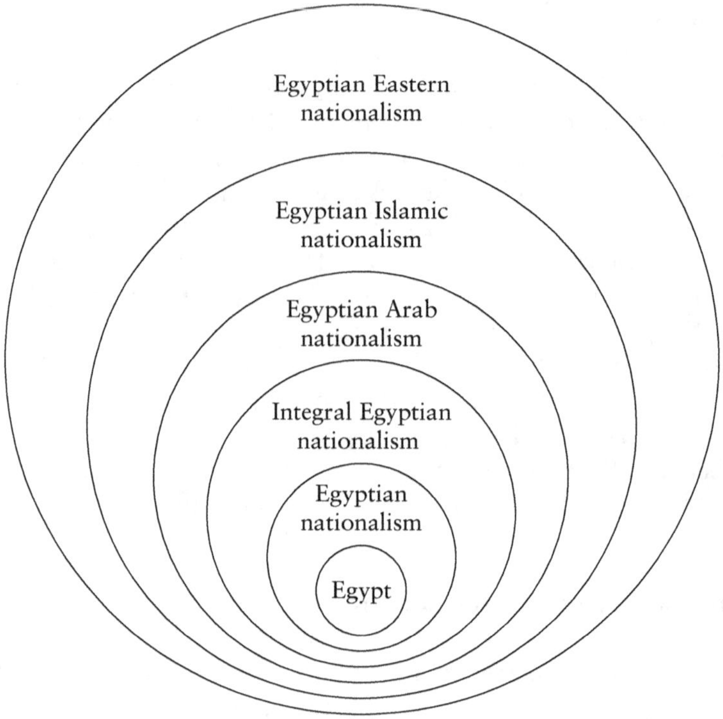

Figure 7.1 Suleiman's (2008) conceptualisation of Egyptian supra-nationalisms

Closer to the core is a more separatist nationalism that views Egypt as entirely removed from the Arab world, while integral Egyptian nationalism captures a view of Egypt as distinct from the Arab world, but 'with strong non-national links with the Arabic-speaking countries' (ibid.). Suleiman's notion of Eastern nationalism also warrants glossing; this, according to him, 'emphasises Egypt's separate national identity but highlights its similarity of culture with nations such as China and Japan' (ibid.). This chapter focuses on the first concentric circle in this diagram (Figure 7.1); that of separatist or territorial Egyptian nationalism.

While the flame of the *nahḍa* was all but snuffed under British occupation (1882–1922) through the downgraded status of Arabic, intellectual nationalism flourished as a mode of ideological resistance. Egyptian territorial nationalism in particular was given an enormous boost in the 1920s due to:

> the pride the country felt in the 1919 revolution against British colonial rule, the establishment of a parliamentary democracy in 1922–3, the excitement following the discovery of the tomb of Tut-Ank-Amon in 1923 and the success of Mustafa Kemal Atatürk in promoting Turkish nationalism with its keen interest in language reform, which the Egyptian territorial nationalists looked to as a model. (Suleiman, 2008: 32)

Suleiman (2008) summarises the ideological positions of Egyptian nationalists in two main attitudes. First, that '*fuṣḥā* was not seen to be invested with the power to define Egypt's national identity' (p. 37). To accept *fuṣḥā* as a marker of Egyptian identity would be to concede that Egypt is an Arab country. To refute this connection, Egyptian nationalists resorted to an 'acute application of the principle of *alterity* in national self-definition: the greater the substantive linguistic similarities between national Self and significant Other, the greater the desire to deny or explain away these similarities as a basis for a shared national identity between this Self and the Other' (p. 38). Second, Egyptian nationalists showed 'a strong and sustained interest in language reform [which was linked] to the socio-economic modernisation of their country' (ibid.). The reforms they proposed ranged from reforming the grammar of *fuṣḥā* (Husayn [1937] 1996), Egyptianising *fuṣḥā* (Al-Sayyid 1937), to replacing the Arabic script with a Latin script (Musa [1945] 2012).

Egyptian nationalists shunned the link to Arabic-speaking countries and looked elsewhere for self-definition. They felt a direct racial and psychological link to the ancient Egyptians, and as heirs to such an ancient civilisation, they felt superior to and more advanced than Arabs (Suleiman 2003, 2008). Suleiman (2008: 33) observes that 'some territorial nationalists went so far as to claim that to be true to their history, the Egyptian Copts, as the legitimate heirs of ancient Egypt, must abandon Arabic and revert to Coptic'. This claim was usually anchored in projecting 'the seventh-century conquest of Egypt as an Arab invasion or occupation', and in painting 'Arabic as an imperial language, equating it symbolically with English as the language of the British colonial rule' (ibid.). The Arab component of Egypt's past was treated 'as historical rupture', which Egypt repaired through its 'historically proven' assimilatory powers' (ibid.).

One of the earliest and most influential figures of Egyptian nationalism was Ahmad Lutfi al-Sayyid (1872–1963). Unlike later nationalists whose nationalism was characteristically anti-Arab, al-Sayyid's nationalism was anti-colonial in essence. Nevertheless, he took a strong stance against pan-Arabism, holding the view that Egyptians had their own distinct culture. He took particular pride in Egypt's pharaonic past and romanticised the Egyptian countryside. He was also opposed to pan-Islamism on the basis that religion could not serve as a means of national definition (Al-Sayyid 1937). Al-Sayyid was behind the first political party in Egypt, *al-Umma* (the Nation), which was established in reaction to the repressive policies of the British administration, and in particular to the violent Denshawai incident of 1906. Influenced by European philosophers such as John Stuart Mill, al-Sayyid embraced liberalism, the Egyptian nation he envisioned was therefore based on the principle of individual liberty which he considered 'not only the criterion of political action, but a necessity of life' (Hourani 1962: 173).

Al-Sayyid became the first director of the Egyptian University (which later became Cairo University) in 1925 and presided over the Arabic language academy in Egypt from 1945 until his death in 1963. His reformist position on language can be fully appreciated only in the context of his nationalist views. While al-Sayyid did not support *ʿāmmiyya*, but rather held it in contempt 'as a corrupt form of Arabic' (Suleiman, 2003: 173), he called for 'linguistic tolerance' towards the use of colloquial words and foreign loanwords with the intention of closing the gap between *fuṣḥā* and *ʿāmmiyya* (al-Sayyid 1937). He 'was aware that *fuṣḥā* was in need of lexical and stylistic modernisation, a task he tackled from the perspective of an Egyptian nationalist who believed in the Egyptianisation of *fuṣḥā* (*tamṣīr al-lugha*), perhaps to make it fit for defining Egyptian national identity at some future date' (Suleiman 2008: 32). Al-Sayyid referred to the product of this process as 'the Egyptian language' (*al-lugha al-miṣriyya*); Egyptians' own version of Arabic.

Al-Sayyid's reformist attitude towards Arabic was shared by the Azhar-educated Taha Husayn (1889–1973), who succeeded him as president of the Arabic language academy in Egypt. Husayn believed that education was 'the most secure basis for bringing about cultural redefinition of the national identity in a manner which preserves and enhances the national unity of Egypt' (Suleiman, 2003: 192). In his book, *The Future of Culture in Egypt*, Husayn expresses his great dissatisfaction with the state of education in Egypt and places language at the heart of necessary educational reforms (Husayn [1937] 1996). He says that the dated emphasis on teaching grammar had made learning *fuṣḥā* akin to learning a foreign language to students. He also reassures the Azharis and the language conservatives that the Arabic he wishes to be taught in schools is *fuṣḥā*, but points to the necessity of simplifying and reforming its grammar lest it becomes a mere liturgical language. He acknowledges the religious significance of Arabic, but argues that it should not be monopolised by al-Azhar, effectively calling for the secularisation of Arabic. Husayn was concerned that those who resisted language reforms on religious grounds would be contributing inadvertently 'to depressing literacy in the schools and to heightening the danger which the colloquial poses to the standard form of the language in Egypt' (Suleiman 2003: 193). Husayn also called for the reform of the Arabic writing system, but categorically opposed the adoption of the Latin script. He was also against teaching *ʿāmmiyya* because he felt that it was 'unfit for literary expression, and that its adoption would deprive Egyptians of a link with their literary heritage' (Suleiman 2003: 194). Husayn talks of a distinctive 'Egyptian culture', but stresses the importance of the Arabic language as a component of this culture.

Like al-Sayyid, Husayn looked to Europe as a model; he argued that the very foundations of European culture were influenced by ancient Egyptian civilisation, and hence Egypt would be betraying its own historical legacy if it were to stay outside the scope of modern European culture (Suleiman 2003). However, unlike al-Sayyid, Husayn did not 'see Egypt as distinct from the surrounding countries' (Suleiman 2003: 197). Rather than isolate itself from the region, he felt that Egypt should assert its national strength by reaching out to its Arab neighbours. In particular, he encouraged inviting Arab students to study in Egypt and opening Egyptian educational institutions in Arab countries. In other words, Husayn's nationalism was characterised by an integral disposition towards the Arab world (the second concentric circle in Figure 7.1).

Husayn's position is in sharp contrast to the 'radical' nationalism of one of his contemporaries, Salama Musa (1887–1958). One of the founding figures of socialism in Egypt, Musa spent a chapter of his youth in Europe where he was deeply taken by European culture. The cultural ideas he encountered during this period, most notably Marxism and secularism, would shape much of his future writing. He returned to Egypt full of nationalistic fervour and produced several books expressing his ideas about society, culture and language. Salama's nationalism was subdued as his writing career progressed, especially towards the end of his life as he assimilated into Nasserist socialism.

In his earlier writing, Musa shunned language as the basis for national self-definition, while paradoxically showing 'a sustained interest in it as the object and means of modernisation' (Suleiman 2008: 35). Musa 'constructed a dire picture of *fuṣḥā*, painting it as lexically defective in dealing with the exigencies of science, industry, and modernity at large owing to its origins in a desert ecology and culture from which it has been unable to break completely free' (Suleiman 2008: 34). He claimed that *fuṣḥā* had 'fossilised to the point where it could be declared (almost) a dead language' (ibid.). Deeming Arab literary heritage inferior, he called upon Egyptian writers to break from the Arab mould of literary writing and to emulate the superior European model instead. Musa 'strongly promoted the Pharaonic theme in the nationalist ideology, considering this theme as the major authenticating and motivating force for Egypt' (ibid.). He called for the revival of the Coptic language and proposed using Latin script to write *ʿāmmiyya* to facilitate borrowing from European languages and keep up with modern technology (Musa [1945] 2012, [1956] 2013).

Musa's views are echoed by Louis Awad (1915–1990) who 'believed that Egyptian creativity was permanently handicapped' by *fuṣḥā*, and that Egyptians needed to nurture *ʿāmmiyya* to embark on a modern era 'unfettered by the linguistic shackles of the past' (Suleiman 2008: 37). The original introduction to his volume of free verse poetry, *Plutoland* (Awad [1947] 1989), is a heated 'manifesto' for two projects: doing away with the Arab(ic) poetic tradition which he repeatedly declares dead, and writing in *ʿāmmiyya*, with some poems in the volume serving as a model (Jabr 2011). Louis Awad argued that Egyptian *ʿāmmiyya* 'has developed its own phonology, morphology, syntax, lexicon, and prosody, and that it had done so under the influence of an Egyptian substratum (Coptic) that made it distinct from other *ʿāmmiyya* varieties outside the borders of Egypt' (Suleiman 2008: 37). Influenced by evolutionary ideas, Awad went as far as to claim that Egyptian *ʿāmmiyya* was 'an outcome of the special physiology of the Egyptian vocal tract', and that it 'therefore separated Egyptians from non-Egyptians in a genetically coded manner' (ibid.).

Awad's book, *An Introduction to the Jurisprudence of the Arabic Language* (Awad [1981] 2006), was famously banned in Egypt for a long time because it questions the dominant account of the origin and history of Arabic. The book suggests that Arabic is a recent language, belonging to the Indo-European family, which has been influenced by ancient Egyptian. Awad's critics accused him of slyly spreading misinformation in order to serve his nationalist ideology by implying that Arab civilisation is inferior to Egyptian civilisation.

According to Suleiman, Egyptian nationalism dwindled towards the middle of the twentieth century as Egyptian nationalists were engulfed by 'the currents of political thinking towards supra-forms of national identification' (Suleiman 2008: 35). Suleiman adds:

> The attempts of some Egyptian nationalists to endow *ʿāmmiyya* with ideologically impregnated symbolic meanings, to make it a durable marker of a territorial national identity, failed because of the historically sanctioned position of *fuṣḥā* in Egyptian society, the lack of political will to go down this nationalist route, and the lack of resources – for example dictionaries, grammars and school curricula – that could carry this nationalism forward institutionally. (Suleiman 2008: 42)

It did not help either that some of the advocates of the most separatist form of Egyptian nationalism like Salama Musa and Louis Awad came from the Coptic minority in Egypt, which made their motives immediately suspect. A telling example is Shaker's (1972) fierce criticism of Louis Awad, where the latter is called a 'charlatan', a 'clown', a 'missionary', a puppet of foreign intelligence, and a begrudging and malevolent 'lie-telling crusader' harbouring ill-intent towards Islam and its people.

A new wave of Egyptian nationalism: surveying the evidence

The surge in pan-Arab nationalism and heightened sense of Arab identity abated as the Nasserite era drew to a close (1970), particularly following the signing of the peace treaty with Israel in 1979 during the presidency of Anwar El-Sadat (1970–81), resulting in Egypt being excommunicated by many Arab states. During this time, feelings that Egyptians were different from other Arabs began to fester once more, and Egyptian nationalists, such as Louis Awad, marginalised for decades, found a fresh voice (Bassiouney 2009).

These conditions have clearly favoured the revival of territorial Egyptian nationalism – a point which receives little attention in the academic literature. A nod to this revival is made by Haeri (1997): in the same article where she states that Egyptian nationalism has been overtaken by pan-Arab nationalism, she reports in a footnote that during her fieldwork in Egypt, she heard of 'a group with a Pharaonic name' which opposed *fuṣḥā* on the grounds that it was the language of 'Arab invaders' (1997: 798).

Only a few years earlier, specifically in 1990, Bayoumi Andil published, at his own expense, a book titled *The Present [Condition] of Culture in Egypt*. The book was republished in three subsequent editions, the latest in 2008 (Andil 2008). The book is chiefly concerned with language as a cultural vessel. Andil's main arguments can be summarised as follows: while *fuṣḥā* is a Semitic language brought to Egypt from west Asia by the Arabs, the Modern Egyptian Language (*ʿāmmiyya*) is a Hamitic language indigenous to Egypt and a descendant of ancient Egyptian. The two languages voice two competing cultures: the foreign Semitic-Arab culture versus the native Hamitic-African culture. The latter is Egyptians' mother tongue and is naturally more capable of expressing the Egyptian sensibility (*al-wijdān al-miṣrī*). The grammatical complexity of *fuṣḥā* makes it impossible to learn for Egyptians. Egyptians are regrettably oblivious to the glory of their own culture/language. As Andil repeatedly proclaims his allegiance to Egyptian nationalism, these arguments about language are predictably impregnated with a wider ideological message about national definition.

A writer, translator and journalist, Bayoumi Andil (d. 2009) was an active proponent of Egyptian nationalism. With others, he applied to register an Egyptian nationalist political party in 2004, under the name 'Mother Egypt' (*Maṣr il-Umm*), espousing secularism and democracy. This significant step heralded a new wave of Egyptian nationalism that was descended from the classical wave in more than name: the initiative arose from a weekly cultural salon at the house of a noted Egyptologist, Muhsin Lutfi al-Sayyid (d. 2009), nephew to none other than Ahmad Lutfi al-Sayyid. It is possible that this is the group Haeri had heard of while conducting her field work in Cairo in the 1990s. With conditions impossibly difficult for the registration of new political parties at the time, Mother Egypt's application was conclusively rejected in 2006 after several attempts to overturn the ruling. Almost immediately, an offshoot of the original group decided to make a fresh application with the same principles but under a different name: the Liberal Egyptian Party (Mazen 2006).

In September 2007, the Liberal Egyptian Party (still unofficial at that point) organised a large celebration of the (ancient) Egyptian New Year under wide media attention (Darwish 2007). Darwish noted that Egypt was experiencing a 'surge in Egyptian nationalism', evidenced in attempts at 'raising the nation's awareness of its ancient spirit' (Darwish 2007: 22). He remarked that 'for the first time in modern history Egyptians publicly revived the old rituals in Giza', and linked 'this feverish revival by Egyptians of their ancient spirit' to the momentum of Egyptian nationalism, which he argued was at its strongest since the early twentieth century (ibid.).

A formal application for the establishment of the Liberal Egyptian Party (LEP) was made in May 2008. The party was keen on making itself conspicuous through cultural activities and an established web presence. A 'Liberal Egyptian Party' page was added to Wikipedia in May 2010. The writer's username was 'The Egyptian Liberal'. The page described the LEP as:

> a grassroots movement and a secular political party in Egypt. The party builds on previous attempts by native anti-colonial activists in the early 20th century to re-assert ethnic Egyptian identity, based in part on national independence from the British and the Ottomans, the establishment of a secular and democratic national government, and the formalization of the local Masri language. It also seeks to revive the indigenous Egyptian language and to disassociate Egypt from the Arab nationalist policies introduced by Gamal Abdel Nasser. The Liberal Egyptian Party calls for separating religion from politics and most civil affairs.

The same year that the application for the LEP was submitted, Wikipedia approved a proposal for the first (and to date only) version of the online encyclopaedia in a regional variety of Arabic and *Wikipedia Masry* (WM) was officially launched at the end of 2008 (Panović 2010). Unsurprisingly, the Masry Wikipedian that Panović interviewed had been a member of the Mother Egypt 'political movement' and subsequently the LEP. According to the description given on WM, which Panović summarises (2010: 98), Masry or the Modern Egyptian Language is described as 'the language spoken by Egyptians in Egypt', noting that it 'is actually a separate language of Hamitic (African) origin, an extension of ancient Egyptian languages, with syntactic and morphological rules that are different from those of Arabic'. Panović traces the claim about the Hamitic origin of *ʿāmmiyya* to the ideas of Bayoumi Andil, who receives a lengthy entry in WM like other Egyptian nationalists. Noting the contrasting brevity of many other WM articles, Panović states:

> it is clear that Masry Wikipedians are the proponents of Egyptian territorial nationalism of a kind that sets itself apart from Arab or Islamic nationalisms, seeking to carve out a specifically Egyptian identity, the uniqueness of which is confirmed by the alleged existence of a separate, Egyptian, language, and is reaffirmed by an imagined continuity of territorially-bound Egyptianness that uninterruptedly stretches back to pharaonic times. (Panović 2010: 99)

The LEP remained culturally active even though their application for registration was not successful. Aboelezz (forthcoming) interviewed one of the four founding members of the LEP in the summer of 2010. This was Abdel Aziz Gamal El-Din, who described himself as a researcher in Egyptology with a particular interest in the 'evolution of the Egyptian language'. Gamal El-Din was vehemently opposed to the term *al-ʿāmmiyya al-miṣriyya* (Egyptian *ʿāmmiyya*), which he stated was being deliberately used to demean the Egyptian Language. He believed that there is no such thing as an Arab(ic) *fuṣḥā* and an Egyptian

ʿāmmiyya, but rather that there is an Egyptian Language which is a direct descendant of ancient Egyptian languages and which has been influenced by the languages of multiple civilisations over the ages, but has maintained its own grammar. On the other hand, he denies that an Arabic *fuṣḥā* ever existed, claiming that the people of the Arabian Peninsula spoke an assortment of underdeveloped dialects (*alsina*). In fact, he argues that what 'Arabs in the region' speak is the Egyptian Language because they have been taught by – the more civilised and accomplished – Egyptian teachers.

Gamal El Din's conceptualisation of the Egyptian Language is clearly a combination of the earlier ideas of Ahmad Lutfi al-Sayyid, Salama Musa, Louis Awad and Bayoumi Andil, even though the end-product is not identical to any one view of these earlier Egyptian nationalists. Particularly worth noting is his wholesale replacement of the 'Arabic Language' with the 'Egyptian Language', which may be traced back to al-Sayyid's idea of a distinctly Egyptian Language. According, to Gamal El-Din, the Egyptian Language comprises a literary level and a popular level, and it is the latter that the LEP seek to make the official language of Egypt, since it is the true language of the people (Aboelezz forthcoming). He expounds this view in the introduction to a book he later published, *On the Evolution of our Modern Egyptian Language*:

> From the outset, we must acknowledge that every living language, including our Egyptian language, has a popular everyday level in common use by all the people of this language. In addition to its widespread use, this level has its popular disciplines and art forms such as folktales, poetry, puppet theatre (*masraḥ al-arāgōz*) and traditional theatre (*masraḥ al-sāmir*). Indeed, it also possesses the language of modern theatre, cinema and [TV] soaps.
>
> From this popular level emanates the official level which some scholars and intellectuals formulate into [grammar] rules and a writing system to be used in the state's official documents. However, this does not mean that this level of the Egyptian language (i.e. the official level) does not have the capacity for literary creativity for those who wish to employ it.
>
> Thus, we see that the popular level of the language provides its grammatical basis and evolutionary grounds, and we cannot imagine a language without this level. (Gamal El-Din 2011: 5, translation)

Following the 2011 uprising and in the lead-up to the 2011–12 parliamentary elections, the LEP assimilated into the Social Democratic Egyptian Party (SDEP). The latter shared the LEP's overarching principles of liberalism and democracy, but notably not its Egyptian nationalism which was absent from the new party's manifesto. The SDEP formed a coalition, The Egyptian Bloc (*al-kutla al-Miṣriyya*), alongside two other parties in the 2011–12 parliamentary elections to counter the political influence of Islamists. The largest party in the coalition was the Free Egyptians (FE) Party (*il-Maṣriyyīn il-Aḥrār*). This was another 'liberal' party established by a number of well-known public figures, among whom was Naguib Sawiris, a Coptic media magnate and business tycoon.

It has been argued that Sawiris' investments in several cultural and media (and now political) institutions is part of his attempt to counter 'Egypt's Islamisation' and transport a vision of a 'liberal Egyptian identity' which is removed from Arab identity (Gemeinder 2009). Sawiris' pro-*ʿāmmiyya* stance was clear in his launch of the satellite channel OTV (now ONTV) in 2006 (Bassiouney 2009, 2014; Doss 2010). The channel, which was aimed at young people and carried the slogan *qanā maṣriyya miyya fī l-miyya* ('a 100 per cent Egyptian channel'), introduced news bulletins in *ʿāmmiyya* for the first time (a domain traditionally associated with *fuṣḥā*). Very much like in the case of WM, the actual product was not 'pure' *ʿāmmiyya* but 'elevated *ʿāmmiyya*'; an intermediate level between *fuṣḥā* and *ʿāmmiyya* (Doss 2010). It is worth noting that the association between the channel, on the one hand, and *ʿāmmiyya* and a young audience, on the other, is difficult to assert today. In 2009, Yosri Fouda, a former al-Jazeera presenter joined ONTV. Fouda had already established an illustrious career as a news presenter and, consistent with the language policy of his former employers, he continued to use *fuṣḥā* in his programme on ONTV. Moreover, the channel gained wide viewership during and after the 2011 uprising for siding with the protestors and providing an alternative to the state media narrative. It could be argued that ONTV today attracts both young and old viewers, albeit with a particular political orientation.

To understand the ideological significance of OTV/ONTV it is useful to dwell on a similar earlier project in Lebanon; that of the Lebanese channel Lebanese Broadcasting Corporation International (LBCI). Established in 1991, the channel 'is strongly connected to the Maronite-dominated Phalange Party, which is committed to maintaining a Lebanese identity for Lebanon in which the Maronites play a pivotal role' (Suleiman 2006: 131–2). Significantly, LBCI's local news bulletin is broadcast mainly in Lebanese colloquial Arabic (Al Batal 2002). Al Batal (2002: 112) relates this to a tension between the ideologies of '[pan-]Arabism' and 'Lebanonism', where 'the former ideology perceives Lebanon as an integral part of the Arab world both culturally and linguistically, while the latter stresses the cultural and linguistic uniqueness of Lebanon vis-à-vis the rest of the Arab world'. According to Suleiman (2006: 132), while the former perceives Lebanon as '*of* the Arab Middle East', the latter sees it as merely '*in* the Arab Middle East'. Clearly, there are many noteworthy parallels between LBCI and OTV/ONTV; not least 'their symbiotic association with the centres of political power in the country' (Suleiman 2006: 131).

While Islamist parties and coalitions predictably won the overwhelming majority of seats in the 2011–12 lower house parliamentary elections, the Egyptian Bloc was still able to secure thirty-four seats (out of a total of 498), fifteen of which went to the Free Egyptians Party, while sixteen went to the SDEP. It is worth noting that while there were no explicitly Egyptian nationalist parties (in the separatist sense) in the 2011–12 elections, many parties touted 'Egyptian identity', and most of these were either secular or secular-leaning, and significantly several were formed by former National Democratic Party members from the political right.

In contrast, there were a handful of parties with explicit pan-Arab ideology (both on the left and the right, but mostly Islamist or Islamist-leaning rather than secular). However, none of these were major political players. Even the most prominent of these did not attempt to 'sell' pan-Arabism in their parliamentary campaigns. A good example is al-Karama Party, the most prominent Nasserist and pan-Arab party on the political scene. Although not itself an Islamist party, in the 2011–12 parliamentary elections, al-Karama was part of the Islamist Freedom and Justice alliance which won 47 per cent of seats in parliament. The founder of the party, Hamdeen Sabahy, joined the presidential race in 2012 and finished third in the first round with 20.7 per cent of votes (2012 Presidential Elections Official Website 2012).[1] Arguably, what attracted his large voter base was not his pan-Arab ideology (which was not a prominent part of his campaign), but his leftist, socialist orientation. Indeed, Sabahi was famously supported by the late *ʿāmmiyya* poet Abdel Rahman El-Abnoudi; what Sabahi and El-Abnoudi had in common is not pan-Arabism, but rather their leftist ideology.

This proposition about the approximate positions of pan-Arabists and Egyptian nationalists on the political map of the 2011–12 parliamentary elections is supported by the findings of Aboelezz (2014). In a web-based survey of language behaviour and attitudes conducted in 2012–13, Aboelezz asked participants to choose which statement best described Egypt's position in relation to the Arab world:

- Egypt is an integral part of the Arab world. Egypt and other Arab countries are one and the same. They have a shared identity, heritage and language.
- Egypt is part of the Arab world, but it has its unique identity and heritage. It is misleading to think of Egypt and Arab countries as the same thing.
- Egypt is very different from the Arab states. It has its unique identity, heritage and language. It is wrong to link Egypt with Arab countries since they have very little in common.

Participants were also asked about the party they had voted for in the 2011–12 parliamentary elections. The parties were then arranged along a two-dimensional ordinal spectrum for the purpose of analysis, with the Islamist parties on one end of the spectrum and liberal/secular parties on the other end. There was a highly significant relationship between participants' responses to the two questions: those who voted for parties at the liberal/secular end of the spectrum were more likely to see Egypt as different from the Arab world, while those who voted for parties at the Islamist end were more likely to see Egypt as integral to the Arab world.

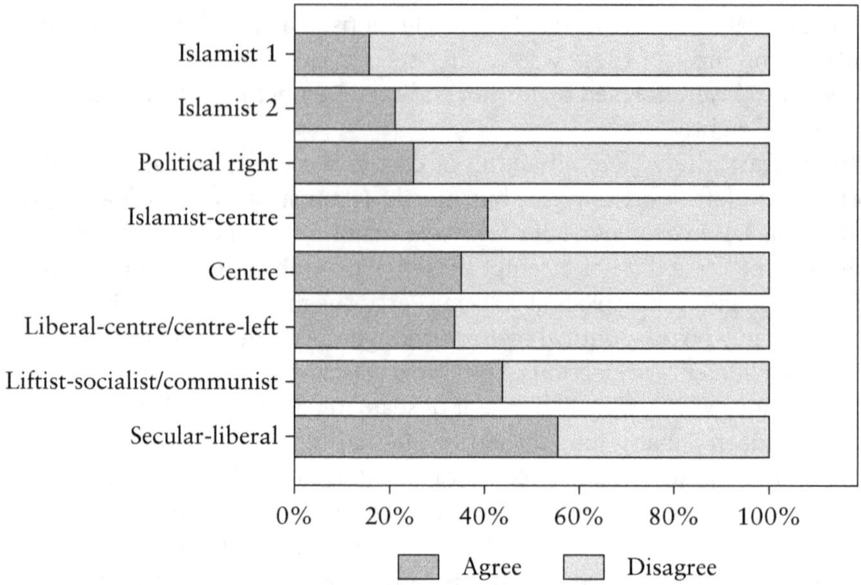

Figure 7.2 Survey participants' agreement/disagreement with the statement 'I think [WM] is a threat to the Arabic language' against the political orientation of the party they voted for in the 2011–12 parliamentary elections ($N = 295$, $Wald = 14.020$, $p = .000$) (Aboelezz 2014: 220).

Unsurprisingly, participants who saw Egypt as different and who had voted for liberal/secular parties were also significantly less likely to perceive marked uses of *ʿāmmiyya*, such as Wikipedia Masry (Figure 7.2), as a threat to the Arabic language.

It is important to return to the term 'Egyptian identity' that featured prominently in the manifestos of many political parties during the 2011–12 parliamentary elections. When interviewed in 2010, Gamal El-Din clearly situated the LEP as an extension of the Egyptian nationalist current of the early twentieth century, but he emphasised later on in the interview that the LEP was not about nationalism (*qawmiyya*) but rather Egyptian identity (*huwiyya maṣriyya*) (Aboelezz forthcoming). This is in line with the description given by Mahmoud El-Pher'oni, one of the other founding members of the LEP, in an article published in 2013 while the Muslim Brotherhood's Mohamed Morsi was still president. The lengthy article lays out the programme of the LEP which was 'rejected before the [25 January] revolution' under four main principles: Egyptian identity, political secularism, liberal democracy and a free economy. El-Pher'oni glosses the first principle as follows:

> Egyptian identity: Identity is the modern expression of nationalism – identity is a political and legal expression away from the racist chauvinism which characterises all nationalisms. Identity is comprised of two elements; belonging (*intimāʾ*) and

> benefit (*maṣlaḥa*), for there is no belonging without benefit. Belonging to Egypt means belonging to the history and culture of this fatherland regardless of origin or race. The history of Egypt is a continuous chain stretching from ancient Egyptian history through the Greek, Roman and Coptic periods to the Islamic period. We at the Liberal Egyptian Party are particularly proud of pharaonic history as the oldest civilisation in the history of mankind; serving as a basis for belonging rather than seeking its reproduction. Egyptian identity takes pride in and emphasises the heritage of tolerance and acceptance of the different Other and resists any culture which contradicts this heritage such as Wahhabism and the culture of hate and religious discrimination. Egyptian identity is the real link between Egyptians. The shared benefit of Muslims and Christians is the guarantor for the continuity of this identity regardless of the population size of either because benefit is not based on numbers. (El-Pher'oni 2013, translation)

El-Pher'oni's explanation of political secularism (*al-ʿilmāniyya al-siyāsiyya*) also deserves attention. This, he says, 'means the separation of the state apparatus from religious institutions and does not necessarily mean individual secularism'. In particular, he notes that the term secular (*ʿilmāniyyīn*) is used by the Egyptian Church in this sense. What is most notable in El-Pher'oni's article, is that it does not contain any mention of language in the party's programme (ibid.).

The term 'Egyptian identity' was frequently flaunted in the media and in political discourse following the deposal of Mohamed Morsi. Early in 2014, the annual International Cairo Book Fair was launched under the slogan 'Culture and Identity' (*al-thaqāfa wa-l-huwiyya*) in a declared attempt 'to revive Egyptian identity' (Ali 2014). Reportedly, the slogan was changed following the toppling of the Muslim Brotherhood government, which was said to have 'deprived Egypt of many elements of its identity' and 'tried to twist the Egyptian cultural traditions to serve the pure [Islamist] interests of the Brotherhood' (ibid.). The fixation on identity is hardly surprising given the successive sharp changes in how national identity was constructed at government level in the preceding few years.

Aboelezz (2014) maps these changes by comparing items related to language and identity in the 1971, 2012 and 2014 constitutions, pointing to a significant difference in how they are handled. The 1971 constitution, which was drafted at the beginning of Sadat's term in office at a time when pan-Arab feelings were high, emphasises the 'Arab' character of Egypt, but the Arabic language itself – except being named official language – does not receive further specific mention. The 2012 constitution reinforced the emphasis on Arab belonging and added numerous stipulations specifically addressing the Arabic language (which is arguably an extension of that belonging). As well as introducing African belonging (and an Asian extension), the first article of the 2012 constitution also introduced belonging to an Islamic nation. This Islamic dimension was stressed by introducing a number of other items in the constitution which lend it prominence, most notably describing al-Azhar in the preamble as having been throughout its history 'the mainstay of the nation's identity' and the 'custodian of the immortal Arabic language and the noble Islamic Shari'a'. Most of the articles dealing with language and identity introduced in the 2012 constitution were either scrapped or significantly altered in the 2014 constitution. Instead of the implied Islamic identity in the 2012 constitution, the 2014 constitution refers to 'Egyptian identity', which is defined within a new chapter on the 'cultural constituents' of Egypt and associated with diversity and pluralism, and – for the first time – incorporates Coptic and ancient Egyptian dimensions.

While the emphasis on Islamic identity in the 2012 constitution drafted under the Morsi government is expected, the emphasis on Arab identity is less so. Indeed, the attention that Arab identity receives in the 2012 constitution is unrivalled even by the constitutions drafted under Gamal Abdel Nasser at the height of pan-Arab nationalism. The most plausible explanation is that, by and large, Islamic and Arab nationalisms are not perceived as at odds with each other: 'In intellectual, if not political terms, Islamic nationalism could imperceptibly fade into pan-Arabism without subscribing to its secularism, thus underpinning the move towards the strongest expression of the [Arabic]-national identity link that is so characteristic of pan-Arabism' (Suleiman 2008: 40). Significantly, the Arabic language is an important symbol in both nationalisms. It would appear, then, that the emphasis on Arab identity in the 2012 constitution was incidental to Islamic identity, perhaps even a means of stressing the latter without being accused of religious bias.

The irrelevance of Arab identity in the 2012 constitution is supported by the findings of Aboelezz (2014), who asked survey participants to rank the identities Egyptian, Arab and their religious identity (which only appeared if they had answered this optional question earlier in the survey) based on how much they felt they belonged to each of them. Out of the rankings for Egyptian, Arab and Muslim identities in the survey, Arab was by far the most likely to be ranked last while Muslim identity was most likely to be ranked first. Moreover, while the rankings of Islamic and Egyptian identities correlated significantly with pro-*fuṣḥā* and pro-*ʿāmmiyya* language attitudes, respectively, the ranking of Arab identity was not a significant explanatory variable.

In this light, the emphasis on Egyptian identity in the 2014 constitution must be understood as a reaction to the weight that Islamic identity was given in the 2012 constitution. So, too, must the results of the 2015 parliamentary elections. With the Muslim Brotherhood, the largest Islamist political player, as well as other Islamist or Islamist-leaning parties (such as al-Wasaṭ) forced out of the political scene, the most successful party was the largest party pitching Egyptian identity, the Free Egyptians, which secured sixty-five seats (High Elections Committee 2015).[2] This lends credence to Phillips' (2014: 143–4) observations about nationalism in the Arab world following the Arab Spring, where Islam 'appears the main source of mass identity and secularist opposition is framed through national rather than Arab discourses most visibly the post-2013 surge in secular Egyptian nationalism'. In other words, if we are looking for an identity binary in Egyptian politics, then the prominent binary at present is not pan-Arabism versus Egyptian territorialism, but rather Islamic identity (which has an incidental pan-Arab element) versus Egyptian identity.

Discussion: qualifying the new wave

After surveying the evidence which demonstrates beyond doubt that Egyptian nationalism is alive and well, it is possible to sketch the features of this new wave of Egyptian nationalism, particularly how it compares with the classical Egyptian nationalism of the early twentieth century. One way in which the new wave is inseparable from its predecessor is in the revival of old nationalistic themes: glorifying ancient Egyptian civilisation; asserting that Egyptians are different from Arabs; regarding Arabs as invaders; claiming the superiority of Egyptians over Arabs; and paying special attention to the Coptic element in Egyptian history. The two waves also have two important features in common: the link to political liberalism and a clear interest in language.

Indeed, like their predecessors, new wave Egyptian nationalists used language as a proxy in expressing their nationalist views. By claiming that Egyptians have their own distinct language and that it is superior to Arabic, Egyptian nationalists are arguing that Egyptians are not only different from Arabs but are also superior to them. However, even though classical and new wave Egyptian nationalists refer to some kind of 'Egyptian Language', there is considerable variation in how they define this. While al-Sayyid called for linguistic tolerance towards *ʿāmmiyya*, he did not consider it fit for literary expression. On the other hand, Musa and Awad considered *ʿāmmiyya* to be the true language of Egyptians and claimed that it descended from Coptic. This is the view held by Andil and Gamal El-Din, but the latter goes a step further to claim that both *fuṣḥā* and *ʿāmmiyya* are Egyptian and that what Arabs speak is in fact the Egyptian Language.

Another feature that the two waves have in common is their association with Egyptian Copts. Egyptian nationalism has particular appeal to Copts for two main reasons: on the one hand, it provides an alternative means of national self-definition against Islamic and pan-Arab nationalisms (which are often conflated); on the other hand, it promotes an Egyptian identity that emphasises continuity from ancient Egyptian and Coptic civilisations, hence privileging Copts as rightful heirs of these civilisations. Central to this nationalism is the claim that *ʿāmmiyya* is a direct descendent of Coptic, bestowing symbolic importance on *ʿāmmiyya* for Copts.

Seen in this light, it becomes quite understandable that the most separatist classical Egyptian nationalists were Copts, that many of the 'Masry Wikipedians' are Copts (Panović 2010), and that an important *ʿāmmiyya* advocate who subscribes to Egyptian nationalist ideology, Naguib Sawiris, is also a Copt. Noting the role of Coptic editors in WM, Panović (2010: 100) states that this should not be underestimated: 'Members of the minorities or marginalised groups tend to be more active in the field of identity politics, more eager to look for alternatives to practices and ideologies which members of the dominant group(s) might comfortably and unreflectively adhere to.' It is also not surprising that Coptic votes in the 2011–12 parliamentary election coalesced around the secular end of the political spectrum, particularly the Egyptian Bloc (Marroushi 2012). The attractiveness of 'secular' parties to Copts can be fully understood only in the context of the 'political secularism' that El-Pher'oni (2013) defines. These parties adopting political secularism are therefore more usefully seen as the antithesis of parties representing political Islam.

One feature in which the new wave of Egyptian nationalism differs markedly from the classical wave is in the abandonment of the term 'nationalism' in favour of 'identity'. This is likely because, while the classical nationalism contended with a concrete form of nationalism (that is, pan-Arabism), the new wave corresponds to the rise of political Islam, which is more concerned with Islam as an identification frame than with unitary Islamic nationalism. The fact that *fuṣḥā* doubles as a symbol for Islamic identity as well as pan-Arabism means that *ʿāmmiyya* can still be deployed as an effective counter symbol in the new wave of Egyptian nationalism.

It is useful here to apply Suleiman's (2013) strategies in establishing the language identity link: identification, differentiation and distanciation. Addressing the role of language as proxy in identity politics, he writes:

> The ability of language to act as proxy is intimately linked to its symbolic function. Language acts in this capacity in the public sphere, especially in the political domain, because of its ability to express meanings of identification, differentiation and distanciation in inter- and intra-group situations. The fact that language does not seem to be overtly political makes it supremely suitable to express these meanings under the cover of politeness, dissimulation or as a way of escaping censorship or what is politically taboo. (Suleiman 2013: 47)

Identification is where language is constructed as a means of identifying with different groups, such as the use of Arabic as a unifying symbol in pan-Arab nationalism. Distanciation applies when 'the same language [is] constructed to designate different identities across nation-state lines' (Suleiman 2013: 30). This could be said to apply to integral Egyptian nationalists who do not subscribe to the separatist stance of territorial nationalists, but believe that Egyptians have distinctive cultural constituents, including their own version of *fuṣḥā* (cf. Aboelezz forthcoming).

Distanciation can also form the first step towards differentiation. Suleiman points out that they both 'operate within the same domain of boundary-setting, but they differ from each other in that distanciation operates in inter-group settings, while differentiation marks intra-group inflections' (2013: 40). Differentiation may be seen as the polar opposite of identification; it is when 'the same language is conceptualised in different ways to signal different inflections of identity within the boundaries of the same nation-state' (Suleiman 2013: 30). Differentiation 'aims to shift the basis for national identification from *fuṣḥā* to the colloquials of each nation-state', effectively downgrading 'the role of the existing standard language as a medium of national identification' (Suleiman 2013: 31). The claim that *ʿāmmiyya* is a completely different language that descends from a different language family to *fuṣḥā* is a clear act of differentiation aimed at differentiating Egyptians as a group from Arabs.

Differentiation relies heavily on the concept of alterity; 'pointing to the fact that it is not possible to posit identity without speaking of difference, of Otherness' (Suleiman 2013: 16–17). This may be seen in the reactionary emphasis on Egyptian identity in post-Morsi social and political discourse where this identity is more significantly defined not in terms of what it *is*, but in terms of what it is *not*. For example, the declared motives for changing the slogan of the 2014 Cairo Book Fair imply that Egyptian identity is not (predominantly) Islamist without offering alternative means of identification.

With the focus of differentiation shifting from Arabist to Islamist ideology in recent years, so too has the differentiation strategy. In their post-2011 political manifestos, 'secular' parties such as the FE and the SDEP, which have notable Egyptian nationalists in their ranks, emphasised the special character of Egypt and Egyptians but without any mention of promoting *ʿāmmiyya* or adopting the 'Egyptian Language'. Given that such calls are likely to put off many potential voters, dropping language from the agenda is undoubtedly a calculated move intended to ensure wider public appeal.

A similar differentiation strategy is exemplified in withdrawing or downplaying articles relating to the Arabic language in the 2014 constitution which were introduced in the 2012 constitution under the Muslim Brotherhood government. This removal of emphasis may still be regarded as differentiation through language proxification as it effectively downgrades the existing standard language as a medium of national identification. The current Egyptian government is clearly keen to distance itself from the ideology of its Islamist predecessors. What is interesting here is that this government belongs to the (traditionally linguistically conservative) political right, which has long upheld a standard language ideology championing *fuṣḥā*. By applying the concept of alterity to distance itself from Islamist ideology and shifting the emphasis to Egyptian identity, the current government is potentially signalling a shift in language ideology as well; that is, as the 2014 constitution indicates, it is difficult to reject an ideology without rejecting its symbols.

If the post-Nasser period has provided the conditions conducive to a political atmosphere that tolerates a new wave of Egyptian nationalism, then the post-Morsi period has boosted it to the forefront of Egyptian politics. The eagerness at the official and public levels to counter the Islamist ideology of the Muslim Brotherhood has resulted in embracing the rhetoric of Egyptian nationalism. Another factor that has aided the revival of Egyptian nationalism is technology, which Egyptian nationalists were deploying effectively even before the 2011 uprising. Wikipedia Masry is a case in point: defying official marginalisation, nationalist parties were able to disseminate their ideology to a wider audience on the web. Today, not only is Egyptian nationalism enjoying support from an extension of the same regime that had censored it for many decades, it arguably has greater popular appeal than at any other point in its history.

Conclusion

Throughout this chapter I have argued that, contrary to popular belief, territorial Egyptian nationalism was not supplanted by pan-Arabism. Evidence suggests that Egyptian nationalist sentiments were brewing from the 1980s onwards, giving rise to a new wave of Egyptian nationalism that has been exponentially growing since the turn of the century, culminating in great political gains in recent years owing to the post-Muslim Brotherhood political atmosphere which has favoured Egyptian nationalism as an alternative identity frame. The new wave of Egyptian nationalism shares many characteristics with classical Egyptian nationalism, but differs in that it contends more clearly with Islamic identity than with pan-Arab nationalism. It also enjoys farther reach due to the communicative power of technology. Language is still an important symbol of new wave Egyptian nationalism, but political parties with a nationalist underpinning have been adopting alternative differentiation strategies, consistently dropping language from the agenda in an apparent bid for wider popular appeal.

Notes

1. Hamdeen Sabahy also ran in the 2014 presidential elections, but withdrew before voting closed.
2. The Social Democratic Egyptian Party, which the LEP had assimilated into, only won four seats (compared with sixteen in 2011–12). Many of its former members had joined the FE party. It is worth noting that 325 parliamentary seats were occupied by independent candidates in the 2015 elections.

References

Works in Arabic

Al-Sayyid, Ahmad L., *Al-Muntakhabāt* (Cairo: Dār al-Maʿārif, 1937).

Andil, B., *Ḥāḍir al-Thaqāfa fī Miṣr*, 4th edn (Cairo: n.p., 2008).

Awad, L., *Plutoland, wa-Qaṣāʾid min Shiʿr al-Khāṣa*, 2nd edn (Cairo: Al-Hayʾa al-Miṣriyya al-ʿāmma li-l-Kitāb, [1947] 1989).

Awad, L., *Muqadimma fī Fiqh al-Luga al-ʿarabiyya* (Cairo: Ruʾya, [1981] 2006).

El-Pher'oni, Mahmoud 'Barnāmaj al-Ḥizb al-Miṣrī al-Librālī alladhī Rufiḍ Qabl al-Thawra': *Al-Hewar*, available at: http://www.ahewar.org/debat/show.art.asp?aid=340496, last accessed 10 January 2016.

Gamal El-Din, Abdel Aziz, *Ḥawl Taṭawwurāt Lughatinā al-Miṣriyya al-Muʿāṣira* (Cairo: Manshūrāt Miṣriyya naḥw Thaqāfa Waṭaniyya Dīmuqrāṭiyya, 2011).

Husayn, T., *Mustaqbal al-Thaqāfa fī Miṣr* (Cairo: Dār al-Maʿārif, [1937] 1996).

Musa, S., *al-Balāgha al-ʿaṣriyya wa-l-Lugha al-ʿarabiyya* (Cairo: Kalimāt ʿarabiyya li-l-Tarjama wa-l-Nashr, [1945] 2012).

Musa, S., *al-Adab li-l-Shaʿb* (Cairo: Hindawi Foundation for Education and Culture, [1956] 2013).

Shaker, Mahmoud M., *Abāṭīl wa-Asimār* (Cairo: Maktabat al-Khānjī, 1972).

Works in English

Aboelezz, M., 'Deconstructing diglossia: language ideology and change in revolutionary Egypt (2010–2014)', PhD thesis, Department of Linguistics and English Language, Lancaster University, 2014.

Aboelezz, M., 'The politics of pro-ʿāmmiyya language ideology in Egypt', in Jacob Høigilt and Gunvor Mejdell (eds), *Writing Change: The Politics of Written Language in the Arab World* (Leiden: Brill, forthcoming).

Al Batal, M., 'Identity and language tension in Lebanon: the Arabic of local news at LBCI', in Aleya Rouchdy (ed.), *Language Contact and Language Conflict in Arabic: Variations on a Sociolinguistic Theme* (London: Routledge Curzon, 2002), pp. 91–115.

Ali, I., 'Cairo Book Fair aims to revive Egyptian identity', *Al-Monitor*, 23 January 2014, available at: http://www.al-monitor.com/pulse/culture/2014/01/cairo-book-fair-egypt-identity.html, last accessed 5 April 2014.

Bassiouney, R., *Arabic Sociolinguistics* (Edinburgh: Edinburgh University Press, 2009).

Bassiouney, R., *Language and Identity in Modern Egypt* (Edinburgh: Edinburgh University Press, 2014).

Brugman, J., *An Introduction to the History of Modern Arabic Literature in Egypt* (Leiden: Brill, 1984).

Chejne, A., *The Arabic Language: Its Role in History* (Minneapolis, MN: University of Minnesota Press, 1969).
Darwish, A., 'The surge in Egyptian nationalism', *Middle East*, October 2007, pp. 22–5.
Doss, M., 'Ḥāl Id-dunyā: An Arabic news bulletin in colloquial (ʿāmmiyya)', in Reem Bassiouney (ed.), *Arabic and the Media: Linguistic Analyses and Applications* (Leiden: Brill, 2010), pp. 123–40.
Gemeinder, S., '"We're not Arabs – we're Egyptians": the struggle for identity in Egypt', Paper presented in *Ninth Mediterranean Research Meeting*, Florence & Montecatini Terme, 25–8 March 2009.
Gramsci, A., *Selections from Cultural Writings*, trans. W. Boelhower (London: Lawrence & Wishart, 1985).
Haeri, N., 'The reproduction of symbolic capital: language, state and class in Egypt', *Current Anthropology* 38(5) (1997): 795–816.
Hourani, A., *Arabic Thought in the Liberal Age 1798–1939* (Cambridge: Cambridge University Press, 1962).
Jabr, Fadel K., 'The children of Gilgamesh: A half century of modern Iraqi poetry', *Metamorphoses* (Spring/Autumn 2011): 341–76.
Marroushi, N., 'Egypt's Copts voice fear and optimism', *The Daily Star Lebanon*, 2012, available at: http://www.dailystar.com.lb/News/Middle-East/2012/Jan-06/159029-egypts-copts-voice-fear-and-optimism.ashx#axzz3DI4MTOFL, last accessed 6 January 2012.
Mazen, M., 'New party touts Egyptian nationalism', *Daily News Egypt*, 14 August 2006.
Panović, I., 'The beginnings of Wikipedia Masry', *Al-Logha: Series of Papers in Linguistics* 8 (2010): 93–127.
Phillips, C., 'The Arabism debate and the Arab uprisings', *Mediterranean Politics* 19(1) (2014): 141–4.
Suleiman, Y., 'Language and identity in Egyptian nationalism', in Yasir Suleiman (ed.), *Language and Identity in the Middle East and North Africa* (Richmond: Curzon, 1996), pp. 25–38.
Suleiman, Y., *The Arabic Language and National Identity: A Study in Ideology* (Edinburgh: Edinburgh University Press, 2003).
Suleiman, Y., 'Charting the nation: Arabic and the politics of identity', *Annual Review of Applied Linguistics* 26 (2006): 125–48.
Suleiman, Y., 'Egypt: From Egyptian to pan-Arab nationalism', in Andrew Simpson (ed.), *Language and National Identity in Africa* (Oxford: Oxford University Press, 2008), pp. 27–43.
Suleiman, Y., *Arabic in the Fray: Language Ideology and Cultural Politics* (Edinburgh: Edinburgh University Press, 2013).
Versteegh, K., *The Arabic Language* (Edinburgh: Edinburgh University Press, 2001).

Online sources

2012 Presidential Elections Official Website, 'al-Natā'ij al-Nihā'iyya li-l-Marḥala al-Ūlā 2012', available at: http://pres2012.elections.eg/index.php/round1-results, last accessed 1 September 2014.

High Elections Committee, 'Mulakhkhaṣ Taqrīr al-Intikhābāt al-Tashrīʿiyya', Majlis al-Nuwwāb, 2015, available at: https://www.elections.eg/images/pdfs/reports/2015HoR-ReportSummary_Ar.pdf .

CHAPTER 8

Rakākah and the Petit Quarrel of 1871: Christian Authors and the Competition over Arabic

Rana Issa

The trouble with Arabic

In 1871, Arab intellectuals – who by this time had risen to canonical status in Arab literary modernity – were engaged in a fierce linguistic battle over the correct modes of expression of Arabic. The main protagonists were the aging Aḥmad Fāris al-Shidyāq (1804–87) versus the young Ibrāhīm al-Yāzijī (1847–1906), and their arguments revolved around issues of 'correct' writing style: the orthography of a few words, what was acceptable rhyme and metaphor, and vowel placement according to the rules of Arabic grammar. In short, they argued about whether they suffered from a *rakākah* or solecism in their use of language. By the third exchange, the name of Buṭrus al-Bustānī (1819–83) had been dragged into the fray as he had permitted the publication of al-Yāzijī's articles against al-Shidyāq in his weekly *al-Jinān*. Known for his sharp tongue, al-Shidyāq lashed out, and accused al-Yāzijī and al-Bustānī of being ignorant users of Arabic, which was befitting of '*naṣārā Beirut*', or the Christians of Beirut. The quarrel began when al-Shidyāq published a eulogy for Nāṣīf that the son, Ibrāhīm, found distasteful. It is hard to tell to what degree this exchange was motivated by personal grudges, but it certainly expressed the invisible ideological stakes in language that emerged in the second half of the nineteenth century.[1] This was not the first time the men competed, nor was it the first time clear winners could be discerned.

This quarrel was a rhetorical demonstration of long-lasting language practices initiated by al-Bustānī and al-Shidyāq at the beginning of their careers when they were working with Anglophone missionaries. Al-Shidyāq commenced his scholarship under the patronage of British evangelists in Malta and Cambridge, while al-Bustānī worked with American evangelists in Beirut. In 1857 and 1860, their competing translations of the Arabic Bible were published. Ibrāhīm al-Yāzijī was the son of Nāṣīf al-Yāzijī (1800–71), another key literary figure of the period. Naṣīf assisted al-Bustānī with his translation for several years before he was replaced by a friend of al-Shidyāq's, the Muslim Azharī sheikh Yūsuf al-Asīr (1815–89). Ibrāhīm would also work with the Jesuits on a Bible translation (1877) a few years after the quarrel. Later on in their lives, those translators of the Bible came to occupy a distinguished status in Arabic cultural life, and played a foundational role in turning Beirut into one of the metropoles of textual modernity (Issa 2012; Grafton 2016). Despite their diverging positions on language use, all of them were the main scholars behind the standard language ideology that would shape the next 150 years of Arabic cultural production. This chapter examines their altercations in order to compare their understanding of *rakākah*. As I show, *rakākah* emerged as a conceptual device that enabled Syro-Lebanese Christians to legitimise their contributions to the revered sciences of language to enact two gestures. First, they distanced themselves from their Christian literary predecessors; and, second, they reformulated the relationship between religion and language that had paradigmatically shaped classical Arabic philology until the nineteenth century.

The linguistic turn and the national imagination

The transformation in Arabic philological sciences took place in a marketplace that differed from the earlier period in that it was increasingly globalised. The cultural marketplace of globalisation moved beyond the localised forms of centralised patronage and control, and into what the Indian globalisation studies sociologist, Arjun Appadurai (1996) has called the 'technoscapes' of global cultural production. Those technoscapes relied on mechanical and informational technologies in order to facilitate the accelerated production and dissemination of knowledge and other commodities. In the colonies, those technoscapes depended on the introduction of printing press technologies, as well as on other technologies of international communication, such as an international postal system, as well as new means of transportation.[2] Beirut was such a technoscape, but so was a standardised Arabic expression. In the context of globalisation, Standard Arabic became a vehicular tool that had the power to unify markets and facilitate speedy economic and political as well as cultural transactions (Sheehi 2012: 295). In addition to the speedy transactions that standardisation facilitated, language tallied the imagination of communities within one national grammar and one preferred lexicon. The emergence of language as a technoscape was prevalent across the nineteenth-century world.[3] From Mandarin to Hindi, Swahili to Turkish, Hebrew, and even English, languages in the nineteenth century became vehicles for the construction of national identities.[4] This linguistic turn mediated the global mechanism that vernacularised globalisation and assimilated it to the ecology of local societies.

Like other languages, Arabic in the nineteenth century was produced through the tandem reliance on technological advancements in steam-powered printing press technologies. Also like other cultures, Arabic culture became interested in a mythological approach to a far-away past that severed from memory and interest the immediate past. For the Arab literates, this tendency to repress the immediate past crystallised in describing it as *inḥiṭāṭ*, or decline (also translated as decadence, decay, etc.), that must be overcome by recollecting the glorified, presumed modernity of an Abbasid cultural past (Suleiman 2003). *Fuṣḥa* facilitated the rupture as well as activated the mythology. Proclaimed to be the style of the ancients, it transformed the variant styles of the immediate past into bad Arabic, written by people who were near illiterate. *Rakākah* thus emerged as the stylistic underbelly of *fuṣḥa*, and its function was to complete the rupture with the immediate past. The discourse on *rakākah* was typical of Christian authors who deployed the concept in order to distance themselves from their Christian predecessors.

In the nineteenth century, *rakākah* became a mark of Christian Arabic writing, at a time when Christians were enjoying mainstream access to the Arabic republic of letters. The historical changes in the status of Christians, as well as their improved access to the literary sphere, produced changes in their attitudes towards Arabic. The 1871 debate between key Syro-Lebanese intellectuals who were born to learned Catholic families reveals how *rakākah* was the result of an evolution in access to the literary sphere, which was consequent on larger political and economic transformations. As children, these men received a similar kind of scribal education, and they even lived in the same neighbourhood on the outskirts of Beirut. As they carved their own careers and broke away from the missionaries, their paths diverged, and they came to exercise their authorial profession in different geographical locations and under tutelage from different (and competing) political and economic establishments. Working directly with the Ottomans produced a different context and worldview than working directly with Western missionaries. In some aspects through their understanding of *rakākah* we can discern how those competing worldviews were mediated. One approach to the question of *rakākah* was associated with al-Shidyāq, who at the time was under financial protection from Istanbul. In his view of *rakākah*, he singled out lexical rigour in the selection of words. The other position was exemplified by al-Bustānī, who had earned rich foreign friends during his long years of service with the missionaries as well as in his work as dragoman at the American consulate in Beirut. Al-Bustānī was interested in promoting an Arabic that exercised grammatical rigour. Whereas lexical rigour demands idiosyncratic precision, grammatical conformity requires mathematical agreement to a prescribed style. In the difference between the two definitions, two approaches to error also competed, and both these approaches were connected to how Christian-born authors envisioned their position in a language that prides itself on being the holy language of the Qurʾān.

In his book, *The Arabic Language and National Identity* (2003), Yasir Suleiman connects the medieval interest of Arabic grammarians in the question of solecism, or *laḥn*, to illustrate how linguistic arguments are historically deployed to regulate access to the literary sphere. As he remarks, *laḥn* was historically used as a marker of foreign origins among speakers. Suleiman observes that in the *nahḍa*, as in the Abbasid period, solecism revealed the foreign identity of its speaker. And in the anti-Turkish context of the 1870s that he explores, he shows how the move towards standardisation carried with it ideas about who was a real Arab and who was a Turk. As he explains, for the Abbasids, solecism set boundaries between the in-group and the out-group. As he writes:

> What is significant about these reports [on *laḥn*] is that they locate – in a boundary-setting manner ... the source of solecism outside the community of original Arabic-speakers, attributing it to the linguistic contact which the military successes in early Islam brought about. (Suleiman 2003)

Suleiman draws a historical parallel in his book that shows how solecism was used against Turks, but also to show how Arabic diglossia emerged in this period as a confirmation of Christian belonging and investment in the political stakes of an emerging pan-national identity. My argument is slightly different, and focuses on the internal dynamics between Arabic writers whose linguistic arguments concealed their political differences in the relationship with the Ottomans. Similar to the historical position of *laḥn* as a political concept, *rakākah* also carried the marks of its political context, yet, unlike *laḥn*, it became the marker of a historical transformation that beset a religious group as it ascended from the margins of Arabic letters to become a major arbiter and canon builder of Arabic.

With the arrival of the missionaries to Beirut in the 1830s, and in the context of sweeping political and economic transformations, this first generation of *nahḍa* writers transitioned from being scribes in the employ of Ottoman governors and local emirs, to become intellectuals: cultural entrepreneurs who made a living out of writing original works in Arabic.[5] The move from local Ottoman patrons to foreign Western ones opened new literary markets and networks for them and introduced them to new vistas of literary and textual practices. The multinational economic power of the missionaries was one channel to be exploited, but so was Egyptian occupation of Beirut and, later on, the more explicit forms of French colonial interest, not to mention the continued (if weakened) presence of official Ottoman rule (Hanssen 2005). These diverse and competing forms of patronage were one aspect of literary production. The other aspect was the positioning of philological labour vis-à-vis the long philological tradition that Arabic letters enjoyed.

Even if only obliquely, for a native Christian to become an Arabic philologist in the nineteenth century, he had to position himself in relation to a debate that started between the Asharites and the Mutazila in the ninth century about the holiness of Arabic as the language of the Qurʾān. The works of al-Shidyāq, al-Bustānī and al-Yāzijī in philology, lexicology, grammar and literature reveal different resolutions of this problematic and propose different understandings of what it meant to be modern Arabic writers who had inherited a language and a tradition that is historically tied to Islam.[6] On the surface of the arguments they produced about language, in the 1871 debate and elsewhere, and the differences about weak style and *rakākah* were highly nuanced and hair-splittingly close at times. Yet, as I claim, they also show different treatments to the question of the relationship between religion and language, and between modern Arabic and the rising forms of sectarianism that culminated in the 1860 massacres of Christians in Mount Lebanon, Damascus and Aleppo.

Rakākah and the Christian *nahḍawis*

In the early modern era, *rakākah* did not preoccupy the Christians. In that period, the high literary style of *fuṣḥa* existed in adjacency to permissive styles of linguistic variation. Known to sociolinguists as Middle Arabic, variants of normative Arabic were prevalent among all sects in sixteenth- and seventeenth-century Levant (Blau 1966, 2002; Samir 1982; Lentin 1997, 2012a, 2012b: 32–52). Sociolinguists show a pattern of variation that is more widespread among religious minorities than among Muslim writers, but also show that Muslim writers, even those famous for their high eloquence, sometimes indulged in the use of this style. Christian literature, and other minority literature was more dependent on this style, as sociolinguists claim. One possible reason is that minorities depend on translation as a central activity in the production of their textual canons, and their treatment of Arabic is usually dependent on the historical role translation plays in a particular era. Thus, we find that in the Abbasid period, Christians produced religious literature that attained a high level of stylistic normativity. We also find that translators were less interested in domesticating their texts to Arabic (Griffith 2013).

Also in the early modern period, Christian texts (that is, texts that have a religious value for Christians) fluctuated between the styles. Such is the case in the eclectic style used by the authoritative Roman translation of the Bible in 1671 known as *Biblia Sacra Arabica*. In the introduction, the translators state that:

> In this copy, you will find utterances that are not in concord, and even contradictory to the rules of Arabic language [*al-lughah al-ʿarabiyyah*]: male gender instead of female, single numeral instead of plural, plural instead of dual . . . the reason for this was the naiveté of the speech of Christians [*kalām al-masīḥiyīn*] which became a kind of language to them.[7]

This assertion to write in a *naïve* style, which as the translators claim, marks the speech of Christians, must be understood in the context of the millet system that was installed following the Ottoman annexation of the Levant from the Mamluks (Masters 2001).[8] According to this system, the minorities were left to be governed by their own churches, as long as they paid their taxes to the Ottoman government. In exchange, Istanbul allowed them to live in peace and to administer their affairs according to their own internal laws. In a way, the linguistic attitude towards Arabic that is expressed in the introduction to the *Biblia Sacra Arabica* embodies this separation, for it is consequent on the group's sense that it administers its own codes and rules, in language as in other aspects of life.

In the *nahḍa*, this nonchalant attitude towards Arabic changed.[9] Whereas in 1671, Rome asserted Christian Arabic as a *religiolect*; in the nineteenth century, Christian Arabs were not interested in being marked through their use of variant speech.[10] This transformation could be discerned in the entire generation of early *nahḍawis*, and it had started as early as the first missionary textbooks that were translated or authored by those Christian writers. The *nahḍa* standard style fit the *nahḍawi* interest in refashioning a group belonging that transcends sectarian signifiers, not because the *nahḍawis* were necessarily secular, but because by using an Arabic stripped of sectarian markers, they could service their ambition to become canonical judges of the *kalām* of Arabs.[11]

Also by choosing literary forms that were widely respected among Muslims, texts produced and disseminated at the speed of print had the opportunity to travel quickly and in large numbers. A new Standard Arabic symbolised this industrialisation of the book-making tradition. Like print, Standard Arabic provided vehicular reach and was economically efficient. The economic efficiency was one of the reasons that the American missionary who initiated the famous translation of the Bible (1865), Eli Smith, chose the standard style for his translation of the Bible. As he wrote to his superiors in Boston:

> the work is designed for a race, only a small portion of which are Christians; and consequently, are on our guard in reference to the many words which are current among Christians, in a meaning not sanctioned by Mohammedan usage, lest by using them we convey a wrong idea to a Mohammedan mind. (Van Dyck and Smith 1900)

Expecting that the Muslims would also want to read the new translation of the Bible, Smith preferred from the outset to conform to a style this majority would appreciate. Al-Bustānī, who worked with Smith on the translation, also preferred to use the standard style. He was not only motivated by economic efficiency, but went further than Smith to underscore the political importance of the standard. He specified that the lexicon ought to be trimmed, and rid of archaic words, but that the grammar ought to be preserved to maintain transhistorical textual continuity. Arabic had to ensure that it does not become a dead language like Latin. 'We cannot imagine a bigger loss for the Arabs than this one,' he wrote. By trimming the lexicon from archaic words and concepts, al-Bustānī preserved the grammar because he saw a danger in breeding future readers who were unable to read the classical texts. This would turn Arabic into 'the language of the learned class and the owners of inquisition [*ʾṣḥāb al-taftīsh*]' (Bustānī [1859] 1981: 98). Al-Bustānī had Islam in mind in his parallel with the courts of the Inquisition, and grammar ensured the continued lay access to the most foundational Scriptures and texts. By giving authoritative remedies to the fate of Arabic grammar and lexicography, al-Bustānī widened philological participation to also include Christians. As a cultural mediator, al-Bustānī envisioned his role as a corrector of an epidemic *rakākah*, which was a sign of social 'decadence' and a weakness that would end up with Islamic inquisitions. The people are illiterate; they had only read the Psalms or the Qurʾān and some stories from folkloric literature. The elite were especially to blame for this illiteracy, for even among them 'we hardly ever find someone we can point out with the finger and say he knows his language or its grammar sufficiently' (Bustānī [1859] 1981: 106). With his pulse on grammar use, al-Bustānī charted out what came to be the great interest of generations of *nahḍa* intellectuals whose prescriptive attitude promoted the need to adhere to classical rules of grammar and succeeded in turning *fuṣḥa* into the hegemonic writing style for published texts.

Arabic was not only in danger of losing its connections with its grammar, its lexicon was in danger of being replaced by Western concepts. In his famous '*Khuṭba fī 'ādāb al-'arab*'(1859), which al-Bustānī's delivered one year before the outbreak of the 1860 massacres, he warned that borrowing from Western expression into the Arabic language was tantamount to 'killing the mother tongue'. He toned down the intensity of his proclamation with some humour, which nevertheless insists that code-switching between foreign languages and Arabic is detrimental to the health of the nation. What was needed was curative linguists that would:

> Administer enough opium to *komisiūn* and *al-sikurteh* and *skūzi* and *afandim* and the like so that it swoons with no hope of ever awakening, and then put a flacon of ammonia by the nose of *'amāla, ḍamāna,* and *lā twākhithnī* and *ya sīdī* and other such Arabic words that signify the required meanings so that Arabic awakens from its stupor. (Bustānī [1859] 1981: 97)

After the outbreak of war, in a series of pamphlets known as *Nafīr Sūriyya* (*Clarion of Syria*), al-Bustānī lost his earlier humour, but went on to emphasise the urgent need to provide adequate language instruction to raise the nation from its barbarity, for language, as he wrote, fosters 'bonds of unity and concord'. He demanded that his countrymen learn from the missionaries and sustain an effort in perfecting their language. As he wrote:

> The missionaries are in agreement that the sons of the nation must be taught in the language of the lands, that is, in Arabic, because this benefits the language and makes the educated more useful and protective of their country and more accepted by their brethren. As for those who claimed that it was not possible to become civilised under the banner of Arabic, perhaps they underestimated its usefulness/effectiveness and did not understand that civilising the Arabic language, rather than the Arabs themselves, would be easier and more effective. Otherwise the destiny of Syria would be a Babel of languages as well as a Babel of religions. (Al-Bustānī [1860] 1990: 60)

Today, scholars remember al-Bustānī for his deep-seated commitment to the cause of secularism in his homeland, but in his own words, this commitment was mediated through linguistic attentions (Abu-Manneh 1980: 287–304; Sheehi 2004; Hanssen 2005; Makdisi 2008). And, indeed, his engagement in linguistics reveals a more complex story. In his encyclopedic contributions to Arabic philology, particularly in his dictionary *Muḥīṭ al-Muḥīṭ*, the question of religion in political identity was resolved through a reformulation of the words that must enter a modern lexicon. In this work, al-Bustānī showed an interest in making linguistic room for Christian expression and culture in the lexicon. The final product was a general dictionary of the language that strategically shifted and adjusted in the etymological information of key Arabic words. Through etymology, al-Bustānī made space for the biblical Levantine languages as adjacent and sometimes more important for lexical precision than the Arabic of the Qurʾān, and its desert origins – origins that continue to be so important to the foundational myth of the Arabic language (Suleiman 2003; Issa 2017: 465–84).

At the time, despite his proclamations of national obligations, his linguistic work was vigorously critiqued by al-Shidyāq for being unable to resolve the problem of religious hegemony over language.[12] In 1871, al-Shidyāq belittled his adversaries by pronouncing them mere translators from the West who hid their lack of original thought with a series of empty signifiers. 'Most of those Arab Christians that learned *ifranjī* (Western) languages started thinking that Arabic is a follower of those languages.' So they calque Western expressions and pen ambiguous constructions that 'cannot be considered speech but are an assortment of word sequence' (Shiblī 1950: 153). Al-Shidyāq emphasised the Christian identity of his interlocutors, and repeated what, by now, had become a stereotype that Christian Arabs were weak in the rules of normative Arabic. His blunt expression of the religious identity of the Beiruti intellectuals brings to the fore the context of sectarian hostilities that structured the 1871 exchange, a decade after the outbreak of civil war in Lebanon. Accusing them of harbouring Christian political loyalties, al-Shidyāq was implicitly also claiming that their loyalties were not the traditional local ones that linked them to Istanbul, but that they were more loyal to Westerners who were threatening Ottoman interests. Put in the terms of the argument in this chapter, this linking of linguistic acumen to sectarian belonging shows that by 1871, language emerged as a site for the formation as well as contestation of national identity.

In 1860, al-Shidyāq converted to Islam in Tunis before he moved on to a new life in Istanbul.[13] That did not mean that he became a practising Muslim, and I have argued elsewhere that his critical stance to major theologians and texts in the Islamic tradition undermines any attempt at understanding his conversion in terms of piety. Rather, al-Shidyāq's conversion was motivated by a deep dedication to the long scholarly tradition of philology and *kalām* that defines major epochs of philosophical and literary pursuit among the Arabs. In his linguistic work, he sought to separate the science of language from the science of religion, and repeatedly claimed and demonstrated the human origins, as well as historically changing dynamics of language.

Like the other writers of the period, he viewed work in the linguistic and literary fields as a contribution to public good, but for him the first task of this good is in the alleviation of the boredom of the readers. The entertaining aspect of writing also made him defend an interest in error as the indisputable mark of individuality and humanness. His corpus of works is dotted with recollections of an Arabic philological tradition that is dedicated to the defence of error, for its entertaining and instructive value (Issa forthcoming). As he wrote in *al-Sāq ʿala l-sāq*, 'few books on the oddities of language are completely without errors . . . the author confesses his shortcomings, confessions erase commission, and none is perfect but God alone, from whom we ask forgiveness and aid' (al-Shidyāq 2013: vol.1, 19). Error was not the same as *rakākah* for him. In his works, he often attacked the style prevalent among Christian writers for what he claimed to be a notorious *rakākah* that plagued most of their writings. According to him, the Christians preferred convoluted expression to simple, clear ideas. His satirical style, which al-Yāzijī would eventually suffer was acerbic. And in *Sāq* he directed his satire at various Christian writers who fell short of a good turn of phrase. Such is his lampoon against the Christian style that he associated with one of his native colleagues that he knew in Malta and London:

> It had become an established fact to them that the books of the Christian religion should be written in as feeble and corrupt a style as possible, because 'the power of religion requires it, so that everything be of one piece', as stated by the Arabic-language-challenged, Feed-sack-carrying, Sweet-meat-chasing, Marrow-slurping, Rag-sucking, Bone-gnawing, Finger-licking, Half-a-morsel-biting, Cauldron-watching, Drippings-drinking, Bottom of the pot scraping, Scourings-scarfing, Leftovers-off-polishing, Dinner-sponging Allepine Metropolitan Atanāsiyūs al-Tutūnjī in a work of his called *Al-Ḥakākah fī al-rakākah (The Leavings Pile Concerning Lame Style)*. (al-Shidyāq 2013: vol.2, 69)

Al-Shidyāq's caricaturist effect makes a rigorous lexical point through the use of a carefully selected glossary that focused on the eating style of the patriarch. For al-Shidyāq, his adversary suffered from a typical Christian style steeped in a *rakākah* of ideas, of *ʿujmah*, brought about by a penchant for obscure and long-winded language use.[14] The difficulty of the words is not what is at stake for al-Shidyāq, for he is legendary in his recollections of the most forgotten lexical curiosities. Rather, it was the penchant for imprecision in language use that he detected in writers he attacked, and he claimed that Christian authors were more prone to such garbled speech than Muslims. Even for a secularist writer like him, al-Shidyāq, like his adversaries, succumbed to the easy reductions of political problems such as sectarianism and nationalism to the lure of linguistically loaded questions. The context of sectarianism giving way to linguistic problems is obvious in the 1871 debate. The interlocutors were all denouncing their *rakākah* as one way to legitimise their labour as authoritative defenders of the classical language of the Arabs. Only al-Yāzijī was somehow different, for he was younger. Belonging to the second generation of Christian philologists, al-Yāzijī had the easier task of positioning himself not against tradition, but vis-à-vis those two towering figures. By initiating this quarrel with al-Shidyāq, al-Yāzijī acted with the new sense of entitlement that Christian Arabs felt in discussing issues of a philological and linguistic nature.[15]

The Petit Quarrel of 1871

The debate began when al-Yāzijī decided to respond to al-Shidyāq's critical eulogy of his father Nāṣīf. The decision also positioned him in continuation with al-Bustānī's grammatical vision at the level of praxis. Through his corrective methodology, al-Yāzijī underlined the importance of a microscopic attention to grammar. By accusing al-Shidyāq of *rakākah*, al-Yāzijī revealed what would become a lifetime project of correcting mistakes in language use in the work of others. The assumption that structured al-Yāzijī's corrective approach to intellectual labour rested on the idea that the people were 'decadent' and untrustworthy. Their speech had to be corrected in order to preserve the political and civilisational interests of the nation. With national fervour as an alibi, and starting with al-Shidyāq, he held a proverbial red pen and went through the work of his contemporaries with an eye for error. His most famous corrections were published in his newspapers *al-Ḍiyāʾ* and *al-Ṭabīb*, as well as two books that corrected what he claimed to be common errors in the use of Arabic. As he wrote in the first of six articles published in *al-Ḍiyāʾ* (1898):

> Apparently, our writers are too proud to abandon their habits of *rakākah* and error, just like their compatriots in the rest of the country who are now accustomed to error in manufacture, agriculture, the upbringing of children, treating sickness,

> for it is difficult for a human to deal with the unfamiliar . . . We saw enough *taḥrīf, laḥn, w al-ṣiyagh al-ʿāmiyyah, w l-ʾaʿjamiyyah* [deviation, solecisms, colloquialism, and foreign phrases] to worry about the deep roots of linguistic corruption, which will be impossible to fix. (Al-Yāzijī 1984: 11)

But he tried, throughout his career, to fix the 'corruptions' of language. When he targeted al-Shidyāq, he argued that the older author made light of his national responsibilities in his linguistic works. Al-Yāzijī flagged problems of vowelisation, alliteration, colloquialism and examples from European languages in al-Shidyāq's linguistic works, particularly in *Sirr al-Layāl fi al-Qalb wa l-ʾibdāl*, but also in *al-Sāq ʿala al-sāq*. For him, al-Shidyāq's use of the language was unacceptable for an elite writer his size. He wrote:

> I saw in *Sirr al-Layāl* many quotes from the speech of common people to the extent that almost none of his material is free of it. Likewise, he quotes from French, English and other foreign languages to the extent that one can say his book is largely foreign [*ʾaʿjamī*]. Not to mention [*nāhīk*] it is of no use to the Arabs! God forgive him. Lest I belittle the standing of this book and detract from the author's pride, I would have pointed that he sometimes mentions words from Maltese. Is all this of wide service and astonishing knowledge. (Shiblī 1950: 98)

Al-Yāziji's critique of *Sirr* hoped to delegitimise al-Shidyāq in his most significant contribution to Arabic linguistics. In this book, al-Shidyāq charted out, in a large and well-researched volume, a theoretical paradigm for a new lexicon in Arabic.[16] However, al-Yāzijī did not discuss al-Shidyāq's concrete ideas about the origins of human language, which are at the crux of al-Shidyāq's strategic inclusion of many of the details that al-Yāzijī faulted. By flagging perceived grammatical error rather than discussing linguistic ideas, al-Yāzijī deployed a mystified understanding of grammar as the supreme art of Arabic rhetoric.

Al-Yāzijī believed he was defending the honour of his father from a perceived offence in the eulogy that was the cause of this quarrel. Yet when al-Shidyāq returned the petty favour, al-Yāzijī refused to accept a treatment in kind. His corrective ideology was entrenched in power differentials and the ambition to become a linguistic apostle who decreed and judged as if in a court of law. Al-Yāzijī's corrective ideology of language would ultimately prevail in a fast-changing political climate that eventually became anti-Turkish (Suleiman 2003). At the time of this debate, al-Shidyāq, who was under tutelage in Istanbul, was more favourable to the Ottomans than his adversaries. Linguistically though, despite his ill-manners and his politically incorrect slurs, he represented an alternative linguistic model to follow that was less prescriptive and more alert to the dynamics of language change across history. Typical of al-Shidyāq's approach to the language was the eulogy that he wrote for Nāṣīf and that irked the son. In this eulogy, al-Shidyāq started with a reference to another eulogy written by Selim Dyab and published in the Beiruti newspaper *al-Jinān* that al-Shiyāq was good friends with the deceased. This reference suggests that al-Shidyāq would not have written a eulogy at all had his name not been mentioned in Beirut as a friend of Nāṣīf's. As he wrote, they had been friends since their youth, and they exchanged many letters and poems. He also stated that Nāṣīf had written a panegyric for al-Shidyāq which he did not publicly dedicate to him when the poem was eventually published in Nassif's *Dīwān*. Al-Shidyāq mentions that he thinks the neglect of the dedication was 'strange'. After this embarrassing prologue, he took the occasion to comment on the insidiousness of colloquialism that breaks into any speech, no matter how eloquent. As an example, he quotes two words that were used erroneously by Nāṣīf in two different poems. The word *faṭḥal*, rendered by Nāṣīf as *faḥṭal*. This last work is as ancient (and as out of use) as the meaning that it denotes. Al-Shidyāq defines it as the time before the creation of humanity, or the time of Noah. It surely could not have been the term that Nāṣīf had in mind. Because of colloquialism, Nāṣīf confused it with the Beiruti word he intended, which means 'an experienced man', or virile. The other word he mentioned in his eulogy was *marābiḍ*, for stables, when in fact the word denoted the place for sheep and was confused with *marābiṭ*, literally the place where the horses are tied.

To make his jabs at the deceased palatable, al-Shidyāq categorised this type of mistake as *wahm*, or illusion, which is a kind of mistake that 'no one can escape . . . and it is a habit of poets when they distort a word that they repeatedly use it . . . and the sheikh [Nāṣīf] was carved on poetry without convolution or arbitrariness or ostentation' (Shiblī 1950: 64). Al-Shidyāq's coyness remained within the limits of politeness, or so he thought. But then the son attacked him and questioned his linguistic philosophies. In response, al-Shidyāq defended the value of his style by pointing out (with extensive quotes from the classical canon of Arab philologists) that the ancients often quoted dialectical usage and renditions in their treatises, and that foreign-language examples are also extensive in the canon. He then moved on to accuse his adversary of *rakākah*, because he preferred to argue the details of language use instead of discussing linguistic ideas. The *rakākah* was lexical and it was evident in the imprecise use of terms for the expression of meaning, for as he wrote 'words are but the content that relate to the form' (Al-Shidyāq 2013: vol. 2, 111). This structural truth he claimed had escaped the Christians who confused ambiguous wording with eloquence.

He then moved on to attack al-Yāzijī's publisher, al-Bustānī, whom he claimed also exhibited the telltale signs of Christian *rakākah*. As he wrote, al-Bustānī's weekly *al-Jinān* was known for its *rakākah*, which is why the Egyptian intellectuals were not reading it (Shiblī 1950: 169). This newspaper, as he wrote, was 'populated with words that do not signify a full meaning, and lead nowhere. It is charged with phrases that are not Arabic or foreign, even if the words were

Arabic' (ibid.: 147–51). As he contended, by attacking him *al-Jinān* was legitimising the positions of its intellectuals and not their ideas, as if they say to the people of Beirut '[we are] your supreme leaders'(ibid.: 221). But he did not end it there, and went further to equate between this convoluted style and the desire to subvert Ottoman rule. According to him, his adversaries were known to make their style so ambiguous that subversive anti-Turkish messages would go undetected by the censor. 'Perhaps [al-Bustānī] thinks no one reads his newspaper for its *rakākah* and *sakhāfah* [triviality] so he made a vocation out of taking stabs at the government in a kind of linguistic code, rampant with symbolisms that reveal his thoughts: and if he dismisses my claims I would extract thousands of examples' (ibid.: 145). In this allegation that the ambiguity of *rakākah* could be used to transmit subversive political ideas, al-Shidyāq placed the political responsibility of intellectual pursuit on the relation an author constructs between the signifier and the signified. He also demanded that the Ottoman censor investigate his enemies for sedition.

The nationalist turn that al-Shidyāq accused his adversaries of possessing was indeed prevalent in their writings, even if calling it anti-Ottoman, especially in the case of al-Bustānī, is not entirely accurate. In the service of this nationalism, Arabic was promoted as a global vernacular, corrected against comparisons with what other nations were doing. Through demanding an elevated linguistic style that would lift the nation from its stupor, those authors promoted a conception of the *nahḍa* as a site of rupture from a decayed and immediate past full of Christian *rakākah* not worthy of preservation or remembrance. Al-Shidyāq too linked public good with language, but, unlike his adversaries, his national fervours were dramatically more demure. Despite their divergent choices and conceptions of the links between language and national progress, al-Bustānī and al-Shidyāq were founding figures who set the scene for the kind of linguistic concerns that would interest subsequent generations of native Arabists.

Conclusion

The consequence of those divergent attitudes towards Arabic was a shared commitment to a standard language. Yet the origins of the quarrel delineate two different approaches to error, and two competing ideologies of Standard Arabic. Those two linguistic views clashed over issues of authorial licence, respect for grammar and lexicon, and intellectual imperfection in the pursuit of meaning. The consequent polemical tone of the rivals differed on what kind of error was permissible and what was *rakākah*. Whereas for al-Shidyāq error was part of the creative process, and thus had its place among the other literary matters a critic could discuss and historicise through recourse to tradition, for al-Yāzijī and his teacher, error of this kind cheapened an author's text, a *rakākah*.

The obsession with *rakākah* reproduced itself in subsequent writings by *nahḍa* authors; in al-Yāzijī's later work, but also in the writings of other authors in Egypt, Lebanon and Damascus. In the years following this debate, the reproduction of the concept of *rakākah* mostly reproduced one definition and chastised one type of error. A classic example was Salīm Shamʿūn's publication of al-Yāzijī's corrections of al-Bustānī's errors in his lexicon *Muḥīṭ al-muḥīṭ*. Salīm Shamʿūn, who was the grandson of al-Yāzijī, and the son of Warda, Ibrahim's daughter, explained that 'we found that al-Yāzijī had left comments and symbols in the margins of his books, and he left many of them in Muḥīṭ al-Muḥīṭ' (Salim Shamʿun and Gibrān al-Naḥḥās 1970: 2). The marginal notes inspired their collection into a single volume, and so he took up the task of deciphering the author's cyphers. Shamʿūn's promotion of al-Yāzijī's notes on the margins of an important lexicon as '*tanbīhāt*', or cautionary notices – as serious critique – reveals how discursively powerful the obsession with correctiveness would become. In the meantime, al-Shidyāq's idea that permits human error could have taken root, but with time his playfulness in his approach to the standard language remained rather lonesome and has tended to lose detail.

Notes

1. The quarrel was collated by Anṭōnius Shiblī,in *Al-Shidyāq Wa Al-Yāzijī*, collection of articles, p. 159.
2. For the introduction of the printing press in the Syria mission, see Auji (2016).
3. Suleiman made a similar argument by relying on the comparative method and by quoting secondary literature from English and French. I suggest here a structural approach that positions this chapter as a contribution to the study of globalisation. See Suleiman (2014).
4. Studies that have examined the connection between language and ideology are many. See Fabian (1986); Bourdieu and Thompson (1991: 46–9); Liu (2004: 181–209).
5. The move into modern authorial work began with al-Shidyāq's publication of his novel, *Leg over Leg*, in 1855.
6. The social precepts of the religious question continue to occupy historians; however, outside Yasir Suleiman's work on language and sociology in the Middle East, the function of language as a marker of sectarian identity is not adequately studied. On the former theme, see, for example, Makdisi (2008); on conversion, see Deringil (2013); on the latter, see Suleiman (2004).
7. 'Introduction', *Biblia Sacra Arabica*, Rome, 1671, 5.
8. The political context is yet to be studied in connection with the language ideology that emerged then, particularly in the active endorsement of Middle Arabic as a permissible writing style in some genres.

9. On the transformation from the millet system to modern sectarianism, see Makdisi (2003); Traboulsi (2012). On al-Bustani's contentious relationship with the missioanries, see Makdisi (2008).
10. In contrast to the early modern period, the sectarian violence in this period emerged in parallel with the Christian preference for *fuṣḥā*. For more on the modernity of sectarianism, see Makdisi (2003).
11. The American missionary Cornelius Van Dyck embodied this dedication and became the most eloquent American writer of Arabic in this period. For a recent short biography that includes some of his texts, see Grafton (2016).
12. In his critique of Arabic lexicology, al-Shidyāq singles out al-Bustānī's main lexical source, al-Fayrūzabādī's *al-Qamūs al-muhīt* for critique on this point specifically. This was not an arbitrary choice and, to a large measure was to do with al- Bustānī's reliance on this text. See Issa (forthcoming).
13. For al-Shidyāq's Islam, see Issa (forthcoming).
14. Tutūnjī (d.1874) also worked for a time with the missionaries as a translator, and was in London at the same time as al-Shidyāq.
15. In the classical period, whereas Christians were often mainstream contributors to poetic literature, derivative discourses such as philology and linguistics were generally the purview of Muslim scholars, who were sometimes also trained as theologians.
16 Al-Shidyāq did not live long enough to work on a lexicon himself. But the linguist Abdallah al-ʿAlāylī let himself be inspired and began to produce a *Shidyaāqian* lexicon that was eventually interrupted for lack funds, see Al-ʿAlāylī (1954).

References

Al-ʿAlāylī Abdallah. *Al-Muʿjam: Mawsūʿah Lughawiyyah ʿilmiyyah faniyyah* (Beirut: Dar al-Jadīd, 1954).

Al-Bustānī, Buṭrus, *Nafīr Suriyya*, ed. Yusuf Quzmā al-Khoury (Beirut: Dār Fikr, [1860] 1990).

al-Shidyāq, Aḥmad Fāris. *Leg over Leg. Or the Turtle in the Tree: Concerning the Fāriyāq, What Manner of Creature Might He Be*, vols 1 and 2 (New York: New York University Press, 2013).

Al-Yāzijī, Ibrahim, *Lughat al-jarāʾid*, ed. Naẓīr ʿAbbūd (Beirut: Dar Marun Abboud, 1984).

Abu-Manneh Butrus. 'The Christians between Ottomanism and Syrian nationalism: The ideas of Butrus Al-Bustani', *International Journal of Middle East Studies* (May 1980): 287–304.

Appadurai, Arjun, *Modernity at Large: Cultural Dimensions of Globalization* (Minneapolis, MN: University of Minnesota Press, 1996).

Auji, Hala, *Printing Arab Modernity* (Leiden: Brill, 2016).

Blau, Joshua, *A Handbook of Early Middle Arabic*. (Jerusalem: Hebrew University of Jerusalem, 2002).

Blau, Joshua, *A Grammar of Christian Arabic: Based Mainly on South-Palestinian Texts from the First Millennium* (Secrétariat du Corpus SCO: Louvain, 1966).

Bourdieu, Pierre and Thompson, John B., *Language and Symbolic Power*, Ce que parler veut dire l'économie des échanges linguistiques (Cambridge: Polity Press, 1991).

Bustānī, Butrus, 'Khuṭbah fī ʾādāb Al-ʿarab', in *Al-Muʿallim Buṭrus al-Bustānī: Dirāsat wa waṯāʾiq*, ed. Jean Dayeh (Beirut: Majalat Fikr, [1859] 1981), pp. 81–112.

Deringil, Selim, *Conversion and Apostasy in the Late Ottoman Empire* (Cambridge: Cambridge University Press, 2013).

Van Dyck, Cornelius and Smith, Eli, 'Brief documentary history of the translations of the Scriptures into the Arabic language', ed. American Presbyterian Mission Press (Beirut: American Mission Press, 1900).

Fabian, Johannes, *Language and Colonial Power: The Appropriation of Swahili in the Former Belgian Congo, 1880–1938* (Cambridge: Cambridge University Press, 1986).

Grafton, David D., *The Contested Origins of the 1865 Arabic Bible: Contributions to the Nineteenth Century Nahḍa*, History of Christian–Muslim Relations, vol. 26 (Leiden: Brill, 2016).

Griffith, Sidney, *The Bible in Arabic: The Scriptures of the People of the Book in the Language of Islam* (Princeton, NJ: Princeton University Press, 2013).

Hanssen, Jens, *Fin de Siecle Beirut: The Making of an Ottoman Provincial Town* (Oxford: Oxford University Press, 2005).

Issa, Rana, 'The fallibility of tradition in Al-Shidyāq: The case of Islam' (forthcoming).

Issa, Rana, 'The Arabic language and Syro-Lebanese national identity: Searching in Buṭrus al-Bustānī's *Muḥīṭ Al-Muḥīṭ*', *Journal of Semitic Studies* 63(2) (2017): 465–84.

Issa, Rana, 'Biblical reflections in the Arabic lexicon', *Babylon Nordisk Tidsskrift for Midtøstenstudier* 2(10) (2012): 58–67.

Lentin, Jerome, 'Recherches sur l'histoire de la langue au Proche-Orient à l'époque Moderne', dissertation, University of Paris III, 1997.

Lentin, Jerome. 'Middle Arabic', in Rudolf de Jong Lutz Edzard (ed.), *Encyclopedia of Arabic Language and Linguistics* (Leiden: Brill Online, 2012a).

Lentin, Jerome, 'Reflections on Middle Arabic', in Gunvor Mejdell and Lutz Edzard (eds), *High vs Low and Mixed Variety Status: Norms and Functions across Time and Language* (Wiesbaden: Harrassovitz, 2012b), pp. 32–52.

Liu, Lydia H., *The Clash of Empires: The Invention of China in Modern World Making* (Cambridge, MA: Harvard University Press, 2004).

Makdisi, Ussama, *The Culture of Sectarianism: Community, History, and Violence in Nineteenth-Century Ottoman Lebanon* (Oakland, CA: EScholarship, California Digital Library, 2003).
Makdisi, Ussama, *Artillery of Heaven: American Missionaries and the Failed Conversion of the Middle East* (Ithaca, NY: Cornell University Press, 2008).
Masters, Bruce, *Christians and Jews in the Ottoman Arab World: The Roots of Sectarianism* (Cambridge: Cambridge University Press, 2001).
Samir, Khalil Samir, *Actes du premier congres international d'etudes Arabes Chretiennes*, vol. 218 (Rome: Pontificium institutum Orientalium studiorum, 198).
Shamʿun, Salim and al-Naḥḥās, Gibrān, *Tanbīhāt al-Yāzijī ʿalá Muḥīṭ al-Bustānī, Bāb 1* ([S. l.]: [s. n.], 1970).
Sheehi, Stephen, *Foundations of Modern Arab Identity* (Miami, FL: Univeristy of Florida, 2004).
Sheehi, Stephen, 'Towards a critical theory of al-Nahḍah: Epistemology, ideology and capital', *Journal of Arabic Literature* 43(2/3) (2012): 269–98.
Shiblī, Anṭōnius (ed.), *Al-Shidyāq wa al-Yāzijī: Munāqashah ʿilmiyyah ʾadabiyyah 1871* (Jounieh: Maṭbaʿah al-mursalīn al-lubnāniyyīn, 1950).
Suleiman, Yasir, *The Arabic Language and National Identity: A Study in Ideology* (Washington, DC: Georgetown University Press, 2003).
Suleiman, Yasir, *A War of Words* (Cambridge: Cambridge University Press' 2004).
Suleiman, Yasir, 'Arab(ic) language anxiety: Tracing a "Condition"', *'Arabiyya: Journal of the American Association of Teachers of Arabic* 47 (2014): 57–81.
Traboulsi, Fawwaz, *A History of Modern Lebanon* (London: Pluto Press, 2012).

CHAPTER 9

Orchestrating Multimodal Protest and Subverting Banal Nationalism in the Linguistic Landscape of the Tunisian Revolution[1]

Sonia Shiri

Introduction

During the second half of December 2010, Tunisians started to mobilise in solidarity with a young southern street vendor who self-immolated in protest against youth unemployment and economic hardship. More and more protesters joined in the mass demonstrations that spread around the country and took a political turn when they reached the capital, Tunis, leading to the departure of their president of twenty-three years by mid-January. These events kicked off what became known as the 'Arab Spring' and shortly after that the 'Occupy' movement in the United States. Protest signs were displayed, especially during the last weeks of this period, exploiting the diglossic and multilingual repertoire of the protesters and effectively co-constructing dissent in the transient and ephemeral linguistic landscapes of the demonstrations (Shiri 2015). However, protest signs were not the only means by which protesters expressed their discontent and caught the attention of the authorities, their fellow citizens and of the world. In fact, protest signs were few compared with the number of signs typically displayed at protests in Europe and the United States, for instance. As the video footage and still images from that period show, protesters effectively combined other semiotic resources in conjunction with protest signs to collectively construct the linguistic/semiotic landscapes that simultaneously expressed and shaped their dissenting messages. This study uses a multimodal approach to examine the Tunisian demonstration of 14 January 2011 and the way protesters exploited a variety of peaceful multimodal strategies, including street theatricality and commonly used national symbols, or 'banal nationalism' (Billig 1995), in order to subvert the linguistic/semiotic landscape of the capital city and effect political change. The study focuses particularly on this critical demonstration because it led to the flight of Tunisia's president, Ben Ali.

Background: street protests

The Tunisian street protests that occurred between 17 December 2010 and 14 January 2011, were performed in public spaces such as the main avenue of a city or town, the square or other space in front of government buildings or labour union offices. Protests were typically performed on the streets for short periods of time before being engulfed then dispersed by police. Many protestors clashed with police when trying to cross police blockades when marching from an initial assembly point to a designated destination. Protesters often re-assembled later to be dispersed again. The mass demonstration in Tunis on 14 January 2011 was by far the biggest and was among the few that lasted long enough for thousands of protesters to assemble and express themselves, deploying all their multilingual and multimodal resources. It is images from this demonstration that reached world media the most, perhaps also because it culminated in the departure of the president that same day.

Participants in mass protests were unarmed civilians. When clashes occurred with armed police in the provinces and disadvantaged suburbs of cities, some protesters hailed stones upon police cars. Police stations were burned after civilians were killed and injured and others were arrested. Approximately 260–300 citizens were killed, while hundreds more were injured within that twenty-eight-day period of unrest. Protests spread gradually from the periphery to the centre. They started with a small sit-in in front of the governor's office in the southern town of Sidi Bouzid in reaction to the self-immolation of the young street vendor, Mohamed Bouazizi, in the middle of the street on 17 December 2010, following a wave of protest suicides or suicide attempts among Tunisian youth (Mabrouk 2011). As news of the suicide and video footage of its aftermath spread, mass demonstrations gradually sprang up in the neighbouring towns in the central and southern provinces, leading to the death of unarmed civilians and the injuring of others at the hands of the security forces. A wave of protests started on 25 December in the capital city, Tunis, and in northern provinces in solidarity with the demands of the youth of the centre and the south and in protest against the violent treatment of civilians. As more civilians were killed and injured in the following days, more Tunisians came out on to the streets, culminating in the ousting of the president on 14 January 2011 and his sudden departure to Saudi Arabia. The majority of protesters during this period were initially younger and mostly male, but a stronger presence of older generations and women was visible on 14 January and in the wave of protests against the interim government that ensued.

It is believed that the mass demonstrations were spontaneous and decentralised. No leaders were identified and no particular political ideology, religious or otherwise, appeared to govern the direction of the uprising. The movement appeared to be driven by the general discontent with high unemployment rates among youth in particular, dissatisfaction with the prevalent level of corruption, and the concentration of the country's resources in the hands of the president's family. Discontent with the curbing of freedoms such as freedom of expression and access to information were also widespread, thus affecting all socioeconomic classes including the upper middle class and the business elite.

Labour unions and civil society representatives such as lawyers and human rights activists along with others such as actors and artists joined in. As news of the protests and violence against civilians spread through video footage and images captured with phone cameras and posted on social media, unprecedented numbers of protesters poured onto the streets. Updates about the events were posted both on dedicated blogs and social media pages and were shared widely reaching greater numbers of citizens around the country, contradicting the government version of events broadcast on official media outlets.

As an Arabic-speaking country, Tunisia is diglossic and therefore uses Standard Arabic, the language of literacy and religion, alongside vernacular Tunisian Arabic. The colonial language, French, remains widely used despite the growing popularity of English, especially among the younger generation. Despite this rich linguistic repertoire that supports the country's long-standing tradition of cultural openness, dissent had been silenced by decades of heavy-handed state control and censorship of journalistic, literary or other forms of expression. When it came to new media, discrepancies in treatment arose. Facebook grew in popularity at percentages akin to those of Europe and Latin America and exceeded by far countries in the Middle East and Africa. YouTube, on the other hand, was considered dangerous because of its potential to spread anti-government propaganda and remained banned until 13 January 2011, when during his final speech as president, Ben Ali lifted the ban in an effort to show openness to civil liberties and freedom of expression. Arts and sports were encouraged by the government, leading to the spread of seasonal music and other festivals as well as soccer clubs throughout the country. While public assembly for subversive purposes was heavily suppressed, artistic and sports events remained sanctioned venues for large crowds to gather for entertainment purposes. Similarly, Facebook was perceived as a form of entertainment and hence remained accessible, opening access for connecting large networks of individuals.

Linguistic landscapes and the study of mass protests

Research within the emerging, interdisciplinary field of linguistic landscapes (LL) initially investigated commercial and road signage in public spaces as a means of understanding language vitality in multicultural and multilinguistic environments (Landry and Bourhis 1997). The field was further expanded through Scollon and Scollon's (2003) development of 'geosemiotics' and Jaworski and Thurlow's (2010) approach to 'semiotic landscapes' that include signs and other semiotic forms that go beyond the written text. LL further illuminated multilingualism by also focusing, for instance, on language policy and minority language studies in a variety of contexts (for example, Backhaus 2006, 2007; Gorter 2006, 2013; Frekko, 2009; Shohamy and Gorter 2009; Shohamy, Ben Rafael and Barni 2010; Stroud and Mpendukana 2009; Lado 2011; Gorter, Marten and Van Mensel 2012). Interest in the role of LL, and graffiti in particular, in shaping social change and urban development, rather than merely reflecting it, further expanded the boundaries of the field (Nwoye 1993; Dragićević-Šešić 2001; Pennycook 2009, 2010; Hanauer 2011; Papen 2012; Rubdy and Ben Said 2015).

Attention has just started to turn to even more transient linguistic landscapes characterised by conflict and dissent, such as those constructed during recent mass demonstrations from movements in different parts of the world. Rubdy and Ben Said's (2015) edited volume contains four studies addressing this particular LL context, including two studies involving Arab countries by Messekher and by Shiri. In the same volume, Hanauer investigated demonstrations from the 2011 Occupy movement in Baltimore. Hanauer examined the multimodal representational genres used in the demonstration to convey a public message, the political functions of these genres, and political messages of the movement and the manner in which they interacted with broader discursive positions within society. He found that a multitude of genres were deployed, turning the encampment site into 'a very large interactive political message board' and reflecting the 'bottom-up, public and participatory nature of the political messages themselves' (2015: 215) that give voice to the '99% of the population' who believed themselves to be unfairly treated, politically and economically, by a system that favoured the '1%' (ibid.: 220). Hanauer concluded that 'the construction of participation through different acts of public literacy was the actual message of the Occupy Baltimore site' (ibid.: 221). Seals' study in the same volume, for its part, explored demonstrations in Montreal and Auckland as well as the National Immigration Reform March of 2010. It revealed that the dialogic nature of the protest messages and the multimodal discourses injected in the linguistic landscape of these mass demonstrations helped protesters to combat erasure, gain visibility in the public space and become part of the landscape.

Shiri's and Messekher's studies in the Rubdy and Ben Said (2015) volume focus on mass demonstrations from the movement that was later called the 'Arab Spring' in the neighbouring North African countries of Tunisia and Algeria, starting in late 2010. Shiri (2015) examines the themes addressed and the discourse strategies employed on the written protest signs during the four-week period of unrest that started in December, led to the ousting of the president, and set in motion mass demonstrations in most other Arab countries and beyond. The study uncovers a move away from the initial compliance with the official signage policy that dictated the use of Arabic on signs, to a strategic exploitation of the multilingual linguistic repertoire that included French and English, reflecting in the process the protesters' evolving socio-political concerns and aspirations. The written signs also intertextually referenced previous movements, dialogically engaged with the president's economic and political agenda, and interpellated local and international audiences. A similar reliance on the multilingual linguistic repertoire was observed in Messekher's study of the linguistic landscape of the 2011–12 protests in Algiers. In addition to Arabic, she noted the use of the stigmatised former colonial language, French, and the use of the marginalised indigenous language, Tamazight, reflecting a conflict between the declared language policy and the actual language practices, and potentially signalling a power struggle between the users of the different languages. Other studies focusing on protest signage remain rare. A comparative study conducted by Ben Said and Kasanga (2016) examined the discourse of mobile, or 'non-fixed', protest signs from Tunisia, Egypt and the Democratic Republic of Congo focusing on frames of identity, intertextuality and interdiscursivity. Using a critical discourse analysis perspective, Al Masaeed (2013) explored the Egyptian slogans that developed in early 2011 and were in circulation during the mass demonstrations against the regime and the president.

Research on signage in Arab countries remains rather limited overall, however; not only research on the ephemeral, subversive kind associated with protests. Ben Said (2010, 2011) offered one of the few studies fully dedicated to street signage in LL in an Arab country. He revealed discrepancies between the development of official government policies and their implementation or rejection by the public in bottom-up linguistic representations in the LL in the capital Tunis and in a nearly suburb. In investigating the relationship between LL, identity and modernity, Suleiman (2011) surveyed studies that focused on the use of foreign or Western names in commercial signs in a number of Arab countries, revealing a propensity to 'ascribe the use of foreign names to the inferiority complex in Arab society towards the West', and the false belief that the use of these names enhances their status among their peers (2011: 214). Questioning the degree to which such views are representative of the ordinary speakers' attitudes, Suleiman wondered whether the anxiety about the use of foreign names in signs had a grassroots dimension or whether it was an elite phenomenon enacted by the 'culture guardians who use language as a proxy to protest the traditional values of society in the face of the forces of modernization and globalization' (ibid.: 217). Focusing on signage in Egypt, Starrett (1995) examined the pervasive use of religious signs on monuments in public spaces in urban centres. Starrett argued that monumental writing actually outdid broadcast media in contributing to message saturation and in making God omnipresent throughout public spaces in Egypt.

It is noticeable that despite the rapid development and the international scope that the LL field has witnessed, the study of LL in Arab countries in general and in mass demonstrations in particular remains in need of further exploration. Likewise, so far, only a limited number of studies of the LL of the region or studies of LL at large have investigated the multimodal nature of protests (Hanauer 2012, 2015; Messekher 2015).

The present study tries to tackle these research gaps by examining the interplay between the various types of multimodal meaning-making resources deployed during the mass demonstration of 14 January and the days leading up to it, and the political messages and movement they served. In addition, the study investigates the way these forms of expression in this counter-power, citizen-led, transient linguistic landscape connect with banal nationalism in society.

Data collection and analysis

Photographs of protests were collected from a variety of print and online sources documenting the 14 January 2011 mass demonstration. These sources include international Arabic-, French- and English-speaking media as well as Tunisian media and Facebook pages dedicated to the revolution. Media outlets and social media were extensively searched for photographs of the protest using keywords in Arabic, French and English. A total of twenty-seven articles containing forty-four photographs of the protest were examined. Several components of the protests seemed to have attracted attention and were featured in more than one photograph. These elements were treated as separate artefacts only if new combinations were detected within the photographs.

As previously noted in my study focusing on written protest signs (Shiri 2015), collecting data for this transient, ephemeral and now eternally lost LL of mass demonstrations is challenging for a number of reasons. The photographs that constitute the data sets are dependent on the perspective of the photographer, and their public existence has depended on the decision of the media or social media editor to publish them. The subjectivity of the author and editor will thus remain interposed or interjected between the data and the researcher. Moreover, the scenes depicted were dynamic and fluid because of the constant motion of the crowds and therefore the constant reconstruction of scenes from the protest. They were also short-lived and impossible to reconstruct because they disappeared forever with the end of the protest. The data set representing this transient linguistic/semiotic landscape is in itself an amalgam of partial representations of the event at best and may therefore be considered a construct in its own right. Despite these shortcomings, the data sets managed to document a wide array of rich, albeit not exhaustive, citizen-driven forms of creative and effective multimodal forms of protest.

Multimodality

Multimodality is a theory of communication that is concerned not merely with language, written or spoken, but with other modes such as gesture, gaze, colour, font choice, other visual modes and interactions between them (Kress and Van Leeuwen, 2001; Kress 2009). This approach has recently gained relevance because of the increase in technology tools and their use allowing for easy combinations of multiple modes of communication in daily interaction and expression. Furthermore, people orchestrate meaning through mode choice and configuration of interaction between modes. The interests and motivations operating in interactions within social contexts affect meaning-making beyond the established norms for the use of an individual mode. 'Modes are semiotic resources which allow the simultaneous realisation of discourses and types of (inter) action' (Kress and Van Leeuwen 2001: 21–2). Modes, 'the material resources which are involved in making meaning' (Kress 2010: 105), are socially shaped over time in order to gain their meaning making capacity. According to Page (2006: 6), a mode is 'a system of choices used to communicate meaning. What might count as a mode is an open-ended set, ranging across a number of systems including, but not limited to, language, image, colour, typography, music, voice quality, dress, gesture, spatial resources, perfume and cuisine. Modes are assembled and configured according to the interest of the meaning-maker during the process of design: 'In the process of *representation* sign makers remake concepts and "knowledge" in a constant new shaping of the cultural resources for dealing with the social world' (Kress 2010: 62, original emphasis).

In addition to written signs, examined in Shiri (2015), a plethora of other modes were employed and combined to express and co-construct dissent in the transient semiotic landscape of the Tunis mass protest of 14 January 2011. The following sections survey the most salient ways in which protesters orchestrate various semiotic resources in order to multimodally construct and disseminate their message of discontent and rebellion. All along, protesters seemed to be aware of the media and social media gaze embodied in other protesters' or attendees' potential role as chroniclers and disseminators of the event, and the importance of the visual dimension of this communicative context where being seen is of ultimate value and significance.

Multimodal protest signs

An examination of the written protest signs reveals that they were themselves multimodal to varying degrees. They were multimodal in the limited sense in that they used different fonts or different ink colours to represent the written word (Kress 2003; van Leeuwen 2006). The ink colour red was used extensively, for instance, possibly to denote the importance and urgency of the message, on the one hand, and to symbolise or evoke the colour of blood when accusing the president of being a killer, on the other. When selected as the background colour of the paper on which the signs were inscribed, it might have been emulating the colour of the (red) background of the Tunisian flag.

Signs were also multimodally constructed by combining symbols with words on the protest signs not merely for effect, but also possibly for succinctness. By emulating a street sign superposed on the president's name transcribed in Roman letters, a protest sign seemed to 'ban' Ben Ali in the same way it would have banned fishing or loitering. Capitalising on the brevity yet eloquence of the message as well as its widely recognisable symbol, the sign was thus intended to communicate with local and international audiences alike. The combination of text and symbol can make the message of the text even more poignant. Moreover, it can also make the overall meaning of the sign much more heteroglossic (Bakhtin 1981), bearing multiple meanings at the same time, some of which are derived from historical uses or from uses in other social contexts. The image of an imprinted bloody hand on a second sign that demanded a trial for Ben Ali in Arabic text, is an example of this multiplicity of meaning. First, it acts as a symbolic explanation for the demand to topple the president; he is believed to be implicated in the killing of unarmed civilians by directly ordering those killings. Second, it acts as an analogy that further incriminates the president by connecting him to the French 'Main Rouge' ('Red Hand') movement that assassinated nationalist leaders and trade unionists during Tunisia's struggle for liberation from France in the first half of the twentieth century. By analogy, the symbol is saying that Ben Ali is as ruthless as the oppressive former colonial power was over sixty years before, and, consequently, that he is not the patriot or protector of Tunisia that he purports to be. The unionist undertones of the symbol also resonate with the demands for jobs witnessed in the text of other signs (Shiri 2015).

Protest signs were also combined with symbols outside of themselves, either by their own carrier or and from within their vicinity, as will be discussed below.

Orchestration and ensembles of meaning

Multimodal expression in the context of the Tunis protest relied on pre-existing signs and symbols, as well as newly formulated symbols and combinations thereof. The combination or 'orchestration' of multiple modes into 'ensembles', to use Kress' (2010) terms, is of particular relevance in this highly dynamic and unstable context of communication where the semiotic landscape is in constant movement and re-configuration. As Kress (2010: 162) expounds, 'orchestration and ensembles are entirely related yet distinct; the former names the process of assembling/organising/designing a plurality of signs in different modes into a particular configuration to form a coherent arrangement; the latter names the results of these processes of design and orchestration'.

One of the most salient orchestrations of citizen dissent during the Tunisian revolution was the very act of assembling. This typically meant occupying and/or marching on non-pedestrian spaces such as streets or squares, unauthorised by the state, for a purpose other than attending a sports event, a concert or a social procession such as a funeral or a wedding, for instance. Illegally assembled crowds typically attracted and eventually clashed with large numbers of security forces that tried to restrict their mobility or access to certain public spaces. The mere fact of assembling, especially when combined with chanted slogans, speeches or protest signs, seemed to attract authorities whose response was to show up to control and disperse the protesters (Shiri 2015). On many occasions, this encounter and the ensuing contestation over public space escalated into violence, leading to deaths among unarmed civilians. Within the illegally assembled masses, carrying protest signs and chanting slogans, crowds orchestrated more multimodal ensembles to construct and unequivocally express their counter-hegemonic discourse. These fell into three main categories, drawing on modes such as attire/appearance, theatrical performance of group movement or *tableaux vivants*, subverted symbols of banal nationalism and combinations thereof.

Symbolic attire

Prior to 14 January, protests held by journalists, lawyers and doctors, all of whom belong to unionised professions, were reported in the capital as well as in other parts of the country in the case of lawyers. While journalists looked indistinguishable from regular citizens as they demanded freedom of expression, doctors and lawyers chose to wear their distinct work attire or 'uniforms' during the protests. Doctors wore white coats while lawyers wore black gowns with white ties. Lawyers were particularly visible in the protest data in different parts of the country. While doctors and healthcare professionals protested the civilian deaths and injuries that they treated as first responders after the security forces opened fire on civilians, lawyers protested human rights violations and demanded a free legal system. By choosing to wear their judicial gowns, the lawyers used the authority bestowed upon them by the legal system and that their uniform represented to counter the authority of the intimidating uniform of the police. The culturally and socially recognised authority of judicial dress is a power statement that typically commands respect and perhaps even intimidation in most citizens. In this context, it was used to lend credibility and legality to the messages of dissent that lawyers voiced along with the rest of the population. It might also be conversely used to indicate solidarity and levelling with the plight of the people, and was thus expressing the profession's humility in its service to the people, especially when combined with the patriotism associated with raising the flag, as some lawyers were observed to do. Perhaps it was also hoped that the reverence granted the legal gown would serve as a form of shield from the violence or intimidation that they might otherwise risk suffering at the hands of the police.

At the 14 January demonstration, a group of lawyers dressed up in full legal gear were seen congregating on and around a raised platform a step above other demonstrators, with police forces behind them guarding the Ministry of the Interior. A female and a male lawyer are seen, centred, in two different photographs. In the first image, the female lawyer is waving a large Tunisian flag above her head. In the second image, she is still holding the flag but lower, while the male lawyer is displaying high up a sign written in French ordering the president to leave in capital Roman letters, 'DEGAGE'. Although it is not possible to judge which of the actions depicted in the images came first, the semiotic interplay in this multimodal ensemble that they paint is infinitely rich and complex in meaning. While the patriotic raising of the re-appropriated flag and the repudiatory protest sign were foregrounded and received primacy through centring and the depiction of movement, their counter-hegemonic message derived strength from the authority of the judicial gown in its solidarity with the people, the pulpit-like raised platform enforcing the entitlement to speak for and represent the people, and the tension in the background between the sea of illegally assembled people and the thin rows of anti-riot police wrapped around the government building. The alternating focus between the male and female in judicial dress, although perhaps purely a result of the semiotic affordances of the event, added a secondary layer of meaning. It emphasised women's and men's equal support for the uprising, while also acting as a reminder of the importance of gender equality issues in Tunisia, women's visibility in society and their right to hold positions of power, including legal power. This stands in contrast to some other Arab countries where women are not allowed to act as judges, for instance.

Although the image of the Che Guevara lookalike, in beret and beard, brandishing up high a small flag as he shouts in unison with protesters raising their fists in his vicinity pales in front of the authoritative visuals of the lawyers' gowns, its revolutionary and leftist undertones earned it the attention of the camera. The image of this fully engaged Tunisian Che marching a step ahead of a man wrapped in the flag is in a dialogic relationship with, and in total rejection of, media-imagined and constructed images of a fanatical, Muslim Arab world that is 'irrational' and intent on curbing already limited freedoms. Che's beret and beard, symbolising the survival of the revolutionary, secular Tunisian left that had remained oppressed since the 1970s, inspired and later re-appeared in photographic representations from other countries such as Algeria that actively protested against their regimes in the following months.

Tableaux vivants

Choreographed group movements which other protesters could spontaneously join constituted another meaning-making resource during this major protest.

Apart from the marching, chanting, dispersing and re-assembling that characterised group behaviour in all demonstrations, newly construed group movements that could perhaps be best categorised within the general boundaries of the tableau vivant genre were noted during the Tunis demonstrations and at other group events. A tableau vivant typically involves a group of performers arranging their bodies in certain positions or stances, then staying still as if they were part of a painting.

On 12 January, and leading up to the major Tunis protest, unique aerial images and a short video were circulated of about a hundred youth gathered next to a metro station in Tunis. The youth assembled themselves by sitting on the ground in such a way that they would form the slogan phrase 'No Killing' in large Arabic letters, recognisable as letters only from a distance. The youth then scrambled the phrase and re-assembled themselves to create the phrase 'Tunisia is Free/ Free Tunisia'. Both times, the youth held the arrangement long enough for aerial photos from neighbouring buildings to be captured. This behaviour whereby a group of people arrange themselves to create words that make up slogans that are legible from a distance has not been noted in any other data collected on the Tunisian protests. In addition to the direct linguistic message, this tableau vivant emphasised the youth's ability to unite, albeit briefly, and to work collaboratively in order to peacefully express opposition to violence as well as their yearning for freedom. Moreover, it highlighted their creativity and media savviness as demonstrated by their theatricality, their use of space and their awareness of the importance of distance from the camera/audience to capture the meaning of their message. The reference to killing was in dialogue with the president's assertion that thugs were responsible for the unrest in the country, that they did not represent the people and that he would deal with them 'resolutely'. A rejection of that claim and of the violence against youth in remote and historically marginalised parts of the country was explicitly conveyed in these two collectively orchestrated and executed two-word tableau vivant.

It is worth noting that the second choreographically inscribed slogan enjoyed an ambiguity allowed by Arabic syntax whereby the two words could mean both 'Free Tunisia' and 'Tunisia is Free'. While 'Free Tunisia' is a phrase that functions as a call or a demand to liberate the country, the declarative nature of the sentence, 'Tunisia is Free', lends a matter-of-fact optimism or even assuredness about the positive outcome of the uprising as perceived by these peaceful young demonstrators. The monolingual choice of Arabic emphasises the intimate character of the message and the national nature of the interpellation directed towards the president, compared with other signs intended for international audiences and hence put out in French or English. The multimodal messages co-constructed through this combination of writing and artistic choreography are among the most dynamic and unique in the data. Unlike in demonstrations where it was difficult to distinguish between protesters and passers-by, participants in the choreographed inscription were clearly and undoubtedly involved in the peaceful protest. Each one of them performed a particular role in order to form the letters and the dots that go with them in a precise manner. Although there is no record of this, rehearsal must have been necessary for the successful performance of these *tableaux vivants*.

Other group movements that were performed and involved much larger numbers of participants were noted in three photographs in the data from 14 January in Tunis. The first two images feature protesters holding their arms above their heads making fists joined at the wrists as if they were in imaginary shackles. The gesture, which can be considered as a form of semiotic synecdoche, whereby the part is used to represent the whole, symbolises servitude. It was unlikely that this performance was rehearsed by participants prior to the demonstration. The gesture was probably spontaneously picked up by participants in the demonstration the way they pick up chanted slogans or other behaviour during a march for example. Usually, this gesture or variants on it are performed with the arms in front of the body not above the head. At the demonstration and because of the large number of participants, the fists had to be held above the head to be visible from a distance. This element underscores once more the protesters' level of consciousness of the collective, performative nature of their actions and their acute awareness of the camera gaze.

The third photograph captured one more gesture that was performed simultaneously by a large number of people at the same demonstration. Protesters held their open hands above their head and motioned from right to left in a gesture that rhythmically echoed the resounding order 'Degage' that they were chanting in unison. The gesture this time constituted a translation of the verbal message of 'Degage'. Participants seemed to join in by copying their neighbours the way they did with the shackles gesture and the way they do with chanted slogans. This multimodal combination of the spoken language with the equivalent gesture reinforced the collective message of repudiation addressed towards the president by making it unequivocally clear, thus making it even more impressive and more demeaning.

Towering over the masses

Protesters engaged in another behaviour that included combining embodied communication with either sound, text or symbol. A few of the images in the data depict young women protesters being carried on shoulders during the demonstration as they shouted slogans, displayed protest signs or waived flags. One of the women appeared in three photographs in the data. While she was carrying a protest sign in the first and waving a flag in the second, she was photographed in the third wearing a traditional Tunisian hat, raising her fist in the air and standing in proximity to another young woman being carried on shoulders, who displayed a sign in Arabic that read 'Release all the Detainees'. Because of their visibility above the crowds, the women primarily act as a vehicle for better exhibiting the rejection of despotism and corruption and the demands for freedom for which the protests stand while emphasising female participation in the uprising. A secondary meaning might possibly be detected in the visual parallelism that exists between these women towering over the crowds and the practice of using female statues to represent freedom or to stand for the nation in other settings, such as in depictions of the French Revolution.

Two other images with a twist on the subject involve carrying an older woman and young man on shoulders. The older woman may have been carried on shoulders to represent a number of issues. First, she may have represented the older generation and therefore the wider reach of the uprising. Second, judging by her attire, she may have represented the poorer classes or the uneducated and their discontent with the government. This stands in contrast to the younger women, who look like they may have been college students or new graduates and symbolised youth, on the one hand, and the educated but still unemployed youth, on the other.

The young man on shoulders was for his part unique in that no other men were seen being carried in this way in the protest data. He was also unique because he used a creative yet widely recognisable multimodal metaphor to represent the demands of the protest. This form of expression might have earned him the ride on other protesters' shoulders perhaps and the opportunity to gain visibility. The man displayed up high an empty bird cage with the door open and a small Tunisian flag attached on top of the door. Presumably, the bird had flown out of the cage to freedom. The closely positioned flag may suggest that Tunisia, metonymically represented by the flag that is perched on the cage door, is now free or at least aspires to be free. Once again, it is clear that the protesters were acutely attuned to the importance of the reach of their collective message, and were willing to orchestrate their collective meaning by giving prominence to other participants where needed.

Another symbol – trope – that protesters were observed using in a few images in the data is the loaf of bread. The common baguette that Tunisians consume as the main staple in their diet, is brandished over the head to represent the demand for a decent livelihood. The word 'loaf of bread' itself is used in Tunisian Arabic to metonymically represent livelihood. The physical use of the baguette in this context transfers the metonymy from the verbal mode to the visual, or semiotic, mode. This strategy works in concert with other visual and verbal strategies to reinforce the protest message and ensure its clarity to the still camera that does not capture the chanted slogans.

Banal nationalism and flags

When ranking national symbols, Geisler (2005) places flags at the top of the list, followed by the national anthem and other symbols such as national monuments, the currency and national holidays. However, national symbols do not operate in isolation. There are 'countless ways in which different national symbols work in concert to establish a web of signification' (Geisler 2005: xxix). Comparing them to mass media that 'construct our everyday lives', Geisler adds that 'national symbols, through redundancy and recursive communication, stabilise our sense of national identity' (2005: xxix). This pervasive reproduction of national symbols in 'mundane', and 'unnoticed' aspects of daily life is what Billig (1995: 6 and 8) calls 'banal nationalism' (Skey 2009). Flags hanging in yards, on government buildings or displayed on food items; the national anthem recited at schools or at sports events; using the name of the country or its map in everything from weather forecasts to names of sports clubs are among the numerous routine manifestations of banal nationalism that contribute to the reinforcement of the sense of national identity that is constructed over time. Billig warns that 'banal nationalism can be mobilised and turned into frenzied nationalism . . .' (1995: 5). That is the kind of nationalism that is needed to wage war or rally the nation around the flag when under real or perceived threat.

At the mass rallies organised during the period under study, the Tunisian national anthem and the flag were used by citizens as they protested *against* the state. The Tunisian national anthem was chanted by protesters from the very first day of the uprising when outraged citizens congregated in front of the governor's office in Sidi Bouzid. The Tunisian flag took longer to adopt by citizens, however. This might have been because it was not easily accessible to the public or perhaps because it took a while for the initially economic protest demands to take a political turn days before the departure of the president (Shiri 2015). The flag was, however, visibly waved, worn and displayed at the 14 January Tunis demonstration that demanded the ouster of the president. In re-contextualising these top national symbols within the discourse of dissent as instantiated in illegally assembled mass rallies where protest slogans were carried and chanted, Tunisian demonstrators subverted what was merely banal nationalism for over fifty years and re-injected it with new meaning.

The linguistic/semiotic landscape data for the 14 January protest is replete with images capturing citizens engaged with the flag in a variety of semiotic combinations lending patriotic meaning to the acts of the crowds around them and by the same token removing that authority from the state. Prior to 12 January, when the flag appeared in images of the protests, it was hanging in the background on government buildings or on the street the way it was intended by the state. It had not yet changed hands and was not yet deliberately claimed by the demonstrating crowds in composing their multimodal message of patriotism. In fact, contexts where citizens practiced banal nationalism abounded. One situation akin to the protest environment with which most of the protesters would have been familiar is that of singing the national anthem and flying or draping oneself in the flag at soccer matches at international tournaments. Tunisia, as is the case with other states, uses sports and entertainment to 'distract' its citizens from political matters. Feeling as one with total strangers in a stadium while singing the national anthem as the flag is flying was sanctioned by the state during matches. By using these and other national symbols in this subversive manner well outside the norms previously dictated by the state, protesters effectively took these symbols away from the state. They thus indirectly declared the state unfit to act as custodian of these symbols that represent the ideals of the nation.

Protesters thus revitalised mundane banal nationalist practices by imbuing them with a renewed meaning that brings them closer to those original ideals that they bore at the birth of the nation and on the heels of independence from French colonialism. Protesters therefore re-appropriated what they perceived as belonging to the nation but had been misused in the hands of the despotic state and reclaimed it as theirs, as their voice, as their symbol. The fight against the government, by extension, became a fight for the nation that the symbols represent and which the citizens will defend, through blood sacrifice if necessary. With the symbols of the nation on their side, the messages of the protesters now acquired more legitimacy and solemnity. The protesters now are soldiers so to speak that are ready to act on behalf of the nation, liberating it from the oppressor who previously held the flag. The introduction of the flag to the linguistic/semiotic landscape of protest can be considered a turning point in (the construction of) the discourse of dissent. The struggle went from one of citizens asking for better economic performance and more freedoms from their ruler to citizen soldiers defending the nation from oppression at the hand of a non-patriotic and disloyal ruler who is killing unarmed innocent fellow citizens.

Several of the most noteworthy subversions of banal nationalism through the use of the flag will be enumerated below. The first observed pattern of use of the flag as an openly subversive strategy was when combined in a multimodal ensemble with protest signs written in Arabic, French or English. The juxtaposition and interplay with the text of the signs made this subversion at its most explicit and perhaps most powerful compared with the use of the flag alone. Thus, on the one hand, the flag lent its authority to the messages of the protesters, elevating their demands to a patriotic, and therefore legitimate, level that benefits the nation as a whole. On the other hand, the subversive messages of the signs made it clear that the flag was now being used in its renewed revolutionary meaning and was now different to its previously authoritarian use by the state.

In instances of intentional juxtaposition, young protesters climbed on streetlights or on the edges or balconies of buildings besieged by demonstrators and flew the flag along the signs that they displayed. The flag is hence seen next to two of the French signs, for example: one sign read 'Ben Ali Degage', while the second read 'Ben Ali Assassin'. When arranged next to 'Ben Ali Assassin', the flag is held down to signify that the nation is in mourning. In some photographs, the flag was in the vicinity of a sign that was being photographed but the two were not intentionally held together by the same protester. They just happened to be framed, intentionally or unintentionally, by the fellow citizen who is responsible for the composition of the photograph and therefore for orchestrating this ensemble. The juxtaposition is inherent to the heteroglossic nature of the protest and the multiplicity of voices and strategies interacting during the protest to collectively express dissent and rebellion against the status quo. In one of the most widely distributed photographs, the sign 'Game Over' is seen emerging, alone, from a large crowd of people in between two flags, as if declaring victory in a battle. The flag on the far right was held by two young men who climbed over streetlight poles. The other widely distributed sign in English that said 'Freedom' equally had a Tunisian flag right in the background. In some photographs, the flag appeared in between signs in different languages. For example, it appeared in between a sign in Arabic that read 'True to our Martyrs' and a sign in English that read 'You killed your people Ben Ali'.

In its second and most common subversive use, the flag was displayed alone by a variety of protesters in a variety of ways. The size of the flag also varied. There were smaller as well as larger flags, some attached to poles and some not. However, all flags were combined with motion from their carrier. As mentioned above, a few young protesters climbed up lamp posts and waved the flag from their more visible vantage points. One of the young women who were carried on shoulders waved a small flag, while an older woman who was carried on shoulders waved a large flag. The Che Guevara look alike was seen in another photograph brandishing a small flag as he moved and shouted in harmony with the surrounding protesters, with a bilingual French–English sign that reads 'I Have a Dream Une Tunisie Libre'. In another photograph, a close-up shot showed a man kissing a small flag, clearly for the benefit of the photographer as the direction of his gaze suggests. Another way of displaying this national symbol that was observed at this demonstration entailed wearing a large flag as a cape. This method was commonly used in international sporting events, especially soccer matches, a venue where banal nationalism was widely practiced by fans at the stadium. Finally, in a non-verbal metaphorical message, the man who was carried on shoulders, jubilant, and holding an empty bird cage with an open door and with a small Tunisian flag on top of the cage. The flag, standing in for Tunisia and uniting Tunisians, represented a desire for liberation and independence from captivity under decades of single-party rule.

Grounded in the context of a large illegal assembly chanting and displaying protest messages, the re-appropriation of the flag by the protesters and its renewed revolutionary message become unmistakable. The flag went from a banal symbol of nationalism that is displayed by the state at state-sponsored events or by citizens at international sports events, to a re-appropriated symbol of the revival of nationalism as the nation feels attacked by an enemy from within, an enemy who is shooting at fellow citizens with live bullets. As it changed hands, the flag lost its status as a banal national symbol and transformed into a symbol of revived nationalism and a banner behind which citizens from all walks of life and ideological background rallied to defend the nation under attack.

Conclusion

The peaceful mass demonstration in Tunis on 14 January 2011 constituted a turning point in the wave of protests of the previous four weeks. Protesters managed to send a unified message to their president of twenty-three years, leading him to flee the country the same day. To this end, they orchestrated a variety of multimodal messages sharing their rejection of his oppressive rule and violent handling of protests, and demanding his departure. Displaying multimodal signs and performing choreographed group movements accompanied by a subversion of banal nationalism, protesters created ensembles that took over the transient linguistic/semiotic landscape. The ensembles were documented by other protesters or onlookers and turned into historical artefacts commemorating this ephemeral moment of union across social groups for what was believed to be the public good. More aspects of these protests remain unstudied, however. These include, for instance, the chanted slogans from this critical period and the graffiti that became prevalent during the weeks that ensued as security forces withdrew from public spaces. A better understanding of the impact of this period in effecting such profound political change will be enhanced with a more thorough examination of the protests and the messages that they created.

Note

1. Images relating to this chapter can be found in the following links: http://www.alriyadh.com/594886, last accessed 5 June 2013; http://du-photographique.blogspot.com/2011/01/chronique-dune-journee-historique.html, last accessed 5 June 2013; http://blueprinteditor.blogspot.com/2011_01_01_archive.html, last accessed 30 May 2013; http://www.bbc.co.uk/arabic/middleeast/2011/01/110114_tunisbenali_ballout.shtml, last accessed 30 May 2013; https://tinyurl.com/ld3yvbf, last accessed 16 March 2013; https://tinyurl.com/kncuohy, last accessed 16 March 2013.

References

Al Masaeed, K., 'Egyptian revolution of 2011 and the power of its slogans: A critical discourse analysis study', *Cross-Cultural Communication* 9(6) (2013): 1–6.

Backhaus, P., 'Multilingualism in Tokyo: A look into the linguistic landscape', *International Journal of Multilingualism* 3(1) (2006): 52–66.

Backhaus, P., *Linguistic Landscapes: A Comparative Study of Urban Multilingualism in Tokyo* (Clevedon: Multilingual Matters, 2007), vol. 136.

Bakhtin, M. M., *The Dialogic Imagination: Four Essays*, ed. M. Holquist, trans. C. Emerson and M. Holquist (Austin, TX: University of Texas Press, 1981).

Ben Said, S., 'Urban street signs in the linguistic landscape of Tunisia: Tensions in policy, representation, and attitudes', unpublished PhD dissertation, ProQuest LLC, 2010.

Ben Said, S., 'Data triangulation as a resource in multilingual research: Examples from the linguistic landscape', *Proceedings of the International Conference: Doing Research in Applied Linguistics*, King Mongkut's University of Technology Thonburi and Macquarie University, Bangkok, Thailand, 2011, pp. 62–70.

Ben Said, S. and Kasanga, L. A., 'The discourse of protest: Frames of identity, intertextuality, and interdiscursivity', in R. Blackwood, E. Lanza and H. Woldemariam (eds), *Negotiating and Contesting Identities in Linguistic Landscapes* (London: Bloomsbury, 2016), pp. 71–83.

Billig, M., *Banal Nationalism* (London: Sage, 1995).

Dragićević-Šešić, M., 'The street as political space: Walking as protest, graffiti, and the student carnivalization of Belgrade', *New Theatre Quarterly* 17(1) (2001): 74–86.

Frekko, S. E., 'Signs of respect: Neighborhood, public, and language in Barcelona', *Journal of Linguistic Anthropology* 19(2) (2009): 227–45.

Geisler, M., *National Symbols, Fractured Identities: Contesting the National Narrative*, Middlebury Bicentennial Series in International Studies (Lebanon, NH: Middlebury College Press, 2005).

Gorter, D (ed.), *Linguistic Landscape: A New Approach to Multilingualism* (Clevedon: Multilingual Matters, 2006).

Gorter, D., 'Linguistic landscapes in a multilingual world', *Annual Review of Applied Linguistics* 33 (2013): 190–212.

Gorter, D., Marten, H. F. and Van Mensel, L. (eds), *Minority Languages in the Linguistic Landscape* (Basingstoke: Palgrave Macmillan, 2012).

Hanauer, D., 'The discursive construction of the separation wall at Abu Dis: Graffiti as political discourse', *Journal of Language and Politics* 10(3) (2011): 301–21.

Hanauer, D., 'Transitory linguistic landscapes as political discourse: Signage at three demonstrations at Pittsburgh, USA', in C. Helot and M. Barni (eds), *Linguistic Landscapes, Multilingualism and Social Change* (Frankfurt-am-Main, Peter Lang, 2012), pp. 139–54.

Hanauer, D., 'Occupy Baltimore: A linguistic landscape analysis of participatory social contestation in an American city', in Rani Rubdy and Selim Ben Said (eds), *Conflict, Exclusion and Dissent in the Linguistic Landscape* (Basingstoke: Palgrave Macmillan, 2015), pp. 207–22.

Jaworski, A. and Thurlow, C. (eds), *Semiotic Landscapes: Language, Image, Space* (London: Continuum, 2010).

Kress, G., Literacy in the New Media Age (London: Routledge, 2003).

Kress, G., *Multimodality: A Social Semiotic Approach to Contemporary Communication* (London: Routledge, 2009).

Kress, G., Multimodality: A Social Semiotic Approach to Contemporary Communication (London: Routledge, 2010)

Kress, G. R. and Van Leeuwen, T., *Multimodal Discourse: The Modes and Media of Contemporary Communication* (London: Arnold, 2001), vol. 312.

Lado, B., 'Linguistic landscape as a reflection of the linguistic and ideological conflict in the Valencian community', *International Journal of Multilingualism* 8(2) (2011): 135–50.

Landry, R. and Bourhis, R. Y., 'Linguistic landscape and ethnolinguistic vitality: An empirical study', *Journal of Language and Social Psychology* 16(1) (1997): 23–49.

Mabrouk, M., 'A revolution for dignity and freedom: Preliminary observations on the social and cultural background to the Tunisian revolution', Journal of North African Studies 16(4) (2011): 625–35.

Messekher, H., 'A linguistic landscape analysis of the sociopolitical demonstrations of Algiers: A politicized landscape', in Rani Rubdy and Selim Ben Said (eds), *Conflict, Exclusion and Dissent in the Linguistic Landscape* (Basingstoke: Palgrave Macmillan, 2015), pp. 260–79.

Nwoye, O. G., 'Social issues on walls: Graffiti in university lavatories', *Discourse & Society* 4(4) (1993): 419–42.

Page, R. (ed.), *New Perspectives on Narrative and Multimodality* (New York: Routledge, 2010).

Papen, U., 'Commercial discourses, gentrification and citizens' protest: The linguistic landscape of Prenzlauer Berg, Berlin', *Journal of Sociolinguistics* 16(1) (2012): 56–80.

Pennycook, A., 'Linguistic landscapes and the transgressive semiotics of graffiti', in E. Shohamy and D. Gorter (eds), *Linguistic Landscape: Expanding the Scenery* (New York: Routledge, 2009), pp. 302–12.

Pennycook, A., 'Spatial narrations: Graffscapes and city souls', in A. Jaworski and C. Thurlow (eds), *Semiotic Landscapes: Language, Image, Space* (London: Continuum, 2010), pp. 137–50.

Rubdy, R. and Ben Said, S. (eds), *Conflict, Exclusion and Dissent in the Linguistic Landscape* (Basingstoke: Palgrave Macmillan, 2015).

Seals, C. A., 'Overcoming erasure: Reappropriation of space in the linguistic landscape of mass-scale protests', in Rani Rubdy and Selim Ben Said (eds),

Conflict, Exclusion and Dissent in the Linguistic Landscape (Basingstoke: Palgrave Macmillan, 2015), pp. 223–38.

Scollon, R. and Scollon, S. W., *Discourses in Place: Language in the Material World* (London: Routledge, 2003).

Shiri, S., 'Co-constructing dissent in the transient linguistic landscape: Multilingual protest signs of the Tunisian Revolution', in Rani Rubdy and Selim Ben Said (eds), *Conflict, Exclusion and Dissent in the Linguistic Landscape* (Basingstoke: Palgrave Macmillan, 2015), pp. 239–59.

Shohamy, E., Ben Rafael, E. and Barni, M. (eds), *Linguistic Landscape in the City* (Clevedon: Multilingual Matters, 2010).

Shohamy, E. and Gorter, D. (eds), *Linguistic Landscape: Expanding the Scenery* (London: Routledge, 2009).

Skey, M., 'The national in everyday life: A critical engagement with Michael Billig's thesis of Banal Nationalism', *Sociological Review* 57(2) (2009): 331–46.

Starrett, G., 'Signposts along the road: Monumental public writing in Egypt', *Anthropology Today* 11(4) (1995): 8–13.

Stroud, C. and Mpendukana, S., 'Towards a material ethnography of linguistic landscape: Multilingualism, mobility and space in a South African township', *Journal of Sociolinguistics* 13(3) (2009): 363–86.

Suleiman, Y., *Arabic, Self and Identity: A Study in Conflict and Displacement* (New York: Oxford University Press, 2011).

Van Leeuwen, T., 'Towards a semiotics of typography', *Information Design Journal* 14(2) (2006): 139–55.

CHAPTER 10

The Arab Jews and the Arabic Language in Israel: An Ongoing Ambivalence between Positive Nostalgia and Negative Present[1]

Maisalon Dallashi

Introduction

In addressing the debate over knowledge and narratives within the Israeli–Palestinian context, I faced a dilemma over where to begin. Should I go back to the year 1948 and give a proper introduction of the Palestinian–Israeli conflict? Or perhaps start even earlier going back to 1917? As I was driving and pondering exactly how to begin the chapter, I heard a song by legendary Egyptian singer Umm Kulthūm. The volume was a bit loud and suddenly I noticed my fellow drivers start to stare at me. Some had nostalgic looks on their faces, as if the song reminded them of their childhood. Others seemed curious, while others appeared hesitant, confused – even hateful. I found myself wondering, as a Palestinian woman living in Israel/Palestine, how can one imagine any other reality outside the one in which we live? Is it possible for a language to constitute a bridge between the different narratives of the two nations that share this land, yet simultaneously be a cause of separation?

The other dilemma I faced was over explaining the choice of nomenclature 'Arab Jews' (*al-Yahūd al-ʿArab* اليهود العرب), Jews from Arab countries, as referred to by Shohat (1988) and Shenhav (2006). They suggested that the term constitutes an alternative definition to the common use of the Hebrew term 'Sephardi' or 'Mizrahi' (oriental), which refers to people with 'Eastern' roots, including Arab countries as well as non-Arab Muslim countries such as Turkey and Iran. The intention of using this term is to challenge the contrasting binary in Zionist discourse, which dichotomises Arabs and Jews and blurs or distorts the connection between Arabs and Jews, East and West. For methodological reasons, however, the definition of Arab Jews includes only those who themselves, their parents or grandparents immigrated from Arab countries to Israel.

I discuss in this chapter the complex relationship between Arab Jews in contemporary Israel and the Arabic language, based on a survey that for the first time directly addressed this topic. The chapter analyses the command of Arabic among three generations of Arab Jews, and compares them with other non-Arab Jews living in Israel – towards a general claim about ethnicity and language in Israel today. My main argument is that language is two sides of the same coin: it serves as a tool to connect cultures, languages and soften conflicts, on the one hand, while, on the other hand, it can be a tool to encourage segregation and conflict among different groups and cultures when it is studied for security purposes.

By focusing on the Arab Jewish community in Israel, I shed light on the processes that have resulted in the dialectical relations in which Arabic concomitantly represents various, contradicting and even dissonant values of fear, love and hate. In other words, Arabic as a language that is aesthetically admired (for instance, in relation to music) and represents the language of 'the grandparents' generation', while at the same time is hardly spoken and is viewed as the language of 'the enemy'.

The status of Arabic in Israel

Arabic is one of the two official languages in Israel; however, the actual implementation of this language policy is perpetually in question. In the past and even more so today, there is an intense public debate surrounding the use of Arabic. Given the nature of the Israeli–Palestinian conflict, the weak status of Arabic in Israel should come as no surprise. Some proponents of weakening Arabic's status as an official language have tried to establish Hebrew as the exclusive, official language of the state. Indeed, recent attempts have been made to revoke the status of Arabic as an official language,[2] and various studies (for example, Amara 2002: 199; Ben-Rafael et al. 2006; Pinto 2011) show that in the last decade its status as an official language has been challenged in an unprecedented way. In contrast, there are those who believe that Arabic's official status should be used as a springboard to create a more democratic and inclusive society that, among other things, respects and values the Arabic language and culture.

The history of the relationship between Jews in Israel and Arabic is extremely complex, and can be examined from cultural, social and political points of view.

The social, cultural and political issues on Arabic in Israel

The social aspect

Jewish and Palestinian citizens of Israel account for approximately 75 and 20 per cent of the total population, respectively. The majority of Jews and

Palestinians live in ethnically segregated communities, although the extent of segregation between the two groups has changed and widened over time. Historically, the small Jewish minority that lived in urban sections of Palestine before the creation of the State of Israel at the turn of the twentieth century resided alongside the Palestinian population in cities such as Jaffa, Safed and Hebron. During the decades of violence leading up to Israel's establishment in 1948, Jews left most of these cities, and moved to mainly Jewish areas such as Tel Aviv. Most of the Palestinian inhabitants fled or were driven from their lands that fell under Israeli control, while Jews – mainly new immigrants – settled in many of the homes left behind by Palestinian refugees (Cohen 2002a; Shwed et al. 2014). In this context, it is worth highlighting the fact that the Palestinians who remained within the borders of the nascent Jewish state after 1948 received Israeli citizenship, unlike the remaining Palestinians in the West Bank, Gaza Strip or the refugees in the diaspora. Due to the difference in the type of citizenship, it is customary to refer to Palestinians living in Israel as 'Israeli Arabs', '48 Arabs', '48 Palestinians', 'Arabs inside the Green Line', etc. The controversial term 'Israeli Arabs' did not take hold due to syntactic convenience or linguistic preferences, but rather because it reflects the Israeli state's attempts to blur or erase its citizens' Palestinian nationhood.

The circumstances surrounding the establishment of the State of Israel heightened the separation between the two groups. Today, 90 per cent of Israel's Palestinian population resides in Palestinian-only towns and villages, while much of the remaining 10 per cent reside in separate Arab neighbourhoods inside Jewish cities (Smooha 2012). Similarly, the majority of Jews reside in Jewish-only towns, with only 22 per cent residing in mixed localities (Khamaisi 2009). The result has been the near-total segregation of the two communities. For example, the vast majority of Jewish Israelis and Palestinians study in separate schools, regardless of whether they live in the same city or even the same neighbourhood.

Hebrew is the language of instruction in Jewish schools, yet Arabic – despite being one of two official languages of the state – is taught as an elective subject (the students can choose between Arabic and French), at times it is not taught at all (the majority of the state religious schools) and generally suffers from a very negative image and status. When Arabic is taught, it is done so in a passive manner or as a Latin language – one that is read but not spoken. In other words, Arabic becomes an unnecessary language that no longer has any 'natives' with whom to speak (Mendel 2014). According to our survey, less than 1 per cent of Jewish Israelis can read and understand a book written in Arabic, and the education system places little emphasis on the need to learn Arabic as a language or culture. While the language of instruction in Arab schools is Arabic, Palestinian students study Hebrew extensively. Thus, the basic conditions for inter-group communication barely exist.

In this context, language plays a crucial role in social interaction and the transmission of cultural and social values (Fishman 1970). Thus, it has been argued that Arabic should be taught in schools in order to promote dialogue with the Palestinian 'other' (Bekerman and Horenczyk 2004). Many scholars (Suleiman 2004; Shohamy 2006; Mendel 2014) highlight the huge gap between Arabic as a lingua franca of the Middle East as opposed to its poor status in Israel – a country located in the heart of the Middle East. Accordingly, they argue that improving the study and status of Arabic is necessary for any kind of integration in the region. The ideological framing of the way Arabic is viewed is in line with Suleiman's (2004) approach, which highlights the connection between language and conflicts. Suleiman characterises language (especially Arabic) as not only an instrumental or technical tool for communication, but rather a cultural, identity and social issue in which ideological competition is not created between languages or language varieties, but among non-homogeneous groups in the country over resources and values in their milieus in inter- and intra-group situations. Suleiman, however, highlights that language is not the cause or reason for conflicts, but merely constitutes an additional side of the conflict. He shows the connection between power and language through his personal experience as a Palestinian who refuses to speak in Arabic with Israeli soldiers at checkpoints in the West Bank, and insists on speaking with them in English. As he concludes: 'While power may be allocated differentially between competing individuals and groups, it is nevertheless possible to achieve some reordering of this allocation by exploiting the linguistic resources available' (Suleiman 2004: 13).

The cultural aspect

The 1950s saw the peak of Jewish immigration to Israel, as more than 400,000 Jews immigrated from the Middle East and Asia. Despite the fact that they shared the same religion with Ashkenazim, their non-European roots caused them to be looked down on as inferior. Alongside discrimination in distribution of budgets, the labour market and education, Arab Jews continue to suffer from a process of 'de-Arabisation' – the result of the Israeli establishment's 'melting pot' policy that sought to assimilate and unite new immigrants under a new Israeli identity. Language loss is a major feature of this process of modernisation and de-Arabisation, and while it is true that other languages have been lost – Yiddish, for example – yet the case of Arabic is entirely different for two main reasons: Arabic's official status in Israel, and the fact that it is the lingua franca of the region in which Israel is located.

Among some Arab Jews, Arabic is seen as the traditional language and culture of their grandparents. This connection is not obvious in Israel, and in the last decades critical voices in the public Mizrahi discourse have challenged the very idea of a 'homogeneous' Israeli identity. Activists belonging to the second generation of Arab Jews established organisations, movements and independent periodicals through which they demanded fundamental changes in three areas: language, identity and social inequality. In doing so, they highlighted the complex relationship between language, identity and status (Shenhav 2006).

Shenhav (2006) argues that unlike the 'Moroccan Jews' or 'Egyptian Jews', the term 'Arab Jews' carries with it an explosive potential of solidarity with those considered the Arab enemy. Arabism appears in Israeli society and culture as a generic name for the enemy of the state. The use of the non-linear category of Arab Jews allows for challenging the identity hierarchy and to disrupt its complacency.

Various explanations have been offered for Arab Jews' de-Arabisation process, the most common of which concentrates on 'orientalisation' and Westernisation (Khazzoom 2003). Aziza Khazzoom looks at the way in which Germany and France 'orientalised' their Jewish populations towards the end of the eighteenth century by offering them economic and social inclusion in return for secularisation of their community. Interestingly, a similar process occurred to Eastern European Jewry by Western European Jews, who derogatorily nicknamed their eastern co-religionists '*Ostjuden*' ('Eastern Jews'), since they did not undergo a Westernisation process. In this way, Western Jews marked the differences between the two groups such that the latter were considered the primitive 'other'. Khazzom (2003) claims that a similar process took place in Israel against Jews from Arab countries, and finally against Palestinians – a process that she terms 'chain of orientalism'. However, Khazzom (2003) and Shenhav (2006) indicate that the orientalisation process of Arab Jews took place at an earlier stage, *prior* to their immigration to Israel, through Zionist emissaries who travelled to Arab countries in the early 1940s to promote Jewish immigration to Israel. There the emissaries met Jews who differed from those in Europe and were far closer to Arab culture.

The Zionist emissaries were bothered by the fact they saw Jews who were indistinguishable from Arabs (Shenhav 2006). This disrupted their binary thinking that formed the chain of orientalism – one that is based on the distinction between tradition and modernity, religiosity and secularism, Ashkenazi and Mizrahi, Jewish and Arab, Israeli and Palestinian, etc. Moreover, Shenhav claims that this disruption threatened the Zionist project, since it fundamentally viewed the Jewish–Arab conflict as a reductive binary of historical and natural ongoing hostility between Jews and Arabs.

The political aspect

The last category suggested in this context is the political aspect, which includes 'security considerations'. A large number of Israeli Jews view Arabic as a language of the enemy – the surrounding Arab countries and particularly the Palestinians. Proponents of this approach argue that Arabic should be taught in Jewish schools, where Arabic serves particular security needs for 'knowledge of the enemy' (Mendel 2014). Therefore, over the years, the Israeli intelligence establishment has become a natural partner and supporter of Arabic in the educational system. Indeed, Mendel shows how 'Israeli Arabic' was created as an artificial, passive and limited language, which directly corresponds with instrumental motivation to serve in military intelligence units and to a certain extent revolves around the needs of Israeli intelligence and security. As such, the creation of 'Israeli Arabic' was a process that largely excluded native Arabic-speakers from taking part in the debate as well as teaching the language. Over time, Israeli 'military-motivated' Arabic was created and developed as both distant and detached from the Arabic spoken by native speakers.

Though Jewish schools in Israel include only sparse Arabic instruction, researchers have paid much attention to the role that schools and universities play in providing a significant learning environment for Arabic (Donitsa-Schmidt, Shohamy and Inbar, 2001; Amara 2016). A recent, extreme incident highlighted the complexity of Israelis' various attitudes vis-à-vis teaching Arabic: Jewish Israeli students (Surkes 2016) complained that a Jewish Arabic teacher instructed ninth graders to translate phrases such as 'I want to kill Jews', 'I want to free Al-Aqsa [Mosque]', 'I want to be a Shahid [martyr]' and 'The Arabs want peace? They want war!' into Arabic. One of the students who complained wrote the following on his Facebook page: 'The teacher is known for his right-wing views. He wears a kippa – not that that really matters. You mainly see his worldview and his attempt to preach to pupils that all Arabs are terrorists who only want to murder Jews' (ibid.).

This example shows how easily Arabic teachers can become a part of the problem due to their negative attitudes towards Arabic. Teachers who are entrusted with language instruction can sometimes be the ones who urge their students to hate Arabic and those who speak it. As can be seen from the student's response, the attempt to disparage Arabic or Arabs in general does not always work.

Since the previous example reveals that Arabic may have different or totally opposite meanings for Israeli Jews – and considering the fact that Arabic is, at least on paper (Pinto 2009), an official language, and that 1.8 million Palestinian citizens of Israel represent a fifth of the total population (Gharrah 2015) – one could expect that Arabic be taught and used on a wider scale. Furthermore, various surveys (Central Bureau of Statistics (Israel) 2013; Shenhav et al. 2015) since the 1990s show that over 60 per cent of the Jewish population supports Arabic instruction in schools. In addition, almost 50 per cent of the Jewish population has Arab origins, many of whom spoke Arabic as their mother tongue. And yet today, Jews hardly speak or read Arabic.

Data and methods

I briefly present the findings of the survey (2015) that examined command of Arabic and attitudes towards the Arabic language among the Jewish population in Israel. The report, *Command of Arabic among Israeli Jews* (Shenhav et al. 2015) is based on a representative sample of the Jewish population in Israel (*N* = 500). Collection of data is based on information gathered through a telephone survey. The survey was written and conducted by the authors of the aforementioned report, along with the B. I. and Lucille Cohen Institute for Public Opinion Research, and was based on a representative sample (*N* = 500) of the Israeli Jewish adult population, with another 261 respondents who were later added to the sample (producing an enlarged sample of *N* = 761). Respondents who are first-, second- or third-generation immigrants from Arab countries (referred to below as 'immigrants from Arab countries' or 'Arab Jews') were compared with other 'non-Arab Jewish' participants. The questionnaire was divided into two sections: the first, focused on knowledge and command of Arabic; the second, dealt with attitudes towards Arabic, including questions on whether Arabic should be an official language, taught in schools, is integral to life in the Middle East, etc. The respondents were asked if they felt comfortable speaking in Arabic outside their home, and about their attitude vis-à-vis listening to Arabic music or hearing spoken Arabic. Those who answered that they do not feel comfortable speaking in Arabic were asked (through an open questionnaire) about the reasons why, and whether they felt more comfortable speaking Arabic when they were younger.

In what follows, I present the major findings of the survey and add new findings and analyses that are not present in the original report.

Results

As shown in Table 10.1, 10 per cent of Israeli Jews say they speak or understand Arabic well. The figure plummets with regard to reading or understanding texts: the percentage of Jews who report that they can read a newspaper in Arabic is 2.6 per cent, while the percentage of readers of Arabic literature is no more than 1 per cent. Moreover, the percentage of those who can actually read a book in Arabic is negligible. It is worth mentioning here that the data indicates that 76.6 per cent of respondents previously studied Arabic in school. However, the Arab Jews among them benefit less than other Jews, since they choose to study Arabic in school at a significantly lower rate.

Furthermore, 21.1 per cent of respondents answered that they were taught Arabic at home, with a noticeable difference in favour of Arab Jews; 4.5 per cent learned Arabic in the army; 3.4 per cent studied Arabic at university; while only 3 per cent learned Arabic independently. It is important to note that the rate of non-Arab Jews who studied Arabic in the army, at university or independently was three times higher than the Arab Jews. We believe that there is a gap between reality and the percentages in our survey data, since

Table 10.1 Knowledge of Arabic among Jews

Type of knowledge	*Representative sample (N = 500) (%)*	*Arab Jews (N = 500) (%)*	*Non-Arab Jews (N = 261) (%)*
Understanding conversations in Arabic	17.2	30.0	3.1
Understanding song lyrics	10.4	18.8	0.8
Speaking	10.0	17.0	1.1
General level of knowledge in Arabic	9.8	15.8	1.1
Familiarity with letters	6.8	7.6	3.1
Reading (newspaper, news)	2.6	3.8	0.4
Writing (email, letter)	1.4	2.6	0.4
Reading fiction (novel, textbook)	1.0	2.2	–

Unit 8200 – the army's prestigious central intelligence-gathering unit – is the largest unit in the Israeli army, and its impact on the field of Arabic studies is crucial (see a wider discussion in Mendel 2014). However, it is important to mention that the majority of respondents who said that they learned Arabic in school were motivated to make use of Arabic in the army. As a previous study (Hayam-Yonas and Malka 2006) has shown, 60 per cent of those who chose to study Arabic in school mentioned their desire 'to join the Intelligence Corps' as the initial reason that led them to to do so. In the expanded report (Shenhav et al. 2015) we have suggested that perhaps this stems from the respondents' sensitivity to stating that they studied Arabic during their military service. Because we gave the opportunity to select more than one answer for this question, respondents preferred to indicate that school was their source of learning, because of their reluctance to discuss issues related to Arabic and their military service in a telephone survey.

Attitudes towards Arabic

Pursuant to the proposed division into the three categories indicated above, I will first deal with the *social* attitudes towards Arabic. Table 10.2 indicates that over 60 per cent of the representative sample (*N* = 500) believe that Arabic should be taught in schools, while 55.8 per cent stated that Arabic is important for Israel to integrate into the Middle East. The majority of the interviewees

(57.8 per cent) stressed the importance of Arabic for living in Israel. A comparison of the two groups' answers (Arab Jews versus non-Arab Jews) reveals no significant differences; that is, both believe knowledge of Arabic is important for social integration inside Israel and among its neighbours.

Regarding *cultural* attitudes, there was a dramatic change in the participants' responses when they were asked about Arabic music, as displayed in Table 10.2. Arab Jews expressed reasonably positive attitudes towards Arabic music (19 per cent versus 7 per cent, respectively), and said they felt a sense of comfort when listening to it (28 per cent versus 21 per cent, respectively). Meanwhile, approximately one-third of the participants viewed Arabic as important, since it is part of Jewish heritage, with no significant difference between Arab Jews and the rest of the respondents.

As for *political* and *security-based* attitudes, roughly 65 per cent of the respondents ascribe major importance to using Arabic for Israeli security needs, or as a matter of 'knowing your enemy'. According to the research, Arab Jews (second- and third-generation) tend to express more negative views towards Arabic (74 per cent) than non-Arab Jews (60 per cent). Other significant differences between Arab Jews and non-Arab Jews were found among those who claim that Israeli citizens should only speak Hebrew (39 per cent of those from Arab countries compared with 29 per cent non-Arab Jews). This shows that, paradoxically, Arab Jews are less supportive of Arabic as an official language. Appropriately, nearly half of them (49 per cent) claimed that Arabic should be an official language, as opposed to 57.9 per cent of non-Arab Jews.

In fact, the percentage of Jews who think there are important cultural reasons for learning Arabic is almost half that which cite security as a reason to learn the language. The relatively wide variability in Jewish attitudes towards Arabic, as shown in Table 10.2, seemingly stem from the reflection of the complex ways Arabic is viewed in Israel. The majority of Israeli Jews believe that Arabic is important and necessary to teach in schools. At the same time, the results provide evidence that, consistent with Mendel's (2014) findings, knowledge of Arabic is primarily considered important for 'knowing the enemy', and the vast majority feels uncomfortable with speaking or using the language.

Focusing on Arab Jews, however, I detected another layer of complexity in their attitudes towards Arabic in particular – one that reveals a constant interplay between conflicting tendencies. On the one hand, people may express fear, revulsion and hatred by using terms such as 'know your enemy' and 'feeling uncomfortable with hearing or using the language'. On the other hand, they may express identification, love and nostalgia for the language through attitudes such as 'I like to hear Arabic music', 'Arabic is important for daily life in Israel' or 'Arabic must be taught in Jewish schools'.

Overall, Arab Jews tend to report more negative attitudes towards Arabic than non-Arab Jews; however, as one type of feeling increases, the other tends to

Table 10.2 Attitudes towards Arabic

Statement	*Representative sample (N = 500) (%)*	*Arab Jews (N = 500) (%)*	*Non-Arab Jews (N = 261) (%)*
Arabic should be an official language in Israel	52.6	49.0	57.9
All citizens of Israel should speak Hebrew only	36.4	39.2	28.7
Arabic should be taught at Jewish schools	60.2	56.8	61.3
Arabic is a very important component of Mizrahi Jewish heritage and should be preserved	33.0	35.6	32.6
Arabic is very important for daily life in Israel	57.8	58.6	58.2
Bilingual education in Arabic and Hebrew is necessary from first grade on for both Jews and Arabs	38.8	37.6	37.2
Arabic is very important for Israel's integration into the Middle East	55.8	58.4	54.0
It is very important to know Arabic as a matter of 'knowing your enemy'	65.4	74.2	59.8
I feel comfortable speaking Arabic outdoors	29.4	18.2	7.7
It bothers me when people speak Arabic next to me	18.0	14.8	18.4
I like to listen to Arabic music	12.0	19.0	7.3
I feel comfortable when hearing Arabic music	25.0	28.0	21.1

decrease. For instance, there were strong significant correlations between the statement 'bilingual education in Arabic and Hebrew is necessary from first grade on for both Jews and Arabs' and the statement 'Arabic is very important for Israel's integration into the Middle East'. The Pearson correlation coefficient (PCC) is 0.46 ($p < 0.01$) indicating that as Arab Jewish participants hold more positive attitudes towards bilingual education, they tend to see Arabic as important for life in the surrounding area. Similarly, other correlations were found between the positive tendency towards bilingual education and the level of comfort with Arabic music (0.28, $p < 0.01$). However, there was a weak and not statistically significant correlation with love for Arabic music. In these equations, the negative PCC for Arabic as a language of the enemy (-0.33, $p < 0.01$) indicates that the more positive attitude towards Arabic arise, the more the negative perception towards Arabic as the language of the enemy is weakened. However, the correlation patterns change when controlling for generational differences; I will elaborate more on this in the next section.

Generational differences

A comparison of the responses of three generations of Arab Jews revealed a loss of fluency in Arabic: fluency in spoken Arabic among the first generation of Arab Jews (25.6 per cent), the vast majority of whom arrived in the country as children and were all educated in the Hebrew education system, is almost twice that of their children (14 per cent) and twenty times that of the third generation (1.3 per cent). However, among first-generation immigrants from Arab countries, the percentage of those who are able to read Arabic texts is very low (2.4 per cent), generally because they arrived in Israel as children and it was before they began acquiring literacy skills in Arabic in their countries of origin.

The loss of Arabic language and culture, or remoteness as Shenhav (2006) calls it, across the three generations coincides with attitudes vis-à-vis the language, as shown in Table 10.3.

The fact that first-generation Arab Jews hold more positive attitudes towards learning and using Arabic does not necessarily mean that they tend to like the language. Rather, these attitudes may only explain, to some extent, their relationship to the language: the more one knows the language (or was exposed to it at a younger age), the more sympathy that person has towards it. However, this is only a partial explanation, as the first generation views Arabic as the language of the enemy, almost exactly to the same extent as the third generation – which, as noted, does not know Arabic as well.

When the correlations between different attitudes were examined, controlling for generational differences, no particularly noticeable difference were found. This is in line with the aforementioned result according to which when one type of feeling increases, the other tends to decrease. Interestingly, however, two Pearson coefficients stood out: the first was the correlation between a positive view

Table 10.3 Attitudes towards Arabic among three generations of Arab Jews

Statement	*First generation (N = 78) (%)*	*Second generation (N = 258) (%)*	*Third generation (N = 164) (%)*
Arabic should be an official language in Israel	56.7	46.9	39.7
All citizens of Israel should speak Hebrew only	43.3	38.8	32.1
Arabic should be taught at Jewish schools	59.1	58.5	46.2
Arabic is a very important component of Mizrahi Jewish heritage and should be preserved	47.0	34.9	14.1
Arabic is very important for daily life in Israel	62.8	57.8	52.6
Bilingual education in Arabic and Hebre w is necessary from first grade on for both Jews and Arabs	45.7	35.3	28.2
Arabic is very important for Israel's integration into the Middle East	66.5	56.2	48.7
It is very important to know Arabic as a matter of 'knowing your enemy'	76.2	72.1	76.9
I feel comfortable with speaking Arabic outdoors	30.5	33.3	14.1
It bothers me when people speak Arabic next to me	12.2	15.5	17.9
I like to listen to Arabic music	25.6	18.2	7.7
I feel comfortable when hearing Arabic music	32.3	27.9	19.2

towards bilingual education and a tendency to love listening to Arabic music (as opposed to passively, rather than actively, 'hearing Arabic music') changed dramatically from a weak and insignificant correlation to a significant positive correlation among the second (0.254, $p < 0.05$) and third (0.254, $p < 0.05$) generations of Arab Jews, with no change among the first generation. The second change in the Pearson coefficient was found in the correlation between positive attitudes towards bilingual education and viewing Arabic as 'the language of the enemy' among the third generation alone, such that the correlation was greatly weakened and became insignificant.

Put simply, the first finding suggests that the tendency among second- and third-generation Arab Jews to hold positive attitudes towards bilingual education increases as their love for Arabic increases. This correlation, however, does not exist among first-generation Arab Jews. The second finding suggests that among first- and second-generation Arab Jews, their tendency to hold positive attitudes towards bilingual education increases as their tendency to view Arabic as the 'language of the enemy' decreases. This correlation, however, does not exist among third-generation Arab Jews.

Avoiding the use of Arabic

The response of the interviewees to the statement 'I feel comfortable with speaking Arabic outdoors' reflects the main reason for the lack of Arabic among Jews in Israel. The question was addressed to those who responded that they *do* know Arabic, yet do not feel comfortable speaking it outdoors (the sample included 134 participants). Only 18 per cent of participants felt comfortable using Arabic outdoors, with a far higher percentage among Arab Jews (29 per cent versus 8 per cent, respectively). Differences in ease of using Arabic among Arab Jews were more pronounced among the first (31 per cent) and second (33 per cent) generations compared with the third (14 per cent).

Respondents clarified their decision to avoid using Arabic after we asked for the reasons. The responses mentioned several reasons:

(a) *Lack of skills in Arabic*: 'I do not know proper Arabic, I only know slang' or 'I do not feel that I know enough'. Around 40 per cent of those interviewed based their answers on a lack of adequate language skills, with no significant differences between non-Arab Jews and Arab Jews. The lack of fluency was the main barrier affecting third-generation Arab Jews (56.4 per cent), compared with the first (32.4 per cent) and (34.7 per cent) second generation, among which the percentage was smaller.

(b) *Non-useful language*: there were additional obstacles, such as the lack of a need to use Arabic in Israel. The following are only some of the responses we got that reflected the Jewish Israeli belief that Arabic simply is not a useful language: 'I have no one to speak with', 'since the Gaza Strip was closed, there are no more [Palestinian] workers to speak with in Arabic', 'this is not my language; in Israel Hebrew is the spoken language, not Arabic' or 'there is no reason it will help me in life, so what for?'

These responses reflect a situation common among minority languages in bilingual or multilingual cultures: while they may be carriers of 'tradition' or 'historical identity', the majority language comes to replace the language(s) of minorities, resulting in a situation in which the minority shifts over time to the majority's language (May 2003, 2005). This situation is highlighted by the fact that over 90 per cent of young Palestinians living in Israel know Hebrew well (Central Bureau of Statistics (Israel) 2013).

(c) *Aversion to Arabic*: other interviewees explained their reluctance to speak Arabic by their dislike of the language: 'This is not my language', 'it is considered primitive', 'I am not enthusiastic about the language, I only spoke Arabic at home', 'it requires too much effort from me' or 'it is not a suitable language for the "holiness" of Israel'. Interestingly, the distribution of responses shows that Arab Jews have a greater dislike for Arabic than non-Arab Jews.

(d) *Shame of Arabic:* 3 per cent of respondents stated that they avoid using Arabic because they are embarrassed, claiming the language is 'unacceptable in my surroundings' or 'it is shameful'. These answers were often provided by first- and second-generation Arab Jews.

The aforementioned reasons shed light on the negative attitudes towards Arabic. Whether it stems from lack of knowledge of the language, viewing it as useless, a contemptuous attitude or feeling ashamed, Arabic is neglected, and little by little disappears from among Jews, and especially among Arab Jews.

In order to know whether avoiding Arabic changes with age, the survey asked about how participants had felt about the language in the past. I found that almost half of the participants did not feel comfortable with Arabic when they were younger. Even more interesting was the finding that among Arab Jews, the third generation felt most uncomfortable with Arabic when they were younger (66.7 per cent), as opposed to the second (58.3 per cent) and the first generation (41.5 per cent).

Inter-class differences

The picture that emerges from the data shows that the disappearance of Arabic is not only a process that accelerated with each new generation, but also one that began quite early in each generation. To gain a better understating of Arab Jews' deeply engrained negative attitudes towards Arabic, one should take a few steps back to view the Israeli demographic and political map.

Demographic analysis (not shown here) shows that the gaps in average years of education between Arab Jews and non-Arab Jews is 4.28 versus 5.44 points,[3] respectively, and in income is 2.68 versus 3.00 points,[4] respectively. Clearly, there is a sizeable economic and educational advantage in favour of non-Arab Jews. This should come as no surprise when dealing with ethnic gaps in Israel: socio-economic disparities do not exist independently of racial or ethnic differences. Researchers in the United States have long recognised that there is a strong significant correlation between race and socio-economic status (SES) (Massey and Denton 1988; Jencks and Mayer 1990).

In the case of Israel, this correlation is mediated by the education system and its discriminatory attitude towards the local 'non-white' populations, in which secondary education in Israel uses curricular tracking that has led to the separation of ethno-cultural groups (Shavit 1984, 1990). For instance, historically Ashkenazi Jews were more integrated into government initiatives, ownership of factories, wealth and professional work. Mizrahi Jews, on the other hand, were employed as unskilled or semi-professional labourers (Svirski and Bernstein 1993). The social divide between the two Jewish groups is sustained by residential segregation in which the ethnic cleavage has become largely correlated with socio-economic status and educational attainment: overall Ashkenazi Jews fare better than Mizrahi Jews and tend to be seen as the hegemonic group (Resh and Dar 1996). Moreover, previous studies concluded that closing the educational gaps between Mizrahi and Ashkenazi Jews did not guarantee a decline in the earnings gap between the two groups (Cohen 2002b).

The two other background indicators (degree of religiosity and voting patterns), emphasised the complexity involved in the linkage between politics and religion in Israel. According to the data it would seem that Arab Jews are more religious (2.50 versus 2.07 points,[5] respectively) and tend towards right-wing parties (1.28 versus 1.69 points,[6] respectively). To get a better understanding of the voting patterns among Arab Jews, one must concentrate on the historical treatment of Arab Jews by Zionist left-wing parties in Israel (Labor, Meretz or their previous incarnations of Mapam, Ratz, etc.). The distribution among the political left–centre-right is quite similar to that of many other countries. However, the political discourse in Israel revolves heavily around security issues in contrast to Europe where the division is based primarily on attitudes towards socio-economic issues. In practice, however, this division was influenced by the Israeli Black Panthers, who raised public consciousness over the discrimination and unequal distribution of resources faced by immigrants from Arab or Muslim countries in the 1970s. At that time, Likud – the current ruling right-wing party led by Benjamin Netanyahu – rose to power with the hope of creating an alternative to the Zionist left parties, which deprived the Mizrahi Jews (and the Palestinians, of course) of material and cultural resources. Although Likud did not necessarily benefit Mizrahi Jews, this division between right and left, as it relates to ethnic origin, still exists. It is worth noting that not all Mizrahi Jews are right-wing and not all Ashkenazim are left-wing (Chetrit 2009; Shamir 2015).

When it comes to religiosity, a closer look at the distribution of the answers reveals that 13 per cent of non-Arab Jews consider themselves to be very religious or Orthodox, while only 7 per cent of Arab Jews fit this definition. On the other side of the scale, 27.8 per cent of Arab Jews identified as non-religious or secular, as opposed to the vast majority of non-Arab Jews (59.0 per cent). The picture became more complex when I compared other categories such as 'masorti' (lit. 'traditional', not strictly observant Jews): 48.6 per cent of Arab Jews identify as masorti compared with 18.4 per cent of non-Arab Jews. In this context, I tend to adopt the explanation offered by Shenhav (2006) and Khazzoom (2003), which suggests that Judaism in Arab and Muslim countries has allowed a succession of identities, as opposed to the binary division of Judaism (religious versus secular) in the West.

A closer look at the data can explain, to some extent, that the dissonance in Arab Jewish attitudes vis-à-vis Arabic was a result of the loss of Arabic language and culture, coupled with their historic support for right-wing parties (especially Likud). Moreover, this process feeds off Arab Jews' political affiliation to nationalist, right-wing parties; those parties that, at best, do not help Arab Jews and, at worst, continue to oppress the party's voters. However, a reader may well wonder how the demographic data squares with the attitudes towards Arabic in the context of class differences.

Interestingly, when the correlation between education and attitudes was tested, the results showed significant differences among Arab Jews: 38 per cent of Arab Jews with poor education tended to like Arabic music, compared with only 15 per cent of educated Arab Jews who hold an academic degree. Interestingly, among highly-educated non-Arab Jews, 9 per cent tended to like Arabic music more than their educated Arab Jewish counterparts. The distaste for Arabic music further emphasises the relationship between class and Arabic: among non-educated Arab Jews, 42 per cent tended to dislike Arabic music, compared with 67 per cent of educated Arab Jews, and 64 per cent of the highly-educated non-Arab Jews. Overall, the Arab Jewish 'elite' tended to hold attitudes closer to those of non-Arab Jewish origin vis-à-vis Arabic, especially among the elite. It is therefore unsurprising that an income gap exists between the elite Arab Jews and their Ashkenazi counterparts.

I also examined Arab Jews' cultural connection to Arabic, expressed in positive attitudes towards music and Arabic as part of Jewish heritage. On the one hand, Arab Jews still view Arabic culture more positively than non-Arab Jews (although this attitude has decreased over the generations and among social classes), while, on the other hand, there has been a painful loss of an ancient culture that has been derided as 'low culture' due to its association with Arabic. Thus, it seems that Arabic plays a significant role as a social and cultural dividing mechanism, or what is known as *habitus* (Bourdieu 1984, 1990). In the general sense of the term, habitus 'distinguishes' between high and low status, and must be seen in a proper context. The elite Arab Jews distance themselves from Arabic and Arab identity in this case in order to distinguish themselves from the common Arab Jews who belong to the less educated and less dominant group. And yet, ironically, the Westernisation process has been only partially successful, since the gaps in income still exist between the two elite groups (36 per cent of the Arab Jewish elite say they earn more than average, versus 49 per cent of the non-Arab elite). This is consistent with the findings of the aforementioned studies, which show that closing the educational gaps did not lead to closing the income gaps (Cohen 2002b).

Summary and conclusions

In the context of Arabic and focusing on Arab Jews in Israel, I have argued that in order to understand the current situation of the Arabic language, one must examine the reasons for the lack of knowledge of Arabic. In other words, it is important to deal with the situation as it is on the ground; it is essential to consider the inferior status of the Arabic language in Israel, the wide scale of social segregation between Palestinians and Jews, the role of Jewish identity among Jews from Arab countries (and Arabism in general), and the security context in which Arabic is taught in Israel.

As has been shown, Arab Jews hold more negative attitudes towards Arabic than do non-Arab Jews, an element that was very clear among second and third generations. There seems, however, to be some contradiction among the attitudes of Arab Jews. On the one hand, they hold more negative attitudes towards Arabic as an official language. On the other hand, their attitude softens with regard to the language in a cultural-historical context (music, for example). However, a deeper analysis of the demographics reveals even more complexity, as Arabic becomes a mechanism with which to distinguish the cultural elite in Israel.

The irony is that this detachment and denial of Arab origins testifies to the success of the Western Zionist project, as Khazzom (2003) and Shenhav (2006) argued. This success also includes the exclusionary discourse of Palestinians, such that instead of creating an 'alliance of the oppressed' in terms of culture, society and economy, what ended up happening was a significant disconnect and renouncing of most Arab markers. This manifested first and foremost in the loss of language and ended in orientalising Palestinians as the ultimate 'primitive other'. On the face of it, it does not seem like there is much hope for Jews to reconnect with Arabic. However, I argue that residues of the connection with Arab culture do still exist, and could perhaps serve as a reminder of the connection between Judaism and Arabism.

In the course of writing this chapter, for the first time in its history, the Israeli Knesset marked Arabic Language Day on 24 May 2016. For the first time members of the Knesset – from different parts of the political spectrum – spoke in Arabic in the Knesset plenum or in the conference hall. This event sought to deal with the low official status of Arabic in Israel, and included various discussions in the Knesset committees on issues such as language and road signs, the teaching of Arabic in Jewish schools, and more.

The results of the survey were presented and discussed in the Knesset during Arabic Language Day in order to emphasise the gloomy state of affairs. The good news was the unanimous agreement on the immediate need to improve Arabic instruction in Jewish schools. Meanwhile, the discussion about the relationship between Arabic and security, what Mendel called 'the elephant in the room', was rarely spoken about in the official discussion.

The prevailing view among the Israeli Jewish public towards Arabic is unconscious at best. The vast majority do not have the basic knowledge to communicate with their Palestinian neighbours, let alone surrounding Arab countries. Salman Natour, a Palestinian writer and novelist, distinguished between Jewish–Israelis who wish to become 'permanent residents' and those who will forever remain 'temporary residents', the latter of which come to the Middle East for a temporary period and are uninterested in investing in their surroundings, such as learning the local language. Permanent residents, on the other hand, want to be part of the region and integrate into it, learn its language and learn to live with its landscape.

Natour's proposal requires effort, first and foremost from Arab Jews who abandoned – or were forced to – abandon the language of their grandparents. The first step on the personal level can begin with learning Arabic out of a desire to connect with the people of the region, as well as with the heritage of their grandparents – the heritage of Abū ʿImrān Mūsā ibn ʿUbayd Allāh ibn Maymūn al-Qurṭubī (also known as Maimonides, or in contemporary Hebrew *Ha-Rambam*) – and other important medieval Jewish philosophers whose books were initially written in Arabic. Going back to Arabic is the long bridge needing to be crossed in order to discover the hidden treasures of Jewish heritage. Crossing this bridge will also shorten the path to Palestinian society and the Arab world at large. The journey, however, must begin by changing the image and status of Arabic in Israel. This is essential for life in the Middle East, as a tool for mediation rather than conflict; remembering that language has never been the reason for conflicts nor is it the essence of the conflicts, as Suleiman (2004) concludes.

The second step should come from policy-makers. As a basic and fundamental decision, they will need to disconnect the historical Jewish–Israeli relationship between the Arabic language and state security, and instead move towards fully recognising the rich culture of Israel's Arab Jews as well as its Palestinian citizens and, of course, of the Arab and Palestinian people at large. In this context, the discussion – but also the practical steps taken recently such as a new initiative for building a serious Arabic curriculum in Jewish schools starting in first grade – is certainly a welcomed first step. I do not believe that the close association between Arabic and Israel's military will disappear soon, but I want to believe deeply that there is at least some good will behind such initiatives. As for the long term, I believe that such initiatives could change the balance of social, cultural, linguistic and power relations.

On the last day of working on this chapter, I heard a song by legendary Jewish Yemenite singer Ofra Haza (also known in Arabic as ʿAfrea Hazaʿa عفراء هزاع), who paved the way for Mizrahi music into the Israeli mainstream, in which one could hear the similarities between Arabic and Hebrew – their pronunciation, melody and culture. It sounds like a seemingly banal statement; however, it is important to note that the connection (or disconnect, rather) between Palestinian and Arab Jewish cultural elements is not an obvious one, and often does not exist in the Palestinian–Israeli context. The establishment's attempt to blur Arab Jewish identity, alongside its tendency towards the Israeli right, only added fuel to the fire between Arab Jews and Palestinians, both of whom largely suffer from the same hegemonic Ashkenazi leadership. These contemporary and historical connections between Palestinians, Arab Jews and the Arabic language require further study. Ofra Haza's song, for a moment, suddenly made this connection seem natural again.

Notes

1. This work derives from the Command of Arabic among Israeli Jews study conducted in the B. I. and Lucille Cohen Institute for Public Opinion Research, Tel Aviv University, and the Van Leer Jerusalem Institute. I am indebted to Yehouda Shenhav, Yonatan Mendel and Rami Avnimelech for the unique opportunity to enjoy their cooperation, useful advice and criticism.
2. See the following link for more information: http://www.acri.org.il/en/wp-content/uploads/2011/10/Basic-Law-Jewish-State-ACRI-position-ENG.pdf.
3. According to a 1–8 scale in which 1 = elementary education or less; 8 = Master's degree or higher a degree.
4. According to a 1–5 scale in which 1 = far below average; 5 = well above the average.
5. According to a 1–5 scale in which 1 = very religious or orthodox; 5 = non-religious or secular.
6. According to a 1–3 scale in which 1 = right-wing parties; 3 = left-wing parties.

References

Amara, M., *Language Education Policy: The Arab Minority in Israel* (Dordrecht: Kluwer Academic, 2002).

Amara, M., *Arabic in the Israeli Academy: Historical Absence, Current Challenges, and Future Possibilities* (Jerusalem: Van Leer Institute Press, 2016, in Arabic and Hebrew).

Bekerman, Z. and Horenczyk, G., 'Arab–Jewish bilingual coeducation in Israel: A long-term approach to intergroup conflict resolution', *Journal of Social Issues* 60(2) (2004): 389–404.

Ben-Rafael, E., Shohamy, E., Hasan Amara, M. and Trumper-Hecht, N., 'Linguistic landscape as symbolic construction of the public space: The case of Israel', *International Journal of Multilingualism* 3(1) (2006): 7–30.

Bourdieu, P., *Distinction: A Social Critique of the Judgment of Taste* (Cambridge, MA: Harvard University Press, 1984).

Bourdieu, P., *The Logic of Practice* (Stanford, CA: Stanford University Press, 1990).

Central Bureau of Statistics (Israel), *Social Survey – 2011: Learning Over a Lifetime and Use of Language* (Jerusalem: Central Bureau of Statistics, 2013).

Chetrit, S. S., *Intra-Jewish Conflict in Israel: White Jews, Black Jews* (New York: Routledge, 2009).

Cohen, Y., 'From haven to heaven: Changing patterns of immigration to Israel, challenging ethnic citizenship', in Daniel Levy and Yfaat Weiss (eds), *Challenging Ethnic Citizenship: German and Israeli Perspectives on Immigration* (New York: Berghahn, 2002a), pp. 37–56.

Cohen, Y., 'Rising wage and the wage-gap between Mizrahim and Ashkenazi', Pinhas Sapir Center for Development, Tel-Aviv University, 2002b, available at: http://primage.tau.ac.il/libraries/brender/booksf/1624329.pdf.

Donitsa-Schmidt, S., Shohamy, E. and Inbar, O., 'Students' motivation as a function of language learning: The teaching of Arabic in Israel', in Z. Dörnyei and R. Schmidt (eds), *Motivation and Second Language Acquisition* (Honolulu, HI: University of Hawaii Press, 2001), pp. 297–311.

Fishman, J. A., *Sociolinguistics: A Brief Introduction* (Rowley, MA: Newbury House, 1970).

Gharrah, R., *Arab Society in Israel: Population, Society, Economy* (7) (Jerusalem: Van Leer Jerusalem Institute, 2015).

Hayam-Yonas, A. and Malka, S., *Toward the Development of a Curriculum in Arabic Junior High and High Schools in the Jewish Sector: Evaluation Study* (Jerusalem: Henrietta Szold Institute, 2006).

Jencks, C. and Mayer, S., 'The social consequences of growing up in a poor neighborhood', in L. Lynn Jr. and M. G. H. McGeary (eds), *Inner-City Poverty in the United States* (Washington, DC: National Academies Press, 1990), pp. 111–86.

Khamaisi, R., 'Introduction', in R. Khamaisi (ed.), *Arab Society in Israel, vol. 3: Population, Society and Economy* (Jerusalem: Van Leer Jerusalem Institute and Hakibbutz Hameuchad Publishing, 2009).
Khazzoom, A., 'The great chain of orientalism: Jewish identity, stigma management, and ethnic exclusion in Israel', *American Sociological Review* 68(4) (2003): 481–510.
Massey, D. S. and Denton, N. A., 'The dimensions of residential segregation', *Social Forces* 67(2) (1988): 281–315.
May, S., 'Rearticulating the case for minority language rights', *Current Issues in Language Planning* 4(2) (2003): 95–125.
May, S., 'Language rights: Moving the debate forward', *Journal of Sociolinguistics* 9(3) (2005): 319–47.
Mendel, Y., *The Creation of Israeli Arabic: Political and Security Considerations in the Making of Arabic Language Studies in Israel* (Basingstoke: Palgrave Macmillan, 2014).
Pinto, M., 'Who is afraid of language rights in Israel?; in A. Sagi and O. Nachtomy (eds), *The Multicultural Challenge in Israel* (Boston, MA: Academic Studies Press, 2009), pp. 26–51.
Pinto, M., 'Minority language and language policy: The case of Arabic in Israel', 2011, available at: http://primage.tau.ac.il/day/229124.pdf.
Resh, N. and Dar, Y., 'Segregation within integration in Israeli junior high schools', *Israel Social Science Research* 11(1) (1996): 1–22.
Shamir, M., *In The elections in Israel, 2013* (New Brunswick, NJ: Transaction, 2015).
Shavit, Y., 'Tracking and ethnicity in Israeli secondary education', *American Sociological Review* 49(2) (1984): 210–20.
Shavit, Y., 'Segregation, tracking, and the educational attainment of minorities: Arabs and Oriental Jews in Israel', *American Sociological Review* 55(1) (1990): 115–26.
Shenhav, Y., *The Arab Jews: A Postcolonial Reading of Nationalism, Religion, and Ethnicity* (Stanford, CA: Stanford University Press, 2006).
Shenhav, Y., Dallashi, M., Avnimelech, R., Mizrachi, N. and Mendel, Y., *Command of Arabic among Israeli Jews* (Jerusalem: Van Leer Jerusalem Institute, 2015).
Shohamy, E. G., *Language Policy: Hidden Agendas and New Approaches* (London: Routledge, 2006).
Shohat, E., 'Sephardim in Israel: Zionism from the standpoint of its Jewish victims', *Social Text* 19/20 (1988): 1–35.
Shwed, U., Shavit, Y., Dallashi, M. and Ofek, M., 'Integration of Arab Israelis and Jews in schools in Israel', in D. Ben David (ed.), *State of the Nation Report* (Jerusalem: Taub Center, 2014) .
Smooha, S., *Still Playing by the Rules: The Index of Arab-Jewish Relations in Israel* (Jerusalem: Israel Democracy Institute, 2012).
Suleiman, Y., *A War of Words: Language and Conflict in the Middle East* (New York: Cambridge University Press, 2004).

Surkes, S., 'Jewish teacher of Arabic tells class to translate "I want to kill Jews"', 10 March 2016, *The Times of Israel*, available at: http://www.timesofisrael.com/jewish-teacher-of-arabic-tells-class-to-translate-i-want-to-kill-jews.
Swirski, S. and Bernstein, D., 'Who worked doing what? For whom? And for what?: The economic development of Israel and the constitution of the racial division of labour', in U. Ram (ed.), *Israeli Society: Critical Perspectives* (Tel Aviv: Breirot, 1993, in Hebrew), pp. 120–48.

CHAPTER 11

War Names in the Arab–Israeli Conflict: A Comparative Study

Muhammad Amara

Introduction

Political and ethnic conflicts give language greater influence and more political and ideological power than usual. Ideologised conflicts are more severe than others and give rise to clear and quite powerful linguistic reflections and interactions. Suleiman (2004) maintains that language is fundamentally a cultural practice, but also functions as a focus of ideological competition, because of the unequal power relations between collectives and individuals that it reflects.

A linguistic conflict is not a conflict between the languages themselves, but between their speakers who have a dispute over resources or values in given regions. Language is rarely the cause of a conflict between the quarrelling parties, but it does constitute an active tool with which the competing collectives express and ideologise their conflict. A linguistic conflict uses symbolic and communicative resources in unequal power relationships.

Linguistic conflicts have been called *language conflict* in titles of books and articles (Das Gupta 1970; Inglehart & Woodward 1972; Laitin, 1987; Jahr 1993; Dua 1996), and the phrase *Language and War* appears in Clavet (1998) and Lakoff (2000); occasionally, the term *linguistic invasion* is also encountered (Suleiman 2004: 16).

The clash between Arabic and Hebrew is one of the lesser studied aspects of the Arab–Israeli conflict, one whose role has so far not received its fair share of scholarly attention in contrast to other facets: political, military, economic and social (Amara and Marʿi 2008). The linguistic conflict between Arabic and Hebrew in Israel and Palestine is part of a larger dispute over resources, symbols and political control.

In this chapter, I shall address the issue of how language is used in the Arab–Israeli conflict, specifically through a comparison of the names given to wars by both sides. Such a comparative study will, we hope, shed new and important light on the conflict.

The role of language in the Arab–Israeli conflict

Before entering into our discussion on the names of the wars, we would like to say something about the role of language in the Arab–Israeli conflict. The Arabs in the Arab world in general view Hebrew as the language of the enemy as well as the language of a foreign entity that has been imposed in their midst, a language whose objective is to convince former and new immigrants of Israel's right to exist in the Middle East. At the same time, it serves and abets the continued occupation of Arab land, which is considered Jewish land that the Arabs had taken control of by force and whose time has come to be returned to its rightful owners, in accordance with the Jewish religious and historical view (Lustick 1994).

As Suleiman explains (2004: 215), 'the presence of Hebrew in the Middle East is therefore delegitimised as an intrusion from the outside, aided and abetted by the colonial aspirations of Britain as mandatory authority. Consequently, interest in Hebrew is driven by security considerations.' In other words, Hebrew in this view plays the role of a colonialist language in the Middle East, just as English did in the days of the British Mandate. There are those who encourage the teaching of Hebrew among the Arabs, but only out of security considerations, in order to 'know your enemy' (Abd-el-Jawad and al-Haq 1997; al-Haq 1999).

The peace accords have somewhat taken the edge off the conflict, including its linguistic aspect. Abd-el-Jawad and al-Haq (1997) provide numerous examples of how in the wake of the peace treaty between Israel and Jordan in 1994 the press in Jordan stopped depicting Israel as 'the enemy', 'the Zionist entity' or 'the colonialist entity', all expressions that were in very common use previously. Suleiman (2004) states that something similar happened after the signing of the peace treaty with Egypt in 1979, as well as after the Oslo Accords of 1993 and the Cairo Agreement of 1995 between Israel and the Palestinians, following which the Palestinian Authority was established.

As for Jordanian attitudes towards learning Hebrew, a study by al-Haq (1999) shows that Jordanian college students associated it with utilitarian motivations. In other areas, their attitudes were negative towards Hebrew.

Palestinian Arabs inside Israel, not surprisingly, have a different attitude towards Hebrew, since after the establishment of the State of Israel they were forced to accept Israeli citizenship. Living together with Jews created spaces of encounter and cooperation, and Hebrew became the common language in which the two sides communicated with each other. In other words, the Palestinian Arabs in Israel use Hebrew for various purposes in the public sphere, whether at the work place, in government offices, in higher education, in medical institutions, in the media and in the Knesset (Israeli parliament). Outside their place of residence, it is difficult for Arabs to manage without a sufficient knowledge of Hebrew (Amara 1999, 2013).

The findings of a study by Amara and Marʿi (2002) show great differences in the perception of the three languages, Arabic, Hebrew and English. The symbolic aspect was found to predominate in the perception of Arabic, while Hebrew was perceived as the language of communication with Jewish Israelis in various areas of life, and as such knowledge of the language was considered useful for pragmatic purposes (for example, 'learning Hebrew can improve one's chances of being admitted to university') as well as for socio-economic mobilisation (for example, 'finding work in Israel', etc.). In contrast, English was considered vital for practical purposes (see Ben-Rafael et al. 2006; Amara 2015).[1]

To conclude, although Hebrew is perceived by Palestinian Arab citizens in Israel mainly as a tool for communicating with Jewish Israelis in the various domains of life, there is a very positive tendency that favours the study of Hebrew at as early an age as possible, and that does not perceive this language as a 'language of conflict' or 'the language of the enemy'.[2]

As for the Jews, since the first groups of immigrants came to Palestine a continuous debate has been going on among them concerning the position and status of Arabic and of learning Arabic. Leading Jewish figures such as Ahad Ha'Am and the historian Joseph Klausner opposed the teaching of Arabic, which they feared would result in Levantinisation. But others, such as Joseph Luria, believed that learning Arabic would promote acclimatisation in the region (Elbaum-Dror 1986).

The debate about learning Arabic continued after the establishment of the State of Israel, when the socio-political environment did not promote the teaching of Arabic in Jewish schools, due to the ideological hegemony of Hebrew as the basic language of public discourse, symbolising the hegemony of the Jews in the new state. In addition, there was little public support for teaching Arabic, not to speak of the fact that it faced competition from English and later French, both global languages (Spolsky and Shohamy 1999: 140). However, security considerations motivated the teaching of Arabic, in which the Israeli Defence Forces (IDF) and Israel's intelligence services are deeply involved, as well as the military regime, and the Prime Minter's office (Mendel 2014).

Language in situations of conflict acts as a boundary, separating people from each other and defining the meaning of belonging to ethnic and national collectives (for example, Spolsky 2004; Suleiman 2004; Bassiouney 2009). No extraneous element can belong to the given ethnic or national space without meeting certain identifying conditions, among which language is one of the most basic, since it constitutes an existential expression, possessing meanings of identity and belonging, and so its role in conflicts parallels that of the political and cultural conflicts in its environment.

The Arab–Israeli conflict has multiple facets, beyond the political, the military and the economic, and beyond the struggle over the land. Indeed, it includes symbolic, and cultural aspects, since the Jewish state strives to strengthen its

Jewish nature using various means in different domains. Few Arab studies have focused on acts of geographical Judaisation by means of expropriation and restrictions, but have under-researched the linguistic–cultural dimension (Marʿi 2006; Shohamy and Abu Ghazaleh-Mahajneh 2012).

War names

While naming practices exist in all societies, they vary considerably from one society to another. The variations include the type of names given, the systems through which they are given and their use in social interactions. Although the primary function of a name is to designate a particular entity, human or non-human, its symbolic meaning is normally derived from the set of cultural and ideological values that are associated with it at the points of production and reception. The symbolic meaning of names varies from one context to another and 'assumes greater importance in situations of conflict than in conditions of natural interaction. This is true of place names in the Arab–Israeli conflict where ideological considerations rule supreme . . .' (Suleiman 2004: 159).

As to war names, Suleiman (2011: 221) explains that:

> In the Middle East, Israel has the richest store of code names. In the 1948 War, Israel used about twenty-eight code names; the Arab countries seem to have used none. In the 1956 Suez Crisis, Israel used five code names, while Egypt seems to have used none. In the wars against Lebanon, Israel used at least five code names, whereas Hezbollah used none. These other discrepancies between Israel and Arab countries reflect differences of institutional practice, whereby the Arabs are less attuned to the use of code names than Israel.

Generally speaking, Suleiman is right as to code names, though in the confrontations between Israel and Palestinians in Gaza between 2008 and 2014, the Palestinians did use code names. However, the wars generated many names among Arabs, though not code names. Names of wars reveal yet another aspect of the conflict between Arabs and Jews, one to which Israelis have attached considerable importance for two reasons. One is that Israel was the victor in most of these wars, while the Arab states were defeated, and so it wished to use this way to impose its dominance, in accordance with the ancient maxim that it is the victor who writes history. The other is the manifestation of the state's Jewishness through the use of religious and historical elements in the Jewish nation's past and connecting to the present.

Wars among nations throughout history have been so numerous that names had to be given to them in order to distinguish them from each other. In the past wars have been called after the places in which they took place or after some particular aspect of the war itself. If we take the wars of the Arabs throughout their history as an example, from pre-Islamic times, through the Prophet's raids down to the war against the Crusaders, we find that battles were named either after the place in which they took place, such as the raids of *Badr*, *Uhud* and *Tabuk* and the battles of *Yarmuk* and *Qadisiyya*, or after some peculiarity of the battle or war itself, such as the 'raid of the parties' (*ghazwat al-aḥzāb*), the battle of the 'trench' (*al-khandaq*), the 'wars of apostasy' (*ḥurūb al-ridda*) or the battle of the 'camel' (*al-jamal*).

In the West the names of wars are chosen with extreme care and deliberation (Sieminski 1995), whereas the Arabs choose names that arouse the emotions (Suleiman 2011). For example, in the West the First Gulf War was given the political cinematic name *Desert Storm*, while Arab media used the traditional ritual name *Mother of Battles* (*umm al-maʿārik*). The American name reflects the stormy desert environment in which the troops fought and with which they had to cope, while the Arabs confront America with a verbal system based on rhetoric, hoping to win the war with fiery speeches that feed and satisfy the emotions (see Suleiman 2004).

Most of the Arab–Israeli wars were given names that refer to the time at which they took place, the place in which they occurred or some special feature about them. In fact, most of the wars have more than one name. As Table 11.1 shows, there are clear differences in the names which Arabs and Jews chose for the wars.

In what follows, I will clarify the names of these wars. The most commonly used names will appear in the headings.

The Arab Catastrophe (*nakba*) / The Liberation (of the Land of Israel)

Following UN Resolution 181 partitioning Palestine between the Jews and the Palestinians violence increased and the British withdrew from Palestine in May 1948. The Arab countries neighbouring Palestine together with Iraq and Saudi Arabia sent their armies to help the Palestinians in their war against the Jews. The war resulted in the defeat of the Arab armies. The Jews thus succeeded in establishing their Jewish state, Israel, on the major parts of Palestine (Amara 1999; Rogan 2004).

This was the first war between the Arabs and Israel, generally referred to as 'the first of the Zionist–Arab wars' (Khalidi 1997) or 'the war over Palestine'. This war, considered a watershed with respect to the Arab armies and Israel, confirmed the declaration of the State of Israel and the division of Palestine. During this war more than 700,000 Palestinians were expelled from their homeland and Israel took control of more than 78 per cent of the territory of Mandatory Palestine (Ghanem 2005; Abu Sitta 2007). The expelled residents became refugees.

Table 11.1 Names of wars between Israel and Arab armies*

Year	*Names in Arabic as used in Arab countries*	*Names in Hebrew as used in Israel*	*Arab countries/ sides involved in the war*
1948	The War of 48 (*ḥarb al-thamāni wa-arbaʿīn*) The Catastrophe (*al-nakba*) The Year of the Collapse (*sanat al-inhiyār*) The War over Palestine (*al-ḥarb ʿala falasṭīn*) The Palestine War of 1948 (*ḥarb falasṭīn 1948*)	The War of Liberation (*milḥemet hashiḥrur*) The War of Independence (*milḥemet ha-atsmaʾut*) The War of year 5708 (according to the Jewish calendar) (*milḥemet tashaḥ*) The War of Revival (*milḥemet hakomemiyut*)	Egypt, Iraq, Syria, Jordan, Lebanon, Palestinians
1956	The Suez War (*ḥarb al-Suwes*) The Tripartite Aggression against Egypt (*al-ʿudwān al-thulāthī ʿala Miṣr*)	The Sinai War (*milḥemet Sinay*) Operation Qadesh (*mivtsaʿ kadesh*)	Egypt
1967	The 67 War (*ḥarb sabʿa wa-sitīn*) The Relapse (*al-naksa*) The June Aggression (*ʿudwān ḥuzayrān*) The War of June 67 (*ḥarb ḥuzayrān*)	The Six Day War (*milḥemet sheshet hayamim*)	Egypt, Jordan, Syria
1973	The War of 6 October (*ḥarb al-sādis min October*) The 10th of Ramaḍan (*al-ʿāshir min Ramaḍān*) The War of the Crossing (*ḥarb al-ʿubūr*) The October War (*ḥarb tishrīn*)	The Day of Atonement (*milḥemet yom kipuur*)	Egypt, Syria
1982	The Lebanon War (*ḥarb lubnān*) The Assault on Lebanon (*ghazw lubnān*) The Destruction of Lebanon (*ijtiyāḥ lubnān*)	Operation Safety of Galilee (*milḥemet shelom hagalil*)	The Palestinian organisations in Lebanon
1987	The First Intifada (*al-intifāda al-ʾūla*) The Stones/Rocks Intifada (*intifāḍat al-ḥijārah*)	The First Palestinian Intifada (*ha-intifaada ha-falasṭinit ha-rishona*)	Palestine (the West Bank and the Gaza Strip)

2000	The Al-Aqsa Intifada (*intifāḍat al-Aqsa*) The Second Intifada (*al- intifāḍa al-thāniya*)	The Second Palestinian Intifada (*ha-intifaada ha-falasṭinit ha-shniya*) The Al-Aqsa Intifada (*intifadat al-Aqsa*) The War of Terrorism and Murder (*milḥemet ha-terror ve-ha-retsaḥ*) The War of Protecting the Home (*ha-milḥama ʿal ha-bayit*)	Palestine (the West Bank and the Gaza Strip)
2006	The Sixth War (*al-ḥarb al-sādisa*) The War for Lebanon (*al-ḥarb ʿala lubnān*) The July War (*ḥarb tammūz*) The Invasion of Lebanon (*ijtiyāḥ lubnān*) The Second War for Lebanon (*al-ḥarb al-thāniya ʿala lubnān*)	The Second Lebanon War (*milḥemet levanon hashniya*)	Hezbollah
The campaigns between Israel and Gaza**			
2008	The Battle of the Distinction (*al-furqān*) The Aggression against Gaza (*al-ʿudwān ʿala Ghaza*)	Cast Lead (*ʿofert yetsuka*)	Gaza
2010	Stones of Hard Clay (*ḥijārat sijjil*) The Aggression against Gaza (*al-ʿudwān ʿala Gaza*)	Pillar of Defence (*ʿamud ʿanan*)	Gaza
2014	Eaten Straw (*al-ʿaṣf al- maʾkūl*] Firm Structure (*al-bunyān al-marṣūṣ*) The Aggression against Gaza (*al-ʿudwān ʿala Ghaza*)	Protective Edge (*tsuk eitan*)	Gaza

* Names are given in Arabic and Hebrew transliteration.
** These were not recognised by Israel as wars. Israel never officially or legally declared them as wars, nor were they defined as such in the Arab world. In Arabic they were called 'Aggression against Gaza', perhaps because the war took place between Israel as a state with a regular army and Hamas and other Palestinian groups, which were considered organisations.

The Jews call this war 'The War of Independence', 'The War of Liberation', 'The War of 5708' (the year 1948 in the Jewish calendar) or 'The War of Revival', as proposed by David Ben-Gurion in his memoirs (Ben-Gurion 1982: 1/34). The first two of these appellations are based on the premise of the Jewish religion and the Zionist ideology that the land had been occupied by the Arabs and was now liberated. The third name is taken from the Jewish year, while the fourth is taken from traditional Jewish sources. Both serve to refer to the revival of the Jewish people by establishing its independent state. The Arabs, on the other hand, call it the 'catastrophe' (*nakba*) of the Palestinian people; some call it 'the year of collapse'.

The first person to have used the name *al-nakba* to refer to the events of 1948 was Constantine Zreiq, whose *The Meaning of the Nakba*[3] was published in Beirut several weeks after the establishment of the State of Israel. In it he says (Zreiq 1994:11):

> The Arabs' defeat in Palestine is not merely a simple *nakba*, or some passing insignificant evil. Rather, it is a *nakba* in the full sense of this word, one of the gravest misfortunes to have afflicted the Arabs in their long history of ordeals and tragedies.

Zreiq stresses the *nakba*'s psychological and cultural effects on the Palestinians:

> Hundreds of thousands of that afflicted (*mankub*) land's people were not only expelled from their homes and became aimless wanderers, but their very thoughts and opinions, and those of the sons of their homeland in all their homes, were also expelled and wandered. (ibid.: 17)

Israel's Palestinian Arab citizens have come to call the day on which the country celebrates its Independence Day '*nakba Day*'. The day is devoted to visiting the remnants of the abandoned villages in order to strengthen the collective memory and to acquaint the younger generation with the dispersion that was forced on the Palestinian people during the second half of the twentieth century (see Masalha 2005; Cohen 2010).[4]

The Arabs' expulsion from Palestine has been compared with their expulsion from Spain, both being perceived as catastrophic events in which religious and national elements were combined (Khalidi 2001).

Arab scholars are united in the view that the Palestinian Arab *nakba* and the catastrophe of the Jews are closely intertwined and that the former is a direct and indirect consequence of the latter. According to Emil Habibi (1989: 26) 'the Jews' catastrophe was the cause for ours'. Bishara (1995: 54) states that the Jewish catastrophe occurred on European soil and was executed by Europeans, but that the price is being paid by the people of the Middle East, especially the Palestinians.

The Tripartite Aggression against Egypt / Operation Qadesh

This war is known throughout the world as the Suez War, which broke out after the president of Egypt at the time, Gamal Abdul Nasser, nationalised the Suez Canal, whereupon France and Britain, in coordination with Israel, launched an all-out attack on Egypt on 29 October 1956. Israel explained its participation in the war as vengeance for the attacks against it which had been carried out by the Fedayeen, the Palestinian fighters, from Gaza.

From the Israeli perspective this was a 'preventive war for survival' (Bar-On 1988). It viewed the acquisition by Egypt of weapons from the Eastern Bloc as a grave danger, which had to be met as quickly as possible in order to maintain the balance of power. Concerning this war Menahem Begin, the ex prime minister of Israel, said that he was unhesitatingly in favour of such a preventive war against the Arab states in order to achieve two objectives: to crush the Arab forces and to expand Israel's territory (Bar-On 1988).

Egypt called this war, which lasted fifty days, 'The Tripartite Aggression', because it was attacked by three countries: Britain, France and Israel. In Israel, it received the name given it by David Ben-Gurion, 'Operation Qadesh', named for Qadesh Barnea', the name of an oasis in the Sinai Desert near the Negev that was of great importance in antiquity and is mentioned in the Old Testament. Moshe Dayan proposed calling it 'The Sinai War', because Israel occupied the Sinai Peninsula but withdrew from it in 1957.

The *Naksa* ('The Relapse') / The Six Day War

This war took place between Israel on one side and Syria, Egypt and Jordan, the latter reinforced by Iraqi troops, on the other. The Arab forces were roundly defeated by the IDF in six days.

The war sent shock waves of disappointment through the Arab world, from the Atlantic Ocean to the Persian Gulf. The defeat had repercussions at a number of levels. At the military level, the war destroyed the morale and arms of the Arab forces. Those responsible for the military failure were put on trial. The war brought about the collapse of the concept of a 'comprehensive Arab nationalism' of the kind promoted by the late Egyptian president Gamal Abdul Nasser, which was replaced by the concept of 'local Arab nationalisms'. At the popular level, the memory of this defeat remained alive, as did Israel's claim to be militarily undefeatable.

The war has been described as 'conspiracy and adventure' (in Arabic: *al-muʾāmara wa-al-mughāmara*), that is, as a military adventure by the Israeli side, and as a conspiracy against the Arab armies, despite the Arabs' vaunted strategic mobilisation, by the Arab side. Concerning the 'conspiracy', Saʿad Jumʿa, who was

Jordan's prime minister in 1967, states: 'We entered the campaign unprepared, militarily and psychologically' (Jumʿa 1989). Muhammad al-ʿArabi, editor-in-chief of the journal *Arab Strategic Thought*, adds to 'lured to destruction' (*istidrāj*), 'adventure', 'conspiracy' and 'lack of preparedness' (*ʿadam al-tahayyuʾ*) the additional terms 'impotence' (*ʿajz*), 'backwardness' (*takhalluf*) and 'lack of seriousness' (*ʿadam al-jiddiyya*) (al-ʿArabi 1984). In other words, this war revealed the Arab military command's impotence, backwardness and lack of seriousness in its role of 'Arab opposition', since it did not perceive the fact that its forces were not in proper condition at the appropriate time.

The Arab side gave a number of names to the defeat of 1967, such as 'The War of 67', 'The June Aggression', 'The June 67 War', 'The Great Defeat' and 'The Relapse' (*al-naksa*). The latter term is similar to *al-nakba*, but with a less oppressive connotation.[5] Egypt's official media declared it a grave military defeat. Within a span of six days Israel managed to occupy extensive Arab territories several times its own size. The name which Israelis generally use is 'The Six Day War', in reference to the war's duration. According to Segev (2005), a number of names were proposed to then-Prime Minister Levy Eshkol, among them 'Operation Peace', 'War of Heroism', 'War of Survival', 'Protecting the Peace', 'Zion', 'ShY' (an acronym of *sheshet ha-yamim*, lit. 'the six days'), 'MShH' (an acronym of *milḥemet shelom ha-medina*, lit. 'war for the state's safety'), 'The War of Jerusalem' and more. In July, Eshkol chose the name 'The Six Day War'. Geula Cohen, a Knesset member from 1972 until 1992, admired the name, which she associated with 'the six days of Creation', while Menahem Begin opposed it and instead suggested the name 'War of Salvation'. Both the latter terms are taken from the Jewish religion.

The 10th of Ramadan (*al-ʿāshir min Ramadan*) / Yom Kippur

This war broke out on 6 October 1973 when Egypt and Syria suddenly attacked Israel. This war was launched by the Arab forces in order to return the lands occupied in 1967 War.

The Egyptian forces made an assault on the very strongly fortified Israeli positions on the Suez Canal, known as the Bar-Lev Line after Israel's Chief of the General Staff at the time of its construction. The Egyptians considered their success in breaking through the Bar-Lev Line a veritable military miracle, in the wake of which the Arabs gave the war the name 'The War of the Crossing' (*ḥarb al-ʿubūr*). The war's other names refer to the date of Arab and Jewish religious holidays during which the war broke out: 'The 10th of Ramadan' or 'The 6th of October' among the Arabs, and 'Yom Kippur' or 'Day of Atonement' among the Jews.

Ramadan is a very important Muslim month with great theological significance. The First Battle of *Badr*, in which the Muslims fought the infidels and defeated them, took place in this month. The name 'The 10th of Ramadan' is thus an allusion to an event of great importance in Arab and Muslim history. As for 'Yom Kippur' or 'Day of Atonement', this is an extremely holy day in the Jewish calendar, a day on which the Jews fast and pray for their sins to be forgiven.

It is tempting to consider the fact that the war began on an important religious occasion for both Jews and Muslims. This could be taken as an indication that the Arabs chose the date as a symbol of their desire to revive the glory of their forefathers and to gain a victory over the Israelis just as their ancestors had defeated the infidels, while at the same time perceiving the day's importance for the Jews, who fast and stay at home on that day. The name 'Yom Kippur' for this war, in which Israel was not victorious as it had been in the past, can be taken to indicate a need for a profound re-analysis of Israel's behaviour and the mistakes and sins it had committed.

Operation Peace of Galilee / The Lebanon War

In 1978, Israel carried out a military operation called Operation Litani in which it occupied a broad strip of territory in southern Lebanon that it called 'The Security Band' or 'The Security Belt', which Israel claimed it needed for the purpose of defending itself against Palestinian attacks from Lebanese soil. However, the attacks on Israel's towns and villages near the country's northern border did not cease. As a result, in 1982, Israel began a large-scale operation in Lebanon, aimed at destroying the PLO's bases and included a weeks-long siege of Beirut. As a result of the war, the Palestinian forces and leadership left Lebanon for Tunisia and Israel expanded the 'security belt' it had previously occupied. The Lebanese Falanges committed a massacre in the Sabra and Shatila refugee camps, which were under the protection of the Israeli forces.

The Arabs gave this war a number of names, all of which contain the word 'Lebanon', for example 'The Lebanon War' (*ḥarb lubnān*), 'The Raid on Lebanon' (*ghazw lubnān*), 'The Destruction of Lebanon' (*ijtiyāḥ lubnān*). As for the Israeli leadership, it issued a statement on the first day of the war under the heading 'Operation Safety of Galilee'. This name was criticised in the Israeli media (Schiff and Ya'ari 1985), which considered it misleading since what actually happened was not an extensive military operation but a total war against Beirut. The media therefore called it 'The Lebanon War'.

Israel's prime minister at the time, Menahem Begin, was a very charismatic figure who believed in the power of the word, which he knew how to use. Thus, when the Israeli attack on Lebanon began in 1981 he refused to use the term 'The Lebanon War', but insisted that the campaign be called 'Operation Safety of

Galilee', a formulation that served his political purposes. He aimed at achieving a gradual acceptance of the ruling political party's ideology, and for this purpose he mobilised the media (Nir 1998: 22). The use of the term 'operation' was meant to give the impression that Israel had been dragged into the war and driven to defend itself and protect the people of Galilee, and not that it just attacks its neighbours.

The First Intifada / The First Palestinian Intifada

The Intifada was a revolt against the Israeli occupation of the West Bank and Gaza Strip. It started in Gaza on 8 December 1987 and continued until the signing of the Oslo Accords between Israel and the Palestinians six years later. It was marked by stone-throwing and demonstrations, usually by youth, and strike days observed by the general population of Gaza and the West Bank.

Damj (1997: 185–6) states:

> The intifada started with unremarkable acts such as demonstrations and mass protests, in the wake of the deaths of the four Gazans in the Jibaliya refugee camp. The incidents spread to the rest of the occupied territories. This form of protest remained the hallmark of the uprising against the occupation in all the villages, refugee camps and cities in the occupied territories.

Intifada literally means 'shake' or 'shaking', though it is popularly translated into English as 'uprising', 'resistance' or 'rebellion'. It is 'a protracted grassroots campaign of protest and sometimes violent resistance against perceived oppression or military occupation, especially either of two uprisings among Palestinian Arabs in the Gaza Strip and West Bank, the first beginning in 1987 and the second in 2000, in protest against Israeli occupation of these territories'.[6]

A characteristic of this intifada, which lasted seven years, was the use of rocks as a means for expressing popular protest. The rocks or stones were thrown by youths, the 'rock children'. The intifada ended when the Oslo Accords were signed in September 1993. The intifada was a popular revolt against the Israeli occupation that, at the same time, also brought about a change within Palestinian society by shaping its values and habits, giving them various meanings (Kuttab 1992). The importance of the intifada for the Palestinian national project lies in the fact that it arose from what the Palestinians call 'the inside' (*al-dākhil*), that is, the West Bank and the Gaza Strip, while previously the focus of resistance was usually located outside Palestine and in the refugee camps while 'the inside' remained relatively quiet. However, resistance operations on 'the outside' waned after the PLO left Lebanon in 1982 and settled in Tunisia. Then, in 1987, they broke out anew on 'the inside' and gave the Palestinian issue a new push.

At first the Israeli leadership tried not to give an official name to the intifada, because it believed that the incidents were a temporary matter and would cease in a short while. For this reason they were initially called 'disturbances' and then, when they became more furious, 'acts of violence', and with the increasing participation of the masses in the protests, 'popular protests'. However, eventually it accepted the Arabic terminology and came to call it 'intifada', a word that entered the Hebrew lexicon and came into common use in its Hebrew pronunciation.

The Al-Aqsa Intifada / The Second Palestinian Intifada

The Oslo Accords had not long been in effect when Ariel Sharon, then the head of the opposition, entered Al-Aqsa Mosque's yard (the Temple Mount) on 28 September 2000. The Palestinians attacked him and the army protected him, resulting in confrontations between the two sides. This incident was the first spark that ignited a new intifada, which was named 'The Al- Aqsa Intifada' or 'The Second Intifada', during which the IDF retook control of the Palestinian territories and Israel threatened to withdraw from the Statement of Principles that the two sides had signed. According to Israeli statistics, by the end of 2004 the intifada had caused the deaths of more than a thousand Israelis and about 2,650 Palestinians (Harel and Yisakharov 2005). Israel accused the Palestinian president, the late Yasser Arafat, of causing the intifada to continue and began to use the now-familiar argument of 'there is no partner', describing Arafat as a terrorist. Until he fell into a coma, Sharon tried to stigmatise the Palestinian Authority (PA), whose headquarters in Ramallah he described as a terrorist centre, in order to create a kind of identification between the PA and terrorism in an effort to isolate it and to deprive it of its legitimacy.

Among the names used by the Israelis for this intifada were 'The Al Aqsa Intifada', 'The Random War', 'The War of Terrorism and Murder' and 'The War of Protecting the Home'. A number of IDF operations took place during the intifada that received names of their own, such as 'Operation Defensive Shield' in 2002. However, the name intifada was later widely used by Israelis. The wide use of the term intifada among Israelis, I assume, is due to its widespread use in the various languages of the world, referring to the First Intifada.

The War for Lebanon / The Second Lebanon War

The Second Lebanon War took place in July 2006. It broke out after Hezbollah took two IDF soldiers captive and lasted for thirty-three days. It was one of the longest of the Arab–Israeli wars. The Lebanese resistance was able to withstand

and foil the Israeli offensive despite the huge disparity in strength between the two sides. This was the first conventional war in which the Israeli rear was hit and suffered great losses (Belqiz 2006).

The Arab media called it 'The Sixth War' (since from the Arab perspective the Palestinian intifada was not considered a conventional war) and also 'The War of Lebanon' and 'The War of July 2006'. In Israel, a furious debate raged concerning the name that should be given to this war. Only seven months after the war ended Israel's military and political establishment gave it the official name 'The Second Lebanon War'.

The issue was raised by the bereaved families of the fallen soldiers after they discovered that the IDF considered their loved ones to have fallen 'on the field of battle' rather than 'in the war'. There is a huge difference between the two terms from a military perspective; those killed in a war are accorded a higher status and their families receive greater financial compensation. Among the names that were proposed were 'Defence of the Northern Border', 'Security of the North', 'Getting the Kidnapped Soldiers Back', 'The Second Lebanon War' and 'Fighting Hezbollah'.

The Israeli Knesset's Ceremonies and Decorations Committee held a session in March 2007 in order to give the war an official name. The deliberations were carried out in two stages: first, it was decided that what had happened in Lebanon was a war and not an operation; then, a debate ensued concerning the definitive name that should be given to this war. After consultation it was decided to call it 'The Second Lebanon War', despite the fact that the war of 1982 in Lebanon was not called 'The First Lebanon War'[7] but 'Operation Safety of Galilee', in order to present it as a defensive rather than an aggressive campaign, as noted above.

The campaigns between Israel and Gaza

In 2005, Israel withdrew from the Gaza Strip without any agreement with the Palestinians, in what Israel called a 'disengagement'. This step was undertaken by the then-Prime Minister Ariel Sharon with a view to breaking the political stalemate between Israel and the Palestinians in the wake of the Second Intifada. In 2007, Hamas seized power in Gaza after it accused Fatah of plotting against it. As a result, Israel imposed a harsh land and sea blockade on the Gaza Strip. In order to demonstrate their continued resistance to Israel and in order to lift the siege, Hamas and other Palestinian resistance groups fired rockets at Israel, leading to bloody clashes and battles that claimed thousands of Palestinian and hundreds of Israeli victims. Israel did not call these confrontations wars, for both political (the enemy was not a country) and economic (a war would have deleterious repercussions on the Israeli economy) considerations.

Israel obviously took great care in its choice of names for these campaigns. The one that took place in 2008 was called 'Cast Lead' (*ʿoferet yetsuka*); the campaign in 2010 was given the name 'Pillar of Defence' (*ʿamud ʿanan*, lit. 'cloud pillar'); and the fighting in 2014 was named 'Protective Edge' (*tsuk eitan*, lit. 'solid cliff').

'Cast lead' is a phrase coined by Israel's national poet Haim Nahman Bialik. According to Gavriely-Nuri (2013), the name, associated with the Jewish holiday of Hanukka, was given to a large-scale military operation in Gaza with the intention of arousing a sense of ceremoniousness and heroism, leading to popular support for the operation.

'Cloud pillar' is a classical example of a name taken from both nature and the world of biblical imagery. The phrase alludes to the 'cloud pillar' that moved before the camp of the Israelites as they wandered through the desert. As it is states in Exodus (13:21–22), 'By day the Lord went ahead of them in a pillar of cloud to guide them on their way and by night in a pillar of fire to give them light, so that they could travel by day or night. Neither the pillar of cloud by day nor the pillar of fire by night left its place in front of the people.' The term 'solid cliff' projects power and connects the strong, defending armed forces with the protected citizenry in the rear. In short, Israel used themes from three domains in the names it gave to its operations in Gaza: the Bible, nature and heroism.

The Arabs, on the other hand, usually used the term 'Aggression against Gaza'; this was the common phrase used by Arab satellite stations such al-Jazeera and al-Arabiyya. Hamas and other Islamic groups used names with religious connotations, such as 'The Battle of the Distinction' (*al-furqān*), 'Eaten Straw' (*ʿaṣf maʾkūl*) and 'Firm Structure' (*al-bunyān al-marṣūṣ*). The first of these is the name of a *sura* of the Qurʾān (Q 25); the word denotes 'distinguishing between truth and falsehood'. The phrase 'eaten straw' appears at the end of Q 105 and describes the state of the elephant that had been destroyed by the missiles cast on it by the birds, in an allusion to the rockets that Hamas intended to launch against Israel, hopefully with a similar effect. The 'firm structure' appears in Q 61:4 and implies the unification of all the Palestinian resistance movements for the fight against Israel. To recap, the Arabs in general used the term 'Aggression against Gaza' when describing the state of war between Israel and the resistance movements in Gaza, while Hamas and other Islamic movements used names from the Qurʾān, in order to evoke the Muslims' glorious victories in the past and arouse hopes of victory over the enemy.

Conclusions

Historical memory plays a part in shaping groups and nations into imagined communities; it is an imagined memory in which all members of the group participate. It is thus an important and vital factor in nation construction and shaping. It is not possible to create a nation without a historical memory (Anderson 1991).

Names play an important role in constructing historical memories, identifying the locations that are absorbed by memories. The *nakba*, an indispensable location, is one of the formative elements in the Palestinian identity. It is an historical event, but at the same time affords a place for a collective memory.

Pioneering works that examined the process of nations and identity, such as Benedict Anderson's (1991) book, *Imagined Communities*, Edward Said's (1997), *Culture and Imperialism*, and Eric Hobsbawm's (1990), *Nations and Nationalism since 1780*, highlighted the relationship between identity and places of memory, on the one hand, and the names they bear, on the other.

The linguistic dispute has played a central role in the Arab–Israeli conflict. It manifested itself primarily in the issue of the historical narrative of the conflict, whereby each side uses its own language to assert its right to the land. The linguistic dispute commenced with the naming of locations in the region. The Zionist movement used the name *Eretz Yisrael* (the Land of Israel) instead of Palestine in order to confirm Israel's historical right to the region (Amara and Mar'i 2008).

War names provide rich data for sociolinguistic research. They carry symbolic meanings related to identity and conflict. As Suleiman (2011: 225) explains, 'code names offer us snapshots of symbolic meanings along a moving frame. However, by tracking the major breaks in this frame, we can identify the major sociopolitical ruptures in society.'

We have shown how language in this political and military conflict served not only to reflect events in the political arena and on the battlefield, but also participated in shaping the realities of the conflict.

The Arab–Israeli conflict is multilayered and it is not only confined to political, military, economic and territorial aspects, but it also encompasses symbolic, semantic and cultural issues as well. We have shown how both Hebrew and Arabic, two related languages derived from a common Semitic origin, participated in creating both parties' linguistic concepts. The present study about the names of the wars has revealed how linguistic terminology was used to create a political map that suited the ideology of each side, with the aim of influencing people's perceptions and conceptions as they interrelated with the facts on the ground locally, regionally and globally.

We found clear differences between the Arab and the Israeli names for the wars. Israel focused on religion, culture and history (ancient and modern), and nature in the name it gave, while the Arabs gave more weight to depictions of the nature and results of the wars, as well as the places and times in which they occurred. This difference has a clear explanation. Israel emerged victorious from most of these wars and the victor dictates the narrative. Israel wanted to state that it had rights in this region, that it fought for its rights and its legitimacy, and that it did not steal anyone else's land; while the Arabs, who were defeated in most of the wars, used names that described a state of defeat or depicted the war as an act of aggression against them. The one name that Israelis and Arabs both shared was 'intifada', perhaps because Israel was not victorious and the Palestinians received a great deal of sympathy, or perhaps because the intifada was not a war in the traditional sense, but rather a popular uprising in the case of the First Intifada and an armed insurrection by resistance groups rather than by a regular army in the Second Intifada. Another explanation about the use of the war name 'Intifada' could also be connected to its dominance among Palestinians and its adaptation by Israelis without even careful intention to do that.

I am aware of the fact that whatever interpretation given to names, other possible interpretations may also be provided. As Suleiman (2004: 159) explains, 'discovering the real motivation behind a name is not an easy matter. The same is true of the interpretation given to the name by the receiver. But one thing is certain: the symbolic meaning of a name assumes greater importance in situations of conflict than in conditions of neutral interaction.' The names in the Arab–Israeli context, including war names, are ideologically loaded constructs, shedding interesting light on the Arab–Israeli conflict.

Notes

1. The survey revealed the important fact that most of the respondents agreed that Hebrew did not represent *the language of the enemy*. Nor was learning Hebrew perceived as conflicting with the learners' religious principles. The majority did not agree with the statement 'I do not like to study Hebrew', and most were in favour of introducing the study of Hebrew already in first grade and not later, in the fifth grade, for example.
2. This result is significant especially if compared with attitudes of Jewish Israeli students, many of whom were found to perceive Arabic as the language of the enemy, and of an inferior nation (Brosh 1996; Mendel 2014).
3. According to *Lisān al-ʿArab* (Ibn-Manzur 1994), s.v. '*nakba*', the word means 'a catastrophe of fate'. As Ghanem (2005: 74) explains, 'a *nakba* is a momentous event that strikes a person, a society or nature. In everyday usage, it usually describes a sudden, catastrophic event which leaves a person helpless and whose damage is irreparable.'
4. The revival of '*Nakba Day*' has generated a debate among the Jews, some of whom tacitly agree to this step while many others, especially in the right-wing parties, oppose it. The latter argue that the revival of '*Nakba Day*' is a sign of the Palestinian refusal to recognise Israel, its right to live in peace and security, and the right of the Jewish people to an independent state in the land of Israel.

5. According to *Lisan al-ʿArab* (Ibn-Manzur 1994) the verb *intakasa* means 'was inverted', in the sense of 'disappointment', since if one's affairs are inverted it means one has lost. *Nakasa raʾsahu* means 'bowed his head in shame'. In modern times the word *naksa* has been used in medicine, where it means 'relapse' or a recurrence of a disease that had been overcome. It also means 'temporary retreat'. In reference to a flag, *nakasa* means lowering it to half mast as a sign of mourning.
6. See at: http://www.thefreedictionary.com/intifada.
7. The name 'The Second Lebanon War' was clearly influenced by the wars that preceded it in the Persian Gulf, which were named 'The First Gulf War' and 'The Second Gulf War'.

References

Abd-el-Jawad, H. and al-Haq, F., 'The impact of the peace process in the Middle East on Arabic', in M. Clyne (ed.), *Undoing and Redoing Corpus Planning* (Berlin: Mouton de Gruyter, 1997), pp. 415–43.

Abu Sitta, S., *The Road of Return: Guide to the Abandoned and Existing Cities and Towns and the Holy Places in Palestine* (London: Land of Palestine Society, 2007).

Amara, M., *Politics and Sociolinguistic Reflexes: Palestinian Border Villages* (Amsterdam: John Benjamins, 1999).

Amara, M., 'Arab population of Israel: Sociolinguistic aspects', *Encyclopedia of Hebrew, Language and Linguistics (EHLL)* (Leiden: Brill, 2013), vol. 1, pp. 124–8.

Amara, M., 'Hebraization in the Palestinian language landscape in Israel', in B. Spolsky, O. I. Lourie and M. Tannenbaum (eds), *Challenges for Language Education and Policy* (New York: Routledge, 2015), pp. 182–94.

Amara, M. and Marʿi, A, *Language Education Policy: The Arab Minority in Israel* (Dordrecht: Kluwer Academic, 2002).

Amara, M. and Marʿi, A., *Language and Conflict: An Analytic Reading in Linguistic Concepts on the Arab-Israeli Conflict* (Kafr Qara and Amman: Dar al-Huda and Dar al-Fikr (in Arabic), 2008).

al-ʿArabi, M., 'Introduction', *Arab Strategic Thought* 11(5) (1984): 1–5.

Anderson, B. R., *Imagined Communities: Reflections on the Origin and Spread of Nationalism*, 2nd edn (London: Verso, 1991).

Bar-On, M., *The Sinai War of 1956*, trans. Badr al-Uqayli (Amman: Dar al-Jalil lil-nashr (in Arabic), 1988).

Bassiouney, R., *Arabic Sociolinguistics* (Edinburgh: Edinburgh University Press, 2009).

Belqiz. A., *Hezbollah from Liberation to Deterrence (1982–2006)* (Beirut: Markaz Dirasat al-Wahda al-Arabiyya (in Arabic), 2006).

Ben-Gurion, D., *Memoirs of the War: The War of Independence 1948–1949*, ed. G. Rippin and E. Uri, 3 vols (Tel-Aviv (in Hebrew), 1982).
Ben-Rafael, E., Shohamy, E., Amara, M. and Trumper-Hecht, N., 'Linguistic landscape as a symbolic construction of the public space: The case of Israel', *International Journal of Multilingualism* 3(2) (2006): 7–30.
Bishara, A., 'The Arabs and the Catastrophe: Analysis of the problem of a coordination particle', *Moznayim* 53 (1995): 54–71 (in Hebrew).
Brosh, H., 'Arabic for speakers of Hebrew in Israel: Second language or foreign language?', *Helkat Lashon* 23 (1996): 111–31 (in Hebrew).
Clavet, L., *Language Wars and Linguistic Politics*, trans. M. Petheram (Oxford: Oxford University Press, 1998).
Cohen, H., *Good Arabs: the Israeli Security Agencies and the Israeli Arabs, 1948–1967* (Berkeley, CA: University of California Press, 2010).
Damj, N., *Procedural Shifts in the Course of the Arab-Israeli Conflict* (Acre: Mu'assasat al-Aswar (in Arabic), 1997).
Das Gupta, J., *Language Conflict and National Development: Group Politics and National Language Policy in India* (Berkeley, CA: University of California Press, 1970).
Dua, H. R., 'The politics of language conflict: Implications for language planning and political theory', *Language Planning and Language Problems* 14 (1996): 187–202.
Elbaum-Dror, R., *Hebrew Education in Palestine* (Jerusalem: Yad Ben-Zvi (in Hebrew), 1986).
Gavriely-Nuri, D., *The Normalization of War in the Israeli Discourse* (Lanham, MD: Lexington Books, 2013).
Ghanem, H., 'Living on the summit of a volcano: Presentations of time and place in examples of *Nakba* poetry', *Another Scale* 1:1 (Markaz Mada al-Karmil, Haifa, 2005), pp. 71–83.
Habibi, E., *The Sextet of the Six Days and Other Stories*, special edn (Cairo: Da'irat al-Thaqafa, PLO and Dar al-Thaqafa al-Jadida (in Arabic), 1989).
al-Haq, F., 'A sociolinguistic study of Hebrew in Jordan: Implications for language planning', *International Journal of the Sociology of Language* 140 (1999): 45–58.
Harel, A. and Yisakharov, A., *The Seventh War: How We Won and Why We Lost in the War with the Palestinians* (Yediot Aharonot: Tel-Aviv (in Hebrew), 2005).
Hobsbawm, E. J., *Nations and Nationalism since 1780: Programme, Myth, Reality* (Cambridge: Cambridge University Press, 1990).
Ibn-Manzur, J. D., *Lisān al-ʿArab*, 15 vols (Beirut: Dar Sadir (in Arabic), 1994).
Inglehart, R. F and Woodward, M., 'Language conflict and political community', in P. Giglioli (ed.), *Language and Social Contexts: Selected Readings* (Harmondsworth: Penguin, 1972), pp. 358–77.
Jahr, E. H. (ed.), *Language Conflict and Language Planning* (Berlin: Mouton de Gruyter, 1993).

Jumʿa, S., *The Conspiracy and the Fateful Campaign* (Cairo: Dar al-Mukhtar al-Islami (in Arabic), 1989).
Khalidi, W., *Fifty Years since the Partition of Palestine 1947–1997* (Beirut: Dar al-Nahar (in Arabic), 1997).
Khalidi, W., *Heirs to the Narrators: From the Nakba to the State* (Beirut: Mu'assasat al-aswar (in Arabic), 2001).
Kuttab, A., 'Participation of Palestinian women in the Intifada of the National Liberation Movement', in Sh. Sarsaki and I. Papeh (eds), *The Intifada a View from the Inside* (Tel-Aviv: Mifras (in Hebrew), 1992), pp. 237–309.
Laitin, D. D., 'Linguistic conflict in Catalonia', *Language Planning and Language Problems* 11 (1987): 129–47.
Lakoff, R. T., *The Language War* (Berkeley, CA: University of California Press, 2000).
Lustick, I., *For the Land and Lord: Jewish Fundamentalism in Israel* (New York: Council on Foreign Relations, 1994).
Marʿi, A., *Hebraization of Palestinian Town and Site Names: Reflection and Extension of the Israeli-Palestinian Conflict*, in Muhammad Amara (ed.), Ibn Khaldun Series, Palestinian Society in Israel, No. 2, Ibn Khaldun Association, Tamra, 2006.
Masalha, N. (ed.), *Catastrophe Remembered: Palestine, Israel and the Internal Refugees. Essays in Memory of Edward W. Said (1935–2003)* (London: Zed Books, 2005).
Mendel, Y., *The Creation of Arabic: Political and Security Considerations in the Making of Arabic Language Studies in Israel* (Basingstoke: Palgrave Macmillan, 2014).
Nir, R., 'Political–linguistic correction, clean language and nourishing the language', *Panim* 7 (Winter 1998): 19–26 (in Hebrew).
Rogan, E., 'Jordan and 1948: The persistence of official history', in E. Rogan and A. Shlaim (eds), *The War for Palestine: Rewriting the History of 1948*, trans.to Arabic Asʿad Kamil Elias (Riyadh: Maktabat al-ʿAkiban, 2004), pp. 170–208.
Said, E., *Culture and Imperialism* (New York: Vintage Books, 1997).
Schiff, Z. and Ya'ari, E., *Israel's Lebanon War* (New York: Simon & Schuster, 1985).
Segev. T., *And the Land Changed its Visage* (Jerusalem: Keter (in Hebrew), 2005).
Shohamy, E. and Abu Ghazaleh-Mahajneh, M., 'Linguistic landscape as a tool for interpreting language vitality: Arabic as a "minority" language in Israel', in D. Gorter, H. F. Marten and L. V. Mensel (eds), *Minority Languages in the Linguistic Landscape* (Basingstoke: Palgrave Macmillan, 2012), pp. 89–108.
Sieminski, G., 'The art of naming operations', *Parameters: US Army War College Quarterly* (Autumn 1995): 81–98.
Spolsky, B., *Language Policy* (Cambridge: Cambridge University Press, 2004).
Spolsky B. and Shohamy E., *Languages of Israel: Policy, Ideology and Practice* (Clevedon: Multilingual Matters, 1999).
Suleiman, Y., *A War of Words: Language and Conflict in the Middle East* (Cambridge: Cambridge University Press, 2004).

Suleiman, Y., *Arabic, Self and Identity: A Study in Conflict and Displacement* (Oxford: Oxford University Press, 2011).
Zreiq, C., *General Speculative Works* (al-Wahda al-ʿArabiyya Research Center and Mu'assasat ʿAbd al-Hamid Shuman: Beirut (in Arabic), 1994).

Online source

http://www.thefreedictionary.com/intifada.

About the Contributors

Ashraf Abdelhay holds a PhD in the field of sociolinguistics from the University of Edinburgh. His research focuses on the cultural politics of language in Sudan with specific emphasis on the intersection of discourse, ideology and power relations. He was an ESRC Postdoctoral Fellow at the Department of Middle Eastern Studies, University of Cambridge (2009–10). He also worked as a Research Fellow at Clare Hall College, University of Cambridge (2009–13). He currently works for the Doha Institute for Graduate Studies (Qatar) in the programme of Linguistics and Arabic Lexicography. Some of his research has been published in the *International Journal of the Sociology of Language*; the *Journal of Multilingual and Multicultural Development*; *Concept*; *Current Issues in Language Planning, and Language Policy* among others.

Mariam Aboelezz recently completed her PhD in the Department of Linguistics and English Language, Lancaster University. A certified legal translator, she has lived and worked in Egypt, the United Arab Emirates and the United Kingdom. Her research falls within the field of Arabic sociolinguistics, with a particular interest in the Arabic writing system and the relationship between language, on the one hand, and the religious, political and social structure of the Arab world, on the other. Her PhD research explored the relationship between language ideologies and change in Egypt at the height of the revolutionary period (2010–14).

Abeer AlNajjar is a Visiting Senior Fellow at the Middle East Centre, London School of Economics, and an Associate Professor of Mass Communications, the American University of Sharjah-UAE. She has authored numerous articles and book chapters in political communication, journalism and media studies and a book titled *Conflict over Jerusalem: Covering the Palestinian-Israeli Conflict in the British Press* (2009).

Muhammad Amara is Associate Professor of Linguistics, the head of Graduate Studies at Beit Berl Academic College and President of the Israeli Society for the Study of Language and Society. His academic interests include language education, language policy, sociolinguistics, language and politics, collective identities and the Arab–Jewish divide in Israel. His publications include *Politics and Sociolinguistics Reflexes: Palestinian Border Villages* (1999), *Language Education Policy: The Arab Minority in Israel* (2002), *Arabic in Israel: Contexts and Challenges* (2010) and together with Abd Al-Rahman Mar'i he edited a book titled *Language and Identity in Israel* (2002); and, with Abd Al-Rahman Mar'i, he co-authored *Languages in Conflict: A Study of Linguistic Terms in the Arab–Israeli Conflict* (2008). His forthcoming book (2018) is titled *Arabic in Israel: Language, Identity, and Conflict.*

Reem Bassiouney is Professor of Linguistics at the American University of Cairo. Her recent publications include *Functions of Code-switching in Egypt* (2006), *Arabic Sociolinguistics* (Edinburgh University Press, 2008), *Arabic and the Media* (2010), *Arabic Language and Linguistics* (co-editor, 2012), *Language and Identity in Modern Egypt* (Edinburgh University Press, 2014) and the *Routledge Handbook of Arabic Linguistics* (co-editor, forthcoming). Her research focuses on topics in Arabic sociolinguistics, including code-switching, language and gender, levelling, register, language policy and discourse analysis. She is also an award-winning novelist.

Maisalon Dallashi is a doctoral candidate in the Department of Sociology and Anthropology, Tel Aviv University. Her doctoral dissertation deals with the effect of integrated and segregated education on Palestinian Arab graduates. It emphasises the importance of Arabic and Hebrew in identity construction beginning during primary education and continuing into institutions of higher education and employment. She currently coordinates the Van Leer Jerusalem Institute Arabic-to-Hebrew Translators Forum. Dallashi holds a BA and MA from Tel Aviv University where she studied women and gender and sociology and anthropology. Her master's thesis focused on the sociology of translation between Hebrew and Arabic.

Eirlys Davies obtained a PhD in linguistics from the University of Wales, UK, prior to moving to Morocco. Over the last sixteen years, she has worked as a lecturer at the King Fahd School of Translation, Tangier, and currently teaches French–English translation, translation theory, academic reading and research methodology. Her research interests include translation and inter-cultural communication, bilingualism, code-switching, sociolinguistics and stylistics. Due to her extended stay in Morocco, she has developed a particular interest in Arabic sociolinguistics and the speech styles of Moroccan bilinguals.

Carole Hillenbrand studied at the universities of Cambridge, Oxford and Edinburgh. She has served as a Professor of Islamic History, University of St Andrews, since 2013. Hillenbrand was a Professor of Islamic History, University of Edinburgh, 2000–8. She served as the Head of Islamic and Middle Eastern Studies, University of Edinburgh, 1997–2002, 2006–8 and was a Professor

Emerita of Islamic History, University of Edinburgh, 2008. Hillenbrand has earned many international awards, including the King Faisal International Prize in Islamic Studies, 2005, and the Corresponding Fellow of the Medieval Academy of America in 2012. In the UK she was granted the Fellowship of the Royal Society of Edinburgh, 2001; the Fellowship of the Royal Historical Society, 2003; the Fellowship of the British Academy, 2007; awarded the Officer of the British Empire (for Services to Higher Education), 2009; and was awarded an Honorary Fellowship at Somerville College, Oxford, 2010. She has published five books, two edited books, and seventy articles and book chapters.

Rana Issa is Assistant Professor of Translation Studies at the American University of Beirut. She is a literary historian interested in issues of translation in the *nahḍa*. Her work includes research on the modern Arabic Bible, Modern Standard Arabic, and the impact of globalisation on language and literature. In addition to her interests in the history of religion and early modern Arabic literature and language, she has been an active cultural producer and public intellectual working with various artistic ventures, including film festivals, theatrical performances, conceptual art and dance. Issa has published in academic and general interest journals. She is currently working on a book about the modern history of the Arabic Bible and on an anthology about the modern cultural history of the Levant.

John E. Joseph is Professor of Applied Linguistics at the University of Edinburgh, and co-editor of the journals *Language & Communication* and *Historiographia Linguistica*. His research focuses on language and identity, language and politics, and the history of linguistics. His books include *Language and Identity: National, Ethnic, Religious* (2004), *Language and Politics* (Edinburgh University Press, 2006), *Saussure* (2012) and *Language, Mind and Body: A Conceptual History* (2017).

Chaoqun Lian is Assistant Professor of Arabic Language and Linguistics in the Department of Arabic Language and Culture at Peking University, China, and Research Associate at the Centre of Islamic Studies, University of Cambridge. He specialises in language planning and language policy (LPLP) and political and cultural semiotics in the Arabic-speaking world. His PhD thesis, titled 'Language Planning and Language Policy of Arabic Language Academies in the Twentieth Century' is currently being turned into a book. Lian is leading a three-year project focusing on language and identity in the core areas along the Silk Road Economic Belt and the 21st-Century Maritime Silk Road funded by the State Language Commission, China. He regularly contributes to the book supplement of *al-ʿArabī al-Jadīd*.

Sinfree Makoni is a Professor at the Pennsylvania State University and is currently a Distinguished Scholar, Graduate School of Education, Division of Educational Linguistics, University of Pennsylvania, and a Research Fellow at the Department of English Studies, University of South Africa, Pretoria. He received his PhD from the University of Edinburgh and also holds degrees from the University of Ghana, Legon, Accra. His areas of specialisation are discourses of terrorism outside the United States, theory and practices of language policy and planning, and philosophies of language and language and health in Africa. Professor Makoni has published a number of academic articles and books on language policy and planning, among them *Disinventing and Reconstituting Languages* (2006), co-edited with Alastair Pennycook, and *Language and Aging in Multilingual Contexts* (2005), co-authored with Kees De Bot.

Yonatan Mendel is a Research Associate at the Centre of Islamic Studies, University of Cambridge. He is author of *The Creation of Israeli Arabic: Political and Security Considerations in the Making of Arabic Language Studies Israel* (2014), and co-author (together with Ronald Ranta) of *From the Arab Other to the Israeli Self: Palestinian Culture in the Making of Israeli National Identity* (2016).

Karin Christina Ryding is Sultan Qaboos bin Said Professor Emerita of Arabic Linguistics at Georgetown University. From 1980 to 1986, she was head of Arabic training at the State Department's Foreign Service Institute. From 1995 to 1998, Ryding was Dean of Interdisciplinary Programs at Georgetown, and she also spent ten years as chair of her department. Ryding is past president (2007–8) of the American Association of Teachers of Arabic (AATA), and serves on the Board of Directors of Georgetown University Press. In 2008, she received the Lifetime Achievement Award from AATA, as well as the Distinguished Service Award from the Faculty of Languages and Linguistics of Georgetown University. Principal publications include *Arabic: A Linguistic Introduction* (2014), *Teaching and Learning Arabic as a Foreign Language* (2013) and *A Reference Grammar of Modern Standard Arabic* (2005).

Sonia Shiri is Associate Professor and Middle East Language Programs Coordinator at the University of Arizona. She is the Director of the Arabic Language Flagship Program and an affiliated faculty of the Second Language Acquisition and Teaching PhD program. Shiri received her MSc and PhD from the University of Edinburgh. Prior to moving to Arizona, she served as Arabic Program Coordinator at the University of California Berkeley, and from 2009 to 2012, she was Senior Academic Director of the Critical Language Scholarship (CLS). Her research focuses on language learning in study abroad, computer-assisted language learning, linguistic landscapes and critical discourse analysis.

Index

Abbasid era, 58, 150, 151, 152
Abdelhay, Ashraf, 9–10
El-Abnoudi, Abdel Rahman, 137
Aboelezz, Mariam, 10
accent, 20
Addis Ababa Peace Agreement, 103
advertising, 9, 74–5
age, 76–8, 195–7, 198
Agha, Asif, 32–3
Alami, Mourad, 70
Algeria, 76, 168, 169
Ali, Muhammad, 127
alphabet, 80–2; *see also* Romanised Arabic; script
alterity, 10, 126, 129, 143
Amara, Muhammad, 12
ʿāmmiyya see Colloquial Arabic
Andil, Bayoumi, 133, 134, 135, 141
Appadurai, Arjun, 11
Aql, Said, 69
Al-Aqsa Intifada, 219
Arab–Israeli War, 60, 207–8, 209–10
Arab Jews, 11, 185–6, 188–9, 191–203
Arab Spring, 140, 165–7, 168–9, 170–7, 171–2, 178–81
Arabic language, 2–4, 5–6, 7, 8–12, 69, 70
  and anxiety, 91
  and al-Bustānī, 154–5
  and al-Shidyāq, 156–7, 158–60
  and al-Yāzijī, 157–8, 160–1
  and Christians, 148–9, 150
  and code-switching, 23–4, 25–6, 113
  and cross-breed speakers, 56
  and discourse, 32–3
  and education, 30–2, 33–4, 39–42
  and ideology, 95–6
  and Israel, 186–203, 209
  and literature, 123
  and Sudan, 98–102, 103–6
  and technology, 149–50
  and Tunisia, 167
  and war names, 210–21, 222–3
  see also Colloquial Arabic; Egyptian Colloquial Arabic; Middle Arabic; Moroccan Arabic; Romanised Arabic; vernacular language; written language

Arabic Renaissance (*nahḍa*), 127, 128, 151, 153
Arabic second language acquisition (ASLA), 31, 38, 42
Arabiyya, 35, 36, 40
al-Asīr, Yūsuf, 149
attire, 173–4
Avicenna, 14
Awad, Louis, 131–2, 135, 141
Awrāq al-narjis (Leaves of Narcissus) (Ramaḍān), 10, 111–12, 118–22, 123

Badawi, Elsaid, 32, 36, 41
banal nationalism, 165, 178–81
banks, 75
al-Bashir, Omar, 9, 99, 100, 103, 104–6
Al-Baṣrah, 2–4
Bassiouney, Reem, 10, 23, 26
battle metaphor, 52, 55, 56, 58, 59, 60–2, 64–5
'Bazra', 1–4
Begin, Menachem, 215, 216, 217–18
Beirut, 148, 149, 150, 151, 155–6
Ben Ali, Zine al-Abidine, 11, 165, 166, 167, 172
Ben-Gurion, David, 214, 215
Berrada, Hakima, 70
Bible, the, 2, 4, 91, 148–9, 152–4
Bouazizi, Mohamed, 165, 166
brain, the, 14–16
Britain *see* Great Britain
al-Bustānī, Buṭrus, 148, 150, 152, 153–5, 159–60

CA *see* Colloquial Arabic
Cairo Academy, 49–50, 57–9, 61
Cantonese, 81
cartography, 2
Chinese, 81
Chomsky, Noam, 15–16
Christianity, 17, 103, 148–9, 150, 152–7; *see also* Copts
cinema, 112–13, 116, 118
class, 198–9
code choice, 10, 23–4, 79
  and Egypt, 112, 113, 116–17, 118, 121–3
cogitatio (reasoning), 14, 15
Colloquial Arabic (CA), 9, 10, 69
  and Egypt, 130, 131, 133, 134–5, 136, 141
  and metaphors, 49, 50–65
  see also dialects
colonialism, 25, 55–6, 57, 63, 91
  and Egypt, 111, 128, 129
  and France, 69
  and Hebrew, 208
  and Sudan, 100, 103
  and Tunisia, 172
Communist Manifesto (Marx), 18–19, 26
Comprehensive (Naivasha) Peace Agreement (CPA), 103
computer-mediated communication (CMC), 71–4, 76, 80–1, 82–3, 84; *see also* social media
Comte, Auguste, 15
Conceptual Metaphor Theory (CMT), 51
conflict, 7, 10, 101, 168; *see also* wars

conspiracy theories, 102, 105
conversation *see* discourse
Conversation Analysis, 23
Copts, 129, 131, 132, 140, 141–2
culture, 17, 18, 24
  and discourse, 33, 38
  and Europe, 130, 131
  and Israel, 193, 197, 200–1
  and language, 92–3, 95, 96
  and Sudan, 99–100, 101, 102, 103, 105

Dallashi, Maisalon, 11
Davies, Eirlys, 9
Dayan, Moshe, 215
de-Arabisation, 188–9
dead languages, 16
democracy, 25
demonstrations, 165–7, 168, 169–70, 171–7, 178–81
Derrida, Jacques, 18–19, 20, 21, 22, 26, 27
Descartes, René, 15
descent metaphor, 52, 55, 58, 61, 62, 64–5
dialects, 31, 35, 39, 70–1, 123
dictionaries, 155, 161
differentiation, 143
diglossia *see* vernacular language; written language
discourse, 30–1, 32–3, 34, 38, 39
distanciation, 96, 101, 104, 106, 143
dress, 173–4

educated spoken Arabic (ESA), 36–7, 38, 41
education, 8, 24
  and Arabic, 30–5, 36–7, 39–42
  and Egypt, 130
  and Israel, 187–8, 189–90, 191–2, 195–7, 199, 200
  and Morocco, 69–70, 75, 77
Egypt, 10, 104
  and 2011 revolution, 64–5
  and Beirut, 151
  and Israel, 208
  and literature, 111–12, 114–17, 118–22, 123
  and nationalism, 126–44
  and protest signs, 169
  and RA, 78
  and wars, 215–17
  see also Cairo Academy
Egyptian Colloquial Arabic (ECA), 36, 112, 113, 116–17, 120–2, 135
elite closure, 37–8, 44n18
email *see* computer-mediated communication
emigration, 24; *see also* immigration
English language, 24–5
  and CMC, 82
  and Egypt, 112, 116, 119
  and Israel, 3–4, 6
  and Morocco, 78, 79
  and Palestine, 209
  and Sudan, 100, 103–4
  and Tunisia, 167, 168, 180
ensembles, 172–3, 179–80
erasure, 96, 100, 101, 106
Eshkol, Levy, 216
ethnicity *see* race
Europe, 130, 131, 189

Fahmi, Abdelaziz, 69
Farsi, 80
fashion, 78
Ferguson, Charles, 35–6
First Gulf War, 211
First Intifada, 218–19, 223
flags, 178–81
Fouda, Yosri, 136
framing, 51–6, 57–9, 63
France, 127, 151, 172, 215
Free Egyptians (FE) Party, 135–6, 140, 143
French language, 24–5
  and Algeria, 169
  and CMC, 82–3
  and Morocco, 69, 70, 71, 72–3, 78, 79, 91
  and Senegal, 81
  and Tunisia, 167, 168, 180
Freud, Sigmund, 20–1
Fukuyama, Francis, 18

Gamal El-Din, Abdel Aziz, 134–5, 138, 141
Garang de Mabior, John, 9, 102–3, 104, 105–6
German language, 118
ghosts *see* spectres
globalisation, 24, 149
graffiti, 74, 168
grammar, 33, 78, 97, 130, 153–4
Great Britain, 103, 215
  and British Mandate, 2, 4, 6, 208
  and Egypt, 10, 111, 128, 129
Greek language, 80–1

Haʿam, Ahad, 209
Hamas, 220, 221
Hamitic language, 133, 134
Hamlet (Shakespeare), 21
Ḥaqqī, Yaḥyā, 10, 111, 115
Ḥassān, Tammam, 58
hauntology, 8, 18–21, 22, 24, 26, 27
Hebrew, 2–4, 6, 186, 187, 193
  and Arabs, 207, 208–9
heritage languages, 17–18
historical memory, 19
Hobsbawm, Eric, 21
Husayn, Taha, 130–1
al-Ḥusrī, Sāṭiʿ, 69

identity, 7, 8, 9, 11
  and Egypt, 10, 112, 114–15, 118–21, 126, 138–41, 142–3
  and hauntology, 19–20
  and language, 16–18, 24, 25–6, 94–5, 96, 98
  and psychology, 21–2
  and RA, 80
  and Sudan, 100, 103, 104–5, 106
  and vernacular, 41
ideology, 6, 92–8, 112–13
  and Sudan, 99–102, 104–6
illiteracy, 154
immigration, 17, 18
indexing, 17, 112, 113–14, 118
intellectuals, 148–9, 151–2
Internet, 9, 25, 74, 76; *see also* computer-mediated communication
Intifadas, 218–19, 223
Iran, 119, 120

Iraq, 2–4, 59
Islam, 17, 95, 127
  and al-Bustānī, 154, 155
  and al-Shidyāq, 156
  and Egypt, 129, 136, 137–8, 139–41, 142
  and language, 35, 152
  and RA, 81
  and signage, 169
  and Sudan, 99–100, 101–2, 103, 104–5
  and Turkey, 80
Israel, 2–4, 6, 11–12
  and 1967 War (Six Day War), 60–1
  and Arab Jews, 185–6
  and Arabic, 186–203
  and Egypt, 132
  and Suez, 215
  and war names, 210–21, 222–3
  see also Arab–Israeli War
Issa, Rana, 10–11

Jews, 2, 3, 4, 6
  and Arabic, 186–7, 189–95, 199–200, 201–2
  and war names, 214
  see also Arab Jews; Hebrew
Jordan, 208, 215–16
Joseph, John E., 8
Julius Caesar (Shakespeare), 21

al-Karama Party, 137
Kebab Connection (film), 118
Khojali, Hussein, 9, 100–2, 104, 105–6
Kilito, Abdel Fattah, 37–8
Klausner, Joseph, 209
Knesset, 202
koinè, 35–6
Koussa, Elias, 6

laḥn (solecism), 151
language, 5–7, 80–1, 118
  and anxiety, 90, 91–8, 102, 106–7
  and Egypt, 126, 129–30, 131–2, 133, 134–5, 139–40, 141, 142–4
  and hauntology, 19
  and horizontal/vertical, 36–7
  and identity, 16–18
  and obligation, 23–4
  and pluralism, 79, 83
  and politics, 127
  and road signs, 1–4
  and technology, 149
  and war, 207–8, 209, 210–21, 222–3
  see also Arabic language; computer-mediated communication; English language; French language; Hebrew; vernacular language; written language
Latin, 16
laypeople, 97
Leaves of Narcissus see *Awrāq al-narjis*
Lebanon, 60, 136, 217–18, 219–20; *see also* Beirut
letters, 9
Levinas, Emmanuel, 22

Lian, Chaoqun, 9
Liberal Egyptian Party (LEP), 126, 133–4, 135, 138
liberalism, 129
Liberation (of the Land of Israel), The, 211, 214
Libya, 119–20
Likud, 199, 200
linguistic landscapes (LL), 167–70
linguistics, 26–7; *see also* sociolinguistics
literacy, 16–17; *see also* illiteracy
literature, 10, 16, 21, 70
  and Egypt, 111–12, 114–17, 118–22, 123
Luria, Joseph, 209

Macbeth (Shakespeare), 21
al-Maghribī, ʿAbd al Qādir, 50–2, 53, 54–5, 56, 63
Maimonides, 202
Makoni, Sinfree, 9–10
Mamluks, 153
Marx, Karl, 18–19
Marxism, 131
Mejdell, Gunvor, 41–2
memory, 14, 15, 19, 21, 221–2
metaphors, 9, 49–65
Middle Arabic, 152
Middle East *see* Iran; Iraq; Israel; Jordan; Lebanon; Palestine; Syria; Turkey
minority languages, 17, 107
al-Miqdādī, Darwīsh, 55
missionaries, 148, 150, 151, 154–5
mobile phones, 9
Modern Standard Arabic (MSA), 9, 10
monolingualism, 101, 102
Moroccan Arabic (MA), 9, 37–8, 69–80, 83, 84–5, 91
  and code-switching, 23–4, 26
Morsi, Mohamad, 10, 126, 139
Mother Egypt (*Maṣr il-Umm*), 133
motifs, 10
Muḥīṭ al-Muḥīṭ (al-Bustānī), 155, 161
multiculturalism, 103
multilingualism, 167–8, 168–9
multimodality, 165, 166, 169–77
Musa, Salama, 69, 131, 132, 135, 141
music, 74, 193, 197, 200, 203
Muslim Brotherhood, 139, 140, 143, 144
Muslims *see* Islam
muwallada, 50–1, 56
mythology, 150

Nafīr Sūriyya (Clarion of Syria) (al-Bustānī), 154
nahḍa see Arabic Renaissance
al-Nakba (catastrophe), 211, 214, 222, 223n3–4
al-Naksa see Six Day/1967 War
naming, 210–21, 222–3
Napoleon Bonaparte, 127
Nasser, Gamal Abdel, 140, 215
national anthems, 178, 179
nationalism, 10, 22, 65n2
  and banal, 165, 178–81
  and Egypt, 126–44
  and Sudan, 101, 102, 103
  see also pan-Arabism

Natour, Salman, 202
North Africa, 25; *see also* Algeria; Egypt; Libya; Moroccan Arabic; Sudan; Tunisia

Occupy movement, 165, 168
Old English, 16
ONTV, 136
Operation Qadesh, 215
Operation Safety of Galilee, 217–18
orchestration, 172–3
organic metaphors, 49–51, 64
orientalism, 189
Other, the, 22, 112
Ottoman Empire, 150, 151, 153, 158, 160

Palestine, 7–8, 11–12, 186–8, 190, 198, 201, 202
  and Gaza Strip, 220–1
  and Hebrew, 208–9
  and Intifadas, 218–19, 223
  and road signs, 2–3, 4, 6
  and Six Day War, 60–1
Palestinian Catastrophe (*Al-Nakba*), 211, 214, 222, 223n3–4
pan-Arabism, 50, 55, 57, 59, 61, 63–4
  and Egypt, 126, 129, 132, 137, 140
Persian, 59
Petit Quarrel (1871), 157–60
phantasia (imagination), 14, 15
Pharaonism, 126, 129, 131
El-Pher'oni, Mahmoud, 138–9
philology, 151–2, 155, 156
poetry, 64
politeness, 76–7
politics, 5, 6, 7, 16
  and Egypt, 133–4, 135–41
  and Israel, 3, 4, 189–90, 193, 199, 200
  and language, 90, 92, 93, 96, 98, 127
  and protest, 168
  and Sudan, 9–10, 100–1, 102, 104–5
  see also wars
polyphony, 25
power, 6, 10
  and language, 90, 92, 93, 97, 98
Present [Condition] of Culture in Egypt, The (Andil), 133
printing, 84, 149, 150
pronunciation, 3–4
protest signs, 165, 168–9, 170, 171–2, 179–80
psychology, 21

Qindīl Umm Hāshim (The Saint's Lamp) (Ḥaqqī), 10, 111–12, 114–17, 118, 122, 123
Qudsī, Ilyās, 53–4, 55–6, 63
Qurʾān, the, 101–2, 105, 152

race, 21–2, 95, 101, 103, 199
rakākah (solecism), 10–11, 148, 149, 150, 151, 152–7, 159–61
Ramadan, 216–17
Ramaḍān, Sumayyah, 10, 111, 121
re-articulation, 96, 104, 106

religion *see* Christianity; Islam; Jews
Retsö, Jan, 35
Rhazes, 14
road signs, 1–4, 7, 169
Romanised Arabic (RA), 69, 70, 71–80, 84–5
and critics, 80, 81–2, 83
Russian language, 80, 81
Ryding, Karin C., 8

Sabahy, Hamdeen, 137
Ṣād (letter), 3
El-Sadat, Anwar, 132, 139
Saint's Lamp, The see *Qindīl Umm Hāshim*
Sāmrāʾī, Ibrāhīm, 59–61, 63
Saussure, Ferdinand de, 15, 20
al-Ṣāwī, Muhammad, 64–5
Sawiris, Naguib, 136, 142
El Sawy Culturewheel, 64
al-Sayyid, Ahmad Lutfi, 69, 129–30, 135, 141
al-Sayyid, Muhsin Lutfi, 133
script, 53, 55, 63, 69, 70
and Egypt, 131
and MA, 79
see also Romanised Arabic
Second Intifada, 219, 223
Second Lebanon War, 219–20
Second World War, 2, 3
secularism, 131, 139, 142, 155, 189
security, 189–90, 193, 199, 202, 209
segregation, 187, 199, 201
Semitic language, 133
Senegal, 81
al-Shabībī, Muḥmaad Riḍā, 57–9, 63
Shakespeare, William, 21
Shamʾūn, Salīm, 161
Sharon, Ariel, 219, 220
al-Shidyāq, Ahmad Faris, 11, 148, 150, 152, 155–60
Shiri, Sonia, 11
signage, 169; *see also* protest signs; road signs
Sindhi, 81
Six Day/1967 War, 60–1, 215–16
slogans, 11, 175–6
Smith, Eli, 153
Social Democratic Egyptian Party (SDEP), 135, 136, 143
social media, 31, 40, 70, 73–4, 76
and Arab Spring, 167, 170, 171
socialism, 131
society, 5–6, 7, 30–1
and language, 93–5, 96–7, 98
sociolinguistics, 33–5, 39, 42
solecism, 148, 149, 150, 151
Specters of Marx (Derrida), 18, 26
spectres, 18–21, 22, 24, 25, 26
spoken language *see* vernacular language
Standard Arabic (SA) *see* Arabic language; written language
storehouse, 14–16
street names, 7
street theatricality, 165, 174–7
Sudan, 9–10, 90, 98–106, 107

Sudan People's Liberation Movement/Army (SPLM/A), 103
Suez War, 215
Suleiman, Yasir, 1–2, 4–6, 7–8, 12, 26–7
  and codes, 113
  and conflict, 188
  and Egypt, 126, 127–9, 132
  and identity, 11, 15, 142, 143
  and ideology, 207
  and language anxiety, 83, 97
  and Lebanon, 136
  and script, 80
  and signage, 169
  and sociolinguistics, 33, 42
  and solecism, 151
  and symbolism, 112
  and war names, 210, 223
Surūr, Aḥmad Fatḥī, 61, 62
symbolism, 56, 93–4, 95, 96, 98
  and protest, 172, 173–4, 177, 179
Syria, 54–5, 63, 215, 216
Syrian Science Academy, 49, 50–1, 53, 54

tableaux vivants, 174–6
taboos, 95
Tabṣur, 2
Tajfel, Henri, 22
Tamazight, 169
Tarzī, Ibrāhīm, 61–2, 63–4
technology, 149–50
television, 74, 136
10th of Ramadan, The, 216–17
text messages, 71, 72–3, 76
Tolkien, J. R. R., 18
Tower of Babel, 91
translation, 148–9, 152–4
transliteration, 71–2
Tripartite Aggression, 215
Tsade/Ṣade (letter in Hebrew), 3
Tunisia, 11, 76, 170–7, 178–81
  and Arab Spring, 165–7, 168–9, 171–2
al-Turabi, Hasan, 100
Turkey, 80, 81–2, 118; *see also* Ottoman Empire

al-Umma (the Nation), 129
uncanny, 20–1
unheimlichkeit (haunted house), 20–1, 22
Unicode, 72

Van Dyck, Cornelius, 162n11
vernacular language, 31–3, 34, 35–42, 43n3, 167; *see also* Colloquial Arabic

War for Lebanon, 219–20
wars, 12, 60–1
  and names, 210–21, 222–3
  and Sudan, 101, 102, 103, 105
  see also Arab–Israeli War
Weber, Max, 26
Welsh, 17–18
Wernberg-Møller, Alison, 23–4, 26
Wikipedia Masry, 126, 134, 141–2, 144

Wolof, 81
women, 51–2, 176–7
written language (*fuṣḥā*), 31–2, 33, 34, 35, 39–41, 42
  and Egypt, 129, 130, 131, 133, 134–5
  and metaphors, 49, 50–65
  and *rakākah*, 150
  see also Romanised Arabic; script

al-Yāzijī, Ibrahim, 11, 148, 149, 152, 157–8, 160–1
al-Yāzijī, Nāṣīf, 148–9, 157, 158–9
Yom Kippur/1973/October War, 216–17
Youssi, Abderrahim, 70

Zionism, 2, 4, 189, 199, 201
Zreiq, Constantine, 214

EU representative:
Easy Access System Europe
Mustamäe tee 50, 10621 Tallinn, Estonia
Gpsr.requests@easproject.com

www.ingramcontent.com/pod-product-compliance
Lightning Source LLC
Chambersburg PA
CBHW051114230426
43667CB00014B/2575
* 9 7 8 1 4 7 4 4 5 2 6 5 6 *